THE CRUSADES AND THEIR SOURCES

Essays Presented to Bernard Hamilton

Edited
John France
and
William G. Zajac

ASHGATE

Published by
Ashgate Publishing Limited
Gower House
Croft Road
Aldershot
Hampshire GU11 3HR
England

Ashgate Publishing Company
Suite 420
101 Cherry Street
Burlington, VT 05401-4405
USA

Ashgate website:http//www.ashgate.com

British Library Cataloguing in Publication Data
France, John
    1. Crusades 2. Crusades — Sources
    I. Title
    909'07

Library of CongressCataloging-in-Publication Data
The Crusades and Their Sources: Essays Presented to Bernard Hamilton / edited
    by John France and William Zajac
        p.   cm.
    Includes two contributions in French and one in German. 'Bibliography
    of Books and Articles by Bernard Hamilton, 1961-1996': p.
    Includes bibliographical references and index.
    1. Crusades — Sources I. France, John. II. Zajac, William G. III. Hamilton,
    Bernard.
    D151.C78   1998
    909.07-dc21   97-32580
                                                                        CIP
ISBN 0-86078-624-2

Reprinted 2003

Printed in Great Britain by Biddles Ltd, Guildford and King's Lynn

THE CRUSADES AND THEIR SOURCES

Essays Presented to Bernard Hamilton

Contents

v

Contents

Illustrations

Colin Morris, *Picturing the Crusades: The Uses of Visual Propaganda, c. 1095-1250*

Jaroslav Folda, *The South Transept Facade of the Church of the Holy Sepulchre in Jerusalem: An Aspect of 'Rebuilding Zion'* (Photographs: J. Folda).

Plate   Page

Abbreviations

AA   Albert of Aachen, 'Historia Hierosolymitana', *RHC Oc.*, 4.265-713.

> All citations of Albert of Aachen's work will include book and chapter numbers as well as page numbers from the *RHC* edition – e.g. AA, II:24/pp. 317-18 – in order to facilitate reference to the forthcoming edition by S.B. Edgington.

FC   Fulcher of Chartres, *Historia Hierosolymitana (1095-1127)*, ed. H. Hagenmeyer (Heidelberg, 1913).

GF   *Gesta Francorum et aliorum Hierosolimitanorum*, ed. R. Hill (London, 1962).

MGH   *Monumenta Germaniae historica*

     Libelli   *Libelli de lite imperatorum et pontificum saeculis XI et XII conscripti*, ed. E. Dummler et al., 3 vols (Hannover, 1891-7).

     Schriften   *Schriften der Monumenta Germaniae historica. Deutsches Institut für Erforschung des Mittelalters.* (Stuttgart, 1938-).

     SS   *Scriptores*, ed. G.H. Pertz et al., 32 vols (Hannover, Weimar, Berlin, Stuttgart and Cologne, 1826-1934).

PL   *Patrologiae cursus completus. Series Latina*, ed. J.-P. Migne, 221 vols (Paris, 1841-64).

RHC   *Recueil des historiens des croisades*, ed. Académie des inscriptions et belles-lettres, 16 vols (Paris, 1841-1906).

     Arm.   *Documents arméniens*, 2 vols (1896-1906).

     Lois   *Lois*, 2 vols (1841-3).

     Oc.   *Historiens occidentaux*, 5 vols (1844-95).

     Or.   *Historiens orientaux*, 5 vols (1872-1906).

RRH	R. Röhricht, ed., *Regesta regni Hierosolymitani* (Innsbruck, 1893); *Additamentum* (Innsbruck, 1904).
RS	*Rolls Series: Chronicles and Memorials of Great Britain and Ireland during the Middle Ages published under the Direction of the Master of the Rolls*, 99 vols in 251 (London, 1858-96).
WT	William of Tyre, *Chronicon*, ed. R.B.C. Huygens, 2 vols, *Corpus Christianorum, continuatio mediaevalis* 63-63A (Turnhout, 1986).

Preface

John France

This volume is dedicated to Professor Bernard Hamilton. It is a tribute to a fine scholar and a kind and considerate person. Bernard has worked in many fields, as the bibliography of his works indicates, but his interest in the crusades has been an abiding theme. It is a mark of the contribution which he has made and continues to make in this field that so many scholars have been happy to write essays for this volume. Amongst them are a number of his pupils: Bernard has advanced learning not only by his own research but also by his teaching which has so often inspired a lasting interest in the crusades.

It is now some 900 years since the First Crusade reached Jerusalem and, by its capture, inaugurated a movement which would dominate European history for 200 years and exert a powerful influence long after. It is a fitting tribute to Bernard, therefore, that the contributors have chosen to examine the sources for these events. Their essays cover the period from the inauguration of the crusading movement through to the sixteenth century and refer to a wide variety of materials. These are substantial contributions to our understanding of the crusading movement in all its diversity.

It is one of the great pleasures of editing this collection that I have been able to read all these essays before anyone else. I would like to thank all the contributors for the trouble they have taken and their forbearance in the face of provocation. Special thanks are due to Janet Hamilton for help, advice and knowledge, and to my co-editor, Bill Zajac, to whom the presentation of this volume owes everything. The Seven Pillars of Wisdom Trust made a grant without which it would have been very difficult to produce this volume and I would like to express my gratitude to them and to their Secretary, M.V. Carey of Tweedie and Prideaux. Professor Michael Jones was kind enough to compile the bibliography of Bernard's work. Finally I have received a great deal of help and advice from John Smedley and Ruth Peters of Variorum for which I am very grateful.

But this volume is a presentation to Bernard. It is a small recognition of his services to scholarship and of his kindness to so many people in the world of scholarship and beyond. We offer it as a small token and with it our thanks and our best wishes.

Bibliography of Books and Articles by Bernard Hamilton, 1961-1997

[Works marked with an asterisk (*) have been reprinted in *Monastic Reform, Catharism and the Crusades, (900-1300)* (1979), below.]

1961

'The City of Rome and the Eastern Churches in the Tenth Century', *Orientalia Christiana periodica* 27 (1961), pp. 5-26.*

1962

'The Monastic Revival in Tenth Century Rome', *Studia monastica* 4 (1962), pp. 35-68.*

1963

[With P.A. McNulty] *'Orientale lumen et magistra latinatis*: Greek Influences on Western Monasticism (900-1100)', in *Le millénaire du Mont Athos, 963-1963: études et mélanges*, 2 vols (Chevetogne, 1963-4), 1.181-216.*

1965

'The Monastery of S. Alessio and the Religious and Intellectual Renaissance in Tenth-Century Rome', *Studies in Medieval and Renaissance History* 2 (1965), pp. 263-310.*

1966

[With E.A.F. Watson] *'Lumen Christi - Lumen Antichristi*: The Exegesis of Apocalypse XI, 5 and XIII, 13 in the Medieval Latin Fathers', *Rivista di storia e letteratura religiosa* 2 (1966), pp. 84-92.

1967

'Johannes Gualbertus', 'Benedikt der Kamaldulenser', 'Romuald', 'Neilos der Jüngere' in *Die Heiligen in ihrer Zeit*, ed. P. Mans (Mainz, 1967).

1970

'The House of Theophylact and the Promotion of the Religious Life among Women in Tenth Century Rome', *Studia monastica* 12 (1970), pp. 195-217.*

1973

'The Origins of the Dualist Church of Drugunthia', *Eastern Churches Review* 5 (1973), pp. 115-24.*

1974

The Albigensian Crusade, Historical Association Pamphlet G.85 (London, 1974). Pp. 40.*

1975

'S. Pierre Damien et les mouvements monastiques de son temps', *Studi Gregoriani* 10 (1975), pp. 175-202.*

1976

'The Cistercians in the Crusade States', in *One yet Two: Monastic Tradition East and West*, ed. M.B. Pennington, *Cistercian Studies Series* 29 (Kalamazoo, Mich., 1976), pp. 405-22.*

1977

'Rebuilding Zion: The Holy Places of Jerusalem in the Twelfth Century', in *Renaissance and Renewal in Christian History*, ed. D. Baker, *Studies in Church History* 14 (Oxford, 1977), pp. 105-16.*

'The Cathar Council of Saint-Félix', in R.I. Moore, *The Origins of European Dissent* (London, 1977), pp. 285-9.

1978

'The Cathar Council of Saint-Félix Reconsidered', *Archivum fratrum praedicatorum* 48 (1978), pp. 23-53.*

'The Elephant of Christ: Reynald of Châtillon', in *Religious Motivation: Biographical and Sociological Problems for the Church Historian*, ed. D. Baker, *Studies in Church History* 15 (Oxford, 1978), pp. 97-108.*

'Women in the Crusader States: The Queens of Jerusalem (1100-1190)', in *Medieval Women*, ed. D. Baker, *Studies in Church History, Subsidia* 1 (Oxford, 1978), pp. 143-74.

'The Armenian Church and the Papacy at the Time of the Crusades', *Eastern Churches Review* 10 (1978), pp. 61-87.*

1979

Monastic Reform, Catharism and the Crusades, (900-1300) (London, 1979; reprinted 1983). Pp. 376.

'A Medieval Urban Church: The Case of the Crusader States', in *The Church in Town and Countryside*, ed. D. Baker, *Studies in Church History* 16 (Oxford, 1979), pp. 159-70.

1980

The Latin Church in the Crusader States: The Secular Church (London, 1980). Pp. x, 409.

1981

The Medieval Inquisition (London, 1981). Pp. 111.

1982

'I monasteri di Roma, 900-1050', in *Dizionario degli istituti di perfezione* (Rome 1982).

'Romuald', in *Die Heiligen des Regionalkalendars*, ed. H.J. Weisbender (Leipzig 1982).

1984

'Ralph of Domfront, Patriarch of Antioch (1135-40)', *Nottingham Medieval Studies* 28 (1984), pp. 1-21.

1985

'Prester John and the Three Kings of Cologne', *Studies in Medieval History presented to R.H.C. Davis*, ed. H. Mayr-Harting and R.I. Moore (London, 1985), pp. 177-91. Reprinted in *Prester John* (1996) below.

'The Titular Nobility of the Latin East: The Case of Agnes of Courtenay', in *Crusade and Settlement: Papers read at the First Conference of the Society for the Study of the Crusades and the Latin East and presented to R.C. Smail*, ed. P.W. Edbury (Cardiff, 1985), pp. 197-203.

1986

Religion in the Medieval West (London, 1986). Pp. viii, 216.

1987

'The Ottomans, the Humanists and the Holy House of Loreto', *Renaissance and Modern Studies* 31 (1987), pp. 1-19.

1988

'The Cathars and the Seven Churches of Asia', in *Byzantium and the West, c. 850-c. 1200: Proceedings of the XVIIIth Spring Symposium of Byzantine Studies, Oxford 30th March-lst April 1984*, ed. J.D. Howard-Johnston (Amsterdam, 1988), pp. 269-95.

'Bollandists', 'Maurists', 'Migne, Jacques-Paul', in *The Blackwell Dictionary of Historians*, ed. J. Cannon et al. (Oxford, 1988), pp. 46-7, 273-4, 278-9.

'Manuel I Comnenus and Baldwin IV of Jerusalem', *Kathegetria: Essays presented to Joan Hussey for her Eightieth Birthday*, ed. J. Chrysostomides (Camberley, 1988), pp. 353-75.

1989

[Ed. with B. Arbel and D. Jacoby], *Latins and Greeks in the Eastern Mediterranean after 1204* (London, 1989). Pp. viii, 245.

1992

'Miles of Plancy and the Fief of Beirut', in *The Horns of Hattin*, ed. B.Z. Kedar (Jerusalem, 1992) pp. 136-46.

1994

'The Impact of Crusader Jerusalem on Western Christendom', *The Catholic Historical Review* 80 (1994), pp. 695-713.

'Wisdom from the East: The Reception by the Cathars of Eastern Dualist Texts', in *Heresy and Literacy, 1000-1530*, ed. P. Biller and A. Hudson, *Cambridge Studies in Medieval Literature* 23 (Cambridge, 1994), pp. 38-60.

1995

'Ideals of Holiness: Crusaders, Contemplatives and Mendicants', *The International History Review* 17 (1995), pp. 693-712.

'Eleanor of Castile and the Crusading Movement', *Mediterranean Historical Review* 10 (1995), pp. 92-103.

'Aimery of Limoges, Patriarch of Antioch: Ecumenist, Scholar and Patron of Hermits', in *The Joy of Learning and the Love of God: Studies in Honor of Jean Leclercq*, ed. E.R. Elder, *Cistercian Studies Series* 160 (Kalamazoo, Mich., 1995), pp. 269-90.

1996

[Ed. with C.F. Beckingham] *Prester John, the Mongols and the Ten Lost Tribes* (Aldershot, 1996). Pp. xiv, 315.

'Continental Drift: Prester John's Progress through the Indies', in *Prester John, the Mongols and the Ten Lost Tribes*, pp. 237-69.

'The Latin Church in the Crusader States', in *East and West in the Crusader States: Context, Contacts, Confrontations. Acta of the Congress held at Hernen Castle in May 1993*, ed. K. Ciggaar, A. Davids and H. Teule, *Orientalia Lovaniensia Analecta* 75 (Leuven, 1996), pp. 1-20.

1997

'King Consorts of Jerusalem and their Entourages from the West from 1186 to 1250', in *Die Kreuzfahrerstaaten als multikulturelle Gesellschaft: Einwanderer und Minderheiten im 12. und 13. Jahrhundert*, ed. H.E. Mayer, *Schriften des historischen Kollegs, Kolloquien* 37 (Munich, 1997), pp. 13-24.

'Knowing the Enemy: Western Understanding of Islam at the Time of the Crusades', *Journal of the Royal Asiatic Society*, 3rd Series, 7 (1997), pp. 373-87.

Raymond IV of St Gilles, Achard of Arles and the Conquest of Lebanon

Jonathan Riley-Smith

In a charter dated 17 January 1103 and issued 'in the castle which is called Mont Pèlerin and is established before the gate of Tripoli', Raymond of St Gilles, 'prince, with God's aid, of the Christian knighthood on the Jerusalem journey', considering his sins, the feebleness of the tiny Christian force with him, and the efforts on his behalf of Abbot Richard of St Victor of Marseilles, gave the abbey of St Victor half the port of Jubail and its territory. Invoking the authority of 'St Peter, the prince of the apostles, in obedience and fealty to whom we now bear arms', he made the gift in Richard's presence and 'with the advice, indeed encouragement, of my fellow-workers (or -soldiers: *comilitonibus*) Count William (VI) of Auvergne, Viscount B(ernard Ato) of Béziers (and Carcassonne), ... the most reverend Achard of Marseilles and Berengar of Narbonne'. It was witnessed by William, Bernard Ato, Achard and Berengar, and also by 'William Hugh ... Peter, bishop of Glandèves ... Herbert, abbot of St Everard ... Pons of Grillon ... William Peter ... Berengar William ... Aicfred ... the monks Durand and Raymond, the second of whom wrote the charter, and the clerks Bernard and Stephen'.[1] Jubail was to fall to the Christians in April 1104,[2] but it passed to the Genoese, who had helped to conquer it, and the abbey never held it. Nevertheless the charter remained in the abbey's possession and was copied into its *Liber magnus cartarum*.[3]

---

[1] *Cartulaire de l'abbaye de Saint-Victor de Marseille*, ed. B.E.C. Guérard, 2 vols (Paris, 1857), 2.151-3 [hereafter *St Victor*] (*RRH*, no. 38).

[2] But see J.H. and L.L. Hill, *Raymond IV de Saint-Gilles, 1041 (ou 1042)-1105* (Toulouse, 1959), p. 138 for doubts about the date of Jubail's capture.

[3] *St Victor*, 1.vii.

Although chancery practices in the early years of the settlement are not known,[4] the charter almost certainly dates from 1103 and is closely related to one in favour of the abbey of St Mary of the Latins discovered by Professor Jean Richard, in which the fortress of Mont Pèlerin was 'noviter edificati';[5] in the charter for St Victor it was 'constitutum'. In the charter for St Mary of the Latins Raymond entitled himself 'comes Tholosanus vel gratia Dei Tripolitanus',[6] whereas in the charter for St Victor he gave himself the title of 'princeps ... milicie Christiane in Jerosolimitano itinere' and elaborated this with the statement that God's 'paucissima Christianitas' 'me ... in caput et principem elegit'. After the liberation of Jerusalem in 1099 and a vain attempt he had made to capture Tripoli, he had returned to Constantinople and, when an army of Lombard, French and German crusaders arrived there early in 1101, he was given a force of 500 turcopoles by the emperor, Alexius, and some kind of position on the ensuing campaign. Although he was blamed later for leading it to disaster,[7] the terms used of him by Albert of Aachen – 'primus et collateralis', 'consiliarius et ductor', 'Comes vero de Sancto Aegidio et ceteri comprimores'[8] – suggest that he shared leadership with the commanders from the West, and this appears to be confirmed in Anna Comnena's account.[9] After the debacle he took Tartus (Tortosa) with a large body of crusaders. The other leaders pressed on to Jerusalem to fulfil their vows,[10] but enough men must have remained for Raymond to be elected 'in caput et principem' of a force which was still 'in Jerosolimitano itinere'; this echoed the election of Stephen of Blois as *ductor, provisor, gubernator, caput* and *dictator* of the crusade in the spring of 1098.[11] In Raymond's case the title of *princeps* probably reflected his ambition to rule independently the

---

[4] See *St Victor*, 1.xiv-xvi for the dating of the charters in the *Liber magnus cartarum*.

[5] J. Richard, 'Le chartrier de Saint-Marie-Latine et l'établissement de Raymond de Saint-Gilles à Mont-Pèlerin', in *Mélanges d'histoire du moyen age dédiés à la mémoire de Louis Halphen* (Paris, 1951), p. 610. For another grant to a religious community, see R. Hiestand, 'Saint-Ruf d'Avignon, Raymond de Saint-Gilles et l'église latine du comté de Tripoli', *Annales du Midi* 98 (1986), pp. 327-36.

[6] See Richard, 'Le chartrier', pp. 607-8.

[7] AA, VIII:46/p. 584.

[8] AA, VIII:5, 7, 24/pp. 562, 563, 574.

[9] Anna Comnena, *Alexiade*, ed. and trans. B. Leib, 4 vols (Paris, 1943-76), 3.37-8.

[10] FC, pp. 433-5; AA, VIII:42-4/p. 583.

[11] *Die Kreuzzugsbriefe aus den Jahren 1088-1100*, ed. H. Hagenmeyer (Innsbruck, 1901), p. 149; *GF*, p. 63; Peter Tudebode, *Historia de Hierosolymitano itinere*, ed. J.H. and L.L. Hill (Paris, 1977), pp. 104-5; Raymond of Aguilers, *Le 'liber' de Raymond d'Aguilers*, ed. J.H. and L.L. Hill (Paris, 1969), p. 77.

statelet he was carving out in Lebanon, south of the Byzantine frontier overrun by the Turks in the eleventh century and therefore outside the regions he and his fellow crusaders had promised to return to the Greek empire.[12] At any rate it is clear that in his eyes the crusade was not yet over and would not be — however many vows were fulfilled at the Holy Sepulchre — until the coast was conquered and a secure line of communications from Jerusalem north through Antioch to Asia Minor and beyond had been secured; in 1108 his son, Bertrand, and the Genoese, who were finishing off the reduction of the Lebanese coast and had vowed to serve 'God and the Holy Sepulchre', also seem to have believed themselves to be on crusade.[13]

A feature of the sources for the first crusading expedition of 1096-99 is the portrayal of Christ as the authorizer and leader of the armies and a veneration shown for eastern saints at the expense of western ones, particularly St Peter whose role was stressed only in relation to the siege and battle of Antioch, where he was believed to have been bishop before he went to Rome. The downplaying of St Peter's authority, and the association of Petrine claims with Antioch rather than with Rome, must have embarrassed the papacy and I have suggested elsewhere that there was a reaction to this in papal circles, manifesting itself particularly in 1100 in a letter from Pope Paschal II to the Latins in Asia.

> Since you began this pilgrimage through the vicar of St Peter ... you should abound always in the consolation of St Peter and to the end hold him, whom you accepted as the foundation of such a great work, as your head in faith and obedience ... You ought to submit to (the papal legate) ... and through him to us, in fact to St Peter.[14]

It is of interest to find the patronage of St Peter, 'cujus obediencia ac fidelitate presencia arma gestamus', being stressed in the charter for St Victor, which

---

[12] The title of 'princeps' was probably adopted by Godfrey of Bouillon in Jerusalem. See J.S.C. Riley-Smith, 'The Title of Godfrey of Bouillon', *Bulletin of the Institute of Historical Research* 52 (1979), pp. 83-6.

[13] AA, XI:3-15, 17-19, 34/pp. 664-9, 671-2, 679; Caffaro, 'De liberatione civitatum orientis', in *Annali Genovesi di Caffaro e de' suoi continuatori dal MXCIX al MCCXCII*, vol. 1, ed. L.T. Belgrano, *Fonti per la storia d'Italia* 11 (Genoa, 1890), pp. 122-4; WT, pp. 507-9; *Liber privilegiorum ecclesiae Ianuensis*, ed. D. Puncuh, *Fonte e studi di storia ecclesiastica* 1 (Genoa, 1962), pp. 43-4.

[14] *Kreuzzugsbriefe*, p. 179; J.S.C. Riley-Smith, 'The First Crusade and St Peter', in *Outremer: Studies in the History of the Crusading Kingdom of Jerusalem presented to Joshua Prawer*, ed. B.Z. Kedar, H.E. Mayer and R.C. Smail (Jerusalem, 1982), pp. 41-63.

described a gift made for the benefit and in the presence of Abbot Richard, who was a cardinal and had been a papal legate.

The sixteen men besides Raymond referred to in the charter for St Victor – or at any rate those about whom something can be said – can be divided into three groups. First there were those who had been in Raymond's household from 1096 or had joined it in the course of the First Crusade. William Hugh was William Hugh of Monteil, the brother of Bishop Adhémar of Le Puy, the papal legate on the First Crusade. He had left the West in Adhémar's company, but had transferred his allegiance to Raymond after Adhémar's death in the late summer of 1098. He was to become lord of Krak des Chevaliers, which was already one of the most important castles on the frontier of the new county of Tripoli.[15] William Peter was probably William Peyre, the lord of Cunhlat south-east of Clermont, who had been the employer of the visionary Peter Bartholomew in 1098. By late in that year he was serving Peter of Narbonne, a chaplain whom Raymond had made bishop of al-Bara, the first Catholic diocese in Syria, and he was put in charge of a small garrison at al-Bara by the bishop when the crusaders marched south to take Jerusalem. By 1103 he was Raymond's constable.[16] Abbot Herbert of St Everard must be the man who had been a monk of Chaise-Dieu and prior of Prévezac before accompanying Raymond on crusade as one of his chaplains. He was later to be the prior of the Holy Sepulchre house on Mont Pèlerin and the first Catholic bishop of Tripoli.[17] The Holy Sepulchre priory was established between 1103 and 1105 in a mosque which had already been converted for Christian use[18] and it may be that it had been housing a short-lived abbey dedicated to a St Everard, although this is unlikely; perhaps the word 'Evrardi' is a corrupted transliteration of the name of some eastern saint.[19] The monks Durand and

---

[15] Raymond of Aguilers, *Liber*, pp. 42, 128, 130, 144; Richard, 'Le chartrier', pp. 610-11.

[16] Raymond of Aguilers, *Liber*, pp. 71, 105; WT, p. 358; Richard, 'Le chartrier', p. 610; *Le cartulaire du chapitre de Saint-Sépulcre de Jérusalem*, ed. G. Bresc-Bautier (Paris, 1984), p. 187 [hereafter *St Sépulcre*] (*RRH*, no. 48).

[17] *Acta Sanctorum. Aprilis* 3.330; William of Malmesbury, *De gestis regum Anglorum*, ed. W. Stubbs, 2 vols, *RS* 90 (London, 1887-89), 2.458; *Les miracles de St Privat*, ed. C. Brunel (Paris, 1912), p. 37; *St Sépulcre*, p. 199; *Cartulaire géneral de l'ordre des Hospitaliers de St Jean de Jérusalem*, ed. J. Delaville Le Roulx, 4 vols (Paris, 1894-1906), 1.70 (*RRH*, nos. 58, 78, 107); *Papsturkunden für Templer und Johanniter*, Neue Folge, ed. R. Hiestand, *Vorarbeiten zum Oriens Pontificius* 2 (Göttingen, 1984), p. 199.

[18] *St Sépulcre*, p. 186 (*RRH*, no. 48).

[19] It is interesting that William of Malmesbury, *De gestis regum*, 2.458, refers to Herbert being made bishop 'ex abbate'.

Raymond may have been members of that community; so could have been the clerk, Stephen. William Hugh, William Peyre and Herbert were members of a household in which Raymond obviously inspired great loyalty, since they had stayed with him in spite of all the setbacks he had endured; presumably they had been in the 'Provençal' force which was reported to have been with him during the disastrous advance into Asia Minor in 1101.[20]

Secondly, there was a party from Languedoc, the leaders of which were related by blood or marriage to Raymond and had presumably decided to reinforce him. They included Bernard Ato of Béziers and Berengar of Narbonne.[21] Bernard Ato's grandmother had been the sister of Raymond's mother. Berengar was more distantly related through marriage. William of Auvergne lived further off, but his uncle, Peter of Melgueil, was the husband of Raymond's sister. A further ramification linked these crusaders to the third group, those from Marseilles, because the wife of Bernard of Béziers was Cecilia of Provence and her grandmother, Etienette, had been a member of the family of the viscounts of Marseilles.

The crusaders from Marseilles and its neighbourhood referred to in the charter comprised Abbot Richard of St Victor, Achard of Marseilles, who had been archbishop of Arles and about whom more below, and Bishop Peter of Glandèves, who was probably a member of the family of Castellane which had dominated his bishopric in the eleventh century;[22] his diocese lay some way to the east of Marseilles, around Entreveaux, north of Grasse. Already with these leading figures must have been men who, with Achard of Marseilles, represented the old order in Arles which was in the process of being challenged, since they were with Achard in Syria in the following years: Raymond of Les Baux, a son of the co-lord of Arles,[23] Bertrand Porcellet, of the other great family dominating the town and the hereditary lay sacristan of the cathedral — he must have been elderly because he had been sacristan since at least 1067[24] — and Raymond Decan, the lord of Posquières (Vauvert, south of Nimes) and

---

[20] AA, VIII:15-16/pp. 568-9.

[21] For Berengar, see C. Devic and J. Vaissète, *Histoire génerale de Languedoc*, 3rd edn, ed. A. Molinier et al., 16 vols (Toulouse, 1872-1904), 3.560.

[22] J.P. Poly, *La Provence et la société féodale (879-1166)* (Paris, 1976), p. 268.

[23] *Gallia Christiana in provincias ecclesiasticas distributa*, ed. Maurists et al., 16 vols (Paris, 1715-1865), 1:Instr.97 (*RRH*, no. 44); *St Sépulcre*, p. 187 (*RRH*, no. 48); Poly, *Provence*, pp. 221, 267.

[24] *Gallia Christiana*, 1:Instr.97 (*RRH*, no. 44); Poly, *Provence*, pp. 220, 253 n. 25, 268.

the lay dean of Arles,[25] whose chaplain was a priest called Pons of Grillon. Pons, who provided evidence that Raymond Decan was already in Syria by witnessing the charter for St Victor, came from the region north-east of Avignon,[26] as did Rostaing of Port who was with the group in the East in 1105.[27] Others who seem to have been attached to this party, because they are also to be found alongside them in Lebanon, were William and Bertrand Arvier from Arles,[28] and, from Marseilles and nearby, Geoffrey of Pennes,[29] Pons IV of Fos, who was to remain in the East,[30] and perhaps Raymond of Cornillon-Confoux.[31]

Achard was a member of the family of the viscounts of Marseilles. He had become archbishop of Arles in c. 1067, but had been accused of simony and he had been deposed in 1080, when he had refused to give up control of the cathedral, and had been excommunicated by the papal legates, one of whom had been Richard of St Victor. His successor, Gibelin, who had been chosen by a reform council at Avignon, had still not been able to take possession of the see as late as 1094. Achard had hung on, dating his acts defiantly with the regnal year of Henry IV as emperor; Gibelin had been scared off by threats from Achard's family.[32] So, accompanying Richard of St Victor, a distinguished supporter of the Gregorian reforms, were a group of disgraced anti-reformers, one of them a scandal-ridden figure who had been excommunicated over twenty years before by Richard himself. Since a recruit to the expedition of 1100-1 had been Albert of Parma, the brother of the anti-pope Wibert of Ravenna, it has been suggested that the major opponents of Gregorianism who joined the early crusades signified the triumph of Pope Urban II over his rival.[33] The reasons for their participation, however, were always complex.

---

[25] *Gallia Christiana*, 1:Instr.97 (*RRH*, no. 44); *St Sépulcre*, pp. 186-7 (*RRH*, no. 48); Poly, *Provence*, pp. 253-4, 268, 330.

[26] *St Sépulcre*, p. 186 (*RRH*, no. 48). See Poly, *Provence*, p. 267.

[27] *Gallia Christiana*, 1:Instr.97 (*RRH*, no. 44); *St Sépulcre*, p. 186 (*RRH*, no. 48); Poly, *Provence*, p. 267.

[28] Richard, 'Le chartrier', p. 610; *Gallia Christiana*, 1:Instr.97 (*RRH*, no. 44). For William, see Poly, *Provence*, p. 267 and n. 111.

[29] *St Sépulcre*, p. 187 (*RRH*, no. 48); Poly, *Provence*, p. 267.

[30] Richard, 'Le chartrier', p. 610; *Gallia Christiana*, 1:Instr.97 (*RRH*, no. 44); Poly, *Provence*, pp. 166 n. 18, 208, 267, 322, 352.

[31] Richard, 'Le chartrier', p. 610.

[32] Poly, *Provence*, pp. 262-4, 268, 273; G. Manteyer, *La Provence du premier au douzième siècle* (Paris, 1908), pp. 302-3.

[33] P. Riant, 'Un dernier triomphe d'Urbain II', *Revue des questions historiques* 34 (1883), pp. 247-55.

Godfrey of Bouillon and his brothers, for instance, were lukewarm about the new forces in the Church, and Godfrey had served the emperor, Henry IV, in his wars against the forces of radical reform in Italy, but as important a reason for this as any was the long struggle he had against the fanatical Gregorian supporter, Mathilda of Tuscany, and her agents over his possessions in Lorraine, to which she as his uncle's widow had claims.[34]

Looking more closely at Achard's case in the light of the Levantine charters, the reason for his presence in the East becomes explicable. First, it is clear from the wording of the charter for St Victor that he was on crusade. If he had still been excommunicated this would have been an impossibility. No excommunicate – by definition an impenitent – could be allowed to fulfil a penitential vow[35] and it follows that Achard must have been reconciled with the Church; indeed Richard of St Victor, as the papal legate who had originally excommunicated him, would have had nothing to do with him if he had not. Secondly, in late January 1105 Achard, Raymond of Les Baux, Raymond Decan and Bertrand Porcellet were among those from the region who witnessed a death-bed endowment from Raymond of St Gilles in favour of the church of Arles which specifically referred to Gibelin as archbishop.[36] Thirdly, some of them at least, including Achard, spent a relatively long time in the East. We do not know the date of their departure from Arles and Marseilles, but Bernard Ato of Béziers left southern France no earlier than the end of August 1101,[37] far too late to share in the catastrophe in Asia Minor. Assuming that he and his companions met with Achard and the rest at Marseilles and sailed for the East in September, they would have arrived – perhaps initially in Palestine – late in the year, and could have visited Jerusalem before travelling north to join Raymond of St Gilles in Lebanon. Achard, Raymond Decan, Raymond of Les Baux, Bertrand Porcellet, William

---

[34] H.E. Mayer, *Mélanges sur l'histoire du royaume latin de Jérusalem, Mémoires de l'académie des inscriptions et belles-lettres*, NS 5 (Paris, 1984), pp. 22-31; S. Runciman, *A History of the Crusades*, 3 vols (Cambridge, 1951-54), 1.145-6.

[35] See 'Documents pour l'histoire de Saint-Hilaire de Poitiers', ed. L. Rédet, *Mémoires de la société des antiquaires de l'Ouest* (1847), 128; *Archives administratives de la ville de Reims*, ed. P.J. Varin, 5 vols (Paris, 1839-48), 1.286; and also perhaps *Cartulaire de l'abbaye de Saint-Laon de Thouars*, ed. H. Imbert, *Mémoires de la société de statistique, sciences, lettres et arts du département de Deux-Sèvres*, sér. 2, 14 (Niort, 1875), p. 44.

[36] *Gallia Christiana*, 1:Instr.97 (*RRH*, no. 44).

[37] *Cartulaires des abbayes d'Aniane et de Gellone, 1. Cartulaire de Gellone*, ed. P. Alaus, L. Cassan and E. Meynial (Montpellier, 1898), p. 248. See also *Cartulaire et archives de ... diocèse ... de Carcassonne*, ed. M. Mahul, 6 vols (Paris, 1857-72), 5.155.

Arvier, Geoffrey of Pennes and Rostaing of Port seem to have stayed at least until 1106; the last record of Achard in Lebanon is in August of that year, but his stay may have been longer.[38] He seems to have returned to the West in the end, because there is a record of him bringing back a relic of the True Cross given by the emperor, Alexius, to Raymond of St Gilles and presenting it to his old cathedral.[39] His companion, Pons of Grillon, was in Tripoli as late as 1110,[40] although he returned home eventually, because he was to become bishop of St Paul-Trois-Châteaux.[41]

At any rate, Achard could have spent at least five years in the East and it looks as though he had come to heel over Arles. Perhaps his resistance had been finally crushed in 1096, when it is probable that Pope Urban himself visited the town towards the end of his year-long journey through French-speaking territories.[42] Some time later Achard must have sought an end to his excommunication and he may have been set the crusade, together perhaps with a commitment to spend at least five years in the East, as a penance. He and his supporters, including the lay dean and lay sacristan of Arles and one of the most important figures in the town's patriciate, travelled with Richard of St Victor, who had excommunicated him in the first place. It is not in the least surprising that most of Achard's five years in the East should have been spent helping Raymond of St Gilles conquer the Lebanese coast. Raymond had ruled, or had at least claimed to rule, Provence as well as Languedoc and had been familiar to Achard and to everyone else in the neighbourhoods of Arles and Marseilles.

---

[38] Richard, 'Le chartrier', p. 610; *Gallia Christiana*, 1:Instr.97 (*RRH*, no. 44); *St Sépulcre*, pp. 186-7 (*RRH*, no. 48).

[39] Poly, *Provence*, p. 268 n. 120.

[40] *St Sépulcre*, p. 199 (*RRH*, no. 58).

[41] *Cartulaire général de l'ordre du Temple 1119?-1150*, ed. G.A.M.J.A. d'Albon (Paris, 1913-22), pp. 84-7.

[42] A. Becker, *Papst Urban II (1088-1099)*, 2 vols, *MGH Schriften* 19 (Stuttgart, 1964-88), 2.454.

Frontier Warfare in the Latin Kingdom of Jerusalem: The Campaign of Jacob's Ford, 1178-79

Malcolm Barber

The construction by the Latins of the fortress of Chastellet at the place known as 'Jacob's Ford' or Bait al-Ahzan on the Upper Jordan between Lake Huleh and the Sea of Galilee between October 1178 and March 1179, and Saladin's subsequent and ultimately successful attempt to demolish it in August 1179 offer an interesting case history for the study of Christian-Muslim warfare in the reign of King Baldwin IV. Although the sources are not copious, they tell us enough to be able to draw some tentative conclusions about the military, economic, and religious significance of a site desired by both sides and the nature of the warfare required to make those desires a reality. The picture which emerges is far removed from the traditional images of the gallant leper king and the chivalrous Saladin; rather it is one of grim and often desperate conflict, no less brutal and ruthless than its counterparts on western Christendom's other frontiers in Germany and Spain. Indeed, it could not have been otherwise, for control of this crossing was absolutely crucial to both sides in a way which it had not been in the past. More than any other military event between 1174 and 1187, the loss of this fortification began the process which led to the defeat of the Christians at Hattin. The situation was made all the more critical in that it took place in a year when, according to Imad al-Din, Saladin's secretary and chancellor, drought and famine were especially severe,[1] the effects of which could only have been exacerbated by the wholesale seizure or destruction of the harvest.

According to one of the versions of the Old French chronicle of Ernoul, who was a contemporary with knowledge of high politics in the Latin kingdom, Baldwin IV had agreed not to fortify the place, but was persuaded by the

---

[1] Abu Shama, 'Le Livre des Deux Jardins', *RHC Or.*, 4.195 [hereafter Abu Shama].

Templars to renege on his promises.[2] William of Tyre – who was often hostile to the Templars and had a particular hatred for Odo of Saint-Amand, the reigning Master – nevertheless says only that the king began to build the fortress, although he implies that the Templars were behind it, when he states that, on completion, it 'was surrendered to the brothers of the knights of the Temple, who laid claim to all that region for themselves by concession of the kings'.[3] A truce had indeed been made with Saladin after the Frankish victory at Montgisard (south-east of Ramla) in November of the previous year, but neither side seems to have been very committed to it, since the Franks had attacked Hamah in August 1178, while Saladin's preparations for a new campaign were fairly obvious.[4] However, the Templars did have a particular interest in the area; in 1168 King Amalric had granted them the important fortress of Safad,[5] which was only about fifteen kilometres (or half a day's journey, according to Imad al-Din)[6] to the south-west. Safad – described by Imad al-Din as 'a nest of evil'[7] – dominated northern Galilee, but could not by itself prevent incursions from the east across the Jordan.

William of Tyre says that the castle at Jacob's Ford took six months to build, although it was apparently not finished in mid-April 1179, when the dying constable, Humphrey of Toron, was taken there. It was in the form of a square with very thick walls, described as of 'suitable height' (*ad convenientem altitudinem*), and was situated upon a shallow hill (*mediocriter eminens*).[8] On the Muslim side, the Mesopotamian chronicler, Ibn al-Athir, calls it 'an impregnable fortress',[9] although perhaps exaggerating its strength added further gloss to the Muslim capture and destruction of it. In fact, neither writer actually saw it; much more detailed is the account of the Qadi al-Fadil, Saladin's administrator. His description is contained in a letter to Baghdad

---

[2] *Chronique d'Ernoul et de Bernard Le Trésorier*, ed. L. de Mas Latrie (Paris, 1871), p. 52.

[3] WT, p. 1003. William had in fact set out for the Third Lateran Council in Rome in the same month as work on the fortress began, so he may not have been fully informed of the circumstances which led to the decision to build, WT, p. 997. On William's view of Odo of Saint-Amand, WT, p. 1002. Baldwin IV was at Jacob's Ford on 17 November 1178, and again on 1 and 2 April 1179, *RRH*, nos. 562, 577, 579.

[4] Ibn al-Athir, 'Extrait de la Chronique intitulé Kamel-Altevarykh', *RHC Or.*, 1.632 [hereafter Ibn al-Athir].

[5] *Tabulae ordinis Theutonici*, ed. E. Strehlke (Berlin, 1869; reprint 1975), no. 4.

[6] Abu Shama, p. 194.

[7] Abu Shama, p. 203.

[8] WT, pp. 997, 999.

[9] Ibn al-Athir, p. 635.

incorporated into the patchwork of sources sewn together by the anthologist Abu Shama in the mid-thirteenth century. Al-Fadil either saw it himself or had his information directly from Saladin, since he often wrote letters on the sultan's behalf.

> The width of the wall surpassed ten cubits; it was built of stones of enormous size of which each block was seven cubits more or less; the number of these dressed stones exceeded 20,000, and each stone put in place and sealed into the masonry did not come out at less than four dinars, and even more. Between the two walls extended a line of massive blocks raised up to the proud summit of the mountains. The lime which was poured around the stone in order to seal it was mixed and incorporated into it, giving it a strength and solidity superior to that of the stone itself, and frustrating, with more success than that of metal, all attempts by the enemy to destroy it.[10]

There seems to have been a keep on the western side, as Saladin's forces concentrated their efforts upon mining what Imad al-Din calls 'a tower of extreme solidity' and Ibn al-Athir describes as 'a citadel'. It may have been hexagonal in shape, since al-Fadil believed that mines were dug on five sides of the walls.[11] In another letter, al-Fadil says that there was 'a vast enclosure adjoining the castle', which may have been the quarters of the service community needed to run it. The castle was well-stocked with food, which al-Fadil estimated would have lasted for several years, and it incorporated a cistern so large that, after the castle's fall, the Muslims used it to dispose of the unwanted bodies of their enemies, but failed to fill it with, he claims, 1,000 cadavers. The garrison included 'eighty knights with their squires, fifteen chiefs each having with them fifty men' and 'artisans such as a mason, architect, blacksmith, carpenter, sword-cutter, armourer, and maker of arms of all types'. There were 100 Muslim slaves. The fighting men were appropriately equipped: when the faubourg fell, the Muslims seized many horses, while in the castle itself they found about 1,000 coats of mail.[12]

The castle was apparently built while Saladin was preoccupied with besieging Baalbek,[13] a situation which had arisen out of the complicated internal

---

[10] Abu Shama, p. 206.

[11] Abu Shama, pp. 204, 208; Ibn al-Athir, p. 638.

[12] Abu Shama, pp. 207-8. Compare the forces needed to garrison Safad in the 1240s, where the figures given are 50 knights, 30 sergeants, 50 Turcopoles, and 300 crossbowmen, plus 820 workers of other kinds and 400 slaves, R.B.C. Huygens, ed., 'De constructione castri Saphet', *Studi Medievali*, ser. 3, 6 (1965), p. 384.

[13] Abu Shama, p. 194.

politics of Muslim Syria, and which was not resolved until the city capitulated in the spring of 1179.[14] Saladin's Syrian problems cannot have been unknown to the Franks; perhaps the Templars had been anxious to take this opportunity, despite the existence of the truce. However, once free of Baalbek, Saladin retired to Damascus – only a day's journey from Jacob's Ford, according to Imad al-Din – to assess the new situation. According to Ibn Abi Tayy, a source now lost, but also partially incorporated by Abu Shama, he first offered the Franks 60,000 dinars to dismantle it, gradually increasing the sum to 100,000, but with no success. These figures seem to have been based on al-Fadil's estimate that the Franks had used 20,000 stones costing at least four dinars each. If the Franks could not be bought out, then force would have to be used. Taqi al-Din, the sultan's nephew, advised Saladin to use the money to equip troops instead.[15]

Saladin began by ravaging the region upon which the castle depended, a tactic which suggests that the garrison was unable to prevent Muslim troops from regularly entering Frankish territory. As was usual, large areas were set on fire, but Saladin also sent out raiding parties to seize the harvest. Imad al-Din says that 'it was not long before he [Saladin] saw them return, bringing back their camels loaded with heavy sheafs; it was thus until the complete destruction of the crops'.[16] Evidently the need to feed troops in a year of acute shortage led to a less profligate approach to the ravaging of the enemy's lands than was normal. In late May, he made some preliminary sorties against the castle itself to test its strength, but, according to William of Tyre, retreated when one of his more prominent emirs was killed in the fighting.[17]

During all this military activity, Saladin became involved in a battle he had not sought, for the king and the Templars had brought up an army to stop these attacks. On 10 June 1179, the Christians defeated an advance section of Saladin's forces under Farrukh-Shah, another of the sultan's nephews, at Marj Ayun, but when Raymond of Tripoli and Odo of Saint-Amand, the Master of the Temple, tried to follow this up by charging the main force, they were heavily defeated. Odo of Saint-Amand was among those captured. Imad al-Din reckoned that 270 knights were taken at this time.[18]

---

[14] See M.C. Lyons and D.E.P. Jackson, *Saladin: The Politics of the Holy War* (Cambridge, 1982), pp. 131-3.
[15] Abu Shama, pp. 197, 206.
[16] Abu Shama, p. 197.
[17] Abu Shama, p. 197; Ibn al-Athir, p. 636; WT, pp. 999-1000.
[18] Abu Shama, pp. 198-9.

The actual siege began on 24 August, when Saladin arrived at the ford with numbers which leave no doubt as to the seriousness of the attack. The plain overflowed with troops, says Imad al-Din. The region around Safad was raided for vine-poles and other wood to support the palisades protecting the mangonels.[19] The outer compound was captured by the evening of the first day; Ibn al-Athir says that the troops were inspired by a person he calls 'a man of the people, wearing a torn tunic', who set the example by being the first to climb up onto the wall.[20]

The castle itself was much more formidable, especially as the defenders had lit fires behind each gate to protect against surprise attack.[21] Work on the mining of the citadel therefore began at once and, by Sunday night, they were ready to set fire to the struts placed beneath it. According to Imad al-Din, the mine was thirty cubits in depth for a wall nine cubits in thickness. Even so, it was not enough, and Saladin had to offer a dinar to anyone who would bring a goatskin of water to help extinguish the fire, so that the sappers could re-enter the mine and enlarge it. They finally succeeded at daybreak on Thursday, 29 August, spurred on by the news that the Franks were assembling another army at Tiberias. Imad al-Din describes the scene as follows:

> The Franks had piled up wood behind the wall which crumbled; the current of air which penetrated at the moment of its fall spread the fire, their tents and several combatants were prey to the flames; the remainder who were in the region of the fire implored amnesty. As soon as the flames were extinguished, the troops penetrated the place, killing, taking prisoners, and seizing important booty, [including] 100,000 pieces of iron arms of all types and victuals in quantity. The captives were taken to the sultan, who executed the apostates and the bowmen; of around 700 prisoners, the greater part were massacred en route by the volunteer troops, the remainder taken to Damascus.[22]

Al-Fadil was deeply impressed by the sight. As he watched, the violet shadows were dissolved by the crimson of the fire: 'it seemed that the dawn had invaded the night', he says. According to him, in the morning, the commander of the castle, who must have been a Templar, despaired of the defence. 'When the flames reached his side, he threw himself into a hole full of fire without fear of the intense heat and, from this brazier, he was immediately thrown into another [that of Hell].' So important was the destruction of the

---

[19] Abu Shama, p. 203.
[20] Ibn al-Athir, pp. 637-8.
[21] Abu Shama, p. 204.
[22] Abu Shama, p. 205.

castle to Saladin that he tore at its stones with his own hands. He destroyed it 'as one effaces the letter of a parchment'.[23] Imad al-Din says that Saladin stayed fourteen days in all, including the siege. Before returning to Damascus, though, he ravaged the regions around Tiberias, Tyre and Beirut, in order to spread terror.[24]

The building, siege and demolition of Jacob's Ford all took place in less than a year, but the events nevertheless reveal a great deal about the importance of the frontier in the relations between the Latin settlers and their Muslim enemies. It may be that, in his determination to refute Deschamps's belief that the Franks built castles to defend their frontiers, Smail overstated his case.[25] Jacob's Ford was clearly important to both sides, as can be seen by the large sums of money involved; Saladin's top offer of 100,000 dinars to compensate for its demolition seems realistic. Indeed, his willingness to try negotiation before force should be seen in the context of his belief that the building of the fortress was part of a concerted strategy by the Franks to consolidate and even expand their eastern frontiers. According to Imad al-Din:

> In this year [1179], the Franks resolved to disturb the Muslims from all sides at the same time, in order to prevent their concentration at a single point. As the prince of Antioch [Bohemond III] had violated the truce in invading the country of Shayzar, and the count of Tripoli had attacked a troop of Turcomans after having accorded them a truce, the sultan placed his nephew Taqi al-Din on the frontier of Hamah, adding to him Shams al-Din and Saif al-Din; he also posted Nasir al-Din on the frontier of Hims in order to oppose the count of Tripoli. Beyond this he wrote to his brother al-'Adil, who was his lieutenant in Egypt, to detach a squadron of 1,500 Egyptian horsemen to reinforce the army of Syria which was going to attack the enemy.[26]

Saladin may well have been right, for Latin strategy seems to have been driven more and more by the military orders, who perhaps had a better appreciation of the need to adopt such a policy than any individual lord or even the king. The Templars were acutely conscious of the frontiers: they were already established in the north in the Amanus Mountains, in the centre in southern Tripoli, and in the south around Gaza. The reinforcement of their enclave around Safad in Galilee was a logical further step. Imad al-Din says that Saladin's advisers told him that 'Jacob's Ford was built to command the weak

---

[23] Abu Shama, pp. 206-7.
[24] Abu Shama, pp. 205-6.
[25] R.C. Smail, *Crusading Warfare (1097-1193)* (Cambridge, 1956), pp. 207-8.
[26] Abu Shama, p. 198.

points of the Muslim frontier and render passage very difficult'.[27] Moreover, for the Templars it had an added advantage. Ibn Abi Tayy, quoted by Abu Shama, says that 'this strong castle appertained to the Templars who had furnished the garrison abundantly with victuals and weapons of all kinds, in order that they could pillage Muslim caravans'.[28] This was, indeed, an established part of the Templar repertoire, and had already proved very profitable in the south, most notably in the attack on the caravan of Nasir al-Din of Egypt in 1154.[29] Smail's impression that there was no coherent frontier policy may well therefore have been derived from his observation of the piecemeal and inconsistent approach which resulted from extensive noble autonomy in the earlier part of the twelfth century: the military orders seem to have been in the process of changing that in the years before Hattin.

As the account of the conflict shows, the warfare which resulted from these suppositions was devastating. Setting aside the defeat at Marj Ayun which preceded the siege, the Franks lost the entire garrison, either killed or enslaved. Imad al-Din says that of the 700 or so prisoners taken, the greater part was massacred, while the rest went to the Damascus slave markets. This includes the eighty knights of the garrison, all or most of whom must have been Templars. Nor was the victory without cost to the Muslims for, soon after, disease broke out among Saladin's troops, 'as a consequence of the extreme heat and the stench of the cadavers'. Ten of his emirs died from this.[30] The material costs were also immense. Apart from a castle worth at least 100,000 dinars, the pillaging and wasting of the surrounding countryside in, it must be remembered, a year of drought and famine, meant that it was never again practical to consider erecting a castle at the ford. It may, indeed, have been the beginning of the decline of Safad, described by the bishop of Marseilles in 1240 as little more than a heap of stones in which lived an impoverished Templar garrison.[31] In April 1180, Farrukh-Shah devastated the region around

---

[27] Abu Shama, p. 194. Recent studies confirm the increase in the relative importance of the military orders. See S. Tibble, *Monarchy and Lordships in the Latin Kingdom of Jerusalem, 1099-1291* (Oxford, 1989), pp. 158-61, for the growth of the influence of the military orders in Galilee, and A. Jotischky, *The Perfection of Solitude: Hermits and Monks in the Crusader States* (University Park, Pa., 1995), pp. 61-2, for the way that monastic foundations sought the protection of the orders in vulnerable areas.

[28] Abu Shama, p. 197.

[29] WT, pp. 822-3. William gives this story an anti-Templar slant, but however the incident is interpreted, it is clear that the Templars were using their base at Gaza in this way.

[30] Abu Shama, pp. 205-6.

[31] Huygens, 'De constructione', p. 379.

Safad, apparently without opposition.[32] According to al-Fadil, after the destruction of Jacob's Ford there was nowhere habitable for the Franks in that region 'other than the fortresses and the towns'.[33]

However, the implications of the destruction of Jacob's Ford, costly as they were in men and materials, went far beyond the fighting of 1178-9, for its fall transformed the whole strategic position. There is little evidence to suggest that, during the 1170s, the Muslim threat was likely to be fatal to the kingdom of Jerusalem. According to al-Fadil, when Nur al-Din died in May 1174, his political structure fell apart so rapidly that even Saladin's capture of Damascus in October could not compensate.

> Hardly had we returned to our country, when we learned what was happening in the empire of Nur al-Din: confusion of spirits, discords, and anarchy reign throughout. In each strong place a chief has installed himself, each country pretending to be its own. The Franks have constructed some fortresses where they terrorize the Muslim frontiers and block Syria in closely. The principal emirs of the court of Nur al-Din are thrown into prison, put to the torture, and their property confiscated. The stupid mamluks created to obey and not to command, present themselves standing before the noble council and do not sit down, elevating their hands, eyes, and sabres; they live only to make evil and to take goods.

The conclusions he drew from this are unequivocal. 'We are convinced that, if a means is not found of taking Jerusalem, if energetic action is not taken to extirpate the religion of the infidels, it will extend its roots and bring grave blows to the true religion.'[34]

By the summer of 1176 Saladin was profoundly worried about the situation. Ibn Abi Tayy says that this was one of the main reasons why he made peace with Sinan ibn Salman, the Assassin leader, whose fortress of Masyaf he had been besieging, and concentrated his attention upon the Latins. 'He feared that the Franks would only profit from his removal to stir up troubles in upper Syria and realize great advantages there.'[35] He was correct in this assessment, for the Latins were able to mount two expeditions in the region with the help of Philip, count of Flanders, who had arrived at Acre in September 1177. The Muslims took his presence extremely seriously. Imad al-Din describes him as 'one of the most powerful chiefs among the infidels', who believed that the Muslims should be driven out of Syria entirely, while Ibn al-Athir saw him as

---

[32] Ibn al-Athir, p. 640.
[33] Abu Shama, p. 209.
[34] Abu Shama, pp. 178-9.
[35] Abu Shama, p. 179.

'one of their most redoubtable tyrants'.[36] In October, Philip besieged Hamah in association with Raymond of Tripoli and, the next month, moved against Harim with Bohemond of Antioch. Ibn Shaddad, Baha' al-Din, who, although he only entered Saladin's service in 1188, is a reliable source for these years as well, says that news of dissension between al-Salih, ruler of Aleppo and son of Nur al-Din, and Gumushtigin, his governor of Harim, had 'excited the ambition of the Franks'.[37] Although neither attack was successful, in the estimation of Ibn al-Athir the siege of Hamah was so ferocious that they came very close to taking the place, while William of Tyre thought that Harim had almost been within the grasp of the Christians.[38] But these failures of the Christians were minor compared to Saladin's attempt to take advantage of their activity in Syria by invading the southern part of the kingdom, which led to his severe defeat at Montgisard on 25 November. Imad al-Din does not try to hide the extent of this blow, calling it 'a disastrous event, a terrible catastrophe', while Ibn Shaddad believed that it was so damaging that the Almighty 'had repaired it afterwards with the celebrated victory of Hattin'.[39]

Although Farrukh-Shah inflicted considerable damage on Baldwin's army at Belfort, near Banyas, on 10 April 1179, and Saladin himself managed to turn a dangerous situation to his own advantage at Marj Ayun two months later, the overall military record of the sultan and his allies against the Franks between 1174 and 1179 is at best mediocre, emphasizing even more strongly how important it was for the Muslims to prevent the long-term establishment.of the castle at Jacob's Ford. A comparison of the situations before and after Jacob's Ford brings out the point with some force. In 1174 Saladin had failed to take Aleppo, without which he would be unable to surround the Franks. In the years which followed he had met with relatively little success in his attempts to harass the enemy within its own lands; indeed, it was the Franks who often took the initiative, culminating in the attempt to build Chastellet. Yet, with the notable exception of Reynald of Châtillon, Frankish military activity between 1180 and 1187 was almost entirely reactive, characterized by frantic attempts to plug holes in their defences as Saladin's forces made regular incursions into Galilee in the north, battered away at Kerak in the south-east, and even opened

---

[36] Abu Shama, p. 191; Ibn al-Athir, p. 630.

[37] Abu Shama, p. 191.

[38] Ibn al-Athir, p. 630; WT, p. 995. Both sources agree that the Latins allowed themselves to be bought off at Harim, a circumstance which only increased William's mistrust of Philip of Flanders.

[39] Abu Shama, pp. 188, 189.

up a new frontier on the west by making hitherto unprecedented naval attacks, including one on the port of Acre – 'the Constantinople of the Franks'[40] – in October 1179.

The vulnerability of Galilee following the removal of Jacob's Ford and the weakening of Safad was demonstrated immediately after the expiry of the two-year truce which had been made in May 1180.[41] Saladin had set out from Egypt with a vast array of caravans and merchants because, according to Ibn al-Athir, once again 'scarcity prevailed in Syria',[42] and the Franks assembled their forces at Kerak in an attempt to intercept him. Imad al-Din remarks:

> It was then that Farrukh-Shah came out of Damascus and, finding the territory of the Franks empty of troops, ravaged Tiberias and Acre, and took Daburiya. Arriving in front of Habis Jaldak, on the cultivated territory of Damascus, he took possession of this rock which dominated the Muslim countryside and made from this position an observation post against the infidels who had first possessed it.[43]

Although the fall of this cave fortress was attributed by the Franks to Syrian treachery,[44] its position to the south-east of the Sea of Galilee, almost equidistant from Tiberias and Baisan to the west, was quite isolated. Farrukh-Shah was able to take back 'a rich booty' from this raid, which included 1,000 captives and 20,000 animals. Consequently, by late July Saladin himself was raiding into the districts of Tiberias and Baisan, and fought a hard battle with the Franks below Belvoir from which neither side could claim a clear victory.[45] Although Raymond of Tripoli achieved a rare Frankish success when he recaptured Habis Jaldak in December 1182, this was a minor event compared to the surrender of Aleppo to Saladin on 12 June 1183. The Christians were under no illusions about the significance of this: from now on, they were, says William of Tyre, 'almost besieged'.[46]

The long-term consequences of easy access to Galilee can be seen on 29 September 1183, when Saladin entered Baisan. Ibn Shaddad says that he found

---

[40] Abu Shama, pp. 209-11.

[41] Although this left Saladin free to pursue other goals within the Muslim world, the effort involved in the campaigns of 1178-79 had so exhausted the Franks, they were only too pleased to accept a respite.

[42] Ibn al-Athir, p. 651.

[43] Abu Shama, p. 218. Ibn al-Athir, p. 652, describes the rock fortress as a source of great damage to the Muslims.

[44] WT, p. 1029.

[45] Abu Shama, p. 218.

[46] WT, p. 1047.

it 'abandoned by its inhabitants; they had taken flight leaving there their movable effects, cereals, and other things difficult to transport; the troops pillaged the town, seized this booty and burnt all they could not carry'.[47] Al-Fadil writes as a participant:

> In the morning [the 29th], your servant and his troops, under the eye of God whose cause they were defending, arrived at the Jordan, a river which separates the Muslim lands from those of the infidel, and to a ford protected on this side by a wall ... After the passage of the ford, the country submitted like the stallion breaking fugitive camels; the soil trembled and broke under the weight of the army to which it offered easy booty ... the inhabitants had deserted their country ... there were towns which we could not formerly have dreamed of approaching, prosperous localities which we used not to have any hope of attaining ... for example Baisan, Kerferbela, Zar'in, Jinin, all celebrated cities, encircled by flourishing villages, shady gardens, navigable rivers, high fortresses, and powerful walls in the enceinte of which their palaces were built. The Muslims took their rich provisions; they sated upon them the hatred of their hearts; they delivered to the flames these refuges of impiety, inflicting on them the punishment which awaited those who inhabited them.[48]

The campaign which followed led to the stand-off by the main Frankish army at Saffuriyah when attacked by the Muslims on 8 October, a tactic which kept the army largely intact, but which lost Guy of Lusignan the regency soon after. So dominant had Saladin's troops been during the eight days which this lasted, the army nearly starved, since nobody was able to bring provisions.[49] The repercussions can be seen before Hattin in July 1187, when Guy, acutely aware of this campaign, chose to march to relieve Tiberias rather than stay encamped at Saffuriyah.[50]

The importance to Saladin of the destruction of the Frankish castle at Jacob's Ford is further underlined by his frustration at not being able to take Kerak, which occupied an equally key position to the south-east of the

---

[47] Abu Shama, p. 243.

[48] Abu Shama, pp. 246-7.

[49] WT, p. 1053, on the starvation. The success of the waiting tactic was only relative, for the skirmishing involved took a considerable toll. Saladin's initial attack on the Franks at Saffuriyah on 1 October is described by Ibn Shaddad as a bloody encounter, which cost many dead and wounded, Abu Shama, p. 243.

[50] On the links between these events and their effects on Guy's behaviour, see P. Edbury, 'Propaganda and Faction in the Kingdom of Jerusalem: The Background to Hattin', in *Crusaders and Muslims in Twelfth-Century Syria*, ed. M. Shatzmiller (Leiden, 1993), especially pp. 177-8, 189.

kingdom. Kerak was more difficult to overcome because it was a completed fortress, which made skilful use of its defensive position along a narrow ridge. Even though it was sometimes possible to take the lower town, 'the large and deep fosse, formed by a frightful ravine', described by Imad al-Din,[51] proved impassable, despite really sustained efforts by Saladin in November and December 1183, and again the following autumn. Al-Fadil's lament in one of his letters conveys some sense of what Kerak meant to the Muslims.

> It is the anguish which seizes the throat, the dust which obscures the view, the obstacle which strangles hopes and lies in wait to stop courageous resolutions; it is the wolf that fortune has posted in this valley and the excuse of those who abandon the duty of pilgrimage prescribed by God. Kerak and Shaubak [Montréal] (may God assure final success!) recall this verse in which the poet is speaking of two lions: *A day does not pass that they do not devour human flesh or do not drink blood.*[52]

More mundanely, Ibn Shaddad put it this way: 'This place caused considerable damage to the Muslims because it closed until then [1183] the route from Egypt and obliged the caravans to move under the protection of an army corps.'[53]

Saladin's frustration was increased many times over by the aggressive policies of its lord, Reynald of Châtillon, whose daring raid upon the Red Sea ports in the autumn of 1182, and attacks on Muslim caravans in the Moab at the end of 1186, breaching an established truce, so angered him that Saladin 'swore that he would have his life'.[54] Muslim hostility was partly based on fear that the Franks would find their way into this area regularly, using Kerak as a base. When, in February 1183, some of the Franks involved in the attack along the coast of the Hidjaz were captured, Saladin ordered that there should not 'remain among them either an eye capable of seeing nor a single man capable of indicating or even knowing the route from this sea'.[55] Ibn al-Athir saw Reynald of Châtillon as 'the most hostile of all [the Frankish demons] against the Muslims', while Imad al-Din calls him 'the most perfidious and the most evil of the Franks, the most avid, the most eager to do injury and to

---

[51] Abu Shama, p. 253. For the details of this castle, see H. Kennedy, *Crusader Castles* (Cambridge, 1994), pp. 45-52.

[52] Abu Shama, p. 251.

[53] Abu Shama, p. 250.

[54] Abu Shama, p. 259.

[55] Abu Shama, p. 232.

make evil, ...'.[56] In fact the depth of hatred for Reynald of Châtillon which is conveyed in Muslim sources indicates very clearly just how much damage he was capable of inflicting, partly because of the nature of his personality and partly because of his possession of Kerak. A castle at Jacob's Ford, under the command of a powerful garrison of Templars, would surely have been at least as dangerous to the territory of Damascus and to Muslim armies and caravans travelling there.

It seems therefore that, during the reign of Baldwin IV, the struggle to gain control over the eastern frontier of the kingdom of Jerusalem became the crucial element in the survival of the crusader states. Both sides recognized this and were prepared to throw in resources of manpower and materials on a huge scale. The warfare which resulted was deeply destructive of the environment, in particular of Galilee, and profligate of human life. In such circumstances each new conflict increased the depth of bitterness still further, so ultimately there could be no compromise. Even if Imad al-Din's claim that Raymond of Tripoli would have embraced Islam, 'had he not feared the people of his religion', cannot be substantiated, there is no doubt that Raymond's attempts to secure some favour with Saladin can have done little for his credibility among those who had suffered from the devastation of the frontier warfare of these years. Indeed, whatever may have been the contacts from time to time between individual Christians and Muslims, the basic struggle over possession of places holy to both religions remained. Jacob's Ford had great strategic importance, but it was also a religious site. William of Tyre explained that old traditions say that 'this is the place where Jacob, returning from Mesopotamia, having sent messengers to his brother and divided the people into two parts, said, "With my staff I have crossed the Jordan and now I am returning with two groups".'[57] According to Genesis 32:10 Jacob did indeed cross the Jordan here on the way to meet his brother Esau. However, like so many sites in the region, it also had its significance to the Muslims. There are various legends about Jacob in Islamic literature and he is discussed in the Koran. Early

---

[56] Ibn al-Athir, p. 647; Abu Shama, p. 251. See also B. Hamilton, 'The Elephant of Christ: Reynald of Châtillon', in *Religious Motivation: Biographical and Sociological Problems for the Church Historian*, ed. Derek Baker, *Studies in Church History* 15 (Oxford, 1978), pp. 97-108, who argues that 'in the second half of his public life [i.e. after his release from prison in 1176] he was sincerely committed to the crusader cause in a way in which he had not earlier been' (p. 99). This may be taking the rehabilitation of Reynald a little too far, but whatever his motives, it is evident that almost alone among the Franks he was prepared to take the war to the Muslims, rather than simply waiting to be attacked.

[57] WT, p. 997.

Meccan *surahs* make him the brother rather than the son of Isaac. This fits with Imad al-Din's statement that, after the fall of the fortress, the ford 'became a place of pilgrimage as before, sanctified by the actions of grace and prayers of the Muslims'.[58] At Jacob's Ford, the calculations of the strategists were reinforced by the certainties of belief.

The failure to complete and secure the castle at Jacob's Ford in 1178 and 1179 can be seen, at least in retrospect, as a major turning-point for the Franks. Although the sides settled on a two-year truce after the fall of the castle, William of Tyre believed that Saladin had agreed to this not from fear of the Franks, but because of the problems caused by the recent five-year drought in the region of Damascus. In William's estimation, the balance had already changed, for he knew of no other instance in which the Franks had been obliged to make a truce without laying down at least some conditions.[59] While some allowance needs to be made for William's anxiety to stress to a Western audience the danger which Jerusalem faced,[60] nevertheless the expiry of the truce coincided with the loss of Byzantine support after the installation of the anti-Latin regime of Andronicus Comnenus in September 1182,[61] a notable absence of heavyweight crusaders from the West equivalent to Philip of Flanders, and the increasing mental and physical paralysis of a king now clearly losing his fight against leprosy.[62] What followed was the bleakest period of the existence of the crusader states in the whole of the twelfth century.

---

[58] Abu Shama, p. 206.

[59] WT, p. 1008.

[60] See P.W. Edbury and J.G.Rowe, *William of Tyre: Historian of the Latin East* (Cambridge, 1988), p. 171. See, too, the less than flattering assessment of Lyons and Jackson, *Saladin*, p. 240, on Saladin's overall achievement by early 1186.

[61] See B. Hamilton, 'Manuel I Comnenus and Baldwin IV of Jerusalem', in *Kathegetria: Essays presented to Joan Hussey on her Eightieth Birthday* (Camberley, 1988), pp. 353-75, and M. Angold, *The Byzantine Empire 1025-1204* (London, 1984), p. 193, who argues that the Byzantine defeat at Myriokephalon in 1176 was not the major disaster it has been made out to be.

[62] WT, p. 1020.

Albert of Aachen and the *Chansons de Geste*

Susan B. Edgington

For the past century and a half the *Historia Ierosolimitana* of Albert of Aachen
– until then an unquestioned authority – has been subjected to critical scru-
tiny.[1] Of several unresolved, possibly insoluble, questions about Albert's
sources of evidence, one of the most fruitful concerns the relationship of the
Historia with poetic sources. It is this problem which is to be discussed here,
not because it is any more soluble today than before, but to reclaim as a
historical question a matter which has recently received more attention in
circles of literary scholarship.[2]

The central question relates to the *Chanson d'Antioche* and is complicated
by the fact that the *Chanson* now exists only as part of a late twelfth-century
cycle of crusade *chansons*, along with the *Chanson des Chétifs* and the
Chanson de Jérusalem.[3] Received theory is that all three were reworkings by
Graindor of Douai of existing *chansons*, and for the *Chanson d'Antioche*
Graindor claimed he used an earlier version which he had from Richard the
Pilgrim. The *Chétifs* and *Jérusalem* epics do not show the striking resem-

[1] H. von Sybel, *Geschichte des ersten Kreuzzugs* (Düsseldorf, 1841); translation: *The History and Literature of the Crusades*, trans. and ed. Lady Duff Gordon (London, 1881).

[2] For a survey, see M. Bennett, 'First Crusaders' Images of Muslims: The Influence of Vernacular Poetry?', *Forum for Modern Language Studies* 22 (1986), pp. 101-22. The best modern historical treatment is E.O. Blake and C. Morris, 'A Hermit goes to War: Peter the Hermit and the Origins of the First Crusade', in *Monks, Hermits and the Ascetic Tradition*, ed. W.J. Shiels, *Studies in Church History* 22 (Oxford, 1985), pp. 104-6.

[3] The most recent editions of these last two *chansons* are vols 5 and 6 in *The Old French Crusade Cycle: Les Chétifs*, ed. G.M. Myers (Tuscaloosa, Ala., 1981) and *La Chanson de Jérusalem*, ed. N.R. Thorp (Tuscaloosa, Ala., 1992).

23

blances to Albert's *Historia* which are found in the *Antioche*, and so it is with this last that some inter-relationship seems certain.

The first modern editor of the *Chanson*, Paulin Paris, was anxious to demonstrate its primacy as a source, at the expense of the Latin narratives. The long title of his work, *La Chanson d'Antioche, composée au commencement du XIIe siècle par le Pèlerin Richard, renouvelée sous la règne de Philippe Auguste par Graindor de Douay, publiée pour la première fois* (1848), demonstrates this.[4] However, Henri Pigeonneau (1877) believed that the strong resemblance between the *Chanson d'Antioche* and Albert's *Historia* was the result of Graindor drawing on Albert and reconciling his narrative with that of the *Gesta Francorum*.[5] This was refuted by Paris in the following year on the grounds that Albert was much richer in romantic episodes and these would have been irresistible to the poet if he had the *Historia* before his eyes.[6] These two positions remain the essence of the debate, as will be seen, and the successors of Paris and Pigeonneau have scarcely shifted their ground, nor have they found new ammunition, although they use the old – the texts – with more sophistication.

It was not until 1932 that the question was exhaustively revisited, by Anouar Hatem in a lengthy discussion of the whole Crusade 'cycle' (though, as he pointed out, none of the manuscript compilations he studied manifested any homogeneity).[7] He was severe about Paris's edition of the *Chanson d'Antioche*, which he considered a 'modèle d'arbitraire et d'incoherence'.[8] Hatem was the first critic to attempt to distinguish the work of Graindor from the original *chanson* by Richard. He suggested, for example, that the first part was Graindor's, but the rest was an original eye-witness account owing nothing at all to Albert or to any other of the Latin narratives.[9] He cited as evidence the favourable treatment of Tatikios – 'Estatins' – in the poem, which is at odds

---

[4] P. Paris, *La Chanson d'Antioche* ..., 2 vols (Paris, 1848).

[5] H. Pigeonneau, *Le cycle de la croisade et la famille du Bouillon* (Saint-Cloud, 1877), p. 37: 'La Chanson d'Antioche n'est qu'un remaniement, et souvent une traduction de la chronique d'Albert d'Aix et de celle de Tudebode, fondues avec une certaine habilité et combinées avec les traditions locales dont la trouvère s'est fait l'écho.' (Quoted by L.A.M. Sumberg, *La Chanson d'Antioche* [Paris, 1968], p. 10.)

[6] P. Paris, *Nouvelle étude sur la Chanson d'Antioche* (Paris, 1878), p. 35.

[7] A. Hatem, *Les poèmes épiques des croisades: genèse - historicité - localisation* (Paris, 1932), especially pp. 168-9 and 339. See also R. Goossens's review of this book, 'L'épopée byzantine et l'épopée romane', *Byzantion* 8 (1933), pp. 706-26.

[8] Goossens, 'L'épopée', p. 706; cf. Hatem, *Poèmes épiques*, p. 83.

[9] See S. Duparc-Quioc, ed., *La Chanson d'Antioche*, 2 vols (Paris, 1977), 1.19-30 and notes (lines 1-267).

with his presentation by all the Latin writers.[10] In Hatem's opinion Richard the Pilgrim was not only an eye-witness, but he could be located with Robert of Flanders's army. He wrote before 1101, Hatem believed: otherwise he would not have been so harsh in his condemnation of Stephen of Blois, who redeemed his reputation by a martyr's death. By inference, any resemblances with Albert had to be the result of Albert's drawing on the *chanson* by Richard the Pilgrim. Hatem's examination of the *Chétifs* and *Jérusalem* concluded that both were written in the East and much later; Robert Goossens postulated a Syrian origin for the *Chétifs* (and dated it to the 1140s), and suggested, almost in passing, Byzantine and/or Arabic literary sources for at least one episode in *Antioche*, thus that this too was perhaps written in Syria.[11] In passing, it should be said that a more recent study of the *Chanson des Chétifs*, by Geoffrey Myers, proposes a first version of the *Chétifs* written around Fécamp c. 1160 and attached then or soon after to the *Chanson d'Antioche* of Richard the Pilgrim.[12]

Claude Cahen, writing in 1940, believed the relationship between Albert and the *Chanson d'Antioche* to be less clear-cut; he suggested that the similarity was because Albert recorded the tales told by merchants and troubadours, which also fed the *chansons*, that is, they shared a common source. At this point Cahen believed the *Chanson d'Antioche* was composed in the West, in 'les régions mosanes'.[13] He was influenced in this, as he later reported (1957), by 'le fait que Albert d'Aix l'avait connue'. This was when Cahen presented his revised opinion, agreeing with Duparc-Quioc that the *Chanson* was written for a clientèle of lords in northern France.[14] At the very end of his working life Cahen returned to the problem, and this time he proposed that Albert had in fact lived in the East until 1119, basing this supposition on the wealth of accurate detail in books VII to XII and the internal consistency of Albert's narrative.[15] Albert's sources for the years 1099-1119 are another interesting question, but Cahen's suggestion is unlikely in view of the dating of the

---

[10] Hatem, *Poèmes épiques*, p. 161.

[11] Goossens, 'L'épopée', p. 725 n. 2.

[12] G.M. Myers, 'Le développement des Chétifs: la version fécampoise?', in *Les épopées de la croisade*, ed. K.-H. Bender, *Zeitschrift für französische Sprache und Literatur, Beiheft* NF 11 (Stuttgart, 1987), pp. 84-90 [hereafter *Les épopées*].

[13] C. Cahen, *La Syrie du Nord à l'époque des croisades* (Paris, 1940), p. 15.

[14] C. Cahen, 'Le premier cycle de la croisade (Antioche - Jérusalem - Chétifs)', *Le Moyen Âge* 63 (1957), pp. 311-28, especially p. 314 n. 7.

[15] C. Cahen, 'A propos d'Albert d'Aix et de Richard le Pèlerin', *Le Moyen Âge* 46 (1990), pp. 31-3.

manuscripts and their dissemination. His earlier conclusions were more securely founded.

The most far-reaching analysis of the *Chanson d'Antioche* was undertaken by Suzanne Duparc-Quioc, who identified the material she believed Graindor had taken from Richard the Pilgrim's original *chanson* and that which Graindor added, largely from Robert the Monk, when he reworked it.[16] She believed Albert had used Richard's *chanson* and was sufficiently confident of her case to claim that Albert could be used to 'reconstitute' it.[17] Duparc-Quioc also used a 'Provençal fragment' for her reconstruction of Richard's *chanson*, but it should be noted that the fragment survives only in a manuscript of the early thirteenth century; thus it presents its own textual problems, not directly our concern here.[18]

In 1980 Robert F. Cook published a new study of the *Chanson d'Antioche* which questioned Duparc-Quioc's reading of the relationship between Albert's *Historia* and the *Chanson d'Antioche*.[19] He presented a detailed and forceful case that the *Chanson* was not written until the late twelfth century and can be shown to conform to the rules of epic which prevailed at that time. He pointed out that Richard the Pilgrim cannot be proved to have existed in the late eleventh century; on the contrary the famous phrase in the *Chanson*, 'Ricars le pelerin de qui nous la tenons', suggests direct transmission rather than long tradition: that is, Richard was a contemporary of the author, and if still alive in the late twelfth century could not have taken part in the First Crusade.[20] Cook claimed that Richard's name was used, in fact, as an epic convention and could quite well have been invented to give authority to the fanciful list of Saracen names which followed it. 'Graindor', too, could be no more than conventional usage. Cook, indeed, was impatient of the attempt to use the

---

[16] S. Duparc-Quioc, 'La composition de la *Chanson d'Antioche*', *Romania* 83 (1962), pp. 1-29 and 210-47.

[17] Duparc-Quioc, 'Composition', p. 22: 'Dans la troisième partie nous essaierons de voir ce qui reste de l'ancienne chanson de Richard le Pèlerin, en comparant notre texte à la chronique d'Albert d'Aix, qui en a connu un premier état, et à la chanson provençale de Béchada, qui l'a copiée egalement.'

[18] The fragment may be consulted in an edition by P. Meyer, 'Fragment d'une *Chanson d'Antioche* en provençal', *Archives de l'Orient latin* 2 (1884), pp. 467-509. It is a unique ms., dating probably from the first half of the thirteenth century. See R.F. Cook, review of Duparc-Quioc, *Chanson d'Antioche*, *Speculum* 55 (1980), pp. 788-90, especially p. 789.

[19] R.F. Cook, *'Chanson d'Antioche', chanson de geste: le cycle de la croisade est-il épique?* (Amsterdam, 1980).

[20] Line 9014 (Duparc-Quioc, *Chanson d'Antioche*, 1.443).

Chanson as a historical source for the First Crusade and viewed it as a created work; an instrument for the presentation in late twelfth-century Europe of a past already distant and exemplary: a *chanson de geste*.[21] Hermann Kleber endorsed Cook's ideas and showed in some detail that Graindor of Douai could have been the 'mécène' (patron) who ordered the work.[22]

Cook further made the point that the Paris/Duparc-Quioc hypothesis was very convenient because it allowed the text to be original or to be a reworking just as one pleased. He pointed out that the greater the degree of correspondence between the *Chanson d'Antioche* and the chronicles, the greater the temptation to say that its truth is 'confirmed', when in fact the information in the *Chanson* could have been drawn from the same sources. Furthermore there is a paradox: we value the *Chanson d'Antioche* as a unique source for a few episodes that are not found elsewhere, but at these very points its veracity is uncorroborated. Cook pointed out that the 'historical' content of the *Chanson d'Antioche* was to be found in different chronicles, a circumstance which was most easily explained by the writer's drawing on several of them, including Albert.[23] An example of the eclectic use of Albert which Cook condemns, not to say of ruthless ellipsis, is to be found with regard to Taphnuz the Armenian. Albert describes at separate points his living in the mountains and his advanced age; Duparc-Quioc suggests these references were the source of Graindor's Old Man of the Mountain (Li Viels a la Montaigne). Thus here we have Graindor drawing on Albert, where elsewhere Albert is thought to be using Richard the Pilgrim. There is a fluidity about the perceived relationship which is unhelpful to the historian.[24]

The difficulty with Cook's thesis is that it does not answer the old, but still valid, question as to why the poet, if he had at his disposal all the riches of Albert's *Historia*, selected certain incidents for inclusion and ignored others

---

[21] See the review of Cook's book by H. Kleber, *Zeitschrift für Romanische Philologie* 99 (1983), pp. 404-6. D.A. Trotter also believes there was a propaganda function in these texts dating from the period of the Third Crusade: *Medieval French Literature and the Crusades (1100-1300)* (Geneva, 1988), p. 246.

[22] H. Kleber, 'Graindor de Douai: remanieur - auteur - mécène?', in *Les épopées*, pp. 66-75; H. Kleber, 'Wer ist der Verfasser der Chanson d'Antioche?', *Zeitschrift für Französische Sprache und Literatur* 104 (1984), pp. 115-42.

[23] Cook, *Chanson*, p. 72: He concluded by suggesting an 'analogie avec la création du texte "clérical" d'Albert': 'Disposant de sources multiples, toutes accessibles en Europe du Nord au dernier quart du douzième siècle, cet auteur [of the *Chanson d'Antioche*] ... a fait des emprunts à ces sources, desquelles la tradition orale n'est pas du tout exclue d'ailleurs.'

[24] Line 2457 (Duparc-Quioc, *Chanson d'Antioche*, 1.140-1); AA, III.31/p. 361.

equally dramatic and colourful.[25] It is further worth noting that Graindor's name is also associated with the *Chétifs* and the *Jérusalem chansons*, and neither of these bears the strong resemblance to Albert's work that the *Chanson d'Antioche* does. If they did indeed have the same late twelfth-century author, then it would be extraordinary for him to have used Albert for *Antioche* and not in the other two *chansons*. The most likely relationship remains the one assumed by Paris and by Duparc-Quioc, that Albert used a primitive version of the *Chanson d'Antioche*. However, Albert probably did not have a written copy of the *Chanson* before him as he worked; there are too many differences in detail.[26] On the other hand, although it is likely that we underestimate the aural memory of those generations who lived in an age where writing was uncommon, it seems unlikely that Albert could have memorized the quantity of information which is shared. It is most likely that Albert heard the *Chanson* and wrote his own detailed notes. There is an intriguing hint, indeed, that Albert worked aurally where he describes the meeting of the princes 'between two mountain peaks, where a certain river had had a bridge put across it (inter duos montium apices, ubi per pontem flumine quodam superato)'. This seems to be a misunderstanding of the *Chanson*'s 'aigue', meaning water, as 'aigu', meaning needle or peak. The result is a topographical improbability.[27] Likewise, Albert is the only writer who calls Antioch's Dog Gate, 'Waiferii', and this could well be a transcription, or mis-transcription of the poet's 'vers pont de Fer'.[28] The idea of aural transmission is compatible with Albert's working method, in so far as this can be deduced from the *Historia*, concerning which Cahen concluded:

> Ses informations sont tantôt d'une exactitude qui exclut une longue transmission, tantôt d'un caractère légendaire qui implique au contraire un certain délai d'élabora-tion. Ce double caractère s'explique facilement si l'on suppose qu'Albert a noté, à mesure qu'il les entendait, les récits des masses de voyageurs qu'il pouvait rencontrer à Aix, pèlerins revenant juste de Terre Sainte ou marchands et trouvères colportant des contes de tous genres. Les mêmes sources, mi-historiques mi-romancées, ont alimenté les plus anciennes parties du Cycle poétique des croisades, avec lesquelles on a depuis longtemps souligné les constantes parentés d'Albert ...[29]

---

[25] See Duparc-Quioc, 'Composition', p. 12.

[26] Duparc-Quioc, 'Composition', pp. 11-12, identifies differences between the two accounts of the same events.

[27] Line 2021: 'A un pont a arvolt, u une aigue desserre' (Duparc-Quioc, *Chanson d'Antioche*, 1.114); AA, II:38/p. 329. See Hatem, *Poèmes épiques*, p. 172.

[28] Line 2910 (Duparc-Quioc, *Chanson d'Antioche*, 1.165); AA, III:39/p. 366.

[29] Cahen, *Syrie du Nord*, p. 12.

Such a hypothetical working method helps to explain the difference in content (there is little difference in style or tone) between Albert's first six books and his account of the years 1099-1119 (books VII to XII), which is sober, detailed and, as far as can be ascertained, reliable. The later account differs, in fact, from the narrative of the First Crusade mainly in that it has lost the admixture of legendary, *chanson*-style material. Epic poems on the First Crusade, by Richard the Pilgrim or not, were circulating in Europe early in the twelfth century; there is no evidence for similar poems about the reign of Baldwin I. Settlement is more prosaic than crusade. Albert used whatever materials were available to him and he wove into his narrative every kind of information that came his way. Thus for 1099-1119 he constructed a coherent account from a variety of written and oral sources, as he had for the First Crusade.[30]

Albert's use of *chanson* sources was also the subject of a study by Cola Minis in 1973.[31] Minis was of the opinion that Richard the Pilgrim's *Chanson* was completed c. 1130 and was therefore not known to Albert, whose work was used by Graindor.[32] More significantly, the study identified an impressive number of stylistic elements shared with the *Chanson de Roland* which is thought to date from the end of the eleventh century.[33] These included the wording of warrior-lists; the use of duplication; formal rankings (e.g. 'episcopi, abbates, monachi, canonici et presbyteri'[34]). There may be added to Minis's list a further possible borrowing, if somewhat oblique: Albert is alone in calling the Cilician gates in Asia Minor the Judas gate ('per ualles Buotentrot superatis rupibus, per portam que uocatur Iudas'). This could be a confused or half-memory of the *Chanson de Roland*, for there Butentrot was the provenance of the first rank of Baligant's army. The *Roland* author probably intended Butintro in Epirus, where according to legend Judas was brought up, rather than Butentrot in Cappadocia, but the juxtaposition is suggestive.[35] The

---

[30] He refers to eye-witness accounts on many occasions throughout the *Historia*, e.g. AA, I:23/p. 290, I:24/p. 291, II:33/p. 324, III:65/p. 385, IV:53, 55/pp. 427-8, VI:24/p. 480, VIII:21/p. 572.

[31] C. Minis, 'Stilelemente in der Kreuzzugschronik des Albert von Aachen und in der volksprachigen Epik, besonders in der "Chanson de Roland"', in *Literatur und Sprache im Europäischen Mittelalter: Festschrift für Karl Langosch zum 70. Geburtstag*, ed. A. Önnerfors, J. Rathofer and F. Wagner (Darmstadt, 1973), pp. 356-63.

[32] Minis, 'Stilelemente', p. 362: no reference is given for this dating.

[33] J. Bédier, ed., *La Chanson de Roland* (Paris, 1922), pp. ii-iii.

[34] AA, II:24/p. 317.

[35] AA, III:5/p. 342, cf. Bedier, *Chanson de Roland*, line 3220, p. 268. See R. Fawtier, *La Chanson de Roland* (Paris, 1933), p. 86.

conclusion Minis reached was that Albert's style is closer to vernacular poetry than to other Latin chronicles. That Albert knew and was influenced by poetic sources is a reasonable assumption.

The Latin poem of Gilo of Paris offers a problem not dissimilar from the *Chanson d'Antioche* in that its final version has definite echoes of Albert, but in this case the relationship is more easily explained.[36] It seems clear that Gilo's original poem drew on the *Gesta Francorum*, Robert the Monk and Raymond of Aguilers, and also, probably, on epic sources including an early version of the *Chanson d'Antioche*. The dating of this first poem, Gilo's, is disputed, but it was probably written towards 1120.[37] There was then a version with interpolations, which may have been written as late as the last third of the twelfth century, the date of the Charleville manuscript in which it is first found. The interpolator is often called Fulco, but this is a very late ascription and C. Grocock prefers to call him 'the Charleville poet' from his presumed locality. It is in the interpolated passages that the resemblances to Albert are found, and this is most easily explained by the poet's having made use of the *Historia*: notably, Charleville is within Albert's known sphere of influence (as defined by manuscript dissemination) – Cahen's 'régions mosanes'.

To claim that Albert was aware of and influenced by early *chansons* is not to say that he modelled himself upon them. Critics have sought to categorize the *Historia* as epic, as saga, as romance. The Victorian historian, Thomas Archer, saw Albert as a spiritual ancestor of Sir Walter Scott as well as Froissart:

> Last of all, in Albert of Aix the First Crusade created the historical romance – that form of narrative where historic truth decks itself out with all the pomp and trappings of her sister, Fiction. This peculiar product of the Middle Ages found its first expression in the *Historia Hierosolimitanae Expeditionis* of the Canon of Aix. Nowhere else do we breathe the very atmosphere of mediaeval life ... It has vitality and motion everywhere; the ring of battle is on every page; there is adventure and pathos and mystery, deeds of noble daring, hairbreadth escapes, gallant exploits,

---

[36] *RHC Oc.*, 5.693-800. A new edition of Gilo's work has recently appeared: *The* Historia vie Hierosolimitane *of Gilo of Paris and a Second, Anonymous Author*, ed. and trans. C.W. Grocock and J.E. Siberry (Oxford, 1997). I am grateful to Chris Grocock and Elizabeth Siberry for personal communications in advance of their edition.

[37] C. Grocock in his thesis (Ph.D. London, 1982) thought that it was composed as early as 1107, but he disputed the use of Robert the Monk and argued for a common source with Robert. Duparc-Quioc believed Robert was used, and hence the later date: S. Duparc-Quioc, 'Un poème latin du XIIe siècle sur la première croisade', in *Les épopées*, pp. 35-49. This is the clearest analysis of the poem.

reckless feats of arms by land and sea ... Few works of its enormous bulk had such a popularity as Albert's history enjoyed in the Middle Ages ... the first specimen of quite a new style of historical literature, one that has given pleasure to a greater number of readers than any other that has ever existed. It would not be too much to say that Albert is the spiritual ancestor of Froissart. The Canon of Aix has all the good qualities and all the bad qualities that signalize the Canon of Chimay.[38]

Ernest Barker described the *Historia* as 'genuine saga in its inconsistencies, its errors of chronology and topography, its poetical colour, and its living descriptions of battles'.[39]

But rather than romance or saga, Albert's work has been viewed as an early prose epic. The first reason for this lies in his treatment of Godfrey of Bouillon. Joseph de Ghellinck, for example, wrote: '... c'est le premier stade de l'entrée de quelques héros de la croisade dans l'histoire poétique et la légende; le rôle notamment de Godefroid de Bouillon est trop grandi ...'[40] According to Pierre Aubé in his recent biography of Godfrey:

... le but avoué d'Albert d'Aix est à l'évidence le panégyrique. Il a recueilli avec amour les moindres miettes susceptibles d'ajouter à la gloire de son héros ... Il prête aussi une oreille attentive à d'autres récits, moins purs, d'auditeurs envoûtés, à l'imagination prompte à s'enflammer. Il les accueille, les cisèle en maître artisan, les incorpore à la substance irrécusable de son oeuvre pour en faire ce monument composite au latin rugueux, mené tambour battant, empreint d'un élan irrésistible et d'une communicative ferveur.[41]

An objective reading of the *Historia* does not support this view of it as a deliberate aggrandizement, still less a panegyric, of Godfrey. From his first appearance (book II) to his death (book VII) he is certainly the focus of the narrative. He is portrayed on the journey to the East as a strong leader, negotiating on equal terms with both the king of Hungary and the emperor of Byzantium. In the early stages of the campaign, at Nicaea, he is paired with Bohemond; later he is described as leader of the soldiers from all Gaul, and chief and lord of the army.[42] But at the siege of Antioch he is regarded as

---

[38] T.A. Archer, 'The Council of Clermont and the First Crusade', *Scottish Review* 26 (1895), pp. 274-95, especially p. 293; cf. J.W. Thompson, *A History of Historical Writing*, 2 vols (New York, 1942), 1.313: 'It abounds in action, the ring of battle, mystery, pathos, hairbreadth escapes, gallant feats of arms, and reckless adventures on land and sea.'

[39] E. Barker, *The Crusades* (London, 1925), p. 107.

[40] J. Ghellinck, *L'essor de la littérature latine au XIIe siècle*, 2 vols (Brussels, 1946), 1.119.

[41] P. Aubé, *Godefroy de Bouillon* (Paris, 1985), pp. 357-8.

[42] AA, III:9/p. 345.

part of the co-operative leadership, and not always first mentioned either: Robert of Flanders and he seem to have established a working partnership, and Robert's name often precedes Godfrey's. He is usually referred to as Duke Godfrey ('dux Godefridus'), whereas other leaders are not often given their titles; but it is notable that he is not given the flattering adjectives that, for example, Bohemond attracts in the *Gesta Francorum* (most frequently 'prudens' or 'sapiens', but also 'bellipotens', 'honestissimus', 'fortissimus', 'doctissimus').[43] Only after his election as ruler of Jerusalem – and Albert makes it clear that Godfrey was not the first or even the second choice for the role – does the writer adduce tales of visions and portents to show the appointment as God's will.[44]

In reality, the earlier books show no prescience of Godfrey's future. His generosity as a lord is mentioned,[45] and his piety,[46] but his main attributes are warlike ones. His prowess with a cross-bow is described[47] and his strength as a swordsman. This famous scene, where Godfrey cuts off helmeted heads and then slices an armed and mounted Turk in half, apparently seemed a tall story to Albert, who stresses that he was told by eye-witnesses.[48] Alternatively, he may have wished to stress that he was not just employing an epic cliché, for the story parallels two contemporary examples, one relating to Charlemagne and the other to Roland. Oddly – or perhaps again as a deliberate difference – those two heroes sliced the enemy vertically, while Godfrey's feat of arms was a horizontal dissection.[49] An equally well-known story, where Godfrey was injured saving a poor pilgrim from a bear was later embellished by William of Tyre, but Albert makes it clear that the major wound was sustained as a result of clumsiness with his own sword, and Godfrey himself had to be rescued: scarcely the last word in heroism.[50] Most of the legendary material about Godfrey is to be found not in Albert, but in William of Tyre.[51]

---

[43] *GF*, passim.

[44] AA, VI:33-36/pp. 485-8.

[45] AA, IV:54/p. 427.

[46] AA, VI:25/p. 481.

[47] AA, II:33/p. 324.

[48] AA, III:65/p. 385.

[49] C. Meredith-Jones, ed., *Historia Karoli Magni et Rotholandi ou Chronique du Pseudo-Turpin* (Paris, 1936), p. 177; R.N. Walpole, ed., *An Anonymous Old French Translation of the Pseudo-Turpin Chronicle* (Cambridge, Mass., 1979), p. 71. The same exploit is described in the *Chanson d'Antioche*, lines 3667-71 and 3690-7 (Duparc-Quioc, 1.200-2).

[50] AA, III:4/pp. 341-2; WT, pp. 219-20.

[51] WT, pp. 425-32.

Furthermore, William's translators must be held responsible for fathering some of it, unjustly, on Albert. In a footnote they stated: 'The legend of the swan ancestor is told by Albert. William, whose willingness to accept legends about Godfrey is very generous, could not stretch his credulity quite so far.'[52] Albert never referred to the swan-ancestor myth, which is part of the second group of crusade *chansons*.[53] Its mention by William attests William's use of the *chansons*, not Albert's.

With regard to the primary definition of 'epic' as 'narrating the adventures or deeds of one or more heroic or legendary figures', then, the *Historia* falls short.[54] Even H. von Sybel, no supporter of Albert or of the Godfrey cult, observed:

> After this preface of Albert's,[55] we expect to find Godfrey the leading spirit in the crusading army. But when we examine his work, we are astonished to discover no confirmation of the Duke's fame. ... we seek in vain for any cause of Godfrey's preponderance. From an apparent equality with, or even inferiority to, other princes, the Duke suddenly emerges, for no reason whatever, to this dazzling eminence. And this surpassing glory vanishes, while the words which announce it still ring in our ears.[56]

In other words, although Albert must have known about Godfrey's elevation even as he wrote the earlier books, he did not allow this awareness to colour the account of events before Jerusalem. Godfrey's apotheosis was the work of later writers, notably the authors of the *chansons de geste*.

A second definition of 'epic', 'an imaginative work of any form, embodying a nation's conception of its past history', was explored by P. Knoch in a chapter devoted to the German interpretation of the crusade.[57] In Knoch's view, 'Albert's literary aim was to portray Duke Godfrey, with his trusty army of "Germans" as the true leader of the expedition. He did this ... by emphasizing and manipulating invented material (durch Akzentuierung und Manipulation

---

[52] William of Tyre, *A History of Deeds Done Beyond the Sea*, ed. and trans. E.A. Babcock and A.C. Krey, 2 vols (New York, 1943), 1.388 n. 20.

[53] The grouping and dating of the *chansons* are usefully summarized in an appendix by H. Kleber to *Les épopées*, pp. 177-9.

[54] Definitions here and below are from *The Concise Oxford Dictionary of Current English* (9th edn), s.v. 'epic'.

[55] Sybel was misled by an introductory rubric which does not in fact appear in any of the early manuscripts of Albert's work.

[56] Sybel, *History and Literature*, p. 192; see J.C. Andressohn, *The Ancestry and Life of Godfrey of Bouillon* (Bloomington, Indiana, 1947), p. 6 and n. 1.

[57] P. Knoch, *Studien zu Albert von Aachen* (Stuttgart, 1966), pp. 108-25.

des vorgegebenen Stoffs).'[58] According to this interpretation, Albert's writing was informed by a sense of national identity and he used his material with a high degree of sophistication to convey a false picture of events. Both conclusions are questionable. Albert's pro-imperial bias has been discussed at some length elsewhere.[59] To summarize, it may be argued that he was writing an honestly conceived account of events from the perspective of the participants whose information he gathered and used: such people as returned home to the Rhineland and Flanders at different times by way of Aachen. It was his contemporaries in 'French' territory – Guibert of Nogent, Baldric of Dol and Robert the Monk – who popularized the story as *Gesta Dei per Francos*.[60] This title, Guibert's, truly betrays the intention to write a national epic. It was not an unworthy purpose: if Albert had conceived the idea of writing a parallel *Gesta* glorifying the Germans there was absolutely no reason why he should not do so; there was no point in dissembling his interest in the subtle way Knoch suggests, indeed every point in making it clear. Nationalism is the obsession of Albert's modern German commentators, not his own.

In contrast, Albert's literary aim was to write not *gesta* or prose epic, but *historia*; initially, probably, only of the great expedition, though he later continued the account to 1119. The title *Historia* was probably given the work by Albert himself, since it is found at the head of the two early copies of the earliest surviving manuscript (ms. E, which unfortunately lacks its beginning). Copyist E3 called the work *Hystoria Iherosolimitane Expedicionis*, while ms. K had *Historia Ierosolimitana*. Albert chose to write a 'Jerusalem History' when he could have written *Gesta Godefridi* or *Gesta Dei per Teutonicos*. Too much may be read into a title, particularly since there is no proof that Albert allocated it himself, but in this case it describes well the content of the work. *Historia* was a literary genre quite distinct from chronicle or annals and still held within its meaning the two cognates 'story' and 'history'.[61] Like the modern French *histoire*, it was a narrative structure conveying fact or fiction – or both. Albert described his own literary intention in the prologue:

---

[58] Knoch, *Studien*, p. 151.

[59] S.B. Edgington, 'The First Crusade: Reviewing the Evidence', in *The First Crusade: Origins and Impact*, ed. J. Phillips (Manchester, 1997).

[60] Latin texts of the three accounts are to be found in *RHC Oc.* as follows: Robert, 3.717-880; Baldric, 4.1-110; Guibert, 4.113-262.

[61] B. Smalley, *Historians in the Middle Ages* (London, 1974), p. 7; C.S. Lewis, *The Discarded Image* (Cambridge, 1964), p. 179.

Concerning the way and expedition to Jerusalem, until these days unheard of and greatly to be wondered at. Many times I was fired with longing for that same expedition and with writing a discourse on it. Since I was so inspired, but could not go because of various hindrances to the carrying out of my intention, with rash daring I decided to commend to posterity at least some of the things which were made known to me by listening to those who had been there and from their reports, so that even thus I would take great pains, not in idleness, but as if I were a companion in the journey if not with my body then with all my heart and soul. And therefore I have ventured to write ... about their hardship and misfortunes and the way their faith was strengthened, and the good concord of the strong princes and the rest of the men in the love of Christ; how they left their homeland ... and sought exile in the name of Jesus; how they made the journey to Jerusalem with a strong hand and a lusty army, and their triumphant legions killed a thousand times a thousand Turks and Saracens in a bold attack; how they laid open the entrance and approach to the Holy Sepulchre of our Lord Jesus Christ and completely remitted the taxes and tributes of pilgrims wishing to enter there.[62]

The tone of the prologue is not artless: Albert's protestations about his own lack of literary skills – omitted from the above quotation – are formulaic. But nor is he necessarily disingenuous about his purpose in writing, or his method of gathering information. Had he intended to write about deeds (*gesta*) or Godfrey or the Germans then the prologue would surely have set out this intention. In so far as the narrative focused on Godfrey and his followers, this resulted from two circumstances: Albert's sources of information, described above, and his audience. In writing a literary work Albert presumably had a clear idea of his intended audience, which we can only infer from his chosen content and from his use of language: tone, style and register. As far as content is concerned, his method was that of a compiler. He aggregated disparate information, sometimes with little regard to duplication or even contradiction. It is easy to list chronological or topographical inaccuracies.[63] If there was any selection, then the guiding principle was to construct a narrative of action and to eschew reflection or commentary. Apart from the prophetic visions to do with Godfrey's elevation mentioned above, Albert positively avoided mention of the miraculous or supernatural. The result was a story packed with incident, as rather cruelly parodied by Sybel.[64] The lists of names and the recording of the deeds and fates of quite obscure warriors – many more than in any other source, and most of them quite local to the Rhineland region – are a strong

---

[62] AA, I:1/p. 270.

[63] Though not, perhaps, at such length as Sybel, *History and Literature*, pp. 164-91.

[64] Sybel, *History and Literature*, pp. 162-3.

indication that Albert was writing for members of those same arms-bearing families who, after all, provided the ecclesiastical hierarchy as well as the military ranks of contemporary society.

Furthermore, the tone of Albert's *Historia* is curiously secular. Although it is informed by a simple and unusually ecumenical view of religion,[65] and although there is no reason to doubt that Albert was a cleric, he used remarkably few biblical citations, and those taken chiefly from the gospels and the psalms. Notably he did not draw explicitly the obvious parallel between the experiences of the crusaders and of God's chosen people in the Exodus, even though he signals such a comparison in the prologue (above) when he uses the phrase 'in manu forti'.[66] Nor did he use another inviting biblical parallel with the Maccabees, as did Raymond of Aguilers.[67] Equally striking is Albert's restraint in using classical allusions. Although a sprinkling of phrases shows his familiarity with the language of Ovid and Virgil − and whether he knew their works in their entirety or was merely exposed to them during his education or adult life is not an issue − his vivid descriptions of campaigns, sieges and battles are his own, not drawn from the *Aeneid*, for example, or Vegetius.[68] It is as though in response to the crusade 'until these days unheard of and greatly to be wondered at (hiis usque diebus inaudita et plurimum admiranda)'[69] Albert consciously chose the genre *historia* and matched his diction to its demands.

As with the Bible and classical texts, so with the *chansons de geste*: Albert knew and quarried their content, but he stripped it down to the narrative core which suited his literary purpose. Thus he probably knew a *Chanson de Roland*, as Minis proposes, but he made no reference in the *Historia* to

---

[65] See C. Morris, 'The Aims and Spirituality of the First Crusade as seen through the Eyes of Albert of Aachen', *Reading Medieval Studies* 16 (1990), pp. 99-117.

[66] Exod. 13, passim. See D.H. Green, *The Millstätter Exodus: A Crusading Epic* (Cambridge, 1966), and V. Epp, 'Die Entstehung eines "Nationalbewußtseins" in den Kreuzfahrerstaaten', *Deutsches Archiv* 45 (1989), pp. 596-604, especially p. 604.

[67] Raymond of Aguilers, *Le 'liber' de Raymond d'Aguilers*, ed. J.H. and L.L. Hill (Paris, 1969), p. 53; in general see Alan V. Murray, 'Ethnic Identity in the Crusader States: The Frankish Race and the Settlement of Outremer', in *Concepts of National Identity in the Middle Ages*, ed. S. Forde, L. Johnson and A.V. Murray (Leeds, 1995).

[68] I am grateful to Dr Neil Wright for checking Albert's 'borrowings' for me.

[69] This is from the first sentence of the *Historia*'s first book and chapter, and as such it is Albert's true 'phrase liminaire'. Aubé, like Sybel before him, believed the work began, 'Incipit liber primus expeditionis Hierosolymitanæ urbis, ubi Ducis Godefridi inclyta gesta narrantur, cujus labore et studio Civitas Sancta sanctæ Ecclesiæ filiis est restituta', which is not the case: this incipit was found in Bongars's exemplar, a late manuscript now lost: Aubé, *Godefroy*, p. 357; Sybel, *History and Literature*, p. 160 n. 2.

Charlemagne or to previous wars against the pagans, and the stylistic elements he echoed were either unconscious or perhaps, in the case of warrior-lists and rankings, a mnemonic device. The same applies to the early form of the *Chanson d'Antioche* which seems to have provided some of the information he wove into his narrative, including lists of names.[70] However, Albert did not adopt the ethos of the *chansons de geste.* For example, he distinguished accurately between Turks and Saracens, rather than employing a blanket term. Moreover, he did not portray the false picture of Islam which was current in the West, with its many idols: when the Turks' camp was captured after the battle of Antioch the only religious artefacts found there were books, credibly enough, which Albert imagined as containing sacrilegious prophecies.[71] And – *pace* a long line of historiographers – Albert depicted his protagonists as human beings – even Godfrey, among whose people his *Historia* was to find its audience.

It is not too difficult, therefore, to establish a relationship between Albert of Aachen's narrative account of the First Crusade and the *chansons de geste.* In the case of the *Chanson d'Antioche* it seems very likely that an early version was available to Albert and he used it as a source of information alongside other reports and stories which he gathered from people who returned from the expedition and in succeeding years. This is not a revolutionary conclusion to draw from an examination which has involved the study of nine hundred years' historiography. The real interest of the exercise is that it highlights a new set of questions. Did Albert set out to write *historia*, and if so, what did he understand by that term? How did this affect his collection and selection of evidence? How far did his literary purpose influence his prose style, which is unusually simple and direct? What sort of audience did he envisage for his work? In short: what was Albert's purpose in writing the *Historia Ierosolimitana*?

---

[70] There is a good example of the close correspondence in Duparc-Quioc, *Chanson d'Antioche*, 1.72-3.

[71] AA, IV:56/p. 428. See N. Daniel, *Heroes and Saracens: An Interpretation of the Chansons de Geste* (Edinburgh, 1984), especially his conclusions on pp. 263-79; P. Senac, *L'image de l'autre: l'Occident mediéval face à l'Islam* (Paris, 1985), pp. 74-82. For a full discussion M. Bennett, 'First Crusaders' Images of Muslims'.

The Anonymous *Gesta Francorum* and the *Historia Francorum qui ceperunt Iherusalem* of Raymond of Aguilers and the *Historia de Hierosolymitano itinere* of Peter Tudebode: An Analysis of the Textual Relationship between Primary Sources for the First Crusade

John France

Historians have long noted the strong similarities between the accounts of the First Crusade given by the anonymous author of the *Gesta Francorum*, and by Raymond of Aguilers in his *Historia Francorum qui ceperunt Iherusalem*.[1] The obvious similarity between their accounts of the interview between Alexius I and Count Raymond of Toulouse on or about 22 April 1097 was remarked on by the earliest editors and bibliographers of crusader manuscripts.[2] Jacques Bongars commented on the point in the introduction to his collection of crusade sources. Caspar von Barth, in his commentary on the Bongars collection, stated that Raymond of Aguilers had copied from the *Gesta* in this passage: 'Primi auctoris (i.e. anonymi) verba ipsissima ponit Raimundus iste, cum tamen in alio fuerit exercitu, et aeque rebus gestis ipse adfuerit, quae sane res mira mihi obvenit.'[3]

Discussion of the relationship between the two chronicles had been much influenced by this passage which is reproduced here in parallel texts as Appendix 1. The accounts are startlingly close but Raymond of Aguilers gives more details of the exchanges between Count Raymond and Emperor Alexius and

---

[1] *GF*: other editions of the *Gesta* will be cited more fully. Raymond's work was edited in the *RHC Oc.*, 3.235-309 and this edition will be cited as RA. Reference will also be made to *Le 'liber' de Raymond d'Aguilers,* ed. J.H. and L.L. Hill (Paris, 1969).

[2] All dates are as fixed in H. Hagenmeyer, *Chronologie de la première croisade* (Paris, 1902).

[3] J. Bongars in the 'Historiarum studiosus' of his *Gesta Dei per Francos* (Hanau, 1611); C. von Barth, 'Animadversiones et glossaria manuscripta ad Bongars scriptores Palestinae', in J.P. von Ludewig, *Reliquiae manuscriptorum omnis aevi diplomatum ac monumentorum ineditorum adhuc,* 12 vols (Leipzig and Frankfurt, 1720-41), 3.235.

explains the motive for Count Raymond's anger against the emperor. Further, he notes the arrival of the Provençal army and the Bishop of Le Puy, and adds that the emperor gave Count Raymond few presents. The closeness of the two accounts is striking, and this, together with certain anomalies, has given rise to conflicting views of the relationship between the two chronicles.

Sybel remarked on this passage, but he did not believe that there was sufficient evidence to demonstrate a definite relationship between the two chronicles.[4] Hagenmeyer made a close textual comparison of the two works and suggested that Raymond of Aguilers had used the *Gesta*.[5] Klein also explored the whole of the two texts and in the case of this passage suggested that the Anonymous may well have used the work of Raymond of Aguilers.[6] This view has found some support from Iorga and Cahen, whose comments, however, are confined to a discussion of the interview between Alexius and Count Raymond.[7] No comparable textual analysis has been done for Tudebode's work which modern critical opinion has inclined to view simply as a derivative of the *Gesta*. The work of Raymond of Aguilers has been seen as making a limited use of the *Gesta*. A different view has been expressed by the latest editors of Tudebode, J.H. and L.L. Hill, who have suggested that Peter Tudebode, the Anonymous, Raymond of Aguilers and Daimbert of Pisa were all drawing on a lost chronicle of the First Crusade.[8]

Hagenmeyer produced a concordance of similar passages in the works of Raymond of Aguilers and the Anonymous, which is reproduced here as Appendix 2. He seems to have regarded these passages as sufficient evidence to support the view that Raymond of Aguilers had used the *Gesta* in writing his own work and offered virtually no commentary. It is primarily because of this lack of explanation that Hagenmeyer's view has not firmly established

---

[4] H. von Sybel, *Geschichte des ersten Kreuzzuges* (Düsseldorf, 1841), pp. 17-18.

[5] *Anonymi Gesta Francorum*, ed. H. Hagenmeyer (Heidelberg, 1890), pp. 50-8 [to be cited as Hagenmeyer, *Gesta*].

[6] C. Klein, *Raimund von Aguilers: Quellenstudie zur Geschichte des ersten Kreuzzuges* (Berlin, 1892).

[7] N. Iorga, *Les narrateurs de la première croisade* (Paris, 1928), pp. 1-16, 63-79; C. Cahen, *La Syrie du Nord à l'époque des croisades* (Paris, 1940), p. 8 and n. 3.

[8] For example R. Hill in *GF*, pp. x-xi; J.H. and L.L. Hill in their English translation Peter Tudebode, *Historia de Hierosolymitano itinere* (Philadelphia, 1974), pp. 1-12 [to be cited here as Hills, *Tudebode*]; their Latin text, as revised by Jean Richard, was published as Petrus Tudebodus, *Historia de Hierosolymitano itinere* (Paris, 1977) [to be cited here as Hills, *Tudebodus*]. The edition in *RHC Oc.*, 3.9-117 will generally be used here and cited as PT.

itself. His critics, however, have ignored other work of his which has a bearing on the subject.[9]

The only other writer to have analysed the two texts in detail was Clemens Klein in his study of the *Historia Francorum*.[10] Klein, like Hagenmeyer, found considerable similarities between the texts of the *Gesta* and the *Historia Francorum*. His conclusions were perhaps sometimes eccentric, but his comments extended the range of the discussion very widely indeed. Although his work seems largely to have been based on Hagenmeyer, he did not assign priority to the *Gesta*.

In seeking to establish the relationship between these three chronicles, the matter of dating is crucial. Hagenmeyer believed that the *Gesta* was completed very soon after the crusade. In part, this was because he supposed that the *libellus* containing an account of the crusade which Ekkehard of Aura discovered on a visit to Jerusalem in 1101 was the *Gesta*.[11] In part, it was because he read it as a very primitive piece of work, much of which he believed was written at Antioch and the remainder at Jerusalem shortly after the crusade.[12] But there is no reason to believe that Ekkehard found the Anonymous's work which he certainly never used.[13] Recent writing has shown that the apparently artless narrative of the *Gesta,* with its lack of cross-reference, is in fact much more contrived and literary in form and ideological in inspiration than Hagenmeyer or R. Hill thought.[14]

Raymond's work is incomplete, concluding in the middle of what is evidently an account of the negotiations for the surrender of Ascalon. Thus an important

---

[9] See especially his analysis of the letter of Daimbert of Pisa which has been markedly ignored and which is discussed below pp. 42-3.

[10] Klein, *Raimund von Aguilers*, pp. 103-36.

[11] Ekkehard of Aura, 'Hierosolymita', *RHC Oc.*, 5.21 [to be cited as Ekkehard] and see the edition of F.J. Schmale and I. Schmale-Ott, *Frutolfs und Ekkehards Chroniken und die anonyme Kaiserchronik* (Darmstadt, 1972) which will shortly be reissued under the auspices of the Monumenta Germaniae Historica.

[12] Hagenmeyer believed that part of the *Gesta* text, his chapters I-XXIX, corresponding to books I-IX in the Hill edition, was written at Antioch, and the remainder, his chapters XXX-XXXIX, which correspond to Hill book X, at Jerusalem.

[13] J. France, 'The Use of the Anonymous *Gesta Francorum* in the Early Twelfth-Century Sources for the First Crusade', in *From Clermont to Jerusalem: The Crusades and Crusader Societies, 1095-1400*, ed. A.V. Murray (forthcoming).

[14] On the careful use of language and structure, see H. Oehler, 'Studien zu den *Gesta Francorum*', *Mittellateinisches Jahrbuch* 6 (1970), pp. 58-97; K.B. Wolf, 'Crusade and Narrative: Bohemond and the *Gesta*', *Journal of Medieval History* 17 (1991), pp. 207-16; C. Morris, 'The *Gesta Francorum* as Narrative History', *Reading Medieval Studies* 19 (1993), pp. 55-71.

piece of evidence for dating, the point at which the author terminated it, is missing. Hints in the text suggest that he was writing after the crusade. In his prologue he says that he was writing to correct false stories told by deserters from the army and he later refers to the priest Ebrardus, 'qui Iherosolymis pro Deo postea remansit'. The death of the count of Toulouse at Tripoli in 1105 is not mentioned by Raymond which suggests that he wrote before then.[15] A.C. Krey, without any detailed discussion, suggests 1102 and Runciman plumps for the very early date of 1099 although he does not discuss the matter fully.[16] Hagenmeyer pointed out that Fulcher of Chartres may well have finished his account of the First Crusade by 1101 and he certainly used Raymond's work.[17] An early date finds some further support in another work by Hagenmeyer.

In September 1099, Daimbert, 'Pisanus episcopus ... et Godefridus dux ... et Raimundus comes de S. Aegidii et uniuersus Dei exercitus, ... in terra Israel' wrote 'ad papam et omnes Christi fideles'. The circumstances in which this letter was written are of some importance. In September 1099, Bohemond, in alliance with the newly arrived papal legate, Archbishop Daimbert of Pisa, was besieging Laodicea. Robert of Normandy, Robert of Flanders and Count Raymond, returning from Jerusalem on their way home to the West, persuaded the archbishop to desist, and the siege was raised.[18] Godfrey was not present. The letter, which purports to be a summary of the events of the crusade, gives a very pro-Provençal view, even asserting the genuineness of the Holy Lance, and this suggests that the leading force in its writing was the count of Toulouse. Hagenmeyer analysed the letter, and came to the conclusion, from its content and style, that it was the work of Raymond of Aguilers.[19] He believed that Raymond wrote the letter at a time when his major work was only partly finished, and that he used the appropriate parts of the letter when he completed it in the West. Throughout, the author uses the first person plural, but in one passage he reveals very clearly that his 'we' is the Provençal

---

[15] RA, pp. 235, 283; J.H. and L.L. Hill, *Raymond IV de Saint-Gilles, 1041 (ou 1042)-1105* (Toulouse, 1959), p. 140.

[16] A.C. Krey, *The First Crusade* (Gloucester, Mass., 1958), p. 15; S. Runciman, *A History of the Crusades*, 3 vols (Cambridge, 1951-54), 1.328.

[17] FC, pp. 12, 65-70.

[18] Runciman, *History*, 1.300-2.

[19] *Die Kreuzzugsbriefe aus den Jahren 1088-1100*, ed. H. Hagenmeyer (Innsbruck, 1901), pp. 167-74, 371-403 and H. Hagenmeyer, 'Der Brief der Kreuzfahrer an den Papst und die abendländische Kirche, 1099 nach der Schlacht bei Askalon', *Forschungen zur deutschen Geschichte* 13 (1873), pp. 400-12.

army: 'in interiora Hispaniae progrederemur ... Sed quia exercitus noster non multus erat, et in Hierusalem unanimiter venire festinabant ... Cumque auditum esset Antiochiae atque Laodiciae et Rohas, quia manus Domini nobiscum esset, plures de exercitu, qui ibi remanserant, consecuti sunt nos apud Tyrum.' This standpoint is very close to that of Raymond of Aguilers, and the use of the term *Hispania* for the Islamic lands is so characteristic that it is hard to believe anyone other than he wrote the letter. The figures given in the letter for armies and dead, notably at the battle of Ascalon, are not found in Raymond's work which is a major difference. However both the letter and Raymond tell the story of how captured flocks seemed to swell the army as it approached the enemy before Ascalon.[20] At the very least it would seem that Raymond's work was conceived in its main lines by September 1099 and probably written by 1101.

Peter Tudebode says that he was present at the siege of Jerusalem and records the death during the second siege of Antioch of Arvedus Tudebodus who seems to have been his brother. He is the only source for some important incidents, notably the the attack on the Bridge Gate and the death of Rainaldus Porchetus in April 1098.[21] He gives no clue as to when he was writing – the period covered in his work is precisely that covered by the *Gesta*. Everything depends on what view is taken of the originality of his work. Once Tudebode's was considered the original of which the *Gesta* was an abbreviated version, but modern historians have taken the view that although Tudebode went on the crusade he used the *Gesta,* enhancing it by reference to the work of Raymond of Aguilers and his own experience. However a recent study has reasserted the originality of Peter's work and suggested that the similarities between all three of the chronicles studied here can be explained by reference to a lost chronicle.[22] Irrespective of this suggestion, however, the authentic nature of the information unique to Tudebode's work suggests that he was writing very close to the time of the crusade.

Hagenmeyer's concordance indicates a close textual relationship only between parts of the *Historia* and parts of the *Gesta*:

---

[20] *Kreuzzugsbriefe*, p. 170; for the use of *Hispania* to mean the lands of Islam, see RA, pp. 243, 245, 264-5; for the flocks in Daimbert's letter, *Kreuzzugsbriefe*, pp. 172-3; RA, p. 304.

[21] Hills, *Tudebode*, pp. 57-9, 72-3, *Tudebodus*, pp. 79-81, 97, 116, 138; PT, pp. 50-1, 67, 85, 106.

[22] For the evolution of views, see Hills, *Tudebode*, pp. 1-12.

Table 1: Distribution of the points of similarity in Hagenmeyer's table
(All numbers refer to Appendix 2.　* This passage forms Appendix 1 below.)

Gesta Book	Events Described	Points of Similarity
I	The Journey to Constantinople	1
II	Constantinople to Nicaea	St. Gilles & Alexius*, 2
III	Dorylaeum & the Journey	
IV	The March to Antioch	
V	Siege of Antioch to New Year 1098	3
VI	New Year to the Lake Battle	4, 5, 6, 7, 8
VII	The Forts & the St. Symeon Battle	9, 10, 11, 12
VIII	The Capture of Antioch	
IX	The Second Siege & the Victory over Kerbogah	13, 14, 15, 16, 17, 18, 19
X	Antioch to Jerusalem　　To Fall of Ma'arrat al-Nu'man　　'Arqa　　At Jerusalem	20, 21, 22　23, 24　25, 26, 27, 28, 29

This distribution table indicates that Hagenmeyer saw some 30 points of similarity between the two texts. Of these, no less than 17 occur in the passages of the two works concerned with the sieges of Antioch. Clearly, if a detailed analysis indicates that a substantial number of these cases demonstrate a similarity which can only be regarded as textual, then Hagenmeyer's table can be regarded as having demonstrated a very close relationship between the texts.

It is extremely difficult to decide whether two or more eyewitness writers who chose to describe the same events, at first hand, did so independently or not. The room for coincidence is enormous and we know relatively little about how they actually wrote their works. Modern opinion takes the view that the *Gesta* was written by a single person but we cannot assess the influence of

Raymond's co-author, Pons of Baladun. The clearest possible pointer to a close relationship between the two works would be the existence of sustained common passages but the only one of these is the description of the interview of Alexius and Count Raymond at Constantinople, and even here there are differences. The evidence of this passage on the matter of how the texts are related is, however, ambiguous. Failing sustained common passages, we can look for the use of similar words to describe substantially the same events, or for common tricks of style (which may be characteristic of one writer or the other). Further, we can examine their selection of events; a similar selection between writers who were very different men might be something more than coincidental. Clearly, if none of the factors mentioned are present, then we can only regard the two chronicles as independent. In themselves, however, these are not the clearest and simplest of criteria; inevitably, clear-cut conclusions will not always be possible.

Hagenmeyer's table of similarities can now be examined critically to see how far it provides evidence that the two texts are related.

Analysis of Hagenmeyer's table of similarities
(All numbers refer to Appendix 2.)

1) Everything depends on the word *roga*. Hagenmeyer had a deep preoccupation with national uses of particular Latin words, and seems to have regarded this as peculiarly Italian. In fact there is no evidence to support this. This is Raymond's only use of the word, but then he only refers to Le Puy as *Anicio* once, though he must have been highly familiar with the usage.[23] Note too that each chronicler is talking about different events. In the *Gesta* these are the words of the captured imperial police pleading for mercy before Bohemond. Raymond is speaking of the imperial troops who stirred up trouble at Rodestol. There is little evidence to point to textual similarity here.

Appendix I: The Interview of Count Raymond and Alexius. The similarity of the two texts at this point is patent, though attention is drawn to the much more extensive treatment in Raymond's work.

2) The coincidence of words is very strong here indeed. Both chroniclers are describing the same events in exactly the same terms. This seems to be a very strong point.

---

[23] RA, p. 301.

3) The similarity of wording here is pressed too far by Hagenmeyer. What is striking is that these are precisely similar passages, general comments on the situation, coming after descriptions of the city and outlines of the preparations of the besiegers. This seems to be much more than coincidence and suggests a textual connection.

4) Again, the similarity of wording is built on too far by Hagenmeyer. It must have been obvious that the besieged took advantage of the absence of a large part of the crusader army to mount a sortie. Both chroniclers appear to be describing well-known events independently.

5) The similarity of wording is feeble. The Anonymous was not at the battle around the city, his description of it is brief, and the capture of the bishop's standard was probably the highlight which he later remembered. Raymond's description is much longer and more detailed, and the capture of the bishop's standard occurs amongst other incidents.

6) The force of the similarity is lost in Hagenmeyer's extracts. The two writers give very different accounts of the departure of Tatikios, yet in these passages, at the ends of their accounts, both use similar wording, and consign him to divine punishment. This would seem to indicate a close relationship between the two texts at this point.

7) This is a difficult case. Obviously both writers must have known of the general plan of defence against the Turkish attack. For both it was a perfectly natural thing to comment on. On the other hand the two comments are made in much the same way and in much the same language. Such a similarity occurring in isolation could be ignored but this is not possible when it is met with in association with other much stronger cases.

8) This seems to be a very weak case. Raymond and the *Gesta* give rather different accounts of the Lake Battle itself. Raymond gives an adequate description of the fighting around the city which is only mentioned briefly in the *Gesta*. Raymond links these two victories as the gift of God, while the Anonymous is only celebrating the victory of the knights. The two accounts here would seem to be independent. As for wording, as Miss Hill remarks, there are only so many words to describe the same event.[24]

9) It is rare indeed to find two chroniclers agreeing about numbers, in this case the enemy casualties in the St Symeon road battle. Further, Raymond carefully says 'circiter MD', and the *Gesta* speaks of other casualties besides the 1,500. Put together this might seem a formidable case. On the other hand this figure may have been bandied about in the crusade camp,

---

[24] *GF*, pp. x-xi.

especially as, on this occasion, a head count was made.[25] This case must be classified with 7 as secondary.

10) This is somewhat similar to 3. These passages are general comments, not integral to any narrative. This is, therefore, a fairly strong similarity.
11) The two writers here merely appear to be describing the same events.
12) The connection between these two passages appears to be very strong indeed: 'Secure ambulamus huc et adhuc'; 'secure ire et redire'. This, together with the fact that both are commenting on the consequences of the building of the count's tower, suggests that the two texts are closely connected at this point.
13) Raymond and the Anonymous could simply be describing the same set speech in their own slightly different words. This would be enough to account for the closeness of the two texts at this point. However they are very close indeed, and this may rank with cases 7 and 9.
14) The two passages occur in similar contexts, but the content is not the same, and the language is not very close. This is a rather weak similarity but one which might be possible if other passages establish a context of use. It should be classified with 7, 9 and 13.
15) This is really a very strong case. In these long passages both writers are commenting on the price of food and its scarcity. They mention largely the same commodities:

> *GF*: bread, wine, flesh of horses and asses, cocks (15 solidi), eggs (2 solidi), nuts (1 denarius).
> RA: head of horse (2-3 solidi), goat intestines (5 solidi), cock (8 or 9 solidi), bread (said to have cost 5 solidi for a day's supply).

Both then go on to comment that everything was dear, Raymond adding that this was a consequence of the amount of gold in circulation among the better classes. Both then go on to mention the cooking of leaves and their sale, and the cooking of animal hides. The *Gesta* gives a long list of animal hides cooked; Raymond is shorter but adds 'et alia'. Raymond also adds that knights bled their horses for food, preferring not to kill them in case God gave opportunity for escape. Both end by making it clear that they have described only a part of the horrors of the siege. The passages deal with the same subject matter, in the same form. Clearly a close relationship exists between their texts at this point.

---

[25] *GF*, p. 42; RA, p. 249.

16) In the *Gesta* the tale of Stephen's desertion is only part of a longer story. Raymond's account is in the same context, the sufferings at Antioch. Hagenmeyer may have regarded Raymond's as a summary of the Anonymous's account but this is not evidence of a textual connection.

17) Both are dealing with the clerical demonstrations which accompanied the march out against Kerbogah. Both make it clear that the clergy, vested, marched out of Antioch with the army and later stood on the walls praying; Raymond's phrase 'induti stolis albis' is a characteristic one. Raymond's account is more formal, more ecclesiastical, but both are cast in very much the same form. Neither makes it clear whether the clergy only marched so far, then went up to the walls, or whether they were originally divided into two groups. The similarity, striking though it is, may simply spring from two people describing the same dramatic scene. This may be ranked with 7, 9 and 13.

18) The similarity here rests in their descriptions of the plunder taken. Both mention gold and silver without particularizing (though the *Gesta* adds 'multaque ornamenta'), then speak at length of food and animals captured, including camels. This may only reflect the facts of the case — the sort of things which were plundered. This case should rank with 7, 9, 13 and 17.

19) This is a very strong similarity indeed. The ending of a book with a doxology is a characteristic of the *Gesta*; only book VIII fails to end thus. This is, however, the only time that Raymond ends a passage with·such a device. Raymond's is longer and more elaborate but essentially the same.

20) In these passages both chroniclers tell of the death of the bishop of Le Puy and lament his passing. What is striking is the form. In the *Gesta* it is a brief self-contained passage. This is repeated in Raymond's work, which is surprising; Adhémar was his bishop yet he chooses to give no more details than the Anonymous. This seems to rank with 7, 9, 13, 17 and 18.

21) The two passages say essentially the same thing, but Raymond tells us where the leaders dispersed to. The *Gesta* records that this division took place after the leaders had made arrangements for the holding of Antioch, Raymond that it happened after the death of the bishop of Le Puy, of which, he says, it was a consequence. This must be considered with 20.

22) The passage in the *Gesta* is rather misleadingly quoted by Hagenmeyer. Between 'scalam in murum ... alii statim' a great deal else supervenes. Further the passage does not end at 'per murum'. It is not a sense break. It would seem most likely that both are recording, in slightly similar terms, a rather dramatic turn of events to which they were both witness.

23) Both the chronicles give vague descriptions of the siege of 'Arqa, Raymond's chronologically highly confused, the Anonymous's a simple and thin narrative. Raymond is much concerned with miraculous matters into which he tosses hard information about events. Here he sandwiches a comment on the arrival of the fleet between a piece of conscience-searching and his story of the miraculous end of Anselm of Ribemont. The resemblance lies in the form of the two passages. Raymond records the nationalities of the ships coming to their aid, which the *Gesta* does not mention. Both then give lists of the foodstuffs delivered which are substantially the same. This must rank with 7, 9, 13, 17, 18, 20 and 21.

24) In these passages the *Gesta* reports that the emir of Tripoli offered peace, and then goes on to describe the terms actually agreed. Raymond narrates these same terms in the form of an offer made by the emir. By and large the content of the passages and the wording are very similar. The only strange factor is not made clear in the extracts given by Hagenmeyer. The *Gesta* goes on to tell us that the emir offered the crusaders military aid; Raymond makes no mention of this at all. Nonetheless a close textual similarity between the two passages would seem to be indicated.

25) These are general comments made by both writers on the difficulties of the siege. The fact that both make virtually the same comment in much the same language suggests that here the two chronicles are related.

26) These describe the preparations of the besiegers and the besieged: they are similar, but both are describing a specific set of events. The two passages are very alike. Raymond elaborates what is said a little, but he really is saying it in the same way as the Anonymous.

27) In these passages the chroniclers are describing enemy resistance to the final assault. Both comment on the use of fire (which Raymond makes clear was used in projectiles) and, more ordinarily, stones. Otherwise there seems to be little similarity.

28) These passages narrate the solemn blessing of the army before it set out to Ascalon. In the form in which it is set out here it is not clear that the passage in Raymond's work is very much longer and more elaborate than that of the *Gesta*. Both chroniclers are describing a splendid scene, Raymond at some length, but there seems to be no other connection.

29) Both chroniclers are describing the military measures taken to prepare the army for the battle at Ascalon. What they say is cast in very similar form, and the language is, to say the least, reminiscent. The Anonymous states that the threat to excommunicate looters sprang from the patriarch; Raymond places it amongst other orders of the leaders, perhaps because as

a priest the specific origin of such an order would have seemed unremarkable to him.

In some twelve cases – namely: Interview, 2, 3, 6, 10, 12, 15, 19, 24, 25, 26 and 29 – a clear textual similarity is demonstrable. In nine cases the texts seem rather similar: 7, 9, 13, 14, 17, 18, 20, 21 and 23. This does not, as Hagenmeyer remarks, constitute plagiarism.[26] The distribution conforms largely to the pattern established for Hagenmeyer's own table:

Table 2: Distribution table
(All numbers refer to Appendix 2.)

Gesta Book	Events Described	Points of Similarity	
		Strong	Weak
I	The Journey to Constantinople		
II	Constantinople to Nicaea	St. Gilles & Alexius, 2	
III	Dorylaeum & the Journey		
IV	The March to Antioch		
V	The Siege of Antioch to New Year 1098	3	
VI	New Year to the Lake Battle	6	7
VII	The Forts and the St. Symeon Battle	10, 12	9
VIII	The Capture of Antioch		
IX	The Second Siege and the Victory over Kerbogah	15, 19	13, 14, 17, 18
X	Antioch to Jerusalem To Fall of Ma'arrat al-Nu'man 'Arqa Jerusalem	 24 25, 26, 29	 20, 21 23

---

[26] Hagenmeyer, *Gesta*, p. 50.

The main point to be made from this analysis of distribution is that the two texts are most similar when they are describing sieges. Further, it is clear that book X of the *Gesta*, considering the length of time it describes, does not closely resemble the corresponding part of the *Historia Francorum*. However, although there was clearly a textual relationship between them the analysis of Hagenmeyer's table does not indicate how it came about. This is why many have disagreed with his conclusion that Raymond used the Anonymous's work.

In his comments on the Latin sources for the First Crusade, Cahen suggests that the Anonymous borrowed from the *Historia* in his account of the interview between Alexius and the count of Toulouse: 'Que l'emprunt n'est pas de Raymond aux Gesta résulte de son détail original sur les cadeaux d'Alexis Comnène à Raymond de Toulouse, et de l'absence d'allusion au combat entre Grecs et Provencaux, ce qui rend incompréhensible le désir de vengeance du comte.' This is precisely the case first made by Klein who considered the question of the relationship between the two texts at length. He pointed out that Hagenmeyer had really assumed that the *Gesta* was written before the *Historia*, and came to the conclusion that priority cannot be assigned to either work.[27] Nor was he impressed by Hagenmeyer's concordance. He dismisses most of the similarities pointed to as 'at best a question of reminiscences' springing largely from 'the narrow vocabulary of medieval chroniclers' and he can only see anything resembling a strong similarity in three cases.[28] This does not, however, mean that he believed the two works to be independent. He suggests that each author, in various passages, shows knowledge of the other's work.

He arrives at this singular conclusion by a new method. Klein noted that in each chronicle there are serious anomalies. Above all, he commented at length on the failure of the Anonymous to explain the count of Toulouse's anger against Alexius, and this led him to the general conclusion that: 'a communication in one author, in itself inexplicable, can be clarified in the words of another.'[29] In other words, at points where one chronicler makes an obscure or wholly isolated statement which can only be explained by reference to the other work, we are entitled to assume his dependence: he points to some

---

[27] Klein, *Raimund von Aguilers*, pp. 102-13 considers the Anonymous's use of Raymond's work is 'mathematischer Sicherheit': Cahen, *Syrie du Nord*, p. 7 nn. 2-8, comments that 'l'oeuvre de Klein est inutilisable'.

[28] Klein, *Raimund von Aguilers*, pp. 99-100. The three passages he concludes as reasonably similar are numbered 11, 19 and 25 in Appendix 2.

[29] Klein, *Raimund von Aguilers*, p. 115.

seventeen cases, in nine of which he believes Raymond used the *Gesta*, and in
seven of which the Anonymous seems to have referred to the *Historia*.[30]
Klein does not try to explain how this happened; he leaves that to future
writers who may be able to find out more about how these chronicles were
written.

The difficulties of Klein's method are obvious. Both chroniclers left glaring
gaps which we have to fill in from elsewhere; neither, for example, mentions
the Council of Clermont. The Anonymous may have been ignorant of the event,
but Raymond of Aguilers seem to have left it out deliberately, presumably
because he felt the event was sufficiently well known, at least to his audience,
the southern French. This kind of allusiveness, allied to defective technique and
prejudice produces serious anomalies in both chronicles which we can only
elucidate by reference to each other and to other sources. Scepticism about the
weakness of the method can only be reinforced by reference to particular cases.
Klein points out that both works stress the slack way in which the army began
the siege of Antioch. He believes, however, that Raymond's comment, that if
the enemy had seen this they could have attacked successfully, can only be
understood in the light of the *Gesta*'s remarks about enemy spies coming from
the city. This is just not the case; Raymond of Aguilers's comment makes
perfect sense in its own context. Worse still, he suggests that both chroniclers
give the same reason for Raymond of Toulouse's final decision to march south
from Ma'arrat al-Nu'man. This again is not the case. The *Gesta* suggests that
the other princes would not go because Count Raymond hung back, while
Raymond says that none of these princes would join him if he did go! Klein
points with reason to the general similarity between the two accounts of the
second siege of Antioch, but then suggests that Bohemond's action, recounted
in the *Gesta*, in setting fire to the city can only be understood in the light of
Raymond's information that he was recognized as leader of the army; therefore
it follows that the Anonymous used the *Historia*, but carelessly.[31] In these
terms one might well ask why Raymond of Aguilers does not mention the fire.
None of this aids our understanding of the relationship between the two
sources. Although Klein does point to the existence of some interesting
anomalies, he produces no convincing evidence that each of the chroniclers

[30] Klein, *Raimund von Aguilers*, pp. 116-36.
[31] Klein, *Raimund von Aguilers*, pp. 116-17 referring to RA, p. 242 and *GF*, pp. 28-9 for the
passage roughly corresponding to 3 in Appendix 2; Klein, pp. 130-1 referring to RA, p. 272
and *GF*, p. 81, there is no corresponding pasage in Appendix 2; Klein, pp. 126-8 referring to
RA, p. 258 and *GF*, pp. 60-2, there is no corresponding passage in Appendix 2.

was acquainted with at least parts of the work of the other.[32] His main contribution to the discussion was to suggest that we cannot assume the priority of the *Gesta* over the *Historia*, and to raise the possibility that the Anonymous may have used the work of Raymond of Aguilers.

Klein did not consider the possibility that Raymond and the Anonymous used a common source. It is the case of the latest editors of Tudebode's work that Raymond, the Anonymous and the letter of Daimbert all used a common source, an official account of the First Crusade, which was probably the *libellus* discovered by Ekkehard at Jerusalem, and that selective use of this explains the differences and similarities between the accounts. There are many objections to this: it is not clear that Ekkehard used the *libellus* at all, and it is certainly not clear that it was the same as the work which he says he did use, the letter of Daimbert. Such information as he adds to that letter is very limited and could have been discovered by him while he was in the East. His story about Godfrey's troubles at Constantinople is completely different from that found in any other Latin source.[33] It is impossible to see Daimbert's letter as derived from the same source as the works of Tudebode or the Anonymous. The letter came from the circle of the count of Toulouse, and possibly from the pen of Raymond of Aguilers himself. Moreover, it is highly unlikely that a single 'official' account of the crusade ever existed. The crusade ended in a welter of jealousies and disputes from which no agreed version would be possible. It is a mark of this that Daimbert's letter never even mentions Bohemond who, to say the least, plays a dominant role in the works of Tudebode and the Anonymous and was very influential according to Raymond of Aguilers. However it is possible that some kind of common source underlies the *Gesta,* Tudebode and Raymond of Aguilers.

The closeness of the texts of Tudebode and the Anonymous is self-evident but it has been pointed out that Tudebode's account is not so laudatory of Bohemond.[34] Some of the information common to Tudebode's account and that of the Anonymous is presented differently and Peter contributes a great

---

[32] Klein, *Raimund von Aguilers*, p. 130 referring to RA, p. 268 and *GF*, p. 77 points out that the *GF* refers only to Raymond going to Ma'arrat al-Nu'man, but later says: 'Boamundus cum suo exercitu secutus est *comites*'.

[33] Hills, *Tudebode*, pp. 10-12; Ekkehard, pp. 21-2.

[34] For example, Peter Tudebode does not mention Bohemond's warning to his troops not to plunder in Greek territory given in *GF*, p. 8; Hills, *Tudebode*, pp. 9, 24-5, *Tudebodus*, p. 41; PT, p. 16.

deal of original information.[35] In Tudebode's account there are passages
closely resembling the work of Raymond of Aguilers. The Hills, however,
emphasize that there are differences: in the report of skirmishing between
imperial police and the Provençals Peter does not give the name of one of the
brothers killed, while he says, and Raymond of Aguilers does not, that
Raymond of Toulouse ordered the attack on Roussa.[36] These are, however,
very small differences which could as easily spring from Tudebode's recol-
lections as from using a common source in a different way.

But the major reason why it is difficult to accept that another source
underlies the works of Tudebode and the Anonymous is the issue of standpoint.
The *Gesta* is very much an account of the crusade from the standpoint of an
adherent and admirer of Bohemond. Elements of this attention and adulation
are missing from Tudebode's account, but for the most part this standpoint
does not change. The great exception is in those parts of Tudebode's work corresponding to the tenth book of the *Gesta*: this records a time when Bohemond
was no longer in the crusader army. It is highly significant that this change in
the *Gesta*'s focus of interest is clearly reflected in Tudebode's work.[37]
Tudebode follows the *Gesta* in saying that Alexius sent a *kyriopalatios* to
Bohemond's army in the Balkans 'ut *nos* secure deduceret per terram suam'.[38]
In the account of Bohemond's discussions at Constantinople with Alexius,
Tudebode reports a controversial passage in which Alexius appears to promise
Bohemond a principality in the vicinity of Antioch.[39] The standpoint of

---

[35] This is summarized in Hills, *Tudebode*, pp. 6-7 though oddly they fail to note that while
the *GF*, pp. 35-6, puts Bohemond in charge at the Lake Battle on 9 February 1098, Tudebode
speaks of the leaders as a whole in charge and also gives details about the division of the army
between those around the city and those who sallied out which are not given in any other
source: Hills, *Tudebode*, pp. 50-1, *Tudebodus*, pp. 70-1; PT, pp. 42-3.

[36] RA, pp. 236-7; Hills, *Tudebode*, pp. 27-8, *Tudebodus*, pp. 44-5.

[37] Wolf, 'Bohemond and the *Gesta*', pp. 207-16, argues that the whole structure of the work
is a consequence of this admiration.

[38] *GF*, p. 10; Hills, *Tudebodus*, p. 42.

[39] *GF*, p. 12; the promise occurs twice in most of the manuscripts of Tudebode, except that
used by the Hills, as noted PT, pp. 18, 22; Hills, *Tudebode*, p. 30, *Tudebodus*, p. 48. This
passage was studied by A.C. Krey, 'A Neglected Passage in the *Gesta* and its Bearing on the
Literature of the First Crusade', in *The Crusades and other Historical Essays presented to D.C.
Munro by his Former Students*, ed. L.J. Paetow (New York, 1928), pp. 57-79. The Hills, *Tudebode*, p. 9, argue that this article proves that the *Gesta* was 'a hurried re-editing for propaganda
purposes', yet it is an integral part of Tudebode's text. Krey's work is actually more tentative
and really only proves that the passage is displaced, on which see my forthcoming article 'The
Use of the *Gesta Francorum*'.

Tudebode's work is so markedly that of a companion of Bohemond and so centred on the doings of that leader and his men that if it were based on a now lost chronicle one would wonder why the Anonymous bothered. Moreover it reproduces the shape of the Anonymous's work and many of what can only be idiosyncratic passages. The Anonymous reports the establishment of Tancred outside the St George Gate at Antioch in April 1098 and remarks: 'I cannot tell you all the things which we did before the city fell, for there is in this land neither clerk nor layman who could write down the whole story or describe it as it happened, but I will tell you a little of it'. This is repeated by Tudebode and so is the gap in our knowledge of events between early April and late May 1098.[40] The structural similarity between Tudebode's work and that of the Anonymous is obvious in the opening parts of the two works, and clearly related to the fact that the Anonymous was written by a south Italian, for its emphasis is on their march through the Balkans: he knows nothing of the march of others to Constantinople and this situation changes in Tudebode only because he used Raymond of Aguilers for the march of the southern French.[41] The case for Tudebode having used the *Gesta* is overwhelming.

This means that the relationship between the works of the Anonymous and Raymond of Aguilers must be direct. Either Raymond of Aguilers used the *Gesta* or the Anonymous used the *Historia Francorum* or each chronicler was acquainted with the work of the other. The idea that the Anonymous used the work of Raymond of Aguilers, put forward by Klein, Cahen and others, rests entirely on a the very evident similarity between their accounts of the meetings at Constantinople between Alexius and Count Raymond of Toulouse noted here in Appendix 1.

The vital point is that in the account of the interview given in the *Gesta*, no mention is made of the reason why the count was angry with the emperor. The passage, as it stands in the *Gesta*, is therefore out of context and meaningless, suggesting that it was lifted clumsily from another account. In contrast, it is perfectly clear in Raymond's account because he has already narrated the story of the scattering of the Provençal army by imperial forces, about which the Anonymous was ignorant. The suggestion is that the Anonymous simply lifted a passage from the *Historia Francorum* so clumsily that he did not notice that it lacked vital information. This cannot be sustained. If we compare the two passages closely in the form in which they are printed here in Appendix 1, we can see that what is found in the *Gesta* could not be a clumsily lifted passage;

---

[40] *GF*, p. 44; Hills, *Tudebode*, p. 61, *Tudebodus*, p. 82.
[41] *GF*, pp. 2-9; Hills, *Tudebode*, pp. 16-27, *Tudebodus*, pp. 32-43.

it could only be an abstract fitted with some thought into the Anonymous's own work. And if he abstracted thus, fairly carefully, it seems odd that he should have left out the explanation of the count's anger which is contained in the words of the emperor: 'At Alexius dicit se nescisse nostros depopulatos esse regnum suum; se et suos multas passum esse iniurias. Nihil esse quod comes quaerebatur, nisi quod dum exercitus comitis solito more villas et castra vastaret, exercitu suo conspecto, fugam arripuerit.'[42] Now, the Anonymous was almost certainly not ignorant of the clash between the imperial and Provençal forces when he came to write his account up much later. It was an event of some importance and news of it would have spread. But as so often happens in his work and those of others he simply made an error and forgot to explain what he said. As we have noted, Klein identified several comparable anomalies in both works.[43] There is no reason to believe that the Anonymous used the work of Raymond of Aguilers: the opposite is the case.

To understand Raymond of Aguilers's use of the *Gesta* we need to consider the character of the two works. They are told from very different standpoints: Raymond was in the army of the count of Toulouse and the Anonymous in that of Bohemond. These two leaders were bitter rivals though neither chronicler had entirely unmixed feelings about their patrons: Raymond admired Bohemond, while the Anonymous abandoned his lord and joined the count of Toulouse in 1099 when Bohemond stopped at Antioch. Raymond was close to the high command, while the Anonymous definitely was not.[44] Both chroniclers shared the common belief that the journey was God's work, but Raymond was deeply concerned to defend his lord, the count of Toulouse, and to assert the authenticity of the Holy Lance and the integrity of its discoverer, Peter Bartholemew, in whose trial he was involved. As a consequence he was concerned with the lot of the poor, whom the Anonymous largely disregarded.[45] The Anonymous enjoyed retailing fabulous stories and what was probably camp gossip about, for example, Kerbogah's mother or Emperor Alexius, while the story of Mirdalin and Kerbogah playing chess as the crusaders sallied out from Antioch is the only example in the *Historia*.[46] Raymond of Aguilers,

---

[42] RA, p. 238.

[43] For Klein's comments and those of Cahen see above pp. 40-41, 51-3.

[44] RA, p. 245; *GF*, p. xiii. The Anonymous expresses the rank-and-file view of the dealings with Alexius, *GF*, p. 12; on Raymond see the discussion in J. France, *Victory in the East: A Military History of the First Crusade* (Cambridge, 1994), pp. 128-31.

[45] RA, p. 283.

[46] *GF*, pp. 53-6, 63-5; RA, p. 260. The story is found in the *Historia Hierosolymitana* of Fulcher of Chartres (FC, p. 253), who derived it from Raymond.

therefore, had very different preoccupations from those of the author whose work he decided to use. This explains why his use was so limited.

Table 2 above probably somewhat understates Raymond's use of the *Gesta*. Raymond refers only briefly to the 'People's Crusade' in a passage which is really used as a stick with which to beat Emperor Alexius following the siege of Nicaea. It is very vague but it could be a summary of the Anonymous's account.[47] More interesting is the shape of the siege of Antioch in Raymond's account for it follows that of the *Gesta* with the same significant gap between Tancred's establishing himself outside the St George Gate in early April and the betrayal of the city in early June.[48]

The pattern of Raymond's use of the *Gesta* is fairly clear. He was little interested in what the Anonymous had to tell about the period before the siege of Antioch. In the later stages of his work, Raymond's account is dominated by a theme which had only occurred in a minor key before the defeat of Kerbogah. The victory over Kerbogah was, for Raymond, the result of divine intervention; an army faithless and despondent was inspired by the Holy Lance, the gift of God's grace. Thereafter the theme of his work is that of man's cupidity and avarice, even that of the count of Toulouse, thwarting God's will as revealed in the persons of his prophets, Peter Bartholomew and later Peter Desiderius. This was Raymond's interpretation of the crisis which struck the First Crusade after the defeat of Kerbogah. The *Gesta's* account of the period from Ma'arrat al-Nu'man onwards was of only limited use to Raymond, hence the marked divergence between the accounts given in the two chronicles, and the few borrowings from the *Gesta*. The experience of the crusade convinced Raymond of Aguilers of the wickedness of Emperor Alexius, despite the friendly attitude of Raymond of Toulouse towards him.[49] The Anonymous shared his hostility which is why Raymond used his report of the meeting of the two men at Constantinople, expanding it considerably, and probably also his account of the 'People's Crusade'.

But during the two sieges of Antioch the crusader army was very much acting as one. When, after the crusade was over, Raymond wrote his work, he

---

[47] RA, p. 240; *GF*, pp. 2-5.

[48] RA, p. 251; *GF*, p. 44 and see the comments above p. 55 n. 40. I have noted that the 'Historia belli sacri', *RHC Oc.*, 3 suggests that there were peace negotiations between the crusaders and the citizens of Antioch in May 1098 in my forthcoming article 'The Use of the Anonymous *Gesta Francorum*'.

[49] Raymond of Aguilers's hostility is particularly evident and its contrast with the attitude of Count Raymond is especially clear in the passage about the imperial embassy which arrived at 'Arqa in the spring of 1099, RA, p. 286.

simply used the Anonymous's account as a useful *aide-mémoire*. Even so Raymond made at least one obvious mistake, suggesting that Bohemond's castle was built at the same time as that of the count of Toulouse.[50] Raymond made quite intensive use of the *Gesta* in his account of the second siege of Antioch when the army was driven together by circumstance, but even here his preoccupation with the Holy Lance makes his overall account different. For his account of the siege of Jerusalem, when the army was again acting together, Raymond used the *Gesta* but only in three passages providing information about military matters.

It is clear that accounts of the First Crusade appeared very quickly after its end. The Anonymous *Gesta Francorum* seems to have been the first and that was closely followed by the work of Raymond of Aguilers. Fulcher's version of events was probably produced by 1101. It is possible that there were other major and substantial accounts of the crusade which have failed to survive but there are no traces of any in the texts of these early works.[51] It should be noted that considerable doubt has now been cast on the idea that Albert of Aachen's work depended on a 'Lost Lorraine Chronicle'.[52] Peter Tudebode produced what was to be one of a great wave of accounts based on the Anonymous *Gesta Francorum*. These have always been somewhat undervalued, precisely because they are all so obviously dependent on the *Gesta*.[53] The new edition of Tudebode was valuable precisely because it drew attention to the virtues of one of these works. Tudebode used the Anonymous *Gesta Francorum* much more extensively than Raymond of Aguilers. Yet he provides much extremely valuable information and his work has, like the Anonymous *Historia*

---

[50] RA, pp. 247-8 suggests Bohemond's fort was built at the same time as that of the count of Toulouse in March 1098 when actually it was constructed in November 1097; *GF*, p. 30.

[51] What is possibly a fragment of a lost work has been edited by J. France, 'The Text of the Account of the Capture of Jerusalem in the Ripoll Manuscript, Bibliothèque nationale (latin) 5132', *English Historical Review* 103 (1988), pp. 640-57. There is no way of telling whether there was ever any more than this fragment.

[52] This is the conclusion of Dr S.B. Edgington, *A Critical Edition of the Historia Iherosolimitana of Albert of Aachen*, Ph.D. thesis (University of London, 1991). This edition will shortly be published by Oxford Medieval Texts and will replace that in *RHC Oc.*, 4. I must express my gratitude to Dr Edgington for permission to use this work.

[53] Some important works belonging to the *Gesta* family are: Robert the Monk, 'Historia Iherosolimitana', *RHC Oc.*, 4; Baldry of Dol, 'Historia Jerosolimitana', *RHC Oc.*, 4; Guibert of Nogent, 'Gesta Dei per Francos', *RHC Oc.*, 4; 'Historia belli sacri', *RHC Oc.*, 3. In my article 'The Use of the Anonymous *Gesta Francorum*' I was at pains to point out that all these have much to tell us, particularly the *Historia belli sacri*.

belli sacri and so many others, been undervalued as a source for the First Crusade.

The *Gesta* is an eyewitness source which cannot be proved to depend on any written source. There are anomalies in its structure. During the account of discussions at Constantinople the Anonymous records a promise by Alexius to Bohemond of land near Antioch, but this passage is clearly displaced for it interrupts the sense of the passage in which it is set. At the second siege of Antioch we are twice told of the building of the wall against the citadel in what is a singularly disordered section of the work. Its book X is suspiciously bland.[54] However its textual history is quite clear and as yet no hypothesis has been propounded which allows us to penetrate beyond it.

The *Gesta* is distinguished by its very originality, but this does not mean that it is the best source for the history of the First Crusade.[55] Raymond of Aguilers must have written his work at almost the same time and Fulcher of Chartres very soon afterwards. The *Gesta* influenced both, and not always for the best. The silence of the Anonymous on the period of the later siege of Antioch has been perpetuated in the work of Raymond of Aguilers and almost all who followed him. Mere originality should not be allowed to exaggerate the *Gesta*'s importance or to minimize that of those who used it. Raymond of Aguilers produced an original and equally valuable record of the First Crusade, as did, in a lower key, Fulcher, Peter Tudebode and the rest of the *Gesta* family. It is time we learned to value their contributions.

---

[54] *GF*, pp. 11-12, 57-62 and see my comments in 'The Use of the Anonymous *Gesta Francorum*'.

[55] See my comments on the tendency to regard the *Gesta* as the 'normal' source for the First Crusade in 'The Election and Title of Godfrey de Bouillon', *Canadian Journal of History* 18 (1983), pp. 321-2 and in the forthcoming 'The Use of the Anonymous *Gesta Francorum*'.

Appendix 1

The passages from Raymond of Aguiler's *Historia Francorum qui ceperunt Iherusalem* and the Anonymous *Gesta Francorum* describing the interview between Emperor Alexius I and Count Raymond of Toulouse.

Historia (RA, p. 238)	*Gesta* (GF, p. 13)
Honorificentissime itaque ab imperatore et principibus suis suscepto comite, postulat imperator a comite hominium et juramenta, quae ceteri principes ei fecerant. Respondit comes: 'Se ideo non venisse, ut dominum alium faceret, aut alii militaret, nisi illi propter quem patriam et bona patriae suae dimiserat. Et tamen fore, si imperator cum exercitu iret Iherosolimam, quod se suos et sua omnia illi committeret.' Sed imperator excusat iter, dicens: 'Praemetuere se Alemannos et Ungaros, et Comanos, aliasque feras gentes, quae imperium suum depopularentur, si ipse transitum cum peregrinis faceret.' Interea comes audita morte suorum et fuga, se proditum esse credidit; et imperatorem, per quosdam principes de nostro exercitu, factae proditionis commonefacit. At Alexius dicit se nescisse nostros depopulatos esse regnum suum; se et suos multas passum esse injurias. Nihil esse quod comes querebatur, nisi quod, dum exercitus comitis solito more villas et castra vastaret, exercitu suo conspecto, fugam arripuerit; tamen pollicetur se satisfacturum comiti, atque Boamundum obsidem satisfactionis dedit. Ad judicium veniunt; cogitur comes, praeter jus, absolvere obsidem. Interea exercitus noster Constantino-	Comes autem Sancti Egidii erat hospitatus extra ciuitatem in burgo, gensque sua remanserat retro. Mandauit itaque imperator comiti, ut faceret ei hominium et fiduciam sicut alii fecerant.

Historia (RA, p. 238)	*Gesta* (*GF*, p. 13)
polim venit; et posthaec episcopus consecutus est nos cum fratre suo, quem infirmum dimiserat Dirachii. Mandat et remandat Alexius, pollicetur multa se daturum comiti, si quaesitum hominium sibi faceret, quod et alii principes fecerant.	
Meditabatur autem assidue comes qualiter suorum injuriam vindicaret, et tantae infamiae dedecus a se suisque depelleret. Sed dux Lotharingiae et Flandrensis comes atque alii principes hujusmodi detestabantur, dicentes: 'Stultissimum esse contra Christianos pugnare, quum Turci imminerent.' Boamundus vero se adjutorem imperatori pollicetur, si quicquam comes contra ipsum moliretur, vel si hominium et juramenta diutius excusaret. Consilio itaque accepto a suis, comes Alexio vitam et honorem juravit, quod nec per se, nec per alium ei auferret. Quumque de hominio appellaretur, respondit non se pro capitis sui periculo id facturum. Quapropter pauca largitus est ei imperator.	Et dum imperator haec mandabat, comes meditabatur qualiter uindictam de imperatoris exercitu habere posset. Sed dux Godefridus et Rotbertus comes Flandrensis aliique principes dixerunt ei, iniustum fore, contra Christianos pugnare. Vir quoque sapiens Boamundus dixit, quia si aliquid iniustum imperatori faceret, et fiduciam ei facere prohiberet, ipse ex imperatoris parte fieret. Igitur comes accepto consilio a suis, Alexio uitam et honorem iurauit, quod nec per se nec per alium ei auferre consentiat, cumque de hominio appellaretur, non se pro capitis periculo id facturum. Tunc gens domini Boamundi appropinquauit Constantinopoli.

Appendix 2

Table of resemblances between the *Gesta Francorum* and Raymond of Aguilers's *Historia Francorum* compiled by H. Hagenmeyer in his *Anonymi Gesta Francorum* (Heidelberg, 1890), pp. 50-8.

Each entry here is numbered: this was not the case in the original. All the readings from the *Gesta Francorum et aliorum Hierosolimitanorum* are as found in the Rosalind Hill edition (London, 1962) [= *GF*]: chapter references are also given from the Hagenmeyer edition [= *AG*]. The readings from the *Historia Francorum* are taken from the RHC edition [= **RA**], but references are also given to the edition in J. Bongars, *Gesta Dei per Francos* (Hanau, 1611) [= **B**] and to the recent edition of J.H. and L.L. Hill (Paris, 1969) [= **H**]. The italics here are as given by Hagenmeyer.

Gesta	*Historia*
1) In *roga imperatoris* locati sumus. *GF*, p. 9; *AG*, c. IV, 7	milites de *roga imperatoris*. **RA**, p. 237D; **B**, p. 140, 34; **H**, p. 40
2) *Nocte* uero illa surrexerunt festinanter Turci et *restaurauerunt murum* tam fortiter, ut ueniente die nemo posset eos laedere ex illa parte. *GF*, p. 15; *AG*, c. VIII, 4	Itaque capta esset civitas, nisi *noctis tenebrae* obstitissent. Instauratus est autem *murus per noctem,* et laborem pristinum nobis inane reddidit. **RA**, p. 239F; **B**, p. 141, 57; **H**, p. 44
3) Tantum autem timebant nos undique *inimici* nostri Turci *qui erant intus in urbe, ut nemo eorum auderet* offendere aliquem ex nostris. *GF*, p. 28; *AG*, c. XII, 3	Quumque haec in castris aguntur, *hostes primo ita sese occultabant infra moenia, ut nullus*, nisi vigiles, in muris cerneretur. **RA**, p. 242F; **B**, p. 143, 33; **H**, p. 49
4) Turci *audientes dominum Boamundum et Flandrensem comitem in obsessione non esse*, exierunt de ciuitate et audacter ueniebant preliari nobiscum, insidiantes undique. *GF*, p. 32; *AG*, c. XIV, 1	electus est *Boamundus et Flandrensis comes* ut exercitum propter victualia in Hispaniam ducerent ... *Haec autem quum hostes comperissent*, solitos incepere assultus. **RA**, p. 243E; **B**, p. 144, 14; **H**, p. 50

Gesta	Historia
5) *Episcopus* ... Podiensis in illa amara die perdidit suum senescalcum, conducentem et regentem eius *uexillum.* *GF*, p. 32; *AG*, c. XIV, 2	*Interfectus est ibi vexillifer episcopi,* et captum est *vexillum* ejus. **RA**, p. 244A; **B**, p. 144, 34; **H**, p. 51
6) Faciam et equos conduci ad uendendum, et *mercatum* per terram in fidelitate imperatoris huc aduenire, ... Adhuc quoque et *domestici mei* et papilio meus sunt in campo. ... *Fuit* ille inimicus, omnia sua dimisit in campo et *in peniurio manet et manebit.* *GF*, pp. 34-5; *AG*, c. XVI, 1	Taliter igitur *mercatus* sibi et suis *perpetuum pudorem,* simulato itinere quasi ad exercitum *imperatoris, dimissis tentoriis et familiaribus* suis, cum *Dei maledictione profectus est.* **RA**, p. 246D; **B**, p. 146, 8; **H**, p. 56
7) *Pars peditum* remaneat iugiter *custodire papiliones,* et quibit nimis obsistere his qui in ciuitate sunt. Alia uero *pars militum* nobiscum ueniat *obuiam inimicis nostris.* *GF*, p. 35; *AG*, c. XVII, 1	consultum est ut *pedites castra servarent et milites hostibus obviam extra castra pergerent.* **RA**, p. 246E; **B**, p. 146, 8; **H**, p. 56
8) Illi qui remanserant in *tentoriis, tota die preliati sunt* cum illis qui erant in ciuitate, ante tres portas ciuitatis. *GF*, p. 38; *AG*, cc. XVII, XVIII, 1; 8 Reuersi sunt nostri *agente Deo triumphantes,* et gaudentes de *triumpho quem in die illo haberunt, deuictis inimicis.* *GF*, p. 39: *AG*, c. XVIII, 1	*Eodem* itaque *die tanta pugna in castris fuit,* ut ibi nullus locus fuerit versus civitatem, ubi bellum non esset. Composuerant enim hostes ut, dum ab obsessis acerrime impugnaremur, ab improvisis auxiliatoribus eorem a tergo opprimeremur. Sed Deus, qui *militibus nostris victoriam* conferebat, in peditibus nostris praeliabatur. Nec minorem *suscepimus eo die* de obsessis *triumphum* quam de fautoribus eorum milites nostri gloriam *retulerunt.* **RA**, p. 247D-E; **B**, p. 146, 35; **H**, pp. 57-8

Gesta	*Historia*
9) Numerus eorum fuit mille et quingenti *GF*, p. 41; *AG*, c. XVIII, 8	numerati sunt circiter mille quingenti **RA**, p. 249G; **B**, p. 147, 55; **H**, p. 61
10) Nos itaque ualde fuimus refecti in illa die *multis rebus,* quae satis erant nobis necessariae, et de equis. *GF*, p. 41; *AG*, c. XVIII, 9	Celebrata *itaque* victoria, cum ingenti exsultatione et *multis spoliis, et equis, multis* nostri ad castra redeunt. **RA**, p. 249D; **B**, p. 148, 8; **H**, p. 61
11) *GF*, p. 42; *AG*, c. XVIII, 10	**RA**, p. 249F-H; **B**, p. 148; **H**, p. 61
12) *Peracto itaque castro* ... Nos autem, *secure ambulabamus huc et illuc, ad portam* et ad montaneas. *GF*, p. 42; *AG*, c. XVIII, 11	Rursus *itaque instaurato vallo* et moenibus castri, victualium conductores *secure ire et redire a portu* potuerunt. **RA**, p. 250E, **B**, p. 148, 35; **H**, p. 63
13) '*Seniores* si hoc non creditis esse uerum, sinite modo me in hanc *scandere turrim* mittamque me deorsum, si uero fuero incolumnis, *credatis hoc esse uerum,* sin autem ullam lesionem fuero passus, decollate me aut *in ignem proiicite me.*' Tunc Podiensis episcopus iussit ut adferentur evangelia et *crux* quatinus *iuraret ille si hoc esse uerum.* *GF*, p. 58; *AG*, c. XXIV, 4	Convocata itaque concione, [sacerdos] habuit haec verba *ad nostros principes,* atque ut *verum esse* monstraret, super crucem juravit: incredulis autem satisfacere volens, vel *transire per ignem,* vel praecipitari de *altitudine turris* voluit. **RA**, p. 256G; **B**, p. 152, 25; **H**, p. 74
14) *Nocte* quippe superueniente *ignis de caelo* apparuit ab occidente ueniens et appropinquans *cecidit intra* Turcorum exercitus. Vnde *mirati sunt* et nostri et Turci. *GF*, p. 62: *AG*, c. XXVI, 4	Eo tempore contigerunt nobis plurimae revelationes, per fratres nostros; et signum *in coelo mirabile vidimus.* Nam stella quaedam maxima *per noctem* super civitatem stetit, quae post paulum in tres partes divisa est, atque *in Turcorum castris cecidit* **RA**, p. 257A; **B**, p. 152, 33; **H**, pp. 74-5

Gesta	*Historia*
15) paruus *panis* uendebatur unó bisantio. De uino non loquar. *Equinas* namque carnes aut asininas manducabant et uendebant. Vendebant quoque gallinam XV solidis, ouum duobus solidis, unam nucem uno denario; omnia enim ualde erant cara. Folia fici, uitis et cardui, omniumque arborum *coquebant* et manducabant. Alia *coria* caballorum et camelorum et asinorum atque bouum seu bufalorum *sicca decoquebant* et manducabant. *Istas et multas anxietates ac angustias, quas nominari nequo,* passi sumus pro Christi nomine et Sancti Sepulcri uia deliberanda. Tales quoque tribulationes et fames ac timores passi sumus per XXVI dies. *GF,* p. 62; *AG,* c. XXVI, 5	Inter haec autem tanta fames in civitate fuit, ut, excepta lingua, caput *equinum* II vel III solidis venderetur; intestina vero capreae V solidis; gallina VIII vel IX solidis. De *pane* quid dicam, quod quinque solidi non sufficerent ad depellendam famem unius? Nec erat mirum, nec grave esse poterat his qui tam care mercabantur, quum auro et argento et palliis abundarent. *Haec autem ideo cara erant,* quia conscientiae militum, possessae criminibus, audacia carebant. Ficus autem immaturas ab arboribus decerpebant, atque *coctas* carissime vendebant. *Coria* vero *bovum* et *equorum,* et alia neglecta ex longo tempore, illa *similiter diu cocta,* carissime vendebantur; adeo ut duas solidatas comedere quilibet posset. Plerique milites sanguine suorum equorum vivebant, *exspectantes Dei misericordiam,* nolebant eos occidere adhuc. *Haec autem et alia mala multa* obsessis imminebant, *quae enumerare difficile est.* **RA**, p. 258B-D:**B**, p. 153, 20; **H**, pp. 76-7
16) Imprudens itaque *Stephanus,* Carnotensis comes quem, omnes *nostri maiores elegerant* ut *esset ductor nostrorum,* maxima finxit se deprimi infirmitate *prisquam Antiochia esset capta,* turpiterque recessit in aliud castrum, quod uocatur Alexandreta. *GF,* p. 63; *AG,* c. XXVII, 1	*Stephanus comes, quem ante captam civitatem pro dictatore alii principes elegerant,* audiens famam belli, *aufugerat.* **RA**, p. 258F; **B**, p. 153, 35; **H**, p. 77

Gesta	Historia
17) Episcopi nostri et presbyteri et clerici ac *monachi sacris uestibus induti,* nobiscum exierunt *cum crucibus,* orantes et *deprecantes Dominum, ut hos saluos faceret* et custodiret et ab omnibus malis eriperet. Alii *stabant* super murum portae, tenentes sacras cruces in manibus suis, signando et benedicendo nos. *GF,* p. 68; *AG,* c. XXIX, 2	sacerdotes et multi *monachi, induti stolis albis* ante acies militum nostrorum pergebant, Dei *adjutorium* et sanctorum patrocinia invocando cantantes. **RA,** p. 260F; **B,** p. 154, 43; **H,** p. 80 Egressis namque ordinibus, *stabant* sacerdotes nudis pedibus et induti sacerdotalibus vestimentis *supra muros civitatis, Deum invocantes ut populum suum defenderet,* atque testamentum, quod sanguine suo sancivit, in hoc bello per victoriam Francorum testificaretur. **RA,** p. 260H; **B,** p. 154, 50; **H,** p. 81
18) Et *persecuti sunt eos usque ad* pontem Ferreum, ac deinde usque ad castellum Tancredi. Illi uero dimiserunt ibi *papiliones* suos *et aurum et argentum multaque ornamenta,* oues quoque et boues, et equos et mulos, *camelos* et asinos, frumentum et uinum, farinam et *alia multa,* quae nobis erant necessaria. *GF,* p. 70; *AG,* c. XXIX, 8	*Persecuti sunt eos nostri usque ad* occasum solis ... Omnia autem *tentoria hostium* capta sunt, et *auri* et *argenti* multum, et *spoliorum* plurimum; *annonae vero* et pecorum et *camelorum* sine mensura et numero. **RA,** p. 261D; **B,** p. 155, 30; **H,** p. 82
19) *Hoc bellum factum est in IVº Kal. Julii, vigilia apostolorum Petri et Pauli, regnante domino nostre Iesu Christo,* cui est honor et gloria *in sempiterna saecula.* Amen. *GF,* p. 71, *AG,* c. XXIX, 12	*Facta sunt autem haec in vigilia apostolorum Petri et Pauli, quibus intercessoribus Jesus Christus Dominus noster contulit hanc victoriam* peregrinae Ecclesiae Francorum, qui vivit et manet cum servis suis propitius Dominus per *cuncta saecula saeculorum. Amen.* **RA,** p. 261G; **B,** p. 155, 34; **H,** p. 83

Gesta	Historia
20) Quorum rector et pastor exstitit Podiensis episcopus. Qui nutu Dei, graui aegritudine captus est; et ut Dei uoluntas fuit, *migrauit* ab hoc saeculo et *in pace* requiescens, *obdormiuit in Domino,* in solemnitate scilicet S. Petri, quae dicitur 'Ad Vincula.' Vnde magna angustia et tribulatio *immensusque dolor* fuit *in tota Christi militia,* quia ille erat sustentamentum pauperum. *GF*, p. 74; *AG*, c. XXX, 10-11	Interea dominus *episcopus* Ademarus *Podiensis,* dilectus deo et hominibus, vir per omnia carus, die Kal. Augusti *in pace migravit ad Dominum. Tantusque luctus omnium Christianorum* in morte ejus fuit, ut nos qui vidimus ... comprehendere aliquatenus nequivimus ... Sepulto igitur episcopo in ecclesia Beati Petri Antiochiae ... **RA**, p. 262E; **B**, p. 155, 55; **H**, p. 84
21) Denique *diuisi* sunt *seniores* et *unusquisque profectus est in terram suam,* donec esset prope terminus eundi. *GF*, p. 72; *AG*, c. XXX, 4	Quum inter *se divisi principes,* Boamundus in Romaniam est regressus, et dux Lotharingiae versus Roais *profectus* **RA**, p. 262E; **B**, p. 156, 1; **H**, p. 84
22) *Gulferius de Daturre primus ascendit* per scalam in murum ... *statimque ascenderunt super murum.* Saraceni igitur tam robuste *inuaserunt* illos per *murum* *GF*, p. 79; *AG*, c. XXXIII, 5	*Ascendit ante omnes Golferius de Turribus:* quem subsecuti sunt *plures,* qui murum et quasdam turres civitatis *invaserunt.* **RA**, p. 270A; **B**, p. 160, 10; **H**, p. 97
23) *Naues* quippe *nostrae uenerunt prope nos* in quendam portum quamdiu fuimus *in illa obsidione deferentes* maximum *mercatum,* scilicet frumentum, *uinum* et *carnem* et caesum et *ordeum,* et oleum unde maxima ubertas fuit in tota expeditione. *GF*, p. 85; *AG*, c. XXXV, 3	Quumque *in hac obsidione* aliquam moram fecissemus, *venerunt ad nos naves nostrae* ab Antiochia et Laodicia, et multae aliae naves Veneticorum et Graecorum *cum frumento, vino* et *hordeo, et carne* porcina, et aliis venalibus. **RA**, p. 276B; **B**, p. 164, 5; **H**, p. 103

Gesta	Historia
24) Rex quoque *Tripolis* sepe *nuntios mittebat senioribus*, ut dimitterent castrum, et cum eo concordarentur. *GF*, p. 85; *AG*, c. XXXV, 41 Tandem concordatus est rex Tripolis cum senioribus illisque continuo dissoluit plusquam CCC *peregrinos, qui illic capti erant, deditque illis XV millia bisanteos* et *XV equos* magni pretii. Dedit etiam nobis magnum *mercatum* equorum, asinorum, omniumque bonorum, unde nimis ditata est omnis Christi militia. *GF*, p. 86; *AG*, c. XXXVI, 1	*rex Tripolis mandavit ad nostros principes, si desisterent ab oppugnatione Archados, donaret eis XV milia aureos,* et *equos* et mulas, et vestes, et victualia, atque *mercatum* de omnibus rebus faceret omni populo; praeterea redderet *omnes captivos quos habebat de gente nostra.* RA, p. 286A; B, p. 170; H, p. 125
25) *Saraceni* namque in cunctis *fontibus* et aquis latentes, *insidiabantur* nostris, eosque ubique *occidebant et dilaniabant, animalia* quoque *secum* in suas cauernas et speluncas *deducebant.* *GF*, p. 89; *AG*, c. XXXVII, 8	At ubi *Sarraceni* cognoverunt nostros inermes discurrere *ad fontes* per montana quae sunt asperrima, *insidias* eis *praetendebant,* et multos ex ipsis *trucidabant* et captivabant, *et jumenta eorum et pecora secum ducebant.* RA, p. 294D; B, p. 175, 10; H, p. 140
26) *Saraceni* igitur uidentes nostros *facientes has machinas, mirabiliter muniebant* ciuitatem, et turres nocte accrescebant. *GF*, p. 90; *AG*, c. XXXVIII, 1	*Videntes* autem Sarraceni, qui infra civitatem erant *multitudinem machinarum quae construebantur,* infirmiora murorum loca *adeo* adversum *munierunt,* ut quibusdam desperabile videretur. RA, p. 298B; B, p. 177, 30; H, pp. 146-7
27) Illi autem, qui intus erant, *mirabiliter preliabantur* cum nostris, *igne et lapidibus.* *GF*, p. 91; *AG*, c. XXXVIII, 5	non solum *lapides* et sagittae, verum etiam ligna et stipulae projiciebantur, et super haec ignis et mallei lignei involuti pice et cera et sulphure et stupa et panniculi *igne* succensi RA, pp. 298J-9A; B, p. 178, 5; H, p. 148

Gesta	*Historia*
28) *Clerici* et presbyteri, induti sacris uestibus ad *Templum Domini* conduxere processionem, missas et orationes decantantes, *ut suum defenderet populum.* **GF**, p. 94; **AG**, c. XXXIX, 9	congregati sunt nostri principes et *clerus*, et nudis pedibus incedentes ante Sepulcrum Domini cum multis orationibus et lacrymis, misericordiam a Domino deprecabantur, *ut populum suum* modo *liberaret*, quem hactenus victorem de omnibus fecerat ... Post haec ... ad *Templum Domini* venimus **RA**, p. 303D; **B**, p. 180; **H**, p. 155
29) Sero autem facto, patriarcha *fecit preconari per omnem hostem, ut* in summo *mane cras essent omnes parati ad bellum, excommunicans ne ullus homo intenderet ad ulla spolia donec bellum esset factum* **GF**, pp. 94-5; **AG**, c. XXXIX, 11	Deinde *conclamatum* est *per exercitum ut mane omnes ad pugnam parati essent,* et quisquis principibus de sua gente conjungeretur, et nemo praedam tangeret; et *excommunicati* sunt quicumque eam tangerent *nisi prius bello confecto.* **RA**, p. 242F; **B**, p. 181; **H**, p. 157

Usamah ibn Munqidh: An Arab-Syrian Gentleman at the Time of the Crusades Reconsidered

Robert Irwin

It is possible that it is only those who have something to hide who write their autobiographies. This thought is prompted by a consideration of the life of Usamah ibn Munqidh. Usamah (the name means 'lion') was born on 25 June 1095. A few months later, on 27 November, Pope Urban II preached the First Crusade to those assembled for the Council of Clermont. The unexpected success of the First Crusade led to the establishment of the kingdom of Jerusalem. On 4 July 1187 King Guy of Lusignan and the army of the kingdom of Jerusalem went down to defeat at the hands of Saladin at the battle of Hattin. In the aftermath of that battle the greater part of the kingdom of Jerusalem was reoccupied by the Muslims. On 6 November 1188 Usamah ibn Munqidh, by then a pensioner of the mighty Saladin, died in Damascus at the age of ninety-three. His life had been more or less coterminous with the existence of the twelfth-century kingdom of Jerusalem.

Usamah was born at Shayzar, a small town on a spur of rock above the River Orontes in north-west Syria. He grew up in a region which in the middle ages was thickly wooded and which included areas of marshland and cane brakes, full of lions, gazelles and wild boars – ideal territory for the princely pursuit of hunting.[1] Usamah's father, a keen huntsman, was a member of the Banu Munqidh, the ruling clan of Shayzar.[2] Although the Banu Munqidh princes of Shayzar were Muslims, the majority of their subjects seem to have

---

[1] On Usamah as hunter, see R. Smith, 'A New Translation of Certain Passages of the Hunting Section of Usamah ibn Munqidh's *I'tibar*', *Journal of Semitic Studies* 26 (1981), pp. 235-55.

[2] On the Banu Munqidh in general, see *The Encyclopaedia of Islam* (2nd edn), s.v. 'Munkidh, Banu' (R.S. Humphreys).

been eastern Christians.[3] Once he had reached maturity, Usamah spent very little time in his birth-place. Instead he was to pursue a career in politics and soldiering in Mosul, Damascus, Egypt, and Hisn Kayfa.

Usamah, who was uniquely well-placed to give an account of the crusaders in the Near East, wrote what has been described (somewhat loosely) as an autobiography.[4] So many of the medieval sources to which one turns in the hope that they will shed a new and vivid light on the lives and attitudes of the Christians in the kingdom of Jerusalem turn out to be parsimonious with human details. Therefore by contrast the apparent simplicity, transparency and liveliness of Usamah's memoirs make them very seductive. Ever since Hartvig Derenbourg discovered the manuscript in the Escorial Library in 1880, Usamah's book has been much quoted by modern historians of the crusades in order to illustrate aspects of Muslim-Christian relations in the twelfth century. For example, this passage:

> When I used to visit Nablus [a small town, at that time part of the kingdom of Jerusalem] I always took lodging with a man named Mu'izz, whose home was a lodging house for the Moslems. The house had windows which opened to the road, and there stood opposite to it on the other side of the road a house belonging to a Frank who sold wine for the merchants. He would take some wine in a bottle and go around announcing it by shouting, 'So and so, the merchant, has just ordered a cask full of this wine. He who wants to buy some of it will find it in such and such a place.' The Frank's pay for the announcement made would be the wine in that bottle. One day this Frank went home and found a man with his wife in the same bed. He asked him, 'What could have made thee enter into my wife's room?' The man replied, 'I was tired, so I went in to rest.' 'But how', asked he, 'didst thou get into my bed?' The other replied, 'I found a bed that was spread, so I slept in it.' 'But', said he, 'my wife was sleeping together with thee!' The other replied, 'Well, the bed is hers. How could I therefore have prevented her from using her own bed?' 'By the truth of my religion', said the husband, 'if thou shouldst do it again,

---

[3] On the good relations of the Banu Munqidh with their Christian subjects, see E. Sivan, *L'Islam et la croisade: idéologie et propagande dans les réactions musulmanes aux croisades* (Paris, 1968), p. 18.

[4] The text and translation of the *I'tibar* cited here are *Kitab al-I'tibar*, ed. H. al-Zayn (Beirut, 1988) [to be cited as *I'tibar*] and *An Arab-Syrian Gentleman and Warrior in the Period of the Crusades: Memoirs of Usamah ibn-Munqidh*, trans. P.K. Hitti (New York, 1929) [to be cited as *Memoirs*]. H. Derenbourg's study of the life and works, *Ousama ibn Mounkidh, un émir syrien au premier siècle des croisades*, 2 vols (Paris, 1889-93) remains unsurpassed in many respects.

thou and I should have a quarrel.' Such was for the Frank the entire expression of his disapproval and the limit of his jealousy.[5]

Moreover with its plethora of nostalgic hunting stories, Usamah's book can be seen as a distinguished oriental precursor of the writings of Robert Surtees and Siegfried Sassoon. Of course, simplicity and humour are always seductive, but students of the crusades have learned to their cost that those 'simple' and lively memoirs written by Robert of Clari, Geoffrey of Villehardouin and Jean of Joinville are not at all what they seem at first sight: none of these sources is really simple. Indeed, a distressing number of medieval sources, once they have been expertly examined by an academic eye, turn out to be exercises in special pleading, full of rhetoric, slander, misdirection and evasion. Why should Usamah's book be any different? At the very least his highly literary work needs to be read within its specific literary context – for it is certain that he was not writing to provide twentieth-century infidel historians with accurate documentary information about Christian-Muslim relations in the twelfth century.

His book, the *Kitab al-I'tibar*, is not in fact exactly an autobiography. The book does not plod from schooldays to maturity to old age, nor does it give a coherent account of the political and military matters in which Usamah was a protagonist. Instead it leaps from anecdote to anecdote and it soon becomes obvious that Usamah has reshaped his life in such a way that those who come after him may learn from those anecdotes. *I'tibar* means learning by example. To medieval Arabs this word and cognate words, such as *'ibra* (warning) and *mu'tabar* (object lesson) had a religious resonance. From the Koran they learnt about the fate of those pre-Islamic dynasties to whom God had sent prophets but who ignored the warnings of those prophets and were consequently destroyed. 'In their story was a warning for those with understanding' (Koran XII.111). And 'So take warning those who have sight!' (Koran LIX. 2). Usamah was steeped in the Koran and knew its text by heart. (His father was, if anything, even better acquainted with the book, having copied it out fifty-nine times.)

The themes of *I'tibar* and *'ibra* were popular in medieval Arabic literature. They are prominent in *The Thousand and One Nights*. In the story of 'The City of Brass', when the exploring party, sent by the caliph to find the jinns imprisoned by Solomon in bottles in the desert, arrive at the Black Castle, the ruined place of a people damned and destroyed by God, we learn that *huwa*

---

[5] *I'tibar*, p. 124; *Memoirs*, pp. 164-5.

'ibrah li-man i 'tibara, that is 'it is a warning to whoso would be warned'.[6] Indeed, the themes of vanished and doomed peoples of 'Ad, Thamoud and Pharaoh — and of learning from the example of past lives is the subject of the exordium which prefaces the entire story collection of *The Thousand and One Nights*. 'Let him who knows how to reflect reflect and draw instruction from what he has read.'[7]

Usamah's book is not then just a random grab-bag of everything a slightly senile and rambling old man could remember. It was a book which sought to teach by example and Usamah had specific students in mind — his own progeny. The sole surviving manuscript of the *Kitab al-I'tibar* (transcribed in 1213) includes an *'ijaza* for the book granted by Usamah's son, Murhaf to Murhaf's grandson.[8]

The run of the narrative in the *Kitab al-I'tibar* is guided by likenesses and antitheses which have struck the author. As far as likeness is concerned, Usamah, having finished one tale, will often remark that 'the following case is somewhat similar'. Antitheses are even more important. Usamah suggests that Frankish justice in the kingdom of Jerusalem is bizarre and awful by giving a colourful account of a brutal trial by combat.[9] But Frankish justice is also good and Usamah refers to a case which he himself won in a Frankish court.[10] Frankish medicine is lethally dreadful. Usamah narrates the story of a woman who died after being treated to a trepanation by a Christian doctor. But Frankish medicine is also good. Their practice of washing infected wounds with vinegar works and their use of glasswort as a cure for scrofula is similarly effective.[11] A bad Frank tried to stop Usamah in the Temple area of Jerusalem from praying in the direction of Mecca. A good Frank, very likely a Templar, intervened to protect Usamah.[12] A lion may be an easy creature to kill. On the other hand, Usamah almost died from the attack of an hyena.[13] He has known men more cowardly than women and women braver than

---

[6] D. Pinault, *Story-Telling Techniques in the Arabian Nights* (Leiden, 1992), p. 198.

[7] *The Thousand and One Nights (Alf Layla wa-Layla) From the Earliest Known Sources*, ed. M. Mahdi (Leiden, 1984), p. 56; *The Arabian Nights*, trans. H. Haddawy (New York, 1990), p. 2.

[8] *Memoirs*, pp. 17, 255. (The text of the *'ijaza* is omitted in al-Zayn's edition of the text).

[9] *I'tibar*, p. 126; *Memoirs*, pp. 167-8.

[10] *I'tibar*, p. 66; *Memoirs*, pp. 93-4.

[11] *I'tibar*, pp. 121-2; *Memoirs*, pp. 162-3.

[12] *I'tibar*, p. 123; *Memoirs*, pp. 163-4.

[13] *I'tibar*, p. 131; *Memoirs*, pp. 173-4.

men.[14] To take a final example and one that is closest of all to the central theme of his book, Usamah has seen a man pierced right through by a lance and survive: on the other hand, he has seen another die from the prick of a needle.[15] There are those, like Usamah, who plunged into the thick of every battle and who yet still live. Others took every precaution but could not escape their doom. These are matters to marvel over, but it is God who disposes all things.

Antithesis was similarly an important way of organizing material in *The Thousand and One Nights*. In a ninth-century fragment of the manuscript, we find:

> And when it was the following night said Dinazad 'O my delectable one [i.e. Sheherezade], if you are not asleep relate to me the tale you promised me and quote striking examples of the excellencies and shortcomings, the cunning and stupidity, the generosity and avarice, the courage and cowardice that are in man.'[16]

Usamah's *Kitab al-I'tibar* is (like so many stories in *The Thousand and One Nights*) an account of fate. Man cannot prolong or shorten his life by his own deeds. It is God who determines all things and victory in battle comes from Him, not from planning. Usamah's fatalism of course derived in part from the Koran. But the Koran was not the only source. Fatalism was also a leading characteristic of pre-Islamic poetry in the Hejaz.[17] Usamah was steeped in pre-Islamic poetry. According to the chronicler and biographer al-Dhahabi, 'he knew over 20,000 verses of pre-Islamic poetry by heart'.[18] In the course of the *Kitab al-I'tibar* Usamah quoted from the ancient Arab poets, Antarah ibn Shaddad and Sahl ibn Shayban.[19] Like the creations of those poets, Usamah's treatise is to some extent an exercise in *fakhr* (boasting). Usamah's sensibility and, more specifically, his perception of warfare were shaped by the poets of sixth- and seventh-century Arabia, rather than by treatises on *jihad* (holy war). Even in the concluding panegyric to Saladin, Usamah does not mention the word *jihad* – though, as we shall see, there may be further reasons for Usamah's lack of enthusiasm for the idea of *jihad*.

---

[14] *I'tibar*, pp. 117-18; *Memoirs*, pp. 157-9.

[15] *I'tibar*, p. 47; *Memoirs*, p. 70.

[16] N. Abbott, 'A Ninth-Century Fragment of the "Thousand Nights": New Light on the Early History of the Arabian Nights', *Journal of Near Eastern Studies* 8 (1949), p. 133.

[17] On pre-Islamic fatalism, see W. Caskel, *Das Schicksal in der altarabischen Poesie* (Leipzig, 1926); H. Ringgren, *Studies in Arabian Fatalism* (Uppsala and Wiesbaden, 1955).

[18] Al-Dhahabi, *Tarikh al-Islam*, cited in Derenbourg, *Ousama*, 1.595.

[19] *I'tibar*, pp. 44, 53-4; *Memoirs*, pp. 66-7, 78.

Modelled as it is on bold, pre-Islamic bedouin exemplars, Usamah's book seems full of vigour, courage, flashing swords and triumphant encounters with the enemy. More closely read, however, it is one of the saddest books ever written – a medieval version of *Gone With the Wind*. Usamah himself is his own *mu'tabar*, or object lesson. Too weak to hold a pen, when once he had held a lance, he dictates his book. He is half blind and reluctantly alive, the out-of-favour pensionary of Saladin. Usamah has outlived both his strength and his times and he sadly contemplates his shrinking body lolling like a maid on stuffed cushions in Damascus.[20] He has tried so many times to lose his life in battle, but God would not allow him. He looks back above all to the days when he was young and his father was still alive and he followed his father on the hunt for lions in the forests and swamps around Shayzar.

In medieval Islamic culture longevity conferred an almost religious distinction upon a man. Anyone who lived to the age of forty or beyond was reckoned one of the *mu'amirun* or macrobiots. Al-Dhahabi and Ibn Hajar devoted biographical dictionaries to this category of person. According to a saying of the Prophet Muhammad, the longer a man lived past the age of forty the greater was Allah's esteem for him.

The longevity attributed in both the Bible and Islamic tradition to patriarchs like Noah and Abraham is evidence of the reverence traditionally accorded to old age. Nevertheless, it was recognized that longevity could be too much of a good thing. According to another saying attributed to the Prophet Muhammad, he is alleged to have prayed to God to preserve him from decrepitude and senility. Islamic lore envisaged a phase of life known as *mu'tarak al-manaya*, 'the battleground of fated doom' which one entered at around the age of seventy.[21] Usamah himself recognized that there was really something rather peculiar about someone who had passed through 'the battleground of fated doom' unscathed and he wrote that: 'Destiny seems to have forgotten me, so that I am like an exhausted camel left by the caravan in the desert.'[22] Very likely he lifted this image from the pre-Islamic poet, Zuhayr, who had compared himself in old age to a night-blind camel.[23] It was certainly a stock image.

---

[20] *I'tibar*, pp. 144-5; *Memoirs*, pp. 190-2.

[21] On longevity and 'the battleground of fated doom', see L. Conrad, 'Seven and the *Tasbi'*: On the Implications of Numerical Symbolism for the Study of Medieval Islamic History', *Journal of the Economic and Social History of the Orient* 31 (1988), pp. 57-62.

[22] *I'tibar*, p. 147; *Memoirs*, p. 195.

[23] R.A. Nicholson, *A Literary History of the Arabs* (Cambridge, 1930), p. 118.

Turning now to what Usamah tells us about himself, although the *Kitab al-I'tibar* is hardly about anything except Usamah, in some senses he tells us very little. His memories of his early years in Shayzar are mostly of perilous encounters with Franks and wild animals. But he has the traditional Arab compunction against talking about love, women or even children. Usamah does not indulge in introspection and there is not really much sense of an 'I'. There are more flagrant evasions. (For example, he passes very easily over the incident when he, at the age of ten, stabbed and killed one of his father's retainers in a quarrel over the punishment of a servant-boy.[24]) From 1127 to 1138 Usamah was in service of Zanki, the atabak of Mosul and chief protagonist of the *jihad* against the crusader states. In 1138 he returned briefly to Shayzar. His father, who had previously renounced the lordship of Shayzar to his youngest brother, had died in 1137; Usamah has nothing to say about his being disinherited in this manner.

In 1138 Usamah was expelled from Shayzar by his uncle. He does not tell us why, merely remarking that 'conditions now made it necessary for me to start for Damascus'.[25] It is from other sources that we learn that Usamah's uncle, the ruling prince of Shayzar, 'Izz al-Din Abu'l-Asakir Sultan, was afraid for the safety of his small sons at the hands of Usamah and his brothers, all of whom were older than Sultan's children.[26] Usamah's account of the time he spent in Damascus under the patronage of Mu'in al-Din Unur, the *mamluk* Turkish general who was the effective ruler of that city, is both evasive and extremely brief.[27] However, in sections of the book devoted to Franks and to hunting, we find clues. In the 1130s and 40s Usamah visited the kingdom of Jerusalem on a number of occasions. Sometimes, he was engaged in ransoming Muslim captives.[28] But we also have anecdotes about Mu'in al-Din Unur in the kingdom and how a Frank wanted to show Mu'in al-Din a picture of the baby Jesus.[29] Then there is a reference to William of Bures accompanying Mu'in al-Din and Usamah from Acre to Tiberias.[30] On another occasion when Mu'in a-Din and Usamah were en route for Jerusalem they stopped off in

---

[24] *I'tibar*, p. 132; *Memoirs*, pp. 174-5.

[25] *I'tibar*, p. 11; *Memoirs*, p. 28.

[26] Ibn al-Athir, *al-Kamil fi'l-tarikh*, ed. C.J. Tornberg, 14 vols (Leiden, 1851-76), 11.124-5; Abu Shama, *Kitab al-rawdatayn fi akhbar al-dawlatayn*, ed. M.H.M. Ahmad, vol. 1, pts 1 and 2 (Cairo, 1956-62), 1:1.281-2.

[27] *I'tibar*, pp. 11-12; *Memoirs*, pp. 28-9.

[28] *I'tibar*, pp. 80-1; *Memoirs*, pp. 110-12.

[29] *I'tibar*, p. 123; *Memoirs*, p. 164.

[30] *I'tibar*, p. 125; *Memoirs*, p. 166.

Nablus.[31] On yet another occasion he refers to himself flying hawks with King Fulk near Acre.[32] It is clear then that Usamah spent some time together with the governor of Damascus in Frankish territory in the early 1140s. It is clear too from other sources that, for all Usamah's perfunctory cursing of the Franks, he and his patron were architects in a pact which allied Damascus with the kingdom of Jerusalem. In 1138 Mu'in al-Din sent Usamah to negotiate joint operations with the kingdom of Jerusalem against Muslim Banyas and the following year the two parties joined forces in the siege of that place.[33] No wonder Usamah never mentions the word *jihad* in the *I'tibar*.

Then in 1144 'certain causes made it necessary for me to depart for Egypt'.[34] He does not tell us why he had to leave or why he chose Egypt as his destination. However, we know from another source that Usamah had become very unpopular in Damascus as an intriguer and that he was ordered to leave by his former patron, Mu'in al-Din.[35] As for the choice of destination, Egypt in the early twelfth century was still ruled by the Shi'ite Fatimid caliphs. Usamah's clan, the Banu Munqidh, may themselves have been Shi'ites.[36] It should be noted, however, that they were probably Twelver Shi'ites, whereas the Fatimid caliphs were leaders of Sevener Shi'ism. Another reason that Usamah ibn Munqidh never refers to *jihad* may be that according to strict Shi'ite doctrine, this duty is in abeyance until the Last Days, when the

---

[31] *I'tibar*, p. 127; *Memoirs*, p. 168.

[32] *I'tibar*, p. 169; *Memoirs*, p. 226.

[33] On Mu'in al-Din 'Unur, the Frankish alliance and joint operations against Banyas, see J. Prawer, *Histoire du royaume latin de Jérusalem*, trans. G. Nahon, 2 vols (Paris, 1969-70), 1.327-8, 334. In an anecdote about a deacon setting a tent-church on fire of which Usamah says that he was the eye-witness, there seems to be the implication that he was one of those Muslims from Damascus who had joined with the Franks in the attack on Banyas in 1140. See *I'tibar*, p. 84; *Memoirs*, pp. 115-16.

[34] *I'tibar*, p. 11; *Memoirs*, p. 28.

[35] Ibn al-Qalanisi, *Dhayl tarikh Dimashq*, ed. H.F. Amedroz (Leiden, 1908), pp. 277-8; Derenbourg, *Ousama*, 1.196-8.

[36] On the probable Shi'ism of Usamah (and of his kinsman, the Shi'ite historian, 'Ali ibn Munqidh), see C. Cahen, *Orient et Occident au temps des croisades* (Paris, 1983), pp. 81-2, 263 n. 31. It seems possible that the Banu Munqidh, like their allies, the Banu 'Ammar clan of Apamea, were all Shi'ites. The Shi'i historian, Ibn Abi Tayyi, cited in al-Dhahabi, says that he was acquainted with Usamah, and that he was a Shi'i (extracted in Derenbourg, *Ousama*, 1.602). According to Ibn Zafir, Usamah's enemies in Egypt 1153 were Sunnis; see Jamal al-Din 'Ali ibn Zafir, *Akhbar al-Duwal al-Munqati'a*, ed. A. Ferre (Paris, 1971), p. 104.

Hidden Imam will emerge from occultation and bring justice and victory to the true Muslims.[37]

Usamah had already had some dealings with the regime in Egypt. In 1139 he had used honeyed words to Ridwan, a former vizier in Egypt, who had escaped and joined Zanki's retinue in northern Syria. Usamah talked him into returning to Egypt where Ridwan was promptly imprisoned and then killed. Ridwan's head was tossed into his wife's lap, while people on the streets of Cairo ate his flesh, hoping thereby to acquire his courage. Usamah piously comments: 'His case was an object lesson for learning by example (*mu'tabar*) and a warning, but the divine will must be executed.'[38] An object lesson indeed, but perhaps the lesson should be to not trust the words of Usamah.

At all events, in 1144 Usamah arrived in Cairo. He was welcomed by Ibn Salar, the vizier at that time and as vizier the real power in the land. Ibn Salar gave Usamah a house and an income.[39] Although Ibn Salar was nominally the servant of the Shi'ite Fatimid caliph, he was in fact a Kurd and like most Kurds a Sunni Muslim. He was hoping for an alliance with the Sunni Muslim ruler of Damascus, Nur al-Din (Zanki's son who had succeeded him in 1146). Such an alliance would help to protect Fatimid Egypt from crusader aggression. Ibn Salar was particularly anxious to defend the important Fatimid port of Ascalon on the southern coast of Palestine from the armies of the kingdom of Jerusalem. (As it turned out the murder of Ibn Salar was speedily followed by the Christian conquest of that place.) Usamah presents himself as a·distant and disinterested witness of this murder.[40] Other sources however suggest that Usamah was a prime mover in the plot against his former patron. In 1153 Ibn Salar had sent several emirs off to assist in the defence of Ascalon. One of the leaders was a man called 'Abbas. Another was Usamah. As they were heading out towards war-torn Palestine, 'Abbas lamented the easy life he was leaving behind in Cairo. Usamah then seized the opportunity to suggest that 'Abbas could do something about it. He could remove Ibn Salar from power and become vizier himself. Usamah worked on 'Abbas until he agreed. Then 'Abbas's son, Nasr ibn 'Abbas, was sent back into Egypt to secretly make his

---

[37] On Shi'i doctrines regarding *jihad*, R. Peters, '*Djihad*: War of Aggression or Defence?' in *Akten des VII Kongresses fur Arabistik and Islamwissenschaft, Göttingen, 15. bis 22. August 1974*, ed. A. Dietrich (Göttingen, 1976), p. 284; M. Momen, *An Introduction to Shi'i Islam* (New Haven and London, 1985), p. 180; H. Halm, *Shi'ism* (Edinburgh, 1991), pp. 57-8.

[38] *I'tibar*, pp. 34-7; *Memoirs*, pp. 55-9; Derenbourg, *Ousama*, 1.178-81, 210-12.

[39] *I'tibar*, p. 13; *Memoirs*, p. 30; Ibn Zafir, *Akhbar*, p. 102; Ahmad ibn 'Ali al-Maqrizi, *Kitab al-Mawa'iz wa'l-I'tibar*, 2 vols (Bulaq, 1853-54), 2.55.

[40] *I'tibar*, pp. 24-5; *Memoirs*, pp. 42-4.

way into Ibn Salar's residence. Things went as planned and Nasr ibn 'Abbas did succeed in secretly entering Cairo and killing Ibn Salar.[41]

In doing so, he seems to have been helped by the Caliph al-Zafir, a dissolute young man who had been chafing under the old vizier's tutelage. 'Abbas returned to take over the vizierate and Usamah returned with him. The close-beset garrison of Ascalon were left to defend themselves as best they could. However, Usamah was still unable to rest, though once again he presents himself as the disinterested bystander of the bloody events he had actually instigated.[42] The Caliph al-Zafir and the assassin, Ibn 'Abbas, were both good-looking young men and there were rumours that they were fond of one another. The caliph had also allegedly made threats against Usamah. Usamah was further concerned that the caliph was trying to turn Ibn 'Abbas against his father. So he went to 'Abbas and told him that people were saying that al-Zafir was doing to Ibn 'Abbas 'what one does to a woman'. Usamah urged that the caliph should be killed in order to expunge the threat to 'Abbas's honour. 'Abbas summoned his son and told him what must be done in order to salvage the family pride. Then, when the Caliph al-Zafir turned up to dine with Ibn 'Abbas attended by only one slave, he was murdered by his host. 'Abbas, as vizier, immediately ordered a phony inquiry to be made, which led to the arrest and execution of al-Zafir's brothers. 'Abbas then put an infant scion of the Fatimid line on the throne, intending to use the child as a catspaw for his own rule.[43]

However, 'Abbas and his son and Usamah were by now so unpopular that they were soon forced to flee Egypt. Al-Zafir's sister wrote to certain Templars who now were based in Ascalon offering them 60,000 dinars if they could deliver to her 'Abbas and his murderous son. 'Abbas and his retinue were ambushed at Muwaylih by a Christian force from Ascalon. 'Abbas was killed,

---

[41] Ibn Zafir, *Akhbar*, p. 103; Ibn Khallikan, *Biographical Dictionary*, trans. M. de Slane, 4 vols (Paris, 1842-71), 1.177, 3.352; Ibn al-Athir, *Kamil*, 11.122; Ibn Taghribirdi, *Al-Nujum al-zahira*, ed. M. al-Burhami Mansur and A.L. al-Saiyid, 12 vols (Cairo, 1929-56), 5.309. C. Cahen, 'Quelques chroniques anciennes relatives aux derniers Fatimids', *Bulletin de l'Institut Français d'Archéologie Orientale* 37 (1937), p. 19 n.; *Encyclopaedia of Islam* (2nd edn), s.v. "Abbas b. Abi'l-Futuh' (C.H. Becker - S.M. Stern); N. Elisséeff, *Nur ad-Din, un grand prince musulman de Syrie au temps des croisades (511-569AH/1118-1174)*, 3 vols (Damascus, 1967), 2.446.

[42] *I'tibar*, pp. 25-7; *Memoirs*, pp. 44-6.

[43] Ibn Zafir, *Akhbar*, pp. 104-5; Ibn Khallikan, *Biographical Dictionary*, 3.426; Ibn al-Athir, *Kamil*, 11.126; Ibn Taghribirdi, *Nujum*, 5.288-9, 293, 309; Maqrizi, *Mawa'iz*, 2.30; Elisséeff, *Nur al-Din*, 2.496.

and Ibn 'Abbas was sent in a cage to Cairo. There he lost his nose and his ears to the wives of the murdered caliph before he was crucified. Usamah and his servants somehow avoided any harm in this ambush and Usamah even came away with a saddle cloth which he claims 'Abbas had illicitly taken from him earlier. Usamah sententiously observes that God had not allowed 'Abbas and his son to profit from the example of their slaughtered predecessor, Ridwan.[44] The new vizier in Egypt, Tala'i' ibn Ruzzik, was an old comrade in arms of Usamah's and a fellow enthusiast for poetry. It may be that Usamah and his retinue owed their escape from the Muwaylih ambush to this old friendship. In any case, once Usamah was safely installed in Damascus, Tala'i' sought to use him as an intermediary in his dealings with Nur al-Din (the ruler of Damascus since 1154). A lengthy correspondence in verse ensued, in which Tala'i' put forward the case for joint Egypto-Syrian operations against the Franks in the kingdom of Jerusalem, while Usamah, responding on behalf of his new patron, temporized, for Nur al-Din was not yet ready for a major offensive against the kingdom.[45]

Usamah had returned to Damascus in the year that that city opened its gates to Nur al-Din, Mu'in al-Din's old enemy, and for some years Usamah seems to have been based there. For some of the time he worked as a poet-propagandist for Nur al-Din. At some time in the early 1160s, Usamah left Damascus to reside in Hisn Kayfa, which was then ruled by the Artukid prince Qara Arslan.[46] Usamah does not give any reasons for this move. It may be significant that he did not return to Damascus until after the death of Nur al-Din. But perhaps Hisn Kayfa was chosen as a place for meditation in retirement, for by then Usamah was quite old and he seems to have spent most of his time there writing books and communing with ascetics. In 1174 he was invited back to Damascus by Saladin who had taken over the city after Nur al-Din's death.

---

[44] *I'tibar*, pp. 29-33; *Memoirs*, pp. 48-54.

[45] *I'tibar*, pp. 32, 39; *Memoirs*, pp. 52, 60; Abu Shama, *Kitab al-rawdatayn*, 1:1.247-8, 266-8, 288-98, 311; Prawer, *Royaume*, 1.413; Sivan, *L'Islam et la croisade*, pp. 80-1.

[46] The last occasion Usamah is mentioned in the service of Nur al-Din is during Nur al-Din's abortive attack on Harim in 557/1162, when Usamah, despite his great age, fought valiantly. See Ibn al-Athir, *Kamil*, 11.187-8. Derenbourg (*Ousama*, 1.305-9) appears to be in error in having Usamah participate in Nur al-Din's subsequent and more successful attack on Harim in 1164. Usamah makes no reference to his move to Hisn Kayfa in the main text of the *I'tibar*, although some of the appended tales dealing with religious folk evidently derive from the period of his residence there.

Usamah's son, Murhaf, had won Saladin's favour and it seems that it was Murhaf who 'extricated him from the teeth of calamities in Hisn Kayfa'.[47]

Philip K. Hitti, the translator of the *Kitab al-I'tibar* into English, tells us in his introduction that Usamah was high in the councils of Saladin and was given Beirut to govern, but that, having been given this key post, he surrendered it to the Franks.[48] This cannot be right. Beirut was only captured by the Muslims in 1187 and surrendered to the Franks in 1197. Usamah would have been in his 90s when he was allegedly given this key posting and, of course, dead before he could have got around to surrendering the place. In fact, it is clear if one looks at Hitti's source, a chronicle written by the Lebanese historian, Salih ibn Yahya, that it was another Usamah, a moderately well-known Muslim pirate, who governed Beirut and surrendered it to the Franks in 1197.[49] There is no evidence that Usamah ibn Munqidh and Saladin were ever particularly close and in 1176 they fell out – over what is not clear. The final page or so of rhymed and highly rhetorical prose in the main text of the *Kitab al-I'tibar* seems to be pitched as a sort of begging letter with the aim of regaining Saladin's favour.[50]

The world Usamah was preparing to take his leave of in the 1180s was very different from the one he had grown up in. The politically complex patchwork of little Syrian principalities, some ruled by Sunnis, some by Shi'is, some by Arabs and some by Turks had vanished utterly. So too had the free and easy contacts with Frankish neighbours. Instead, all Syria and Egypt were united under a warlord who was dourly dedicated to prosecuting a *jihad* against the

---

[47] Abu Shama, *Kitab al-rawdatayn*, 1:2.676-7. It is also a curious feature of the *I'tibar* that although Usamah and the Ayyubid Sultan Saladin were, for a while at least, on friendly terms, the only reference to the latter is in the panegyric addressed to him which is tacked on to the main text of the *I'tibar*. (It is important not to confuse the Ayyubid sultan with Salah al-Din al-Yaghisiyani, an officer of Zanki's, who does make frequent appearances in the *I'tibar*.) Although the *I'tibar* in its final form must have been dictated in Damascus in the early 1180s when Usamah was aged about 90 in *hijri* years (q.v. *I'tibar*, p. 144; *Memoirs*, p. 90), its contents suggest that most of the main text must have been composed much earlier – perhaps as early as the 1160s. This may account for the brevity of his account of his second sojourn in Damascus, his lack of interest in Nur al-Din's and, later, Saladin's achievements in the prosecution of the *jihad*, his failure to refer to his own prowess during the siege of Harim in 1162 and his failure even to mention Qara Arslan, his host in Hisn Kayfa.

[48] *Memoirs* (Introduction), p. 11.

[49] Salih ibn Yahya, *Tarikh Bayrut*, ed. F. Hours and K. Salibi (Beirut, 1969), p. 20. (In a note, the editors of this text distinguish between 'Izz al-Din Usamah ibn Munqidh, the pirate, and Mu'ayyad al-Din Usamah ibn Munqidh, the author of the *I'tibar*.)

[50] Derenbourg, *Ousama*, 1.402-3.

last remnants of the crusader states. The age of intrigue and appeasement was over (for a time at least).

The *Kitab al-I'tibar* is not the only work by Usamah to have survived. He also compiled the *Kitab al-Manazil wa'l-Diyar* (The Book of Campsites and Abodes), a collection of poems on the traditional bedouin themes of abandoned campsites, lost homeland, lost loves and nostalgia.[51] Some of the best poems in the anthology are by Usamah himself. In a preface, written in highly coloured rhymed prose, he refers to the great earthquake in northern Syria in August 1157 in which an estimated 10,000 died:

> I was moved to compose this volume by the destruction which has overcome my country and my birthplace. For time has spread the hem of its robe over it and is striving with all its might and power to annihilate it. All the villages have been levelled to the ground: all the inhabitants perished: the dwelling has become but a trace and joys have been transformed into sorrows and misfortunes. I stopped there after the earthquake which destroyed it ... and I did not find my house, nor the house of my father and brothers, nor the houses of my uncles and my uncles' sons, nor of my clan.

In fact almost the entire Banu Munqidh clan had assembled in the castle of Shayzar in the summer of 1157 for a party to celebrate the circumcision of the son of the ruling prince and they perished in the ruins of the castle. Usamah continues: 'Sorely troubled I called upon Allah in this great trial ... and I sought consolation in composing this book ... and I can complain to Allah, glorious and great, of my solitude, bereft of my family and brothers, I complain of my wanderings in alien lands, bereft of country and birthplace.'[52] At the time he he wrote this he had another thirty years to reflect on the mystery of his survival.

The *Kitab al-Manazil wa'l-Diyar* is an anthology of poetry. In his lifetime and in the centuries which followed, Usamah was famed in the Arab lands not as an autobiographer, but as a poet. Medieval Arabs regarded poetry as the chief literary form, while works of prose were hardly esteemed at all. Ibn Khallikan, in his biography of Usamah ibn Munqidh, says that copies of the *Diwan*, or Collected Poems, of Usamah were in everybody's hands, and Ibn Khallikan went on to cite some of Usamah's best known lines.[53] (Revealingly

---

[51] Usamah ibn Munqidh, *Al-Manazil wa'l-diyar*, ed. M. Hijazi (Cairo, 1968).

[52] Usamah, *Manazil*, pp. 3-4; translated in I.Y. Kratchkovsky, *Among Arabic Manuscripts* (Leiden, 1953), pp. 83-4 and see Kratchkovsky's comments on the manuscript in general.

[53] Ibn Khallikan, *Biographical Dictionary*, 1.177-80; see al-Dhahabi in Derenbourg, *Ousama*, 1.596-601.

enough, considering Usamah's chequered political career, those verses dea
with the faithlessness of those whom Usamah had loved and how they accusec
him of crimes he had not committed.)

The twelfth-century *jihad* against the crusaders in the Holy Land wa:
peculiarly a war fought by poets. Poetry played an enormous role in shapin{
the ethos and perceptions of the Muslim combatants – a role comparable to bu
greater than the role of poetry in the British trenches of the First World War
Saladin, the great commander, was a Kurd who probably spoke Turkish to hi:
generals, but he knew Abu Tammam's *Hamasa* by heart. (The *Hamasa*, o
'Fortitude' was an Arabic anthology of pre-Islamic poetry compiled in the
Abbasid period. It celebrated the bedouin virtues of courage and generosity.
Saladin also kept a copy of Usamah's *Diwan* with him.[54] What is more, wher
Saladin took counsel on the conduct of the war against the crusaders, he wa:
flanked by the great administrators, al-Qadi al-Fadil and 'Imad al-Din al
Isfahani. Al-Qadi al-Fadil was, of course, a famous poet as well as a majo
innovator in prose style. 'Imad al-Din al-Isfahani had written verses on the
jihad for Nur al-Din. Together, he and al-Qadi al-Fadil lobbied Saladin anc
others, urging the *jihad* upon them and often drafting their appeals in verse
We have already seen how Usamah and Tala'i' ibn Ruzzik conducted diplo
matic correspondence in verse. The Mosuli chronicler, Ibn al-Athir, was als(
a rated poet. Subsequently, many of the Ayyubid sultans and princes wh(
fought against the crusaders wrote poetry and patronized poets. Al-Kamil, al
Afdal, al-Nasir Dawud and al-Nasir Yusuf all wrote verses. Al-Salih Ayyub
the austere and warlike sultan who presided over the defence of Egypt agains
Louis IX's crusade, wrote no poetry himself, but he was the patron of two o
the greatest Arab poets of the late middle ages, Baha' al-Din Zuhayr and Ib
Matruh.[55]

Ibn Sana al-Mulk (1155-1211) was only one of many poets to write a pane
gyric *qasida*, or ode, for Saladin on the occasion of his victory at Hattin i
1187. The strict form of the traditional *qasida* begins by mentioning desertec
dwelling places and ruins and lamenting them.[56] Obviously, the conventiona

---

[54] M.Z. Sallam, *Al-Adab fi'l-'asr al-Ayyubi* (Cairo, 1968), pp. 232, 257.

[55] On poetry in the Ayyubid period in general, see Sallam, *Al-Adab*, passim; J. Rikabi, *L*
Poésie profane sous les Ayyubides et ses principaux représentants (Paris, 1949); H. Dajani
Shakeel, '*Jihad* in Twelfth-Century Arabic Poetry: A Moral and Religious Force to Counte
the Crusades', *Muslim World* 66 (1976), pp. 96-113.

[56] On the *qasida* form, see *Encyclopaedia of Islam* (2nd edn), s.v. '*madih*' (G.M. Wickens)
J. Stetkevych, *The Zephyrs of Najd* (Chicago, 1993), especially pp. 51-3 for Usamah's ow
work within the tradition of the bedouin *nasib*.

imagery of the first section served Usamah very well when he looked back on the desolation of Shayzar. It could also be put to use in the service of anti-crusade propaganda, for it was useful for poets who wanted to commemorate the sack and devastation of Muslim towns by crusaders — such as Ma'arrat al-Nu'man for example. The *nasib*, which is the second part of a *qasida*, celebrates the violence of the poet's love and the anguish of separation from the beloved. The *nasib* section might be used to lament over beloved women captured or killed by the Franks. In the third part of a *qasida*, the poet was expected to complain of fatigue and suffering as he journeyed by camel to a destination. Then in the *madih*, or panegyric, which usually concluded the *qasida*, the poet put forward his case for being rewarded and increased his chances of getting that reward by praising the patron. In the numerous poems which celebrated al-Kamil's reoccupation of the Delta port of Damietta after the failure of the Fifth Crusade, the panegyric took pride of place. Baha' al-Din Zuhayr was only the most prominent of the poets to celebrate the Muslim victory with a *qasida*, whose main thrust is in its concluding *madih*.

More generally, poems couched in such traditional forms encouraged the Muslim participants in the *jihad* to think of the war in terms of individual heroism and single combat — as a battle between courageous horsemen, rather than as a struggle between two territorial powers or religions. Although secular poetry played a crucial role in shaping the perceptions of the Muslim officer class, more rigorous civilian pietists frequently expressed their distrust of poetry. In a twelfth-century treatise written in Aleppo, its anonymous author (who was a fanatical enthusiast for the *jihad*) warns fathers who are bringing up sons that the 'first evil is frequenting astrologers, poets and physicians: for such people often neglect matters of the Law, even when their own belief is correct'.[57]

To return to Usamah ibn Munqidh, he wrote a number of other books. Some of them seem not to have survived, among them his oneiromantic book on sleep and veridical dreams, his book on women and his history of recent events up to about 1170.[58] A treatise on rhetoric has survived and over the centuries has been much quoted by other Arab writers.[59] For Usamah, rhetoric and belles lettres had moral and exemplary purposes. Besides being a distinguished poet and rhetorician, Usamah was also a keen rhabdophilist and the *Kitab al-*

---

[57] *The Sea of Precious Virtues (Bahr al-Fava'id): A Medieval Mirror for Islamic Princes*, trans. J.S. Meisami (Salt Lake City, 1991), p. 80.
[58] On those works of Usamah which have not survived, see Derenbourg, *Ousama*, pp. 330-9.
[59] Usamah ibn Munqidh, *Lubab al-Adab*, ed. M.H. Shakir (Cairo, 1935).

'Asa, which has also survived, is an anthology of religious citations
reminiscences and poems dealing exclusively with the lore of the stick.[60] The
Kitab al-'Asa was composed in 1171 or 1172, by which time the stick had
presumably become the prop of his old age. This curious literary collection
(which certainly deserves to be translated into English) contains much that is
of interest. At one point Usamah recalls how when he was on a *ziyara*, or
minor pilgrimage, in the territory of the kingdom of Jerusalem, he visited
Sebastea and entered the church of the tomb of John the Baptist. Inside he
found ten old men, with what sounds like a version of the heraldic emblem of
the cross potent on their chests, standing rapt in prayer. Usamah was both
touched by their piety and envious of it. At that time he knew of nothing to
match such devotion among the Muslims. However, later on in Damascus, his
patron Mu'in al-Din Unur took him into a place called the Peacock House and
there he saw a hundred Sufis prostrate on their prayer-mats and, looking on
them, he realized that in these mystical devotees Islam possessed a body of
men whose piety matched anything to be found among the Christians
Thereafter, Usamah became an enthusiastic partisan of the Sufis.[61]

Elsewhere in his book on sticks, he tells the story of the ascetic Jarar who
having just acquired a magic staff and a skullcap of invisibility from a Sufi in
Manbij, was able to pass undetected through the lines of the Franks, who a
that time were investing Shayzar.[62] Usamah also writes about various
skirmishes with the Franks in which sticks were, however tangentially, involved.[63] And he tells the story, which he had from a friend, about a man who
went to the *qadi* to complain about how his wife had taken to beating him
striking at him with such force that she had broken the stick she was using
Seeing the *qadi* looking exceedingly gloomy, the man hastened to add that the
qadi should not get too sad, for the woman only did it from the evil of her
nature and her lack of education, and the man could understand that. But the
qadi replied: 'I would not grieve, even if she killed you. My only worry is tha
she may think that all men are like you.'[64]

So, to conclude, there is much that is comic and much that is stirring in the
Kitab al-'Asa and in the Kitab al-I'tibar. But if one reads Usamah's writing

---

[60] Usamah ibn Munqidh, *Kitab al-'Asa*, ed. H.A. Muhammad (Alexandria, 1981) [to be cited
as *al-'Asa*].

[61] *al-'Asa*, pp. 276-7.

[62] *al-'Asa*, pp. 235-7.

[63] *al-'Asa*, pp. 237-8, 259-60.

[64] *al-'Asa*, p. 340.

attentively, one can detect, behind all the rippling jokes and boasts, a strong groundswell of melancholy. Usamah struggles with his memories, trying to get back to before his falling out of favour with Saladin, before his involvement with political murder in Egypt, before his time as an intriguer and arch-appeaser of the Franks in Damascus, back to the uncomplicated days of his vigour and youth, when the castle of Shayzar was filled by the feasting warriors of the Banu Munqidh, and Usamah hunted lions with his father.

Les colophons de manuscrits arméniens comme sources pour l'histoire des Croisades.

Gérard Dédéyan

On peut donner la définition d'un byzantiniste concernant les colophons des manuscrits grecs. Le mot grec *kolophôn* signifie 'faîte', 'sommet', au sens figuré, c'est-à-dire 'achèvement', 'couronnement' (d'une entreprise, d'un discours), ou souscription, sous forme de note sur un manuscrit (habituellement à la fin), avec une information sur sa date, le lieu où il a été rédigé et, parfois, sur le scribe.[1] Les colophons ne sont pas seulement la principale source d'information sur les copistes, mais sont également importants pour l'histoire sociale et politique, la prosopographie, les aspects économiques et techniques de la production de livres et du commerce des livres (prix, salaires, temps nécessaire pour la copie d'un manuscrit) et l'histoire des centres de copie (en latin, *scriptoria*). Dates et lieux mentionnés dans les colophons sont fondamentaux pour l'étude du développement de l'écriture grecque (principalement la minuscule) et la production régionale de manuscrits. Comme genre, les colophons grecs fournissent des informations moins riches que les colophons de manuscrits syriaques ou arméniens.[2] Cette définition peut-être complétée par celle d'un arméniste à propos des colophons (le mot arménien *hichatakaran* équivalant à 'mémorial') de manuscrits arméniens, portés à la fin et sur les emplacements libres des textes manuscrits.[3]

Dans les colophons sont présentés les conditions de la création d'un manuscrit donné, souvent aussi les événements d'une époque, ainsi que des renseignements biographiques sur le copiste du manuscrit, le relieur, l'enlu-

---

[1] E. Gamillscheg and I. Ševčenko, art. 'Colophons', dans *The Oxford Dictionary of Byzantium*, direct. A.P. Kazhdan, 3 vol. (New York, 1991), 1.481.

[2] Gamillscheg and Ševčenko, 'Colophons', p. 481.

[3] Par exemple, à la fin d'une longue séquence de texte.

mineur, entre autres. Les colophons nous ont laissé les noms des copistes-scribes, des miniaturistes, des enlumineurs, des relieurs, des commanditaires et de tous ceux qui, d'une manière ou d'une autre, sont liés à un manuscrit.[4] Les colophons ont été créés sur le modèle et à la suite des inscriptions lapidaires. C'est au sein de la réalité arménienne que les colophons se sont le plus développés et répandus, gagnant ainsi une valeur spécifique de caractère historiographique. Le colophon arménien manuscrit, né au Ve siècle et connaissant un véritable apogée aux XIIIe-XVe siècles, a persisté jusqu'au XVIIIe siècle.[5]

Dans le monde occidental, le pionnier en matière de présentation des colophons comme sources historiques a été Avédis K. Sanjian, Professeur à l'université de Californie à Los Angeles de 1969 à 1995, dans sa magistrale traduction annotée de colophons de manuscrits de la période 1301-80,[6] choisis dans la collection rassemblée, en trois volumes, par Levon S. Khatchikyan, Directeur du Maténadaran d'Erévan (Bibliothèque des Manuscrits anciens) de 1954 à 1982. Nous lui empruntons les observations suivantes. Les auteurs de colophons arméniens ne se contentent pas d'indiquer les circonstances de la production de manuscrits. Grâce à la situation géopolitique de l'Arménie, grâce aussi à un réseau diasporique s'étendant, du nord au sud, de la Crimée et du Caucase à l'Egypte, et, d'est en ouest, de l'Asie centrale et de l'Iran à Constantinople et à l'Europe, les auteurs de colophons sont des observateurs privilégiés des événements de l'histoire, même s'ils en ont souvent une perception purement locale. Témoins oculaires ou auriculaires, ils fournissent, concernant principalement l'Arménie et le Moyen-Orient, une catégorie de sources primaires qui doit prendre sa place à côté des chroniques et des inscriptions.[7] Outre le principal colophon, écrit par le scribe, on trouve parfois des colophons dûs à la plume du commanditaire, du donateur, de l'enlumineur ou du relieur.[8] Un manuscrit, dans son histoire multiséculaire, peut recevoir de nouveaux colophons de ses propriétaires, restaurateurs, relieurs successifs.[9]

L'utilisation systématique des colophons comme sources historiques primaires n'a pu été mise en oeuvre qu'avec la publication de catalogues de

---

[4] H. Bakhtchinyan, art. '*hichatakaran*', dans *Encyclopédie arménienne soviétique* (en arm.) [= *EAS*], t. 6 (Erevan, 1980), p. 413.

[5] Bakhtchinyan, '*hichatakaran*', p. 413.

[6] A.K. Sanjian, éd., *Colophons of Armenian Manuscripts 1301-1380: A Source for Middle Eastern History* (Cambridge, Mass., 1969), p. vii

[7] Sanjian, *Colophons*, p. vii.

[8] Sanjian, *Colophons*, p. vii.

[9] Sanjian, *Colophons*, p. viii.

manuscrits arméniens, à partir du XIXe siècle.[10] Cependant des historiens aussi notoires que Stép'annos Orbêlian (*Histoire de la province de Siounik'*) au XIIIe siècle, Aŕak'el de Tabriz au XVIIe (*Histoire*) ou, à Venise, le Mekhit'ariste Tchamtchian au XVIIIe siècle (*Histoire d'Arménie*), se sont appuyés, entre autres, sur les colophons pour composer leurs oeuvres.[11] Parmi les divers systèmes de calendriers, le plus répandu chez les auteurs de colophons (comme chez les historiens et chroniqueurs arméniens), est celui dit de la Grande Ere Arménienne, commençant en 552 après J.C. Même s'ils écrivent dans le cercle des classes dirigeantes et de l'Eglise et si leur point de vue est essentiellement politique et religieux, les auteurs de colophons présentent l'avantage d'un témoignage sur le vif, l'événement étant soustrait au prisme déformant que constituent le décalage chronologique et l'élaboration littéraire caractérisant les histoires et chroniques. Ils complètent, en outre, les lacunes de l'historiographie traditionnelle (nombreuses, par exemple, dans la période allant du XIVe siècle au XVIIe siècle).[12] On peut, en grande partie, appliquer aux siècles antérieurs ce qu'Avédis K. Sanjian disait des colophons des XIVe et XVe siècles: les colophons – alors que les sources historiographiques arméniennes (à la différence des sources syriaques) sont très discrètes sur de tels sujets – fournissent des informations sur la vie sociale et économique de la bourgeoisie et du peuple, sur les 'calamités' (épidémies, séismes), sur les conditions matérielles de l'activité culturelle.[13] En outre, ils permettent souvent, par les nombreuses données topographiques qu'ils contiennent, d'entrer dans le détail de la géographie historique de l'Arménie.[14] Dans la forme, les colophons présentent certaines limites: les auteurs, outre que leur langue peut s'éloigner de l'arménien littéraire, suivent souvent des stéréotypes, alourdissent leur récit de références bibliques et ne discernent guère l'enchaînement des événements.

Tout en étant des documents historiques sûrs, les colophons de manuscrits arméniens ont exprimé aussi le goût artistique et la mentalité de l'époque et même enrichi la poésie et la prose arméniennes médiévales. Nous ajouterons que les colophons de manuscrits arméniens ont d'abord été édités dans le cadre de la publication des catalogues de manuscrits arméniens (la plupart d'entre eux figurent dans la 'Bibliothèque arménienne' de la Fondation Calouste Gulbenkian), tâche dans laquelle a excellé, au monastère Saint-Jacques de Jéru-

---

[10] Sanjian, *Colophons*, p. viii.
[11] Sanjian, *Colophons*, p. viii.
[12] Sanjian, *Colophons*, pp. x-xi.
[13] Sanjian, *Colophons*, p. xi.
[14] Sanjian, *Colophons*, pp. xi-xii.

salem, dans une longue vie de recueillement et de travail, l'archevêque Norayr Bogharian (1904-96). Ils ont ensuite fait l'objet d'éditions spécifiques, principalement grâce aux efforts conjoints du Maténadaran (Bibliothèque des Manuscrits anciens) et de l'Académie des Sciences d'Arménie. Il faut cependant rappeler que le pionnier, en la matière, a été Karékin Ier Hovsêp'ian, catholicos de la Grande Maison de Cilicie (1943-52), avec ses *Colophons de manuscrits* (en arm.),[15] recueil qui rassemble, jusqu'à 1250, 459 colophons de manuscrits arméniens, avec d'importantes notes paléographiques, iconographiques, bibliologiques ou de critique textuelle.[16] C'est en Arménie même que l'édition et l'étude des colophons de manuscrits est apparue comme une entreprise de longue haleine et de vaste envergure. L'impulsion, ici, a été donnée par Levon S. Khatchikyan, avec ses *Colophons de manuscrits arméniens du XIVe siècle* (en arm.),[17] comme ses *Colophons de manuscrits arméniens du XVe siècle* (en arm.),[18] sur la base desquels, dans ses travaux de recherches, il a éclairé la vie politique et économique du peuple arménien dans ces périodes, de même que l'histoire des maisons féodales de diverses provinces d'Arménie (Siounik', Artaz, Hamchên), en liaison avec la vie culturelle.[19] Quoique également médiéviste, Vazken Hakobyan, responsable des recherches en histoire médiévale à l'Académie des Sciences d'Arménie de 1971 à 1982, s'est orienté (en collaboration avec A. Hovhannissyan) vers la période moderne, avec ses *Colophons arméniens du XVIIe siècle*.[20] Le matériel disponible pour la période médiévale a fait l'objet d'un nouvel inventaire, exhaustif, de la part d'Ardachês S. Mat'évosyan, infatigable chercheur au Maténadaran, qui a publié les *Colophons de manuscrits arméniens du XIIIe siècle*,[21] et les *Colophons de manuscrits arméniens du Ve au XIIe siècle*.[22] C'est en recourant au matériel fourni par certains de ces travaux que nous tenterons de définir l'apport des colophons de manuscrits arméniens comme sources de l'histoire des Croisades, en nous limitant à la période allant de la conquête d'Antioche (1098) à la chute de Jérusalem (1187), voire à la récupération d'Acre (1191).

---

[15] Antélias, 1951.
[16] S. Kolandjyan, art. 'Hovsêp'ian (K.)', dans *EAS*, 6.580.
[17] Erevan, 1950.
[18] 3 vol., Erevan, 1955-67.
[19] S. Arevchatyan, art. 'Khatchikyan (L.S.)', dans *EAS*, t. 5 (Erevan, 1979), pp. 27-8.
[20] 2 vol., Erevan, 1974-77. S. K'olandjyan, art. 'Hakobyan (V.A.)', dans *EAS*, 6.75-6.
[21] Erevan, 1984.
[22] Erevan, 1988.

I. Un regard de complicité sur la Première Croisade, 1095-1099.

L'un des colophons de manuscrits les plus précieux pour l'histoire de la Première Croisade est celui d'un manuscrit contenant la copie d'une collection canonique, effectuée entre le début de l'automne 1097 et la fin de l'hiver 1099. Le copiste auteur du colophon, un moine du nom de Hovhannês, a intégralement assisté au siège d'Antioche, du 21 octobre 1097 au 3 juin 1098, mais non à la victoire des Francs, stimulés par 'l'invention de la Sainte Lance', sur l'armée turque de secours, le 28 juin 1098. Dans un article intitulé 'Un témoignage autographe sur le siège d'Antioche par les Croisés en 1098',[23] le Père Paul Peeters, tout en dénonçant la boursouflure du style, la confusion de la pensée et le désordre chronologique, en avait jadis souligné l'importance. Hovhannês, plus tard réfugié en Cilicie occidentale, près de Lambroun, avait exécuté la majeure partie de son travail de copie au monastère de Paṙlahou (Barlâhâ, en syriaque, du nom de l'ermite Barlaam à qui l'église était dédiée), situé sur le mont Cassius. Celui-ci s'élève sur la rive gauche de l'Oronte, non loin de son embouchure et fut appelé par les Francs (d'après le nom syriaque) le mont (Saint-) Parlier.[24] Ce couvent et son territoire se trouvaient sous la juridiction du catholicos Grigor II Vekayasêr (le Martyrophile), de là famille des Pahlawouni, dont un parent, Vahram, avait exercé la fonction de duc d'Antioche en 1078, avant d'être évincé, la même année, par un général byzantin dissident, Philarète Brachamios, de souche arménienne, mais de confession orthodoxe. C'est dans le couvent de Paṙlahou que, en 1102, Grigor II qui rend Barlâhâ par 'Paradis de Dieu', effectua, avec la coopération du Grec Théopistos, la traduction en arménien de la vie de saint Jean Chrysostome, comme le rappelle un colophon qui lui est dû.[25]

Quant au témoignage de Hovhannês sur le siège d'Antioche, il compte certes des erreurs, dues à l'éloignement géographique (itinéraire maritime – et non terrestre – des Croisés, durée de cinq mois – au lieu de neuf – pour le siège d'Antioche), mais il reste intéressant, au jugement du Père Peeters (pour lequel

---

[23] P. Peeters, *Recherches d'histoire et de philologie orientales*, 2 vol. (Bruxelles, 1951), 2.164-80. L'auteur donne (pp. 165-8) une traduction latine du colophon, dont on trouvera le texte original dans K. Hovsêp'ian, *Colophons de manuscrits du VIIe siècle à 1250* (en arm.) (Antélias, 1951), n° 120/col. 259-64, et dans A. Mat'évosyan, *Colophons de manuscrits arméniens, VIIe-XIIe siècles* (en arm.) (Erevan, 1988), n° 140/pp. 117-19.

[24] Peeters, *Recherches*, 2.168-73.

[25] Cf. L. Alichan, *Sissouan*, texte (Venise, 1885), p. 406; trad., (Venise, 1899), p. 486. Voir le texte complet du colophon dans Hovsêp'ian, *Colophons*, n° 125/col. 270-2; Mat'évosyan, *Colophons*, n° 168/pp. 135-6.

il n'apporte pas d'informations neuves sur l'histoire de la Première Croisade
par le silence qu'il garde sur la prétendue Sainte Lance, dont 'l'invention'
traditionnellement liée à la victoire du lac d'Antioche, n'aurait, en fait, suscit
que peu de réactions à Antioche,[26] et par l'enthousiasme manifesté à l'occa
sion de l'intervention des Occidentaux, enthousiasme que le Père Peeter
explique par le voisinage d'Arméniens chalcédoniens, nombreux de l'autre côt
de l'Oronte, autour du monastère de Saint-Syméon Stylite le Jeune.[27]

L'intérêt du colophon de Hovhannês est aussi de mettre en évidence la situa
tion d'oppression où se trouvaient les chrétiens orientaux et, parmi ceux-ci, le
Arméniens, après la conquête turque comme on peut en juger ici:

> L'année de l'achèvement de mon testament, il se produisit un ébranlement du peu
> ple des Occidentaux en vue du bannissement et de l'expulsion, par les chrétiens, d
> peuple étranger des circoncis égorgeurs d'hommes, tyrans sur cette terre, qui, dan
> le déshonneur, avaient étendu leur domination sur les saints et les prêtres de Diet
> les saintes églises étaient pour eux un vase de remèdes; ils brûlaient les croix et le
> saints lieux et alourdissaient la vie des chrétiens de pesants tributs.[28]

Hovhannês, comme le souligne le Père Peeters, voit dans la mise en march
des Croisés, 'qui dressent devant eux le signe de la Croix du Christ', un
manifestation de la Providence: 'La même année, le Seigneur visita son peuple
selon qu'Il a dit: Je ne vous laisserai pas et ne vous ferai pas souffrir en vair
la main toute-puissante de Dieu vous conduira.'[29] Hovhannês, évoquant le
difficultés rencontrées par les Francs au lendemain de la prise d'Antioch
(disproportion des effectifs chrétiens et musulmans, difficultés d'appro
visionnement en vivres et en fourrage), souligne leur humilité et leur ferveu

> A bout de forces et terrorisés par la multitude des Infidèles, ils se réunirent dans l
> grande basilique élevée à la mémoire de l'apôtre saint Pierre; d'une voix pleine d
> soupirs et avec des torrents de larmes, la prière de beaucoup, leurs souhaits étaier
> ainsi formulés: 'Notre Seigneur et notre Sauveur Jésus-Christ, en qui nous avor
> mis notre espoir et du nom duquel nous fûmes appelés chrétiens pour la premièr
> fois dans cette ville, c'est Toi qui nous as conduits ici. Si nous avons péché contr
> Toi, Tu peux, à bon droit, nous distribuer des châtiments nombreux. Mais ne not
> livre pas aux Infidèles, afin que nos ennemis, parlant avec jactance, ne disent pa:

---

[26] Peeters, *Recherches*, 2.177-8.

[27] Peeters, *Recherches*, 2.178-80.

[28] Hovsêp'ian, *Colophons*, n° 120/col. 261; Mat'évosyan, *Colophons*, n° 140/p. 118; Peeter
Recherches, 2.166, qui traduit *aman darmanots*, 'vase de remèdes', par *nosocomium*, 'hôpital

[29] Hovsêp'ian, *Colophons*, n° 120/col. 261; Mat'évosyan, *Colophons*, n° 140/p. 118; Peeter
Recherches, 2.166-7.

'Où est leur Dieu?' La prière de certains ayant été exaucée, ils s'encourageaient les uns les autres en disant: 'Le Seigneur donnera la puissance à son peuple, le Seigneur bénira son peuple et lui donnera la paix.[30]

C'est la ferveur de leur prière (non l'invention de la Sainte lance) qui mérite aux chevaliers francs une victoire éclatante, marquée par le massacre des Turcs et l'abondance de blé et d'orge.[31] On peut, ici, s'abstenir d'attribuer le sentiment de solidarité chrétienne exprimé par l'auteur à une influence chalcédonienne. Sa réaction est celle même d'un illustre compatriote et contemporain de Hovhannês, le chroniqueur Matt'êos d'Ouřha (Matthieu d'Edesse), pour lequel l'arrivée des Francs manifeste la réalisation d'une prophétie du catholicos Nersês le Grand, à la fin du IVe siècle: 'Ils venaient briser les fers des chrétiens, affranchir du joug des Infidèles le tombeau vénéré qui reçut un Dieu.'[32] En outre, 'c'étaient des chefs illustres, rejetons de familles souveraines, éminents par leur foi et leur piété, et élevés dans la pratique des bonnes oeuvres'.[33]

On trouverait une éclatante confirmation des bonnes dispositions des Arméniens de la Diaspora proche-orientale – les seuls qui, avec ceux de Cilicie, aient été témoins des victoires des Croisés – vis-à-vis des Francs, dans le colophon d'un Evangile copié par le moine Ahařovn (Aaron), en Egypte, à Alexandrie, 'sous la protection de Saint Jean l'Evangéliste', peu de mois après la conquête de Jérusalem (15 juillet 1099). L'interprétation providentialiste de la Croisade est également présente dans ce texte:

Ce saint Evangile fut copié sous le patriarcat de Têr Grigor et sous l'autocratie du vaillant peuple des Romains c'est-à-dire des Francs. Ceux-ci, se mettant alors en mouvement, s'élancèrent en multitudes innombrables, par la sollicitude céleste et sous l'influence du Dieu Tout-Puissant, et parvinrent jusqu'à Antioche.[34]

---

[30] Hovsêp'ian, *Colophons*, n° 120/col. 262-3; Mat'évosyan, *Colophons*, n° 140/pp. 118-19; Peeters, *Recherches*, 2.167.

[31] Hovsêp'ian, *Colophons*, n° 120/col. 262-3; Mat'évosyan, *Colophons*, n° 140/pp. 118-19; Peeters, *Recherches*, 2.167.

[32] Édit. et trad. par E. Dulaurier, *RHC, Arm.*, 1.25.

[33] *RHC, Arm.*, 1.25. Sur les contacts arméno-francs lors de la Première Croisade et dans les décennies suivantes, cf. G. Dédéyan, *Les pouvoirs arméniens dans le Proche-Orient méditerranéen (1068-1144)*, thèse multigraphiée, 4 vol. (Paris-Lille, 1990: à paraître dans la 'Bibliothèque arménienne' de la Fondation C. Gulbenkìan), passim. Cf. aussi pour la période envisagée, J. France, 'La stratégie arménienne de la Première Croisade', dans *Les Lusignans et l'Outre-Mer (Actes du Colloque Poitiers-Lusignan, 20-24 oct. 1993)*, éd. J.P. Arrignon (Poitiers, 1995), pp. 141-9.

[34] Hovsêp'ian, *Colophons*, n° 121/col. 265; Mat'évosyan, *Colophons*, n° 141/p. 120.

Non content de rapporter la prise d'Antioche et le massacre d' 'Infidèles' de tout poil ('le peuple des Turcs, Perses, Arabes et Tadchik'[35]) avec beaucoup plus de détails que Hovhannês (comme ce dernier, il attribue la victoire finale des Francs à leur prière instante dans l'église Saint-Pierre), l'auteur du colophon, avec quelque approximation chronologique, puisque la prise de Jérusalem eut lieu plus d'un an après celle d'Antioche, rapporte beaucoup plus succinctement, mais avec une égale satisfaction, le premier événement: 'La même année, ils entrèrent dans la grande et célèbre métropole de Jérusalem et, par la puissance du Christ, passèrent les Infidèles au fil de l'épée'.[36] On pourrait comprendre l'enthousiasme de l'auteur pour les succès antiochiens, remportés sur les sultans saldjûkides, Turcs et protecteurs du califat sunnite de Bagdad, et, à ce titre, ennemis jurés des Fâtimides, Arabes et détenteurs d'un califat chî'ite ismaélien. Mais c'est sur ces derniers qu'est conquise la Ville Sainte, sous le vizirat du tout-puissant al-Afdal (1094-1121), qui avait hérité sa charge de son père, Badr al-Djamâlî, un Arménien islamisé. Certes, ce dernier, pour combattre les Turcs, avait encouragé l'immigration en Egypte de plusieurs milliers de cavaliers nobles arméniens et favorisé, pour la desserte spirituelle de cette 'colonie', la création d'une sorte de catholicossat en second, dévolu à un neveu de Grigor Vekayasêr.[37] Mais les massacres de Jérusalem où, de surcroît, le catholicos qui y séjournait alors, avait failli être tué par les musulmans, avaient provoqué un raidissement d'al-Afdal dont un thuriféraire des Croisés, comme Ahaṙon, aurait pu faire les frais. Notons que, sur les liens entre les Arméniens d'Egypte et ceux de Jérusalem, pendant le bref vizirat (1135-37) de l'Arménien, resté chrétien, Vahram (un Pahlawouni, comme Grigor Vekayasêr), nous sommes renseignés de façon concrète grâce à deux colophons de manuscrits syriaques copiés dans l'année 1138, l'un à Marach, en Euphratèse, l'autre à Jérusalem. Ceux-ci font état de la démarche, couronnée de succès, de l'évêque arménien de Jérusalem auprès du tout puissant Vahram, pour la délivrance d'un vaillant seigneur franc, Godefroy de Ascha, compagnon de Godefroy de Bouillon, dont la captivité remontait à la Première Croisade; ces colophons rappellent aussi, contre les revendications domaniales (deux villages possédés par la communauté jacobite) de Godefroy de Ascha, revenu

---

[35] Du syriaque *Tayoyo*, nom donné par les chroniqueurs syriaques à des Arabes d'origine yéménites qui avaient émigré en Syrie. Le terme *Tadchik*, chez les Arméniens, désigne d'abord les Arabes nomades (comme, peut-être, ici) puis l'ensemble des peuples musulmans (Dulaurier dans *RHC, Arm.*, 1.325 n. 2 et p. 815, art. 'Dadjig'.

[36] Hovsêp'ian, *Colophons*, n° 122/col. 266; Mat'évosyan, *Colophons*, n° 141/p. 120.

[37] Cf. A. Kapoïan-Kouymjian, 'Le catholicos Grégoire II le Martyrophile (Vkayaser)', dans son *L'Egypte vue par les Arméniens (XIᵉ-XVIIᵉ siècles)* (Paris, 1988), pp. 7-24.

à Jérusalem, la décision sans appel de la reine Mélisende (née de Baudouin II de Jérusalem et de Morfia, une Arménienne de Mélitène, ville d'Euphratèse à forte communauté syriaque) en faveur de ses anciens 'compatriotes'.[38]

II. L'expédition de Jean Comnène en Cilicie: le fanatisme anti-arménien.

Les colophons de manuscrits éclairent encore, brièvement mais d'un jour nouveau, l'expédition de l'empereur Jean Comnène (1138-43) en 1137, destinée à replacer la principauté arménienne de Cilicie, alors dirigée par Lewon Ier (1129-37), sous la souveraineté de Byzance, et la principauté normande d'Antioche, où Raymond de Poitiers (1136-49) venait de prendre le pouvoir, sous sa suzeraineté. Dans le colophon d'une collection canonique (*Joghovatzou*) de 1143, de la plume même de Nersês Chenorhali (le Gracieux), frère et coadjuteur du catholicos Grigor III (1113-66), et lui-même futur catholicos (1166-73), l'auteur, à l'occasion du rachat, par ses soins, de l'ouvrage en question, évoque la violence de la reconquête byzantine en Cilicie:

> Après tous ceux qui l'ont reçu (le recueil), souvenez-vous, dans le Christ, de moi, de l'indigne Nersês, qui suis évêque et frère du catholicos des Arméniens Têr Grigor. J'ai reçu ce livre, à prix d'argent, sur le butin fait par les Grecs aux dépens des couvents arméniens, lorsque le roi des Romains vint au pays des Ciliciens et l'enleva au prince Lewon, qui était Arménien par la race et par la foi.[39] Il dévasta plusieurs couvents et églises et ils (les Grecs) brisaient les signes (i.e. les croix) du Seigneur et, pleins d'esprit de vengeance, ils portaient de terribles coups à notre peuple. Et cela arriva en l'an 586 (15 février 1137-14 février 1138).[40]

De fait, beaucoup moins ouvert au dialogue interecclésial que ne le sera son fils et successeur Manuel Ier (1143-80), Jean Comnène conduit, au sud-est de l'Asie Mineure, une véritable 'Croisade des Albigeois' pour éradiquer l' 'hérésie' arménienne et mettre fin, en même temps, à l'indépendance de la Cilicie. Il ne le cède en rien à l'émir danishmendide Muhammad: en 1136, les Turcs selon Mattêos d'Ouŕha, brûlent le monastère de Karmir Vank' (en Euphratèse), brisent 'les croix du Seigneur en bois et en pierre', emportent 'celles de fer et de bronze'.[41] Le témoignage de Nersês Chenorhali, qui résidait alors, avec le catholicos, dans la forteresse de Tzovk', à l'ouest du comté d'Edesse, confirme

---

[38] Abbé Martin, 'Les premiers princes croisés et les Syriens jacobites de Jérusalem', *Journal Asiatique* 12 (1888), pp. 471-90 et 13 (1889), pp. 33-79.

[39] Il se différenciait ainsi des Arméniens chalcédoniens, plus ou moins présents dans l'ouest de la Cilicie et relais de la pénétration byzantine.

[40] Hovsêp'ian, *Colophons*, n° 169/col. 355-6; Mat'évosyan, *Colophons*, n° 191/p. 162.

[41] *RHC, Arm.*, 1.149-50.

les données du *Panégyrique* de Jean Comnène composé par l'orateur Michel
Italikos au retour de campagne du Basileus (1138). Lors de la prise d'Anazarbe
sur les Arméniens, en 1137, les Grecs s'emparent des 'très vénérables reliques
des prédicateurs du Christ', c'est-à-dire des saints Barthélemy et Thaddée,
considérés par la tradition nationale comme les premiers évangélisateurs de
l'Arménie; ainsi 'elles ont été sauvées des mains des impies'.[42]

III. Saccages, migrations, esclavage: la fin du comté d'Edesse.

Sur la grande catastrophe du milieu du XIIe siècle, la double chute d'Edesse
(1144/6), ville sainte de l'Orient chrétien en raison de la précocité de sa
conversion (en la personne d'Abgar IX, au tournant du IIe siècle, plutôt qu'en
celle d'Abgar V Ukkâmâ, contemporain du Christ, dont son messager aurait
rapporté le portrait, vénéré à Edesse jusqu'en 944 sous le nom de Mandylion),
sur le démantèlement du comté franco-arménien d'Edesse (1098-1150), les
colophons arméniens complètent les données du Continuateur de Matt'êos
d'Oułha, Grigor Yérêts (Grégoire le Prêtre), de Nersês Chenorhali, auteur
d'une *Elégie sur la prise d'Edesse*, et du patriarche syriaque jacobite Michel
le Grand (1166-99). Un colophon en vers, écrit un an après la première chute
d'Edesse, par un certain Stép'annos, au style lapidaire et à la langue
maladroite, manifeste un attachement passionné de ce dernier pour sa ville:

> Ma subsistance, ma naissance, ma vie, mes années
> C'est Edesse, en Mésopotamie, en pays syriaque.
> Nous étions dans la douleur, car les fortifications furent sans efficacité
> En ce lieu d'habitation de mon lignage et sa patrie.[43]

Il évoque ensuite la violente confrontation des Francs et des Turcs et la
destruction, jusqu'aux fondements, des maisons et des villages, par l'ennemi
musulman.[44] Il s'agit là de la première prise d'Edesse, par le Turc Zankî
(1127-46), maître de Mossoul et d'Alep, en décembre 1144.

> Ce fut ensuite le bannissement, nous gagnâmes Amid,
> Région où il n'y a de ville ni sur la mer ni sur la terre ferme.[45]

C'est, à environ 150 km au nord-est d'Edesse, l'actuelle Diyarbékir. Mais les
fuyards ont les escadrons turcomans sur leurs talons:

---

[42] Cité par Dédéyan, *Les pouvoirs arméniens*, 3.691-2.
[43] Mat'évosyan, *Colophons*, n° 192/p. 163.
[44] Mat'évosyan, *Colophons*, n° 192/p. 163.
[45] Mat'évosyan, *Colophons*, n° 192/p. 163.

La cavalerie arriva sur nous, nous allâmes là-bas,
Nous fûmes vus par les païens, nous supportâmes le vent et la chaleur.[46]

Contrairement à Stép'annos, le scribe Karapet, 'humble prêtre', qui copie un Evangile en 1147, 'dans le canton de Mésopotamie, dans la ville gardée par Dieu et très renommée d'Edesse, sur l'ordre du moine Stép'annos, saint et brillant de pureté, serviteur du Saint Signe (la Croix) qui se trouve au couvent de Tzovk', près du territoire de la forteresse de Hoṙomkla',[47] a pu rester dans la cité d'Abgar, malgré les mesures de rigueur prises à l'encontre des Arméniens par Nûr al-Dîn (1146-74) — fils et successeur de Zankî à Alep –, après la réoccupation temporaire d'Edesse par le comte Josselin II (fin octobre 1146).

Notons ici que les colophons des Syriaques (de la communauté jacobite, en contact étroit avec les Arméniens en Mésopotamie du Nord, dont ils constituaient la population autochtone) nous fournissent de précieuses informations sur les mouvements migratoires qui affectèrent la région d'Edesse après la chute de la ville: dans le colophon circonstancié d'un lectionnaire copié en 1149 à Jérusalem, au couvent de Saint-Simon le Pharisien et de Sainte-Marie Madeleine, le moine Mar Simon nous apprend que, dès 1148, la Ville Sainte est remplie de réfugiés, Syriaques et Francs, dont les premiers ne sortent d'une situation particulièrement précaire que sur l'intervention du métropolite jacobite Ignatius et avec le concours de la régente Mélisende et du jeune Baudouin III.[48] Si les Arméniens ne sont pas mentionnés, d'autres indices suggèrent qu'il y a eu, de leur part, un important mouvement de repli d'Edesse et des villes voisines vers Jérusalem.[49] Cette attitude de loyalisme vis-à-vis des seigneurs francs, et particulièrement d'une dynastie à demi arménienne, ne nous étonne pas, s'agissant des Arméniens; en revanche, venant des Jacobites, dont on a parfois mis en exergue le sens du compromis, voire la turcophilie,[50] elle permet de corriger l'opinion reçue ou, du moins, de montrer que la bienveillance montrée tant par l'Arménienne Morfia, épouse de Baudouin II (1118-31), que par sa fille Mélisende, mariée à Foulque d'Anjou (1131-43), à

---

[46] Mat'évosyan, *Colophons*, n° 192/p. 163. Nous supposons que le terme d'*azgik'*, 'peuples', équivaut ici à *aylazgik'*, 'païens'.

[47] Hovsêp'ian, *Colophons*, n° 170/col. 356-7; Mat'évosyan, *Colophons*, n° 194/p. 165, qui corrige 1144 en 1147.

[48] Cf. G. Dédéyan, 'Un projet de colonisation militaire arménienne dans le royaume latin de Jérusalem', dans M. Balard et A. Ducellier, direct., *Se partager le monde (Actes du Colloque de Conques, avril 1995)* (sous presse).

[49] Dédéyan, 'Un projet de colonisation arménienne'.

[50] R. Grousset oppose trop volontiers les Arméniens, d'une fidélité presque sans faille et d'un courage éprouvé, aux Syriaques, jugés islamophiles et peu combatifs.

l'égard de la communauté jacobite de Jérusalem, avait porté ses fruits. Le démantèlement du comté d'Edesse, malgré un sursaut de Josselin II après la perte définitive de la capitale, se poursuivit inexorablement.

Les Turcs visaient particulièrment Marach, qui était le centre d'un petit comté vassal, au nord-ouest d'Edesse, d'abord, tenu par Baudouin de Marach, frère du prince d'Antioche, Raymond de Poitiers (1136-49); Baudouin étant mort lors de la tentative de reconquête d'Edesse en 1146, c'est son frère Renaud (gendre de Josselin II) qui lui succéda, jusqu'au désastre d'Inab (29 juin 1149) où il périt en même temps que Raymond de Poitiers.[51] Le comte d'Edesse ayant, en l'absence d'héritier, annexé le fief, mais sans en organiser la défense, les Turcs purent s'en emparer, le 11 septembre 1149. C'est cet événement et ses suites que relate un colophon de 1149/50, dû à Grigor de Marach, un célèbre *vardapet* (docteur),[52] fondateur et moine du monastère des Jésuens (ou de Machkewor), dans la Montagne Noire, près de Marach. Grigor rapporte d'abord la prise de Marach, qu'il impute, sans beaucoup de clarté, à Mas'ûd, sultan saldjûkide de Rûm, dont il semble confondre précédemment les attaques avec celles du 'fils de Zangê (Zankî)', c'est-à-dire Nûr al-Dîn, conscient par ailleurs que le comté de Marach est la cible d'attaques convergentes de plusieurs souverains turcs (Nûr al-Dîn, sollicité, avait envoyé son lieutenant, Shirkûh, à la rescousse).[53] Le couvent des Jésuens échappe à la dévastation qui frappe le pays: 'Quant à nous, qui étions dans le 'désert' des Jésuens, nous continuâmes à bénéficier de la miséricorde de Dieu, car, quoiqu'ils (les Turcs) s'approchassent chaque jour de nous, ils ne purent néanmoins réaliser leur projet, en raison des fortifications du lieu'.[54] Les moines n'en sont pas moins incommodés par 'l'odeur consécutive aux dommages causés', particulièrement à Marach (incendies et charniers). L'auteur mentionne encore l'attaque de Tell-Bâchir/Turbessel (résidence de Josselin II) – que la médiation de Nûr al-Dîn empêcha de tomber aux mains de Mas'ûd – et la conquête, 'par ruse', de nombreuses localités qu' 'il serait trop long d'énumérer les unes après les autres'.[55] Grigor de Marach tente d'établir – et c'est là l'intérêt de ce témoignage sur le vif – un bilan précis des dommages causés par les Turcs:

---

[51] Sur tout ceci, cf. M. Amouroux-Mourad, *Le comté d'Edesse* (Paris, 1988), pp. 87-8.

[52] Sur ce personnage, cf. H. Adcharyan, n° 174, dans *Dictionnaire des noms de personne arméniens* (en arm.), 5 vol. réédit. (Beyrouth, 1972), 1.557-8.

[53] Hovsêp'ian, *Colophons*, n° 171/col. 359.

[54] Hovsêp'ian, *Colophons*, n° 171/col. 359.

[55] Hovsêp'ian, *Colophons*, n° 171/col. 359.

Ils tuèrent 1800 hommes à Zaghkhin, 250 à Adchar, 300 à Aweln, 38 à Khoumanos; à Deghnoytoun, ils livrèrent aux flammes 5 autochtones, puis ils entreprirent de déplacer des gens et en amenèrent à Halil, ils brûlèrent 39 localités, grandes et petites, et, réduisant en esclavage ces cantons, ils livrèrent tout en pâture aux flammes, les cultures et les lieux habités.[56]

Après la retraite des Turcs 'pendant l'hiver', Grigor reconnaît: 'Nous n'avons pu vérifier le nombre des captifs.'[57] Précisant que son récit a été rédigé le 5 février (de l'an 598, i.e. 12 février 1149-11 février 1150), l'auteur note ensuite: 'Après j'ai appris qu'il y avait plus de 40.000 prisonniers, mais il y avait encore à venir l'amertume de nombreuses guerres.'[58] Rapportant une expédition de Kilîdj Arslân II, héritier présomptif de Mas'ûd, accompagné de son fils Turkman, dans le territoire d'Antioche, il relève les captures et les ventes: 'Il s'empara de nombreux animaux, de 1500 hommes et d'enfants, qu'il emmena à Marach. on les y vendait 6 *k'artêz*, puis 2 *dahékan*.'[59] Si Grigor Yerêts et le patriarche Michel donnent des détails assez précis sur la nature des dommages commis par les différents princes turcs en Euphratèse en ce milieu du XIIe siècle, Grigor de Marach nous plonge, lui, au coeur de ces 'calamités'.

IV. Le rôle des Arméniens dans la ligue panchrétienne de Manuel Comnène.

Les colophons de manuscrits arméniens fournissent encore d'intéressantes données, sinon sur l'expédition de Manuel Comnène (1143-80), contre T'oros II, prince roubênien de Cilicie (1145-49), et Renaud de Châtillon, prince consort d'Antioche (1153-60), dont le premier avait été le complice lors du sac de Chypre (1155), du moins sur les destinées de la ligue panchrétienne regroupant les Byzantins et, sous la suzeraineté du Basileus, les Arméniens et les Francs, dans la période 1158-69. Si cette ligue remporta des succès (par exemple en Asie Mineure sur Kilîdj Arslân II, en 1161), elle subit une défaite retentissante à Hârim, à l'est d'Antioche, le 11 août 1164, Bohémond III d'Antioche, Raymond III de Tripoli (soutenus par les Ordres Militaires), Coloman, duc byzantin de Cilicie, et T'oros II (qui, depuis l'intervention de Manuel, avait évacué la plaine cilicienne), étaient venus y affronter Nûr al-Dîn, son frère Kutb al-Dîn de Mossoul et les Artukides du Diyar Bakr.[60] Les forces chréti-

---

[56] Hovsêp'ian, *Colophons*, n° 171/col. 359.

[57] Hovsêp'ian, *Colophons*, n° 171/col. 359.

[58] Hovsêp'ian, *Colophons*, n° 171/col. 360.

[59] Hovsêp'ian, *Colophons*, n° 171/col. 360. Monnaies respectivement de cuivre et d'argent (ou d'or).

[60] C. Cahen, *La Syrie du Nord à l'époque des Croisades* (Paris, 1940), pp. 408-9.

ennes s'étant laissées encercler par les Turcs, seuls T'oros et son frère Mleh purent s'enfuir et échapper à la captivité.[61] Un colophon versifié, dû à un prêtre de Hoṙomkla — forteresse du comté d'Edesse cédée en 1150 à Grigor III et à son frère par Béatrice, épouse de Josselin II captif — évoque le sort du souverain ṙoubênien sous un jour paradoxalement laudatif, mais sans se départir de cet esprit de solidarité chrétienne qui caractérise l'historiographie arménienne de l'époque des Croisades:

> Nous avons écrit ceci en l'année
> 613 (9 février 1164-10 février 1165),
> Dans une mauvaise heure de tristesse
> Où les chrétiens étaient tout à fait à terre:
> L'armée d'Antioche fut battue
> Et les généraux furent faits prisonniers
> Le 13 août,
> Un jeudi, jour de tristesse.
> A cause de leurs fautes
> Qui s'étaient multipliées
> La volonté du Créateur se déchaîna,
> Et les livra à ceux qui n'avaient pas de lois (i.e. les Infidèles),
> Parce qu'ils s'étaient détournés de ses lois.[62]

La piété de T'oros II lui vaut d'échapper au désastre et de n'encourir aucun dommage territorial:

> Mais la droite du Père protecteur
> Garda le prince arménien,
> T'oros, qui était plein de majesté
> Issu de la race des Ṙoubêniens.
> Il (Dieu) nous accorda un don généreux
> Et lui conserva le pays qu'il possédait en propre,
> Ecoutant les prières que tous lui adressaient.[63]

L'auteur du colophon ajoute d'intéressants détails autobiographiques:

> Ainsi, j'ai composé cet écrit de peu de valeur
> Dans le pays dont il est maître,
> Au saint monastère de Kastaghôn,
> Mausolée de ses ancêtres.

---

[61] Cahen, *Syrie du Nord*, p. 409.
[62] Mat'évosyan, *Colophons*, n° 213/p. 189.
[63] Mat'évosyan, *Colophons*, n° 213/p. 189.

En fait, c'est sans doute dûment mandaté par Grigor III, qui avait pour résidence, depuis 1150, la forteresse de Hoṙomkla, sur l'Euphrate (qui se trouvait, avec son territoire, sous la juridiction de Nûr al-Dîn, le tout-puissant maître d'Alep et de Damas),[64] que cet ecclésiastique s'est rendu en Cilicie:

> Dieu avait alors guidé nos pas,
> Alors que, venant du château des Romains[65]
> Nous allions le voir
> Selon notre désir.[66]

L'envoi d'un légat catholicossal auprès de T'oros II s'expliquait d'autant mieux que le frère de ce dernier, Mleh (qui, pendant son usurpation, de 1169 à 1175, devait trouver des accommodements avec Nûr al-Dîn) était marié à une nièce du catholicos, fille de son frère Vasil le Vieux.[67]

Dans le cadre de la ligue panchrétienne dirigée par le Basileus, de nombreux contacts interecclésiaux furent établis, souvent à l'initiative de Manuel Comnène lui-même. Dès 1165, Alexis le Prôtostratôr, gendre de l'empereur et résidant, comme duc de Cilicie, à Mamistra/Mesis, invitait à un dialogue théologique le frère et coadjuteur du catholicos Grigor III, Nersês Chenorhali, qui revenait d'une mission – remplie avec succès – de réconciliation entre Ochin, seigneur de Lambroun, à l'ouest de la Cilicie, et T'oros II, qui avait entrepris de faire le siège de cette place.[68] On connaît, certes, l'événement par la profession de foi composée par l'archevêque arménien à la demande d'Alexis.[69] Mais, parmi les sources narratives, ce sont les colophons de manuscrits qui nous paraissent offrir le témoignage le plus proche et le plus précis. L'auteur d'un colophon relatif à l'année 1165, après avoir exposé la mission de réconciliation de Nersês (dont une nièce, fille de son frère Chahan,

---

[64] En fait, Hoṙomkla (Kal'at al-Rûm des sources arabes) se trouvait sous l'autorité de l'Artukide Shihâb al-Dîn, vassal de Nûr al-Dîn (Cahen, *Syrie du Nord*, pp. 386, 405 n. 1).

[65] C'est la signification de Hoṙomkla, par référence à sa qualité d'ancienne forteresse byzantine.

[66] Mat'évosyan, *Colophons*, n° 213/p. 189.

[67] C. Toumanoff, *Les dynasties de la Caucasie chrétienne* (Rome, 1990), Karîn-Pahlavides, 54 'Princes Pahlavouni', A 32, p. 275.

[68] Cf. P. Tékéyan, *Controverses christologiques en Arméno-Cilicie dans la seconde moitié du XIIᵉ siècle (1165-1198)* (Rome, 1939). Plus récemment, et entre autres études du Père B.L. Zékiyan, art. 'Nersês Chenorhali (saint)', dans *Dictionnaire de Spiritualité ascétique et mystique*, t. 11 (Paris, 1981), col. 134-50.

[69] Cf. *Correspondance générale de St Nersês Chenorhali* (en arm.) (Jérusalem, 1871), pp. 87-109.

était l'épouse d'Ochin de Lambroun),[70] s'attarde sur la rencontre entre Nersês et Alexis. Après avoir rappelé qu'Ochin était un fidèle du Basileus, tandis que T'oros II avait un comportement séditieux, et souligné le succès de la mission de Nersês, chaleureusement accueilli par l'entourage d'Ochin et la population de son territoire, il évoque l'entrée de l'archevêque (peut-être accompagné et introduit par le seigneur de Lambroun, comme le suggère très vaguement le texte):

> Il entra dans la ville des *Mamouestatsik'* (habitants de Mamistra), où il y avait un prince de souche impériale, qui avait été établi duc des contrées orientales, car les Romains (i.e. les Byzantins) avaient l'habitude, à chaque changement d'année, de rappeler le gouverneur du pays et d'en envoyer un autre à sa place. Cet homme était venu là en raison de sa perspicacité et de son intelligence; placé à la tête de la cavalerie, il était revêtu de la dignité de *predôstrator* (*prôtostratôr*), comme on l'appelle en grec.[71]

Alexis Axouch, duc de Cilicie, puisque, c'est de lui qu'il s'agit, exprime sa soif de dialogue: 'S'il y avait un souhait dont je désirais l'accomplissement depuis longtemps, c'était de discuter avec vous des Saintes Ecritures et d'étudier la cause de la division de l'Eglise du Christ.'[72] 'Répondant aux questions qu'il lui posait', Nersês accepta de rédiger à l'intention d'Alexis la profession de foi des Arméniens: 'Il accéda à cette agréable demande et fit avec foi ce qui lui était demandé. Il mit par écrit notre profession de foi et la situation de notre Eglise et en remit le texte entre les mains du pieux prince susmentionné.'[73]

Un autre colophon, porté sur une *Histoire des Saints Pères*, concernant l'année 1173 et relatant les péripéties de la vie de Grigor III et de Nersês Chenorhali, évoque en des termes à peu près semblables la rencontre entre le duc de Cilicie et le coadjuteur du catholicos et en décrit les conséquences à proche et moyen terme: dans l'immédiat,

> cet homme intelligent, ayant reçu le texte de la profession de foi, honora le bienheureux de magnifiques présents et le laissa reprendre son chemin en paix; celui-ci retourna au siège patriarcal auprès de son frère, premier en dignité. Le duc, ayant achevé son année de gouvernement, retourna dans la ville royale de Constantinople et montra la lettre contenant la profession de foi des Arméniens au pieux roi, qui s'appelait Manuel, et à leur patriarche, accompagné des clercs de la Grande

---

[70] Toumanoff, *Les dynasties*, Karîn-Pahlavides, 54 'Princes Pahlavouni', A 32, p. 275.
[71] Hovsêp'ian, *Colophons*, n° 187/col. 384-5.
[72] Hovsêp'ian, *Colophons*, n° 187/col. 385.
[73] Hovsêp'ian, *Colophons*, n° 187/col. 386.

Eglise.[74] Le roi fut plein d'étonnement et d'admiration en constatant la force des idées qui transparaissaient dans ces paroles (de la profession de foi); s'étant réjoui, il se laissa convaincre de l'orthodoxie de ces affirmations.[75]

Nersês, devenu catholicos (1166-73), poursuivit le dialogue avec les Grecs, comme l'atteste sa correspondance. On sait que la défaite de Manuel Comnène face à Kilîdj Arslân II, à Myrioképhalon, en 1176, coupa désormais au Basileus la route vers la Cilicie arménienne et la Syrie franque et mit un terme définitif à la réalisation de son programme d'union religieuse et de coalition militaire. La réaction anti-latine se fit particulièrement sentir sous le règne de son cousin, Andronic Comnène (1183-85), puis sous la dynastie des Anges (1185-1204), alliés à Saladin, sultan d'Egypte et de Syrie (1174-93) et conquérant de Jérusalem, le 2 octobre 1187.

V. *De la chute de Jérusalem à la reconquête d'Acre: une douleur et un espoir partagés*

La chute de la Ville Sainte suscita une émotion considérable chez les Arméniens, comme en témoignent aussi bien l'*Elégie sur la prise de Jérusalem*, du catholicos Grigor IV Tegha (1173-93), fils de Vasil le Vieux (le frère aîné de Nersês Chenorhali), que les colophons de manuscrits rédigés dans cette période. L'impression qui ressort des écrits arméniens faisant écho à cette catastrophe du monde chrétien (précédant d'une dizaine d'année le couronnement royal de Lewon le Magnifique sous la suzeraineté du pape de Rome et de l'empereur d'Occident) est, comme pour la chute d'Edesse (où le témoignage de l'*Elégie* de Nersês Chenorhali est sans équivoque), celle d'un sentiment de solidarité chrétienne transcendant largement les litiges doctrinaux, juridictionnels ou disciplinaires. Les mêmes sources rapportent, à l'occasion, l'organisation de la Troisième Croisade (1189-92), conduite par l'empereur germanique Frédéric Barberousse (mort en Cilicie en 1190) et les rois de France et d'Angleterre, Philippe Auguste et Richard Coeur de Lion, qui, le 13 juillet 1191, concluent victorieusement le siège de Saint-Jean d'Acre (Ptolémaïs).

C'est Nersês de Lambroun, fils d'Ochin susmentionné et petit-neveu, par sa mère, de Nersês Chenorhali,[76] qui est le plus sensible à ces événements décisifs pour la vie de l'Orient latin. Nersês, archevêque de Tarse, artisan du

---

[74] Sainte-Sophie.
[75] Hovsêp'ian, *Colophons*, n° 203/col. 430-5.
[76] Cf. Toumanoff, *Les dynasties*, Karîn-Pahlavides, 56 'Hétoumides, Princes de Lambron', A 30, p. 280.

rapprochement avec l'Eglise latine (certains de ses colophons nous font connaître dans quelles circonstances et avec quels concours il traduisit les *Dialogues* du pape Grégoire le Grand et la *Règle* de saint Benoît de Nursie),[77] a été un témoin particulièrement attentif, comme le montrent deux de ses colophons. Le premier, écrit probablement en 1193, est composé sous forme de poème. L'auteur commence par rappeler les prophéties relatives à la chute de Jérusalem et par évoquer les premiers succès de Saladin (Yûsûf), 'chef du peuple que l'on appelle Turk'iman' (par référence aux Turcomans, nombreux dans l'armée ayyûbide et côtoyant les Kurdes, compatriotes de Saladin), puis décrit l'attaque contre les Francs:

> Dans son arrogance, il porta la main
> Sur le territoire réduit des chrétiens,
> Car ceux-ci ployaient sous le poids des péchés
> Et nos princes furent vaincus.[78]

Manifestant, depuis l'avènement de Baudouin Ier (1100-18) une véritable révérence envers les rois de la Ville Sainte,[79] confirmée, même après la chute de celle-ci, par les relations étroites entre le prince Lewon II (Lewon Ier après son couronnement royal en 1198) et Henri de Champagne, qui avait hérité du royaume latin, les Arméniens pouvaient considérer les souverains hiérosolymitains comme *mer ichkhank'*, 'nos princes' (il s'agit ici de Guy de Lusignan). Accusant le vainqueur (qui ménagea pourtant les communautés chrétiennes orientales de Jérusalem) d'avoir plongé la ville dans un bain de sang et de n'avoir pas fait ensevelir les morts, l'auteur ajoute:

> Nos voisins se moquèrent de nous
> Et mirent leurs menaces à exécution.[80]

C'est ensuite l'appel à la Croisade, lui aussi, de caractère prophétique, lancé par la papauté (en la personne de deux pontifes successifs, Grégoire VIII et Clément III), dans un Occident en deuil:

> De l'Occident, une voix retentit jusqu'à nous,
> Celle de Pierre, à Rome, le grand vicaire.[81]

---

[77] B.L. Zékiyan, art. 'Nersês de Lambron (saint)', dans *Dictionnaire de Spiritualité*, 11, col. 134-50.

[78] Hovsêp'ian, *Colophons*, n° 256/col. 571.

[79] Cf. notre article 'Un projet de colonisation arménienne'.

[80] Hovsêp'ian, *Colophons*, n° 256/col. 571.

[81] Hovsêp'ian, *Colophons*, n° 256/col. 571.

Nersês de Lambroun est bien informé de la venue des Occidentaux par vagues successives:

> En ayant reçu l'ordre du patriarche,
> Ils prirent la Croix et se répandirent de ce côté-ci (de la mer).
> Ils s'élancèrent à l'assaut en foule, étant de diverses nationalités,
> Formant une armée unanime de plusieurs dizaines de milliers d'hommes,
> Faisant voile, ils traversèrent la mer
> Et arrivèrent à Ptolémaïs, où ils s'installèrent.[82]

On sait que, avant la Croisade des souverains, vinrent des secours de Champagne, de Sicile et de Souabe. La dureté de l'affrontement, où les Francs, au cours d'un siège de deux ans, deviennent à leur tour assiégés, étant encerclés par l'armée musulmane de secours, est mise en évidence:

> Ils creusèrent un fossé et se fortifièrent
> Et se tinrent là pendant deux ans.
> Ils ne cherchèrent pas à fuir le combat
> Et il y eut des morts de part et d'autre.[83]

Puis:

> D'autres Croisés[84] se dépêchent de monter
> Vers la Jérusalem céleste
> Et leurs frères qui demeurent là
> Ne se lassèrent pas d'aller au combat.[85]

C'est donc de la Troisième Croisade proprement dite qu'il s'agit. Si le 'roi des Romains' (Frédéric Ier Barberousse) meurt avec beaucoup:

> Cependant les survivants ne s'arrêtèrent pas,
> Ils arrivent encore nombreux, par mer.[86]

C'est la présentation, assez optimiste — car la grande armée allemande se débanda après que son chef se fut noyé dans le Sélef — de l'arrivée du fils de Barberousse, Frédéric de Souabe, qui, ayant gagné Antioche avec de maigres effectifs, s'embarqua pour Acre. Arrivent ensuite 'le roi des Francs, Philippe',

---

[82] Hovsêp'ian, *Colophons*, n° 256/col. 571-2.

[83] Hovsêp'ian, *Colophons*, n° 256/col. 572.

[84] En arménien *khatchengalk'*, 'ceux qui ont reçu la croix'. Très réservés vis-à-vis du culte byzantin des icônes, vénérant plus volontiers la Croix, les Arméniens, sensibles à leur signe distinctif, ont vite trouvé le mot juste pour désigner les 'pèlerins' venus d'Occident.

[85] Hovsêp'ian, *Colophons*, n° 256/col. 572.

[86] Hovsêp'ian, *Colophons*, n° 256/col. 572.

et 'celui des Anglais' qui, précise l'auteur, totalement impliqué dans ces événements, viennent 'auprès de nous', ajoutant:

De ceux-ci, nous attendons le salut,
Tout comme (nous attendons) le secours de notre Dieu,
Afin que y accomplisse par eux la parole des prophètes:
'Vous mériterez de vous réjouir'
Amen![87]

Le même Nersês de Lambroun, dans un autre colophon, avant de rappeler comment, en 1192, il avait pu récupérer un précieux ouvrage dérobé par les Turcomans qui avaient attaqué son escorte près de Marach, résume ce qu'il dit ailleurs de façon circonstanciée sur la chute de Jérusalem (datée de 1189) et la Troisième Croisade. Il note que 'les ecclésiastiques et les princes qui étaient au service des Lieux saints furent emmenés en captivité' et aussi que, la nouvelle de la catastrophe étant parvenue en Occident, 'tous les peuples, avec les rois et les princes, sur l'ordre du patriarche de Rome, se mirent en route pour ces contrées'.[88] Nersês de Lambroun est d'autant plus attentif à la Troisième Croisade qu'il avait été envoyé à Grigor IV par Lewon II pour aller, avec le catholicos, au-devant de Frédéric Barberousse, mission que la razzia turcomane, évoquée plus haut, l'empêcha de mener à bien.[89] Le prince arménien, qui s'était rendu à Chypre, auprès de Richard Coeur de Lion, après la conquête de l'île par le roi d'Angleterre,[90] aurait, au moins d'après l'auteur d'un poème en allemand sur la Croisade de Louis de Thuringe, participé au siège d'Acre, avec les souverains d'Allemagne, de Jérusalem et de Chypre.[91] On trouverait d'autres mentions de la catastrophe de 1187 et de ses suites dans les colophons arméniens. La même année 1192, 'Vardan, humble moine, le dernier et le plus vil des scribes', ayant copié un Missel au couvent de Machkewor, 'sur le territoire de Sis, dans la province de Cilicie', rappelle brièvement que, en 1187, 'Jérusalem fut prise' et que 'le soleil s'obscurcit'. Il ne s'intéresse qu'à Frédéric Barberousse et, surtout, à Richard Coeur de Lion: 'Et en 639 (1190), le Franc Alaman s'élança et mourut; et en 640 (1191), le

---

[87] Hovsêp'ian, *Colophons*, n° 256/col. 572.

[88] Hovsêp'ian, *Colophons*, n° 215/col. 466-467, trad. complète dans E. Dulaurier, *Recherches sur la chronologie arménienne technique et historique* (Paris, 1859), p. 327.

[89] L. Alichan, dans *Léon le Magnifique* (Venise, 1888), pp. 102-3, date l'attaque des Turcomans vers la fin mai 1190.

[90] Alichan, *Léon le Magnifique*, pp. 102-3. Lewon y assista au mariage de Richard Coeur de Lion avec Bérengère de Navarre.

[91] Alichan, *Léon le Magnifique*, pp. 109-10.

roi anglais s'élança et prit l'île de Chypre ainsi qu'Acre et Ascalon.'[92] Plus tard, le célèbre juriste Mekhit'ar Gôch (1120-1213), qui avait séjourné en Cilicie, dans un colophon de manuscrit (son *Commentaire de Jérémie*) de 1187 ou 1188, rédigé à Gédik, en Grande Arménie, fait allusion à la perte des reliques de la Vraie Croix (récupérées lors de la libération d'Acre): 'Cette même année,[93] à cause de nos (mauvaises) oeuvres, la Sainte Ville de Jérusalem fut prise par un tyran nommé Salahaddin, en raison de la multiplication des fautes des chrétiens, et le Saint Signe fut emporté, tandis que le roi et une grande partie de ses troupes étaient capturés.'[94] Là encore, la chute de Jérusalem est ressentie comme une catastrophe pour tous les chrétiens, dans laquelle les Arméniens, par leurs péchés, ont leur responsabilité autant que les Francs.

Ainsi, dans la première période des Croisades, les colophons de manuscrits arméniens fournissent des informations, souvent complémentaires de celles émanant des chroniques et histoires nationales, sur les grands événements du XIIe siècle. Ces sources originales, qui sont souvent des témoignages pris sur le vif, éclairent la création des Etats croisés, la campagne de Jean Comnène en Cilicie, la fin du comté d'Edesse (sinon la Deuxième Croisade), la dimension arménienne de la ligue panchrétienne suscitée par Manuel Comnène, ainsi que la chute de Jérusalem, puis la reconquête d'Acre grâce à la Troisième Croisade. Certes, le plus souvent, les auteurs de colophons ne donnent pas de l'événement qu'ils appréhendent une vue complète et détaillée. Mais ils insistent sur des points négligés par les sources historiques classiques: le point de vue francophile d'un témoin oculaire lors de la prise d'Antioche (1098); la sympathie manifestée par un sujet des Fâtimides lors de la conquête de Jérusalem (1099); la décomposition du comté de Marach, localité par localité (avec le compte et le prix des captifs), avant le milieu du XIIe siècle; l'importance – omise par presque toutes les autres sources – des discussions théologiques (à incidence assurément politiques) entre Nersês Chenorhali, coadjuteur du catholicos Grigor III, et Alexis Axouch, duc de Cilicie; l'implication des Arméniens dans les bouleversements qui affectent le royaume latin de Jérusalem entre 1187 et 1192.

La contribution des colophons de manuscrits arméniens à l'historiographie des Croisades se confirme dans la période suivant, celle qui va de la reconquête à la deuxième chute de Saint-Jean d'Acre (1191-1291), événement qui marque la fin des Etats croisés de terre ferme. En effet, pendant ce siècle, le

---

[92] Hovsêp'ian, *Colophons*, n° 250/col. 559-60.
[93] C'est, par erreur, à l'année 1188 que l'auteur se réfère.
[94] Hovsêp'ian, *Colophons*, n° 238/col. 522.

nouveau royaume arménien de Cilicie (1198), contemporain du royaume latin de Chypre (1197), restructuré dans ses institutions, sur le modèle franc (celui de la principauté d'Antioche), resserrant ses liens avec les Etats latins du Levant par de multiples alliances matrimoniales, admettant l'autorité du siège romain, est partie intégrante (Claude Cahen parlait d'un Orient 'arméno-franc') de l'Orient des Croisades et même acteur privilégié (par exemple pour la politique mongole). Son histoire, appréhendée au prisme original des colophons, éclaire alors du même coup celle des Etats latins, voisins et alliés.

The *Tractatus de locis et statu sancte terre ierosolimitane*

Benjamin Z. Kedar

The treatise known as *Tractatus de locis et statu sancte terre ierosolimitane* amounts to a systematic description of the Frankish kingdom of Jerusalem in the years preceding the battle of Hattin. The anonymous author situates the *terra ierosolimitana* at the world's centre, mentions briefly the adjacent countries, and lists the Christian groups that inhabit it. Concentrating then on the Latins, he dwells on the special status of the Pisans, Genoese and Venetians, describes the Templars at length and the Hospitallers in brief, and surveys in detail the structure of the Frankish church. He then specifies the country's most prominent holy places according to their sequence in Christ's ministry, and adds three sites notable for their physical traits. Brief sections on the country's mountains and fauna are followed by a longer passage on its fruit trees. The author then gives the names by which the country's main towns were known in different periods. Only at this point does he speak of the king of Jerusalem, cite his coronation oath and relate that each baron must follow him into battle with a specified number of knights. He then lists the most important barons, remarking that, although the prince of Antioch and count of Tripoli reside beyond the kingdom's borders, they are the king's vassals nevertheless. The treatise concludes with an enumeration of the country's non-Christian inhabitants.

Examination of this unique treatise has been sporadic, with scholars repeatedly unaware of their predecessors' efforts. A survey of the stages of this examination may render intelligible the complex and quite bewildering printing history of the treatise and the conflicting appreciations of it, which persist to the present. The survey may also illustrate the sometimes problematic communication within this area of research.

Sometime in the early 1860s, Titus Tobler, the noted student of *itineraria* literature, found in a Munich manuscript of the fifteenth century, Clm 5307, a treatise he had not encountered before. He brought it to the attention of Georg Martin Thomas, who later discovered the same text in Clm 17060, a manuscript of the early thirteenth century, and in Clm 4351, a manuscript of the fifteenth. In 1865, Thomas, believing himself to be the first to publish the treatise, edited it on the basis of Clm 17060, with variants from Clm 4351 and Clm 5307, and gave it the title *Tractatus de locis et statu sancte terre ierosolimitane*, which appears in Clm 17060.[1] In this manuscript, as well as in Clm 5307, the treatise is followed by a historical account that focusses on the Third Crusade and had already been published by Johann Georg Eckhart in 1723. Thomas printed this account, which he named *De excidio regni et regibus Jerusalem*, right after the treatise, although he doubted that treatise and account were the work of the same author.[2] Thomas did not attempt to date the treatise. His transcription of the texts is occasionally inexact; also, he did not print two important additions to the treatise that appear in Clm 5307, the one on the Teutonic Knights, the other on the Assassins.

A year later, in 1866, Wilhelm Anton Neumann edited the first three-quarters of the treatise from a thirteenth-century manuscript belonging to the abbey of Heiligenkreuz (no. 88), in which it is preceded by a brief pilgrimage account that starts with the words: 'Ego ivi de Accon in Caifa'. Neumann believed that the pilgrimage account and the treatise formed two parts of a single opuscule, which he presented as the work of an anonymous pilgrim, 'Innominatus V'. He suggested that the pilgrim had made his voyage before 1187 but had written down his account (at least its second part) sometime after 1198, probably at the beginning of the thirteenth century, since he remarks that the king of Armenia had recently (*nuper*) received the crown from the archbishop of Mainz, legate of the Apostolic See – and it is known that the papal legate, Conrad, archbishop of Mainz, was present at Leo II's coronation in January 1198.[3] Neumann's transcription is marred by misreadings and omissions; the

---

[1] G.M. Thomas, ed., 'Ein Tractat über das heilige Land und den dritten Kreuzzug', *Sitzungsberichte der Königlich Bayerischen Akademie der Wissenschaften zu München: Philos.-philol. Classe* 1865/2, pp. 141-60. Thomas noted that the beginning of the treatise had been published by Canisius: 'Ein Tractat', p. 142. See H. Canisius, *Lectiones antiquae*, ed. J. Basnage, 4 vols (Amsterdam, 1725), 4.21-2.

[2] Thomas, 'Ein Tractat', pp. 160-71; for his doubts see p. 142. To simplify matters I shall consistently refer henceforth to these two texts as 'the treatise' and 'the *De excidio*' respectively, even when presenting the views of authors who referred to them by other names.

[3] W.A. Neumann, 'Drei mittelalterliche Pilgerschriften: Innominatus V', *Oesterreichische Vierteljahresschrift für katholische Theologie* 5 (1866), pp. 211-82. For the dating see pp. 218-20.

text is provided with copious footnotes. It appears that Neumann became aware of Thomas's edition only when his own article had already gone to the press, for he refers to it just in a footnote and an endnote, noting that the opuscule's second part had been more completely published by Thomas.[4] In 1867, Tobler presented the two parts published by Neumann as two distinct works: the first, an anonymous enumeration of the holy places, which he dated to c. 1180; the second, an anonymous description of the Holy Land, the core of which he dated to 1187 or earlier. He realized that the second work was partially identical with the treatise edited by Thomas; it appears that he regarded the *De excidio* as an integral part of that treatise.[5]

In 1866, unaware of the articles by Thomas and Neumann, Paul Riant put forward a hypothesis about the treatise's genesis and author. In his edition of the poem *De expugnata Accone*, which he attributed to Haymarus Monachus, patriarch of Jerusalem in the years 1194-1202, Riant claimed that in September 1199 Pope Innocent III had asked the patriarch for a report on the Saracen forces and on the state of the Holy Land (*de statu Terrae Sanctae*), and that the latter had submitted it before the end of that year. Riant believed that this report contained three parts: (a) an account about the Ayyubid rulers, together with a largely geographical description of the Holy Land and Egypt, which was later erroneously considered to be James of Vitry's third book and was printed by Gretser in 1608, Bongars in 1611, Martène and Durand in 1717 and Giles in 1846; (b) the *De statu Terrae Sanctae*, which was also printed by Martène and Durand in 1717 – and which, unknown to Riant, is identical with the treatise that Thomas in 1865 believed to publish for the first time; (c) the historical account published in 1723 by Eckhart – which, as we have seen, Thomas re-edited under the title *De excidio regni et regibus Jerusalem*.[6]

---

[4] Neumann, 'Drei mittelalterliche Pilgerschriften', pp. 258 n. 1, and 282.

[5] T. Tobler, *Bibliotheca geographica Palaestinae* (Leipzig, 1867), pp. 19-20, 22-3.

[6] Haymarus Monachus, *De expugnata Accone liber tetrastichus*, ed. P. Riant (Lyon, 1866). My summary integrates Riant's remarks on pp. l-li, 63-4, 92-5 (on p. 63 n. 2, the page numbers 1524-9 should be corrected to 1124-9). The treatise is printed in E. Martène and U. Durand, *Thesaurus novus anecdotorum*, 5 vols (Paris, 1717), 3.275-81. Martène and Durand offered a ludicrous text: for instance, where the manuscripts have 'mercimoniorum ingenio sagaces', they printed 'Mathimoniorum, vel Marthimoniorum, vel Mathematicorum ingenio flagrantes'; 'cana melli, unde fit zucarum' became 'cana melli Zachariae'; 'Ptolomaida' became 'Tholonia Ida', and so forth.

It should be noted that William Stubbs did not accept Riant's opinion that the patriarch's name was Haymarus Monachus, and claimed that it was Monachus Florentinus: see his introduction to his re-edition of the poem in Roger of Hoveden, *Chronica*, ed. W. Stubbs, 4

Riant's hypothesis with regard to the treatise is easily refuted. It hinges on the assumption that Innocent III asked for, and received, a report on the state of the Holy Land:[7] yet Innocent's letters, on which Riant bases this assumption, make clear that the pope did not ask for a general report on the country's population or ecclesiastical and political organization in the pre-1187 period, as contained in the treatise, but for frequent letters on the country's current situation,[8] and that he received – not only from the patriarch but from a number of Frankish dignitaries – 'litteras ... ipsius terrae necessitates et miserias plenius exponentes et postulantes subsidium diutius exspectatum',[9] a characterization that by no means fits the treatise.

Nevertheless, in his *Bibliotheca geographica Palaestinae* of 1890, as well as in later works, Reinhold Röhricht accepted Riant's hypothesis with only slight modifications. Like Tobler in 1867, he dated the first part of Neumann's text to c. 1180, attributing it to 'Innominatus V'.[10] Then, following Riant, he presented the account about the Ayyubid rulers together with the geographical description of the Holy Land and of Egypt as a single work that Haymarus Monachus wrote in 1199 in response to Innocent III's request. Finally, he asserted that in 1200 Haymarus Monachus wrote the work, *De statu Terrae Sanctae*, comprising two parts: the treatise and the *De excidio*.[11] Röhricht listed in his *Bibliotheca* twenty-eight manuscripts that contain the Latin version of *De statu Terrae Sanctae* and seven giving the Old French one; unfortunately he did not specify which of the manuscripts contain both parts (that is, the treatise and the *De excidio*) and which just one of them.[12] Neither did he

---

vols, *RS* 51 (London, 1868-71), 3.cv. On the patriarch's career see R. Hiestand and H.E. Mayer, 'Die Nachfolge des Patriarchen Monachus von Jerusalem', *Basler Zeitschrift für Geschichte und Altertumskunde* 74 (1974), pp. 109-10 (reprinted in H.E. Mayer, *Kreuzzüge und lateinischer Osten* [London 1983], Study XII); B. Hamilton, *The Latin Church in the Crusader States: The Secular Church* (London, 1980), pp. 243-8.

[7] Haymarus Monachus, *De expugnata Accone*, pp. l-li, 92 (summary of document xxix), 94 (summary of document xxxiii), 95 (summmary of document xxxix).

[8] '...exhortamur...quatenus...statum Jerosolymitanae provinciae nobis per litteras vestras frequenter et veraciter intimetis.' *PL*, 214.738 (Ep. 189).

[9] *PL*, 214.828 (Ep. 270), 833 (Ep. 271).

[10] R. Röhricht, *Bibliotheca geographica Palaestinae* (Berlin, 1890), no. 99/p. 41.

[11] Röhricht, *Bibliotheca*, no. 109/pp. 43-5. See also *RRH*, nos. 760, 762; R. Röhricht, *Geschichte des Königreichs Jerusalem (1100-1291)* (Innsbruck, 1898), p. 682.

[12] For the list of manuscripts and printed editions see Röhricht, *Bibliotheca*, no. 109/pp. 44-5, and the addendum to no. 109 on p. 666. To these manuscripts should be added Cambridge, Magdalene College: F.4.22 (first half of the thirteenth century), fols 1ra-3va, and Berlin, Preussische Staatsbibliothek: Görres 111, a manuscript of the thirteenth century, which, on fols 105r-106v, contains sections on three sites notable for their physical traits, on the country's

consider the consequences for Riant's hypothesis of the chronicle of Richard of San Germano, of which an edition by Georg Heinrich Pertz appeared in 1866. Richard includes, under the year 1214, the account about the Ayyubid rulers but not the largely geographical description of the Holy Land and Egypt.[13] Röhricht simply refers to this edition as if it contained the account as well as the description.

The exertions of Riant and Röhricht were ignored by Aubrey Stewart, who, in 1894, printed an English translation – the only one to date – of the treatise, on the basis of Neumann's 1866 article. Apparently influenced by Tobler, Stewart ascribed the brief pilgrimage account that starts with 'Ego ivi de Accon in Caifa' to 'Anonymous Pilgrim V.1', and the treatise (that is, the first three-quarters of it printed by Neumann) to 'Anonymous Pilgrim V.2'; yet, with regard to the date, he reverted to Neumann's view that both parts refer to a pilgrimage that took place before 1187 and was described after 1198. Probably misunderstanding Neumann's endnote, he remarked that 'Dr Thomas ... has given a complete edition of this fragment'; at any rate, he did not

---

mountains, animals and fruit trees, and on its non-Latin inhabitants. From Röhricht's list of printed editions one might deduce that the treatise had been printed in 1733 by Muratori in volume 23 of the *Rerum Italicarum scriptores*; in reality, the *Historia Montisferrati* by Benvenuto di San Giorgio (d. 1527) that is printed there (cols 367-72) contains only the *De excidio*. On the other hand, Röhricht appears to have been unaware of the fact that the treatise had been printed in 1717 by Martène and Durand (see note 6 above), although he knew that the account about the Ayyubid rulers together with the geographical description of the Holy Land and Egypt was printed by them.

The *Tractatus de locis et statu sancte terre ierosolimitane* appears also in the following manuscripts: (1) Charleville-Mézières, Bibliothèque Municipale: No. 275, fols 217ᵛ-219ᵛ (thirteenth-fourteenth century); (2) Besançon, Bibliothèque Municipale: No. 671; (3) Bourges, Bibliothèque Municipale: ms. 162 (145); (4) Cambridge, Corpus Christi College: ms. 315, fols 73ʳ-75ᵛ; (5) Uppsala, University Library: ms. C 43; (6) Košice, Biskupská Knižnica: ms. 156, fols 311ᵛ-329ʳ (a. 1467). I would like to thank Dr Theresa M. Vann of the Hill Monastic Manuscript Library, Saint John's University, Collegeville, Minnesota, for having kindly provided this information.

Only one of the two Brussels manuscripts listed by Röhricht contains the *Tractatus*. This is Bibliothèque Royale: ms. 10147-58 (thirteenth-fourteenth century), fol. 21ʳ-22ʳ (Röhricht listed it as ms. 10149). My thanks to Professor Baudouin Van den Abeele for having examined the two manuscripts for me.

[13] *MGH SS*, 19.336-7; the chronicle was re-edited by C.A. Garufi in *Rerum Italicarum scriptores*, new series, vol. 7/2 (Bologna, 1937-38), pp. 56-9. Riant might have consulted the chronicle as edited by Ughelli or Muratori.

translate the last quarter edited by Thomas, nor did he provide a usable reference to that edition.[14]

Auguste Molinier gave some further publicity to the Riant-Röhricht hypothesis in the sections of his well-known survey of sources that appeared in 1902-3 (Molinier referred mainly to Riant).[15] But in 1909 the hypothesis suffered a blow when Philipp Funk (who referred only to Röhricht) showed that the account about the Ayyubid rulers is independent of the geographical description of the Holy Land (and Egypt) and claimed that, at most, Haymarus Monachus could have had something to do with the first of these two works but certainly not with the second, which should be dated after 1217. He did not waste a word on Haymarus Monachus's purported authorship of the treatise and the *De excidio*. Funk, who knew Thomas's edition of these works, was the first to show that in 1717 Martène and Durand had printed all four texts – the account about the Ayyubids, the geographical description, the treatise and the *De excidio* – one after another, and he persuasively argued that all four were among the materials that James of Vitry had at his disposal when preparing his *Historia orientalis*.[16] Funk's view appears to have been influential: Max Manitius in 1931 attributed to Haymarus Monachus only the poem on the conquest of Acre (although in a footnote he listed Röhricht's entry in the *Bibliotheca*), and the *Repertorium fontium historiae medii aevi* did likewise, noting that Röhricht (not Riant!) attributed to Haymarus Monachus the account on the Ayyubids and the geographical description.[17]

In 1906, Girolamo Golubovich, unaware of Thomas's and Neumann's editions of the treatise and of the Riant-Röhricht hypothesis, printed from ms. Verona 317 an anonymous account that comprises a brief description of the holy places and the beginning of the treatise, in which the Christian groups inhabiting the Holy Land are listed. Golubovich knew that Röhricht had presented the brief description as the work of 'Innominatus IX', dated it to c. 1175, and commented on its similarity to 'Innominatus V'; nevertheless, Golu-

[14] The translations appear in *Palestine Pilgrims' Text Society*, 13 vols (London, 1890-97), 6.22-36, with the quotation on p. 36.

[15] A. Molinier, *Les sources de l'histoire de France des origines aux guerres d'Italie (1494)*, 6 vols (Paris, 1901-06), 2.291 (no. 2145), 3.36-7 (nos. 2338-9).

[16] P. Funk, *Jakob von Vitry: Leben und Werke* (Leipzig and Berlin, 1909), pp. 136-7, 157-69.

[17] M. Manitius, *Geschichte der lateinischen Literatur des Mittelalters*, 3 vols (Munich, 1911-31), 3.701-3; *Repertorium fontium historiae medii aevi*, 6 vols to date (Rome, 1962-), 5.391.

bovich ascribed the account in its entirety (that is, also the treatise's beginning) to an anonymous compiler and dated it to the early thirteenth century.[18]

In 1973, Anna-Dorothee von den Brincken, in her detailed discussion of Latin perceptions of oriental Christians from the mid-twelfth to the later fourteenth century, repeatedly made use of the texts published by Thomas, Neumann and Golubovich. Apparently unaware of the earlier literature, she presented the three texts as distinct works. She considered the oldest of the three to be the account published by Neumann, which she ascribed to an unknown pilgrim, 'Innominatus V', who visited the Holy Land before 1187 (or relied on a pre-1187 description) and wrote soon after 1198; the second to be the *Tractatus* published by Thomas, which she believed to have been written after 1199 by an anonymous author who may or may not have visited the Orient, and who depended almost verbatim on the account by 'Innominatus V' or on a source common to both; and the most recent to be the text published by Golubovich, written after 1216, by a Franciscan who did travel to the Orient and who made use of the two previous works.[19]

In 1983, Sabino De Sandoli, unaware of Thomas's edition and Funk's work, reverted to the Riant-Röhricht hypothesis (which he cited only according to the data appearing in Röhricht's *Bibliotheca* of 1890). He evidently misunderstood it, for he reprinted the treatise (with a translation into Italian) twice. In the first place, he reprinted Neumann's 'Innominatus V' – which consists in reality, as we have seen, of a brief pilgrimage account plus the treatise's first three-quarters. Like Neumann in 1866, he considered the two parts to be components of a single work and dated it to c. 1180 – without realizing that Röhricht, to whom he refers, distinguished between the two parts and dated to c. 1180 only the brief pilgrimage account. De Sandoli observed that the work of 'Innominatus V' differs from ordinary pilgrim descriptions and appears to have been written by a cleric well versed in Palestinian affairs, being the first to introduce descriptions of the three realms of nature into the reports about the country. De Sandoli then proceeded to conjecture that Haymarus Monachus imitated this

---

[18] G. Golubovich, *Biblioteca bio-bibliografica della Terra Santa e dell'Oriente francescano*, 9 vols (Quaracchi, 1906-27), 1.405-8; he refers (p. 405 n. 2) to Röhricht's entry (*Bibliotheca*, no. 97/pp. 40-1) for 'Innominatus IX'.

[19] A.-D. von den Brincken, *Die 'Nationes christianorum orientalium' im Verständnis der lateinischen Historiographie von der Mitte des 12. bis in die zweite Hälfte des 14. Jahrhunderts*, Kölner historische Schriften 22 (Cologne, 1973), pp. 4, 52, 84-5, 107-8, 185-6, 215, 293-4, 364-5, 426, 446 et passim; see also J. Richard, '"Manières des Crestiens": les Chrétiens orientaux dans les relations de pèlerinages aux Lieux-Saints (XIIᵉ-XVᵉ s.)', *Columbeis* 5 (1993), pp. 94-5.

work of 'Innominatus V' in 1199 when, in response to Innocent III's request, he composed two tracts, the one on the Saracen forces and the other on the state of the Holy Land. De Sandoli went on to print from Clm 4351 what he presented as the latter tract – without realizing that this fifteenth-century Munich manuscript had been used by Thomas back in 1865 in his edition of the treatise, and that the treatise was followed in that manuscript by a description that – as Thomas had noted – partly corresponds to Bede's *De locis sanctis*. Thus, De Sandoli's *De statu Terrae Sanctae*, which he presented as the work of Haymarus Monachus, contains, in addition to the treatise, about ten chapters of Bede's work, as well as some other texts.[20] The Latin text of Clm 4351 – transcribed inaccurately, with entire phrases missing – is translated into Italian. Elsewhere in the volume De Sandoli reprinted (and translated into Italian) the anonymous account which Golubovich had published in 1906 and which comprises the beginning of the treatise. De Sandoli presented the entire account as the work of 'Innominatus IX' of c. 1175, though Röhricht, on whom he appears to have relied, ascribed to 'Innominatus IX' only the brief description of the holy places that precedes the treatise's beginning.[21]

In 1984, Aryeh Grabois reprinted, and translated into Hebrew, Neumann's edition of the treatise's first three-quarters and, like Stewart in 1894, presented it as the work of 'Anonymous Pilgrim V.2'. In an article devoted to this fragmentary text he appraised it – as Neumann had done in 1866 – as the work of a pilgrim, probably a German cleric who may have come to the Levant in 1197-8 in the retinue of Archbishop Conrad of Mainz, and who was writing in the early years of the thirteenth century. Grabois asserted (not unlike, unbeknownst to him, De Sandoli a year earlier) that the treatise amounts to a new departure in the *itineraria* literature, breaking with the tradition of concentrating on the holy sites in the order the pilgrim visited them and striving instead to describe the country realistically and comprehensively.[22] When the existence of Thomas's edition was brought to his attention, Grabois asserted that the manuscripts Thomas had used postdate the Heiligenkreuz manuscript utilized by Neumann (thus ignoring that Clm 17060 antedates or is coeval with the Heiligenkreuz manuscript) and suggested that the final quarter of Thomas's

---

[20] S. De Sandoli, *Itinera Hierosolymitana crucesignatorum (saec. XII-XIII)*, 4 vols (Jerusalem, 1978-84), 3.29-42, 163-93. De Sandoli's chapters 8-13/pp. 178-90 largely correspond to chapters 1-7, 14-15 and 19 of Bede, 'De locis sanctis', ed. I. Fraipont, in *Itineraria et alia geographica, Corpus Christianorum, Series Latina* 175 (Turnhout, 1965), pp. 252-65, 275-6, 279.

[21] De Sandoli, *Itinera*, 3.91-9.

[22] A. Grabois, 'From "Holy Geography" to "Palestinography": Changes in the Descriptions of Thirteenth-Century Pilgrims', *Cathedra* 31 (1984), pp. 43-66 [in Hebrew].

text contains a medieval scribe's additions to the original text transmitted by the Heiligenkreuz manuscript.[23]

In 1986, Robert B.C. Huygens noted that two English manuscripts of the first half of the thirteenth century containing William of Tyre's chronicle include also the treatise in question.[24] An examination of the treatise as transmitted by these English manuscripts has revealed that in both of them it is followed by a survey of Saladin's forces, modelled on the list of Christian groups contained in the treatise.[25]

What may one conclude from this review of 130 years of discontinuous research? First, that unawareness on the part of various authors of their predecessors' work brought forth untenable assertions and the reprinting of a text that should have been recognized as a fragment. Second, that an easily refutable hypothesis about the nature of the treatise in question, enshrined in a renowned research aid, was often accepted uncritically. Third, the fact that each of the manuscripts studied, as well as Martène and Durand's printed version, presents the treatise alongside a different text repeatedly obscured the treatise's true extent. Indeed, there is no cogent reason to consider any of the texts that precede or follow the treatise in the manuscripts, or in Martène and Durand's volume, as an integral part of it. Fourth, that unawareness of previous work, the persistence of a dubious hypothesis, and the lack of certainty about the treatise's true extent have caused considerable vacillation about the treatise's date and character.

As for the date, it is reasonable to assume that the treatise was originally written during the last two decades of the existence of the kingdom of Jerusalem. The enumeration in the present tense of the Latin canons and monks of Jerusalem's churches points to the period before Saladin's conquest in 1187; the same is true of the list of barons. The *terminus a quo* is provided by the mention of the bishopric of Hebron and the archbishopric of Petra, both founded in 1168.[26] The mention of the bishop of Banyas as suffragan of the

---

[23] Grabois, 'From "Holy Geography"', p. 51 n. 29, where he also claims that the suggestion had already been put forward in Neumann's introduction.

[24] See his introduction to WT, pp. 19, 21, 22 n. 42. Huygens refers to Funk and to Röhricht's *Bibliotheca,* where only one of the English manuscripts in question is listed.

[25] See B.Z. Kedar, 'A Western Survey of Saladin's Forces at the Siege of Acre', in *Montjoie: Studies in Crusade History in Honour of Hans Eberhard Mayer,* ed. B.Z. Kedar, J. Riley-Smith and R. Hiestand (Aldershot, 1997), pp. 113-22.

[26] See H.E. Mayer, 'Der kirchliche Neugliederungsversuch von 1168', in his *Bistümer, Klöster und Stifte im Königreich Jerusalem, MGH Schriften* 26 (Stuttgart, 1977), pp. 197-221. Mayer, who repeatedly utilized the treatise and characterized it as 'undoubtedly well-informed'

archbishop of Tyre is inconclusive for dating; for, although Nur al-Din conquered Banyas in 1164, its bishop continued to bear his title. The statement, 'Armenii nuper Romane ecclesie promiserunt obedire, dum rex eorum a Maguntino archiepiscopo Romane sedis legato coronam suscepit', refers – as Neumann realized – to the coronation of Leo II in January 1198. Yet it does not follow, as Neumann and Grabois inferred, that the treatise must have been written after 1198. This statement on the Armenians, phrased as it is in the past tense, stands out starkly in a treatise that consistently uses the present tense in describing the country; it may therefore be deemed an addition.[27]

The author is a visitor from Europe, not a Frankish inhabitant of the kingdom of Jerusalem, for in his account of the country's fauna he mentions 'preter communia terrarum nostrarum animalia'. The fact that he starts the list of Latins inhabiting the country with the *Alemanni* may indicate a German origin; his detailed and enthusiastic description of the Knights Templar may imply that he spent some time with them; his painstaking survey of the Latin church suggests that he was a cleric. But these are mere guesses.

The treatise should be compared not to pilgrimage accounts but to geographical and ethnographical reports about distant countries. The report closest in time and space is the account about Egypt and Syria by Burchard of Strasbourg, the envoy whom Emperor Frederick I sent to Saladin in 1175.[28] For instance, Burchard's statement that 'in Corsica vero sunt homines utriusque sexus compositi, curiales, habiles, hospitales, viri militares et bellicosi'[29] finds a counterpart in the treatise in the characterization of the Latins as 'homines bellicosi, armis exerciti, nudi capite, et soli qui inter omnes gentes barbam radunt'; and his observation that the desert between Egypt and Damascus

---

(*Bistümer*, p. 21), dated it, without specifying his reasons, to the end of the twelfth century *Bistümer*, pp. 92, 113, 172, 222, 235, 259.

[27] The statement appears in all manuscripts consulted, with the exception of Berlin: Görres 111 (note 12 above). However, as this manuscript presents an abbreviated version of parts of the treatise, the absence of the statement cannot be deemed conclusive.

[28] On the envoy's identity see P. Scheffer-Boichorst, 'Der kaiserliche Notar und der Strassburger Vitztum Burchard, ihre wirklichen und angeblichen Schriften', *Zeitschrift für die Geschichte des Oberrheins* 43 (1889), pp. 456-77.

[29] Arnold of Lübeck, 'Chronica Slavorum', ed. J.M. Lappenberg, *MGH SS*, 21.236, lines 1-2, P. Lehmann and O. Glauning, 'Mittelalterliche Handschriftenbruchstücke der Universitäts bibliothek und des Georgianum zu München', *Zentralblatt für Bibliothekswesen*, Beiheft 72 (Munich, 1940), p. 63. Lehmann and Glauning present the version of the manuscript they publish as being close to the original text; but the sentence in question is mutilated there.

'nutrit leones sevissimos, struciones, porcos silvestres, onagros, et lepores'[30] recalls the statement in the treatise that the Holy Land has 'leones, pardi, ursi, cervi, dami,[31] capree silvestres, animal quoddam sevissimum quod appellant loncam'. True, Burchard uses the first person singular throughout and presents a travelogue, whereas the anonymous author of the treatise uses the first person just a few times and does not follow a geographical order. Yet it should be borne in mind that much of Burchard's information was incorporated almost verbatim in the largely geographical description of the Holy Land and Egypt, which was later erroneously regarded as a part of James of Vitry's third book, and which Riant, as we have seen, believed to constitute a part of Haymarus Monachus's 1199 report to Innocent III. In this rendering all of Burchard's first-person phrases have been expunged.[32] One may hypothesize, therefore, that the treatise, too, may be an impersonal rendering of what was originally a first-person account, and regard the few single first-person phrases it contains as lone vestiges.

The treatise was repeatedly utilized by later writers. The German pilgrim, Thietmar, who visited the Holy Land in 1217, used the sections on animals, trees, the Christian and non-Christian groups, and the survey of the Latin church.[33] James of Vitry, bishop of Acre in the years 1216-1228, repeatedly relied on the treatise in his *Historia Hierosolimitana*, usually adding to the information he found in it.[34] And Burchard of Mount Sion, the Dominican

---

[30] Lehmann and Glauning, 'Mittelalterliche Handschriftenbruchstücke', p. 67; Arnold of Lübeck, 'Chronica Slavorum', p. 239, lines 14-15, gives a slightly expanded text.

[31] Probably from *damma*, a general name for beasts of the deer kind. Thietmar, in a passage that evidently depends on the treatise, has 'Leones et leopardi, ursi, cerui, damme, apri siluestres et animal seuissimum, quod incole appellant lonzam': *Peregrinatio*, ed. J.C.M. Laurent (Hamburg, 1857), p. 22.

[32] Martène and Durand, *Thesaurus*, 3.271-5. Compare for instance Burchard's statement: 'Vidi eciam capellam, in qua idem ewangelista ewangelium scripsit et ubi martirium accepit, et locum sepulture sue, unde a Venethis furatus fuit' (Lehmann and Glauning, 'Mittelalterliche Handschriftenbruchstücke', p. 64) with its rendering in the geographical description: 'Est etiam ibi capella in qua evangelia sua scripsit, & martyrium suscepit, est etiam ibi locus sepulturae ejus, sed a Venetis corpus ejus furatum est' (Martène and Durand, *Thesaurus*, 3.275).

[33] Thietmar, *Peregrinatio*, pp. 22, 51-4. Consequently, a future edition of the treatise, to be based on all available manuscripts, should take into account these passages of Thietmar.

[34] See for instance the sections on the Templars, the Christian and non-Christian groups, the fountains, trees, and animals: James of Vitry, 'Historia Hierosolimitana', in *Gesta Dei per Francos*, ed. J. Bongars (Hanau, 1611), pp. 1084, 1095-6, 1098-9, 1109. The Milanese Cambio Bosso relates that he saw in the library of Mount Sion, in 1479, a book from which he copied a survey of the Latin church; the text appears to be identical with James of Vitry's. See

writing late in the thirteenth century, incorporated the treatise's beginning into the first redaction of his description of the Holy Land.[35]

'Historia Hierosolimitana', p. 1077 and Ioannes Philippus Novariensis, *Cronica canonici ordinis* (Cremona, 1535), pp. 29a-b; J. Le Paige, *Bibliotheca Praemonstratensis ordinis* (Paris, 1633), pp. 96-7.

[35] Burchard of Mount Sion, 'Descriptio Terrae Sanctae', in Canisius, *Lectiones antiquae* (note 1 above), pp. 21-2. On the relation between the two redactions, and the connection between the first of them and 'Innominatus V', see E. Rotermund, 'Das Jerusalem des Burchard vom Berge Sion', *Zeitschrift des Deutschen Palästina-Vereins* 35 (1912), pp. 1-6. It may be noted that Burchard's assertion that it is untrue that no rain falls on Mount Gilboa (see A. Grabois, 'Christian Pilgrims in the Thirteenth Century and the Latin Kingdom of Jerusalem: Burchard of Mount Sion', in *Outremer: Studies in the History of the Crusading Kingdom of Jerusalem*, ed. B.Z. Kedar, H.E. Mayer and R.C. Smail [Jerusalem, 1982], pp. 288-9) is prefigured in the treatise, where it is stated: 'In monte Gelboe fabulantur quidam quod non pluat per imprecationem David, sed falsum est.'

Appendix 1

The Treatise according to British Library: Royal 14.C.X

Robert Huygens's observation that the rendering of William of Tyre's chronicle in British Library: Royal 14.C.X and Cambridge, Magdalene College: F.4.22, amounts to a medieval critical edition,[36] applies also to their rendering of the treatise. This rendering is edited below. Limitations of space permit the indication of only the more significant divergences in the manuscripts utilized by Thomas and Neumann, and in a thirteenth-century Berlin manuscript that includes several sections of the treatise.

The sigla used are:

B London, British Library: Royal 14.C.X, fols 1ra-3rb, of the first half of the thirteenth century. Unedited.

W Cambridge, Magdalene College: F.4.22, fols 1ra-3va, of the first half of the thirteenth century. Unedited.

M Munich, Bayerische Staatsbibliothek: Clm 17060, fols 68^r-76^r, of the early thirteenth century. It is on this manuscript that Thomas based his 1865 edition.

H Heiligenkreuz, Stiftsbibliothek: No. 88, fols 156ra-156^v, the thirteenth-century manuscript used by Neumann in 1866. [Incomplete].

G Berlin, Preussische Staatsbibliothek: Görres 111, fols 105^r-106^v (thirteenth century). Unedited. [Fragments].

N Munich, Bayerische Staatsbibliothek: Clm 4351, fols 203rb-204va, the fifteenth-century manuscript utilized by Thomas and printed by De Sandoli in 1983.

O Munich, Bayerische Staatsbibliothek: Clm 5307, fols 120^r-130^v, the other fifteenth-century manuscript utilized by Thomas.

De situ terre jerosolimitane et habitatoribus eius[a]

Terra jerosolimitana in centro mundi[b] posita est, ex maiori parte montuosa, ubere gleba fertilis. Cui ab oriente adiacet Arabia, a meridie Egyptus, ab oc-

---

[a] Tractatus de locis et statu sancte terre ierosolimitane M; Tractatus de locis et statu terre iherosolimitane N; De terra jerosolimitana O   [b] mundi *om.* W

---

[36] See his introduction to WT, pp. 22-31.

cidente Mare Magnum, a septentrione Syria[c]. Hec ab antiquis temporibus communis fuit patria nationum, quia[d] ad loca sancta colenda illuc[e] de quibuslibet partibus convenerunt, sicut in actibus apostolorum legitur in missione sancti spiritus: *Parthi et Medi et Elamite*[37] et cetera. Nunc autem iste sunt gentes[f] que in ea versantur et habent in ea domicilia et oratoria. Quorum alii sunt Christiani, alii non Christiani. Christianorum vero varie sunt gentes que[g] in varias sectas divise.

De Francis. Quorum primi sunt Franci, qui Latini verius appellantur, homines bellicosi, armis exerciti[h], nudi capite, et soli qui inter omnes gentes barbam radunt. Et dicuntur Latini omnes qui latina littera utuntur et obediunt Romane ecclesie. Isti pure catholici sunt.

De Grecis. Alii sunt Greci, ab ecclesia Romana divisi, homines astuti, armis parum exercitati[i], pilleos oblongos portantes, errantes in fidei et iuris articulis, precipue in eo quod dicunt spiritum sanctum non a patre et filio sed a patre solo procedere, et solum fermentatum sacrificant, et in multis aliis errant. Propriam habent litteram.

De Surianis. Alii sunt Suriani, armis inutiles, ex maiore parte barbam non sicut Greci nutrientes, sed ipsam aliquantulum castigantes. Inter Latinorum et Grecorum cultum medii, ubique tributarii[j], Grecis in fide et sacramentis[k] concordantes. Litteram habent saracenicam in temporalibus, in spiritualibus grecam.

De Armeniis. Alii sunt Armenii, armis aliquatenus exerciti[l], a Latinis et Grecis in multis discordantes, ieiunantes tempore nativitatis Christi suam quadragesimam et in die apparitionis nativitatem Christi celebrantes, et multa alia circa[m] ecclesiastica[n] instituta facientes. Hii propriam habent litteram. Inter Armenios et Grecos odium imp<l>acabile est. Armenii nuper[o] Romane ecclesie promiserunt obedire, dum rex eorum a Maguntino archiepiscopo Romane sedis legato coronam suscepit.

De Georgianis. Alii sunt Georgiani, sanctum Georgium solenni pompa colentes, armis plurimum exerciti[p], barbam et comam in immensum nutrientes, gestantes unius cubiti pilleos. Isti tam laici quam clerici coronas habent ad

---

[c] et Mare Cipricum *add.* MHNO   [d] qui W; que MHNO   [e] ad huc W   [f] gentes *om.* W
[g] et WMHO   [h] exercitati WMH   [i] exerciti W; B = MHNO   [j] in terra Latinorum et Grecorum ubique tributarii M; Nec Latinorum et Grecorum cultum tenent, ubique tributarii H; Suriani sunt populi inter Latinorum et Grecorum cultum medii G   [k] per omnia *add.* MHNO; G = BW   [l] exercitati MHNO   [m] contra MHGNO   [n] iura et *add.* MNO   [o] aliquando O
[p] exercitati MNO

---

[37] Acts 2:9.

instar clericorum, clerici rotundas, laici vero quadratas. Fermentatum sacrificant et fere in omnibus Grecos imitantur. Propriam habent litteram.

De Jacobitis. Alii sunt Jacobiti^q sive Jacobite, a quodam Jacobo in Nestorianam heresim depravati, pessime credentes. Caldeam habentes litteram.

De Nestorianis. Alii sunt Nestoriani, in fide heretici, dicentes beatam Mariam tantum hominis matrem fuisse et in multis aliis errantes. Litteram habent Caldeam.

De Latinis. Latini etiam in gentes varias dividuntur: Alemannos, Hispanos, Gallos, Italicos et ceteras gentes quas parit Europa. De Italia sunt in terra jerosolimitana tres populi, ipsi terre plurimum efficaces et utiles, Pisani, Januenses et Veneti, navali exercitio predocti, in aquis invicti, in omni bello exerciti^r, mercimoniorum ingenio sagaces, a cunctis tributis et reditibus liberi, excepti ab^s omnium iudicum iurisdictione, sibimetipsis iura dicentes^t, inter se tamen invidi atque discordes, quod maiorem securitatem exhibet Saracenis.

De Templo et Hospitali. Sunt etiam in eadem jerosolimitana regione due domus religiose^u, Templum et Hospitale^v, divitiis pluribus abundantes, de tota Europa redditus colligentes, in ipsa terra promissionis largissimos redditus et possessiones habentes. Hii dominice cruci procedenti^w ad bellum hinc inde assistunt, Templarii a dextris, Hospitalarii a sinistris. Qui videlicet Templarii peroptimi^x milites sunt, albas clamides et rubeam crucem ferentes. Vexillum bicolor quod balcanum^y dicitur ipsos ad bella procedit. Ordinate et absque clamore ad bella vadunt, primi congressus et acriores ipsos expectant, in eundo sunt primi, in redeundo postremi, et magistri sui iussionem attendunt. Cum autem bellare utile iudicaverint, et iussu precipientis buccine clangor insonuerit, daviticum canitur canticum et devote^z: *Non nobis, Domine, non nobis sed nomini tuo da gloriam*^a,[38] flectentes lanceas in hostes irruunt^b. Cuneos et cornua belli unanimiter et dure requirentes, nunquam ausi cedere, aut penitus frangunt hostes aut moriuntur. In redeundo ipsi postremi sunt et ceteram turbam premittunt, omnium curam et tutelam gerentes. Si quis autem aliquo casu terga dederit aut minus fortiter egerit, vel contra Christianos arma portaverit, dure discipline subicitur. Clamis alba que est signum milicie cum

^q Jacobini MHGNO   ^r exercitati MHNO   ^s exempti ad W   ^t dictantes MHNO
^u religionis W   ^v Domus Teutonicorum *add.* O   ^w precedenti M; procedent N; procedentes O; hii cum ad bellum procedunt H   ^x boni MNO   ^y balzano MN; balzaus H; balza O
^z daviticum illud communiter concinunt MHNO   ^a Non nobis — da gloriam *om.* W   ^b in hostium irruunt cuneos M; flectentes genua in hostium cruorem et cervicem, nisi cuneos H; O = BW

---

[38] Ps. 113:9.

cruce sibi ignominiose aufertur, a comunione abicitur, in terra sine manutergio comedit per annum, canes si eum molestaverint non ausus increpare. Post annum vero si magister et fratres eius satisfactionem[c] condignam iudicaverint, pristine milicie cum omni gloria[d] redditur[e]. Isti vero Templarii in dure religionis observantiam diriguntur, humiliter obedientes, carentes proprio, parce[f] comedentes et induentes, omni tempore extra in tentoriis commorantes.

Hospitalarii vero albam crucem portant in clamide, milites boni, cum ipsa militia[g] pauperum et infirmorum curam gerentes, suam observantiam et disciplinam habentes[h].

De patriarcha et episcopis. Preterea ipsa terra jerosolimitana patriarcham habet, qui est pater fidei et Christianorum et vicarius Jhesu Christi. Qui videlicet patriarcha quatuor habet archiepiscopos, unum in provincia Palestina scilicet Cesariensem, alium in provincia Phenicea scilicet Tyrensem[i], tercium in provincia Galilee scilicet Nazarensem, quartum in provincia Moabitarum scilicet Petracensem, i. de Munt Real. Cesariensis archiepiscopus habet unum suffraganeum, scilicet episcopum Sebastenum, ubi sepultus fuit Johannes Baptista, Helyseus et Abdias prophete. Tyrensis archiepiscopus habet quatuor suffraganeos, Acconensem, Sydoniensem, Beritensem et illum de Bellinas, que est Cesarea Philippi. Nazarenus archiepiscopus habet unum suffraganeum, scilicet Tyberiadensem. Petracensis nullum habet suffraganeum latinum. Habet unum grecum in Monte Synai. Habet etiam dominus patriarcha istos episcopos nullo mediante: Bethleemitanum, Liddensem et illum de Ebron, ubi sepulti fuerunt Adam et Eva et tres patriarche Abraham, Ysaac et Jacob.

De domibus religiosis. In ecclesia dominici sepulcri sunt canonici sancti Augustini. Priorem habent[j] sed soli patriarche obedientiam promittunt[k]. In Templo Domini sunt abbas et canonici regulares. Et sciendum est quod aliud est Templum Domini, aliud Templum Milicie: isti clerici sunt, illi milites. In montis Syon ecclesia sunt abbas et canonici regulares. In ecclesia montis Oliveti sunt abbas et canonici regulares.[l] In ecclesia Vallis Josaphat sunt abbas et monachi nigri. In ecclesia de Latina[m] sunt abbas et monachi nigri. Isti omnes mitrati sunt[n] et[o] cum predictis episcopis[p] patriarche assistunt in ministerio.

---

[c] penitentiam MHNO   [d] milicie cingulo MHNO   [e] reddunt H   [f] MNO pariter; H = BW [g] milites boni, cum ipsa militia *om.* MNO; H = BW   [h] De Alamannis — necessitatibus succurrunt *add.* O [see Appendix 2 below]   [i] et *add.* W; Tirus dicitur Suri *add.* M   [j] cum infula et anulo pontificali *add.* MN; cum infula et bacculo et subtalarabus [*sic*] pontificalibus O; H = BW   [k] Cum vero patriarcha defunctus est, eligendus est quicunque predictis canonicis placuerit et sine ipsorum electione nemo fiet *add.* M   [l] In ecclesia montis Thabor abbas est et monaci nigri *add.* MNO; H = BW   [m] ecclesia latina WN; ecclesia de sancta Maria latina M; O = B   [n] omnes habent infulas MNO; omnes qui numerati sunt H   [o] et *om.* MHNO   [p] sicut predicti episcopi M

De civitatibus episcopos non habentibus. Preterea iste sunt civitates que non habent episcopos: Ascalona, que est sub Bethleem; Joppe, que est sub canonicis dominici sepulcri; Neapolis, que est sub abbate Templi; Cayphas que est sub Cesariense archiepiscopo.

Et licet ipsa terra ierosolimitana per totum sancta sit et solennis, utpote in qua prophete et apostoli et ipse Dominus conversatus est, tamen in ea quedam sunt loca, que inter alia speciali prerogativa homines venerantur. Quorum merita et nomina breviter prosequemur.

De locis diversis. Nazareth in qua nata est beata virgo et mater Christi. In qua etiam angelico premisso legato descendit in uterum virginalem altissimi filius. In qua nutritus etatis humane incrementa suscepit. Bethleem in qua celestis panis natus est, in qua etiam indice stella Christo magi munera optulerunt. In qua etiam latinus interpres Jeronimus requiescit. Jordanis in quo salvator noster baptizatus humane salutis formam instituit et spiritus sanctus in columbe specie visus est et vox patris audita. Locus ieiunii qui dicitur Quarentena, in quo Christus xl. dies ieiunavit et observantiam quadragesimalem instituit. In quo etiam temptatus est a diabolo. Stagnum Genesareth circa quod multum conversatus est et miracula operatus est et discipulos evocavit. Mons Thabor in quo transfiguratus est coram tribus discipulis apparentibus Moyse et Helya. In Ierusalem sunt multa loca venerabilia, sicut Templum Domini in quo presentatus fuit et unde eiecit vendentes et ementes, et unde Jacobus frater domini precipitatus fuit. Mons Syon in quo cenam cum discipulis celebravit et novum instituit testamentum. In quo spiritus sanctus super apostolos visibiliter apparuit, ubi eciam virgo mater domini migravit. Calvaria ubi pro salute nostra crucem suscepit et mortem. Sepulcrum in quo positum fuit corpus eius et unde resurrexit. Mons Oliveti ubi a pueris honorifice susceptus est sedens super asinam. Unde et mirabiliter ascendit in celum. Bethania ubi Lazarum suscitavit. Syloe ubi ceco nato lumen dedit. Vallis Josaphath que dicitur Jessemani, ubi captus fuit a Iudeis et ubi virgo Maria sepulta fuit. Sebaste in quo Johannes Baptista, Helyseus et Abdias prophete sepulti fuerunt. Ebron in quo Adam et Eva et tres patriarche sepulti fuerunt. Ecclesia sancti Stephani in qua ipse fuit lapidatus. Et ut scriptura veteris et novi testamenti solerter revolvatur[q], nullus mons, nulla vallis, nulla campestria, nullus fluvius, nullus fons, nullum stagnum a visitatione prophetarum et apostolorum et ipsius Christi vacant miraculis. Fons Jacob[r] in partibus Samarie quater in anno colorem mutat, pulverulentum, sanguineum, viridem et limpidum. Fons Syloe iuxta montem Syon non singulis sed tribus diebus in ebdomada currit. Lacus Asfaltidis est in

---

[q] resolvatur M   [r] Jacob *om.* MNO; GH = BW

terra jerosolimitana in confinio Arabie et Palestine, ubi fuerunt olim quinque civitates que propter peccatum civium suorum submerse sunt. In quo lacu nil quod habeat animam mergi potest. Quod cum Vespasianus audisset, septem homines ignaros natandi ligatis manibus et pedibus intus proici fecit, et per triduum intus steterunt et non fuerunt mortui. Circa hunc lacum arbores sunt pulcherrime[s] poma ferentes, que cum carpseris fetent et subito in cinerem dissolvuntur.[39]

De montibus. Montes precipui sunt in terra jerosolimitana Lybanus, mons Thabor, Hermon, Gelboe, Carmelus. Lybanus autem altissimus omnium est et spectat[t] Syriam a Phenicea et habet cedros longissimas, sed non ita abundanter sicut antiquitus. In monte Gelboe fabulantur quidam quod non pluat per imprecationem David, sed falsum est.

De animalibus. Animalia autem plura sunt in eadem terra, sed preter communia terrarum nostrarum animalia sunt ibi leones, pardi, ursi, cervi, dami[u], capree silvestres, animal quoddam sevissimum quod appellant loncam[v], a cuius sevicia nullum animal potest esse tutum et ut dicunt leonem terret. Preterea sunt ibi papiones, quos appellant canes silvestres, acriores quam lupi. Sunt ibi cameli et bubali abundanter.

De arboribus. Arbores plurime[w] ibi sunt et[x] omnium fere generum que nascuntur in terra. Sed preter communes arbores quas habet Europa, sunt ibi palme, fructibus quos dicunt dactilos referte. Sunt ibi arbores quas appellant arbores paradisi, habentes folia longa unius cubiti, lata medii cubiti, facientes poma oblonga et in uno ramusculo centum tangentia sese et melleum saporem habentia. Sunt etiam ibi limones arbores, quarum fructus acidus est. Sunt etiam ibi arbores que poma gignunt, que vocant poma adam, in quibus pomis morsus Ade evidentissime apparet. Sunt etiam ibi canne ex quibus succus dulcissimus fluit et vocantur canimelle unde fit zucarum. Sunt etiam ibi arbusta que seminantur sicut triticum, unde colligitur bombicinum. Olim etiam balsamus arbor in toto mundo non erat preterquam in terra jerosolimitana in loco qui dicitur Jericho. Postea supervenientes Egyptii ipsam arbustam transportaverunt in Egyptum et plantaverunt in civitate eorum Babilone et ibi solummodo sunt[y]. In quibus arboribus illud mirabile est hodie etiam, quod si ab aliis quam Chris-

---

[s] pulcherrima GHNO; M = BW   [t] separat MGH   [u] dayni M; damicii G; dani O   [v] lonzam MN and Thietmar; lonham G; unca H; lonzum O   [w] pulcherrime MN   [x] et *om.* W   [y] et plantaverunt. Est etiam ibi ficus pharaonis que non inter folia sicut cetere arbores sed in ipso trunco ficus facit. In civitate vero Babilone solum modo sunt plantationes M

---

[39] Vespasianus — dissolvuntur: see Bede, 'De locis sanctis', p. 272.

tianis[z] excolantur, nullum fructum ferunt sed sterilitate dampnantur perpetua. Sunt ibi arbores cedri que fructum faciunt grossum sicut caput hominis et aliquantulum oblongum et habet fructus ille tres sapores, unum in cortice[a], alium infra corticem[b], tercium in intima[c] medulla[d]. Et est sciendum quod cedrus arbor longissima est et sterilis. Cedrus maritima parva est et fructuosa. Est etiam ibi ficus pharaonis, que non inter folia sicut cetere arbores sed in ipso trunco fructum facit.

De mutatione nominum urbium. Nomina civitatum et locorum propter mutationem gentium que terram ipsam diversis temporibus coluerunt paulatim mutata sunt. Verumtamen quarumdam civitatum antiqua nomina et moderna referam. Jerusalem primo dicta est Jebus, postea Salem, postea ex Jebus et Salem, Jerusalem. Postea Jerosolima. Postea Elya ab Elyo questore romano, qui eam post destructionem a Tito factam reedificavit in loco quo nunc est. Ebron primo Arbe, postea Cariathiarim, postea Ebron, postea sanctus Abraham quia ibi sepultus fuit. Ascalona primo Philistiim urbs primo Philisteorum. Gaza semper vocata sic fuit. Que modo sanctus Georgius dicitur, Lidda fuit. Joppe semper sic vocata fuit. Cesarea primo Dor, postea Turris Stratontis[e], postea Cesarea ad honorem Cesaris est vocata. Cayphas primo Porphiria. Acon primo, postea Tholomais[f]. Tyrus semper sic vocata fuit, urbs nobilis quondam in qua regnavit Agenor, unde fuit Dido. Sydon modo Sagitta dicitur. Sarepta modo dicitur Sarphent. Bethleem primo Effrata vocata fuit. Que nunc Neapolis, primo Sychar dicta fuit. Que nunc Sebaste, primo Samaria dicta est. Que nunc Maomeria, primo Luza, postea Bethel vocata est. Que nunc Belinas, primo Paneas, postea Cesarea Philippi vocata est.

De rege Jerosolimorum. Preterea eadem Jerosolimitana provincia latinum regem habet, qui a suo patriarcha sceptrum accipit et coronam, cui omnes que in eadem terra sunt obediunt nationes. Hic[g] sanctissimo sepulcro iurat defensionem et iudicium et iusticiam inter gentes, consuetudines patrie et mores patrios conservare. Cui barones terre tocius subsunt et ad nutum ipsius ad bellum procedunt, parati semper cum numero militum singulis assignato terram defendere et pro hereditate Christi dimicare.

De magnatibus terre jerosolimitane. Precipui[h] autem barones terre isti sunt: Dominus Berithi[i], Dominus Sydonis, Dominus Cayphe, Dominus Cesaree, Do-

---

[z] a christianis WMGHNO   [a] qui est calidus *add.* MNO; qui est amarus *add.* H; G = BW [b] alium in medietate qui est humidus MNO; alium infra corticem s. in pulpa qui est insipidus H; G = BW   [c] ultima W; intima *om.* G   [d] qui est frigidus *add.* MNO; alium qui est acidus in medulla H; G = BW   [e] Stratonis WMHN   [f] Acaron primo vocata fuit, deinde Ptolomaida, nunc iterum Acaron M   [g] rex *add.* MN   [h] maiores MNO   [i] i. Baruth *add.* M

minus Tyberiadis qui est princeps Galilee. Comes Joppes[j] et Ascalonis. Dominus de Munt Real et totius terre ultra Jordanem. Dominus de Hebelino[k]. Dominus Assur. Dominus de Bethan[l]. Jerusalem vero et Tyrus et Acon et Neapolis ad regem spectant nullo mediante domino. Princeps autem Antiochenus et comes Tripolitanus licet extra confinium regni Jerosolimitani sint, tamen homines regis sunt et ei iurata fidelitate tenentur. Omnes isti certum[m] habent numerum militum, quos semper oportet esse paratos armis et equis, ut cotidie Saracenis insultantibus resistant.

De hiis qui Christiani non sunt. Et quia superius dictum est de sectis et diversitate Christianorum qui in terra jerosolimitana morantur, nunc de illis videndum est qui Christiani non sunt et ibidem sua habent domicilia.

De Judeis. Quorum primi sunt Judei, homines obstinati, plusquam mulieres imbelles, ubique servi, singulis lunationibus fluxum sanguinis patientes. Vetus testamentum ad litteram servant et litteram habent hebream. De istis sunt Saducei qui resurrectionem non credunt.

De Samaritanis. Alii sunt Samaritani, similiter imbelles sicut Judei. Lintheo circinatum caput habentes. Judeis similes in cultu, sed in mente valde dissimiles. Nam crudeles sunt inimici adinvicem. Solummodo quinque libros Moysi servant. Litterarum hebrearum partem habent sed non omnes. Ydiomate saracenico utuntur. Isti ita infelices sunt in generis sui propagatione, quod in toto mundo ex illis non sunt mille, immo[n] vix trecenti inveniuntur.

De Assessinis. Alii sunt Esseie quos vulgo Assessinos dicimus. Isti de Judeis tracti sunt, sed Judeorum ritus in omnibus[o] non observant. Homines religiosi in supersticione sua, sicut Templarii in lege sua[p]. Prelatum pro deo colunt, eique usque ad mortem obediunt. Cum eorum princeps, qui semper senex vocatur quasi sapiens[q], voluerit aliquem principem interficere, in medio cultellorum suorum[r] nominat quem voluerit occidere[s]. Tunc sui certantes ad cultellos currunt et qui potuerit habere grates refert principi et statim ad occidendum qui fuerit nominatus digreditur. Quicumque in obedientia mortuus fuerit, pro angelo colitur. Vita eorum communis est, proprium non habent. Pauciores quam triginta ferre non possunt sententiam. Magistrum habent in profundo orientis, qui est caput ordinis et religionis[t] eorum, illi subsunt et obediunt. Hunc

---

[j] Joppen MNO   [k] Ybelino i. Debelinas M; Ybelino idem Belinas N; dominus de Belina O
[l] Bethania MNO   [m] centum MN; O = BW   [n] ex illis non sunt mille immo *om.* MNO
[o] in omnibus *om.* MGNO   [p] Dei G; sicut Templarii in lege sua *om.* MNO   [q] quasi
sapiens *om.* MG; NO = BW   [r] suorum *om.* W   [s] nominato quem voluerit occidi in medio
suorum cultellos longos proicit et acutos MN; nominato quem voluerit in medio suorum
cultellos proicit acutos O; in medio suorum cultellos nominato quem voluerit occidi proicit G
[t] supersticionis MN; et religionis eorum *om.* G

Saraceni appellant dominum[u] cultellorum[v]. In solos magnates conspiracionem faciunt et hoc non sine culpa vel causa. Plebeios occidere apud ipsos summe ignominie est. Litteram habent ex chaldeo et hebreo permixtam.[w]

De Bedewinis. Alii sunt Bedewini, homines agrestes, quos vulgus silvestres Turcos appellat. Semper in campestribus habitantes, nullam habentes patriam neque domum. Pecudibus[x] et cunctis animalibus abundant, que nunc in terra Christianorum nunc Saracenorum accepta licencia pascuntur. Isti plurimi sunt et per provincias turmatim divisi, carnibus et lacte vescuntur, ovinis pellibus et caprinis vestiuntur, semper sub nudo aere cubant, nisi nimia pluvia ingruente. Tentoria habent de pellibus animalium. Amici fortune sunt. Nam quos viderint viribus prevalere adiuvant, proditores maximi, latrones insignes. Pilleos rubeos portant et peplum circa pilleos circinatum. Quando nos prevalemus adversus Saracenos, tunc fratres et amici nostri sunt. Si vero Saraceni prevaluerint, tunc ipsos adiuvant, furantes Christianos vendunt Saracenis, et similiter Saracenos Christianis. Fides eorum nulla est nisi quam timor fecerit. Maometh de ipsis dicitur fuisse.[y] Litteram habent saracenicam sed valde corruptam.

---

[u] Deum MN   [v] cultellorum *om.* O   [w] Nuper enim — anima privantur *add.* O [see Appendix 2 below]   [x] domos, pecoribus MN   [y] qui sua prava doctrina omnes inficit. Dixit enim sine peccato esse filium cum matre commixtionem habere et cognatum cum cognata et fratrem cum sorore. Unde talis consuetudo aput Sarracenos habetur. Tandem [...] divina clemencia a porcis dilaceratus est. Unde gentiles talibus carnibus porcinis non utuntur *add.* O

Appendix 2

Two Additions from Bayerische Staatsbibliothek: Clm 5307.

Clm 5307 contains a number of interpolations. Two of them – the one dealing with the Teutonic Knights, the other with the Assassins – are printed below.

A) *De Alamannis*. Habent eciam in Accon domum milites Alamanni, viri discreti, in milicia docti, in bello imperterriti, epistulam Pauli per omnia servant. Qui cum essent discordes cum Hospitalariis bona sua eis aufferre volentibus, accesserunt ad Templarios, rogantes ipsos ut eis astarent <si> potestati eorum subditi essent. Qui cum fuissent Templariis subiecti, venerunt Templarii et circulum qui erat circa nigram crucem, quam adhuc portant, deposuerunt; quod erat inter omnia signa maxime honorificum. Isti autem curam gerunt infirmorum et in omnibus eis necessitatibus succurrunt. (fols 122^{r-v}).

This passage appears to refer to an early, little-known stage in the history of the Teutonic Order. The continuations of William of Tyre relate that at the time of Duke Frederick of Swabia's death at Acre (20 January 1191), the Hospitallers insisted that all local hospitals must submit to their authority, and forbade the burial of high-ranking individuals at the House of the Germans; if such were buried there despite their prohibition, the Hospitallers would forcibly transfer the bodies to their own cemetery.[40] The interpolation suggests that at this juncture, with the Hospitallers trying to confine the activities of the new hospital and attempting to deprive it of deathbed bestowals, the Germans sought the protection of the Templars; in return they had to acquiesce in the Templar demand to change their emblem.[41] This temporary German submission to the Temple ties in with the assertion of the *Narracio de primordiis ordinis Theutonici* that the assembly that established the Teutonic Order – probably early in 1198 – took place *in domo Templi* at Acre.[42]

B) Nuper enim aput civitatem Turtus in monasterio beate virginis filium principis Anthiochie predictus senex occidere fecit. Unde Templarii et ipse

---

[40] *La continuation de Guillaume de Tyr (1184-1197)*, ed. M.R. Morgan (Paris, 1972), p. 99.

[41] Cf. M.-L. Favreau-Lilie, 'Alle origini dell'Ordine Teutonico: Continuità o nuova fondazione dell'ospedale gerosolimitano degli Alemanni?', in *Militia sacra: Gli ordini militari tra Europa e Terrasanta*, ed. E. Coli, M. De Marco and F. Tommasi (Perugia, 1994), p. 32.

[42] See 'De primordiis ordinis Theutonici narratio' in *Scriptores rerum Prussicarum*, vol. 6 (Frankfurt am Main, 1968), p. 26, and the discussion by M.-L. Favreau, *Studien zur Frühgeschichte des Deutschen Ordens, Kieler Historische Studien* 21 (Stuttgart, 1974), pp. 64-72.

princeps et pater iuvenis occisi et rex Armenie commoti, expeditionem indixerunt et terram suam penitus destruxerunt, exceptis quatuor castris omnia hostili vastitate destruxerunt. Dicitur eciam de ipso sene quod pueros ablactatos in domo subterranea includi faciat et ipsos usque ad iuventutem pane et aqua et leguminibus nutrire faciat. Postquam autem ad discrecionem pervenerunt, ipsi ad ortum suum, qui omni amenitate plenus est, et deducuntur, et in ipso per aliquot tempus tam delicatis cibariis quam commixtione pulchrimarum virginum deliciantur. Diversa enim fercula in ipso orto et diversi fructus reperiuntur et pulchriores virgines, que in tota provincia illa inveniuntur, ipso includuntur, que libidini illorum iuvenum subiecte erunt. Senex vero ad ipsos iuvenes talem exhortacionem facit, dicens quod domus subterranea sit infernus et qui suis noluerit obtemperare preceptis, tali pena eternaliter sit subiciendus; qui vero ipsius voluntatem fecerit, in tali paradiso eternaliter sit permansurus. Et sic plurimi decipiuntur et sic tam vita quam anima privantur. (fols 129^r-130^r).

The youth whom the Assassins killed at Tortosa was Raymond, the eighteen-year-old son of Bohemond IV; the murder took place at the end of 1213. The reprisal of Bohemond and the Templars was not as successful as the passage would have it. The Franks besieged the Isma'ili fortress of al-Khawabi, but were forced to retreat.[43]

The tale about the Old Man who deceives his Assassin followers by acquainting them with life in a bogus hell and paradise recalls Marco Polo's story about the terrestrial paradise by which the Old Man lures his adherents into absolute obedience.[44]

---

[43] See C. Cahen, *La Syrie du Nord à l'époque des croisades et la principauté franque d'Antioche* (Paris, 1940), pp. 620-1; B. Lewis, *The Assassins: A Radical Sect in Islam* (London, 1967), p. 119.

In a seminar paper written several years ago, my student Sharon Roubach tentatively transcribed this interpolation and identified the incident in question.

[44] See *Le Livre de Marco Polo, rédigé en français par Rusticien de Pise*, ed. G. Panthier (Paris, 1865; repr. Geneva, 1978), pp. 97-101.

The Hospitallers' Early Written Records[1]

Anthony Luttrell

Modern historians of the military-religious Order of Saint John have been able to use a variety of written records dating back virtually to the crusaders' conquest of Jerusalem in July 1099. The Hospital may well have lost some documents when Jerusalem fell in 1187 and others disappeared in 1291 at the fall of Acre; furthermore, whatever records were kept on Cyprus from 1291 to 1310 were somehow lost thereafter, and much of what was in the chancery on Rhodes, where the Hospital's Convent or headquarters moved from Cyprus in about 1310, was destroyed or abandoned in the course of the next two centuries or during the final siege of 1522. A significant portion of the Rhodian archive was, however, taken in 1530 to Malta where it still remains.

After 1099, the Hospital accumulated a collection of privileges and charters, together with its Rule and its own legislation in the form of its statutes, its customs or *usances* and its *esgarts* or judgements, its various liturgical texts, the *Miracula* or Legends concerning the Hospital's origins and much other material.[2] Many documents from the Syrian period were saved by being sent

---

[1] This paper employs various largely unexplored texts to question in interim fashion the accepted impression that the Hospital's legislative corpus survives in a single reliably established version. I am most grateful to Anne-Marie Legras who has collected many manuscripts of the Hospital's statutes on microfilm at the Institut de Recherche et d'Histoire des Textes at Orleans; for the numerous comments of Katja Klement who generously communicated her unpublished doctoral thesis; for important observations from Rudolf Hiestand; for the extensive contributions from Munich sent by Karl Borchardt; and for many points and materials kindly provided by Alain Beltjens.

[2] Many texts are published in *Cartulaire général de l'ordre des Hospitaliers de S. Jean de Jérusalem, 1100-1310*, ed. J. Delaville le Roulx, 4 vols (Paris, 1894-1906) [hereafter *Cartulaire*]; for the archives in general and especially for the papal documents to 1198, see R.

135

to safety, probably in the West, before 1291. An inventory of what remained of these materials from Acre was made at Manosque in Provence in 1531 but documents from this collection were not generally available to the Hospital's historians before the seventeenth century when part of what survived was transferred to Malta; some documents remained in Provence and much was lost or dispersed, but something of the missing materials is known from the summaries in the inventory. A different group of texts was preserved through translations and copies made between about 1278 and 1303 for the Hospitaller Fr. Guglielmo of Santo Stefano. Other early documents from the East were kept in the provincial archives of the Hospital's many Western priories and commanderies, while miscellaneous texts found their way into other archives and libraries.[3] Further collections, such as the records of the Hospital's German house in Jerusalem or of its Syrian centres outside Acre, were lost, as indeed were many registers and other chancery materials kept on Cyprus and on Rhodes between 1291 and 1522.

The Hospital of Saint John originated in a pilgrim hospice founded in Jerusalem probably in about 1070 as a dependency of the Benedictine Amalfitan monks of Sancta Maria Latina.[4] This hospice apparently had no endowments but relied on support from the merchants and Benedictines of Amalfi,[5] so that before 1099 it probably had little or no need for any archive of its own. With a few minor exceptions,[6] the records of Sancta Maria Latina were lost. There

---

Hiestand, ed., *Papsturkunden für Templer und Johanniter, Vorarbeiten zum Oriens Pontificius* 1-2, 2 vols (Göttingen, 1972-84) [hereafter Hiestand, *Templer und Johanniter*].

[3] The Western archives are not discussed here, but many documents are published in *Cartulaire*, which also provides an overall survey of the Hospital's provincial archives (*Cartulaire*, 1.xxvii-ccxxx); Hiestand, *Templer und Johanniter*, adds important details. For provincial chancery practice: S. García Larragueta, 'La Escribanía señorial navarra de San Juan', in *Landesherrliche Kanzleien im Spätmittelalter* (Munich, 1984), and Daniel le Blévec and Alain Venturini, *Cartulaire du Prieuré de Saint-Gilles de l'Hôpital de Saint-Jean de Jérusalem: 1192-1210* (Paris, 1997), pp. xiii-xvii.

[4] J. Riley-Smith, *The Knights of St. John in Jerusalem and Cyprus, c. 1050-1310* (London, 1967), pp. 32-7; R. Hiestand, 'Die Anfänge der Johanniter', in *Die geistlichen Ritterorden Europas*, ed. J. Fleckenstein and M. Hellmann (Sigmaringen, 1980), pp. 32-8; M. Matzke, '*De origine Hospitalariorum Hierosolymitanorum* – Vom klösterlichen Pilgerhospital zur internationalen Organisation', *Journal of Medieval History* 22 (1996); A. Luttrell, 'The Earliest Hospitallers', in *Montjoie: Studies in Crusade History in Honour of Hans Eberhard Mayer*, ed. B. Kedar, J. Riley-Smith and R. Hiestand (Aldershot, 1997), pp. 37-41.

[5] WT, pp. 123, 816-17.

[6] R. Hiestand, ed., *Papsturkunden für Kirchen im Heiligen Lande, Vorarbeiten zum Oriens Pontificius* 3 (Göttingen, 1985), pp. 32-5 [hereafter Hiestand, *Kirchen im Heiligen Lande*].

may have been documents dating before 1099 in the Hospital's later archives, but these would probably have concerned gifts made to the Holy Sepulchre or other bodies some of whose properties or claims subsequently passed, together with their documentation, to the Hospital.[7] Following the conquest, the hospice was detached from Sancta Maria Latina and acquired a measure of autonomy under its *institutor*, Gerard, and from 1099 or 1100 onwards it was receiving privileges and donations in its own name.[8] The Hospitallers must also have had various administrative and other papers, presumably kept in their own house or church. Some early documents remained in the Order's possession; for example, no less than four early versions of the royal confirmation of 1110 are in the Hospital's pre-1798 central archives still in Malta, as are the acts given in 1112 by the patriarch of Jerusalem and the archbishop of Caesarea and the original of the first papal privilege of 1113.[9]

That privilege recognized the Hospital as a partially independent institution and subsequent popes confirmed it in 1119, 1123 and 1135; all these privileges were at Manosque in 1531.[10] After 1113, there were royal charters, episcopal exemptions, property deeds, records of arrangements with other institutions and so on. A *cancellarius* of the Hospital was mentioned in 1126 but thereafter the description lapsed,[11] though the Order evidently employed notaries and scribes, and presumably kept its documents, in its central writing office and treasury.[12] The Hospitallers apparently preserved the two papal letters of 1143 which granted them jurisdiction over Hospitallers in German lands and over the hospital of Sancta Maria Alemannorum in Jerusalem.[13] Many other pre-1291 documents were at Manosque in 1531. Some early materials, apparently including the papal confirmation of the Rule issued in 1185, survived the Muslim reconquest of Jerusalem in 1187, perhaps because they were sent away in good

---

[7] Some early datings once advanced for Hospitaller texts have subsequently been rejected: e.g., *Cartulaire*, 1.1 n. 1; 4.311.

[8] Luttrell, 'Earliest Hospitallers', pp. 40-52.

[9] *Cartulaire*, nos. 20, 25, 29, etc.

[10] Texts in Hiestand, *Templer und Johanniter*, 2.194-201, 206-7, 210-12; discussion in R. Hiestand, 'Feierliche Privilegien mit divergierenden Kardinalslisten? Zur Diplomatik der Papsturkunden des 12. Jahrhunderts', *Archiv für Diplomatik* 33 (1987), pp. 242-56.

[11] *Cartulaire*, no. 77; J. Delaville le Roulx, *Les Hospitaliers en Terre Sainte et à Chypre, 1100-1310* (Paris, 1904), p. 347. After 1126, the title of Chancellor lapsed until the early fourteenth century.

[12] Riley-Smith, *Knights*, pp. 240, 255, 278, 285, 304, 310-12, 427.

[13] *Cartulaire*, nos. 154, 155 = Hiestand, *Kirchen im Heiligen Lande*, pp. 169-72, both texts inventoried at Manosque in 1531 and now in the Hospital's Provençal archive at Marseilles.

time or because those Hospitallers who stayed on in the city were able to preserve them. After Jerusalem fell, the Hospitaller brethren who were still there succeeded in ransoming a number of poor people who then left the city under a guard of Hospitallers and Templars, and ten brethren of the Hospital were permitted to stay in the Jerusalem hospital for a year in order to tend those patients who were too sick to be moved.[14] One remarkable reliquary remained in Jerusalem, buried in the crypt of the Hospital's church.[15]

After 1187, the archives may at first have been kept in one of the Hospital's castles; the Rule and other regulations were available to the chapter general at Margat in 1206. In Syria, a brief gap in the process of copying documents followed the loss of Jerusalem, but the transmission and diffusion of charters and privileges, with copies sometimes being kept in certain Western houses, was soon continued.[16] At some point after 1189, the Convent was established in the new capital at Acre where it accumulated an important archive; after 1255, the documents of the Benedictines of Mount Tabor also passed to the Hospital.[17] The need to conserve records was inescapable and a statute of 1262 decreed that every prior in the West should keep a register listing his priory's rents and properties.[18] Some time before the fall of Acre in 1291, an important part of the archive there was sent to safety. These documents were at Manosque in 1531 when they were summarized in an inventory.[19] What was considered to be the body of a 'beatus Gerardus', presumably the Hospital's founder, was in a 'very precious silver gilt box with many precious stones' in the Hospital's chapel at Manosque by 1283,[20] and the bulk of the

---

[14] Riley-Smith, *Knights*, pp. 108, 247.

[15] J. Folda, *The Art of the Crusaders in the Holy Land, 1098-1187* (Cambridge, 1995), pp. 297-9.

[16] Hiestand, *Templer und Johanniter*, 1.13 et passim, giving diplomatic details and textual variations frequently ignored in the *Cartulaire*.

[17] Texts from Mount Tabor in *Cartulaire*, 2, Appendix nos. I-XXVI; cf. Hiestand, *Kirchen im Heiligen Lande*, pp. 68-70, 92-9, 179-80.

[18] *Cartulaire*, no. 3039 # 23.

[19] An inventory of 1741 was used in J. Delaville le Roulx, 'Inventaire de pièces de Terre Sainte de l'ordre de l'Hôpital', *Revue de l'Orient latin* 3 (1895), and throughout the *Cartulaire*. The 1531 inventory was discovered by Rudolf Hiestand, who will publish it with a detailed study of these important materials, which are not considered here: Hiestand, *Templer und Johanniter*, 1.23, 48-50; 2.19-28 et passim. There is no sign that they were on Rhodes between 1310 and 1522.

[20] F. Reynaud, *La commanderie de l'Hôpital de Saint-Jean de Jérusalem de Rhodes et de Malte à Manosque, XIIᵉ siècle-1789* (Gap, 1981), pp. 141, 195-8; A. Luttrell, *The Hospitallers of Rhodes and their Mediterranean World* (Aldershot, 1992), Study XVIII, p. 9; Addenda, p. 3.

documents from Acre could have been sent there at about that time, possibly in more than one consignment.[21] Other texts, including Lucius III's confirmation of the Rule with his bull, were lost at Acre 'cum aliis rebus non modicis' in 1291;[22] also lost were the copy of the 1206 statutes sealed by Master Alfonso of Portugal[23] and the Hospital's holy relics.[24]

At Acre a number of constitutional texts were available to Fr. Guglielmo of Santo Stefano who always used the French language rather than Italian or Latin but who apparently belonged to the Priory of Lombardy and was probably an Italian. Fr. Daniele of Santo Stefano was presumably a kinsman; in 1315, while acting in the same priory as lieutenant there, he had a copy made of a codex which contained the statutes in a form related to that of Fr. Guglielmo's two codices.[25] Fr. Guglielmo had strong legal and historical interests, and at Acre in 1282 he commissioned Jean of Antioch to translate from Latin into French the *Rhetoric* then attributed to Cicero. While in Acre he had certain documents in the Hospital's archive copied and also translated into French, and these were included in the compilation of Hospitaller texts he made apparently between 1278 and 1283. Subsequently he returned to Lombardy where he had available a collection of documents, at least some of which he had presumably brought from Acre, and between about 1296 and 1300 he produced further works which included his own treatise on the Hospital's legislation and constitution. He was Commander of Cyprus, an office of considerable responsibility, at least from 1299 until probably about 1303, after which he disappeared. Fr. Guglielmo was important for his copying and conservation of Hospitaller records, for his mature attitude to the Hospital's historiography and his rejection of the legendary accounts of its origins, for his appreciation of the importance of preserving the *esgarts* dating after 1291, and for his constitutional treatise. He increased the number of texts available in French, and some of these he arranged in a quasi-historical, or at least chronological, format.[26]

---

[21] Fr. Guglielmo of Santo Stefano's two codices (discussed below) made no mention of any of these documents being either at Acre in about 1283 or in the West.

[22] *Cartulaire*, no. 4496; the 'other things' were not necessarily all writings.

[23] Infra, p. 149.

[24] Luttrell, *Hospitallers of Rhodes*, Study XVIII, pp. 10-11; Addenda, p. 3.

[25] L. Delisle, 'Maître Jean d'Antioche, traducteur, et Frère Guillaume de Saint-Étienne, hospitalier', *Histoire littéraire de la France* 33 (1906), p. 23.

[26] The best appraisal is Riley-Smith, *Knights*, pp. 32-6, 260-1, 272-3; important additions in K. Klement, 'Alcune osservazioni sul Vat. Lat. 4852', *Studi Melitensi* 3 (1995), redating the first codex to probably 1278/1283. Considerable parts of the two codices are published in *Cartulaire* and elsewhere; in addition to Delisle, 'Maître Jean d'Antioche', see *RHC Oc.*, 5.cxx-

A number of these documents related to the grave constitutional conflict within the Hospital between 1295 and 1300 in which Fr. Guglielmo himself played some role. His writings must have buttressed the position of the Conventual oligarchy which was an indispensible element of stability within the Order.[27]

The first codex compiled for Fr. Guglielmo began with a French translation of the Rule as confirmed in 1185 by Lucius III with the later additions of 1206 arranged in the form of a marginal gloss also in French, and with a copy of Lucius's *rota*. There followed Master Jobert's privilege for the sick of 1176; various customs of Master Roger of Moulins of 1181/2; the statutes and other items confirmed or newly enacted in 1206; the statutes of 1262 to 1268 in a *grant chartre* and those of 1270 to 1278 in a *petite chartre*; and, in a new hand, those of 1287. Next came an *ordenement* concerning the Jerusalem hospital[28] and then what were termed the *usances* and the *esgarts*, the final *esgarts* of later codifications naturally being absent. The manuscript was probably compiled in the scriptorium at Acre which was associated with Jean of Antioch, who may well have made the translations from the Latin. This first codex stated that it had used four writings which had leaden bulls, one of

---

cxxv, and on the Acre 'scriptorium', J. Folda, *Crusader Manuscript Illumination at Saint-Jean d'Acre, 1275-1291* (Princeton, 1976), pp. 42-6. Delisle, 'Maître Jean d'Antioche', p. 24, and Riley-Smith, *Knights*, p. 273, claim that Fr. Guglielmo was Commander of Cyprus in 1296. Paris, Bibliothèque Nationale [hereafter BN]: ms. fr. 6049, stated (fol. 298) that his treatise entitled *Saterian* was completed on Cyprus in September 1296, and (fol. 217) that the other *livre* in that codex was done while Fr. Guglielmo was Commander of Cyprus; it did, however, contain a text of 1304: *Cartulaire*, no. 4672. Fr. Guglielmo was Commander by 3 June 1299 and Fr. Simon le Rat was named Commander in November 1303: *Cartulaire*, nos. 4464, 4620.

[27] Riley-Smith, *Knights*, pp. 296-303; A. Forey, 'Constitutional Conflict and Change in the Hospital of St. John during the Twelfth and Thirteenth Centuries', *Journal of Ecclesiastical History* 33 (1982), pp. 20-7; A. Luttrell, 'Gli Ospitalieri di San Giovanni di Gerusalemme dal continente alle isole', in *Acri 1291: la fine della presenza degli ordini militari in Terra Santa e i nuovi orientamenti nel XIV secolo*, ed. F. Tommasi (Perugia, 1996), pp. 87-9.

[28] Klement, 'Alcune osservazioni', pp. 241-3, notes this unknown text at fols 89-104; it is published in K. Klement, *'Von Krankenspeisen und Ärtzen...': Eine unbekannte Verfügung des Johannitermeisters Roger des Moulins (1177-1187) im Codex Vaticanus Latinus 4852* (unpublished thesis: Salzburg, 1996). It is evidently a French version of a text also preserved in an equally unknown Latin version in Marseilles, Archives départementalesdes Bouches-du-Rhône [hereafter Marseilles]: 56 H 4055 no. 2, datable in or after 1181 by a reference to the *casale* of Cole or Chola acquired in 1181: *Cartulaire*, no. 603, wrongly given as of 1189 in A Luttrell, 'The Hospitaller's Medical Tradition, 1291-1530', in *The Military Orders: Fighting for the Faith and Caring for the Sick*, ed. M. Barber (Aldershot, 1994), p. 67. S. Edgington, 'Medical Care in the Hospital of St John in Jerusalem', in *The Military Orders, Volume II. Welfare and Warfare*, ed. H. Nicholson (forthcoming) studies this important text.

Lucius III, one of Master Alfonso of Portugal, and two of Master Hugues Revel; Revel's statutes were contained in two *chartres*, one *grant* and one *petite*, both with a leaden bull, and added to the latter were Master Nicholas Lorgne's statutes of 1278 which had no bull as they were passed before his magistral seal had been made.[29]

Fr. Guglielmo's second codex described more fully the documents he had seen in Acre, probably in about 1282:[30]

Ci testimoigne le conpileor de cest lieure que il uit cestes choses bulles soute la bule de Lucius pape et de maistre Anfons. Et deuise aucunes coustumes et aiostances qui fuerent iointes par aucun leuc de regle au Margat.

Se sont les ordenemens de sus ecris si come la regle et les autres ordenemens. Je vis et tins en mes mains bulles de plomb. Ce est assauoir la regle si come uous laue oye deuant qui estoit bullee de la bulle apostolial. Et de lapostoille Lucius et estoit en latin. Et puis la fais translater et metre en frances, si come est dite et translatee deuant le co[n]trescrit en latin en latin.[31] Quant Je parti dou prioure de Lombardie demora la les autres choses ensi auant. Cest le priuilege que maistre Jobert fit de pain blanc et les autres ordenations que il fist. Et celes qui uienent apres de maistre Rogier de Molix. Et puis la recordation dou Margat atresi. Je vis et tins et oys proprement por faire cont[r]escrire. Et estoit bullee de la bulle de plomb, dou nom de Maistre Anfons les quels Je fis contrescrire autresi en latin. Et [quant] ce lieure[32] fu compile Je auee[33] le dit cont[r]escrit qui proprement fu pris de sous la bulle de maistre Anfons et la uoie[34] en Chipre.

Cestes choses ay ci dit por ce que la dite regle qui estoit bullee de la bulle de lapostoly, et les autres choses que estoient soute la bulle de Maistre Anfons furent perdues ala perte dAcre, si que au jor[35] que cest liure fut compile nous non auions regle bullee dou pape ne les choses desus escrites recordees et confermees au Margat, non auions nous sous nule bulle. Et por ce que elles ne fussent mise en obli par negligence, ou que autre error non fust per aucuns escris descordables des escris qui les freres ont, ay Je dit la ou la uerite seroit trouee. Et qui Je eusse la

---

[29] Rome, Biblioteca Vaticana: Codex Vaticanus Latinus [hereafter Vat. Lat.] 4852; analysed in Klement, 'Alcune osservazioni'.

[30] BN: ms. fr. 6049, fols 240ᵛ-241ᵛ; earlier publication (here amended) in Delisle, 'Maître Jean d'Antioche', pp. 23-4; J. Delaville le Roulx, *De prima origine Hospitaliorum Hierosolymitanorum* (Paris, 1885), pp. 40-1; J. Delaville le Roulx, 'Les statuts de l'ordre de l'Hôpital de Saint-Jean de Jérusalem', *Bibliothèque de l'École des Chartes* 48 (1887), pp. 350, 351 n. 2.

[31] Possibly meaning a copy of the Latin text in Latin.

[32] Ms: 'Et ce lieure ...'.

[33] Ms: 'auce'.

[34] Probably to read 'l'auoie'?; Delaville illogically amends to 'l'a[n]voié'(!).

[35] Ms: 'lor' (or 'ior'?).

regle cont[r]escrite sous la bulle dou pape et les ordenemens desus dis bulles sous la bulle de Maistre Aufons, Je trais a testimoingne frere B[ru]n[36], qui estoit Tresourier au jour, et auoit la dite regle et escrit fait au Margat en sa garde qui les presta por faire contreescrire.

de ce meismes.

Meismes as diz escritz fais au Margat conte[n]oit la regle la qual regle et tous les escritz desus ditz estoient en vne chartre bullee souz la bulle de plomb au nom dou dit Maistre Anfons.

de ce maismes.

Aucunes choses ajosteront lois a la droite escripture de la regle laquel ajostance tient leuc solement destabliment non pais de regle. Et non auons pas juste vser de Tout selonc celes ajostances Car ou la regle parole de .iij. choses que len doit promettre lajostance par la main dou prestre et por liure mas lusance si est que le bailli ou autre des freres qui face aucun frere tieigne en ses mains le liure sur lequel cil qui doiuent estre frere prometent. Et puis le porte sur lauter et le reporte au bailli se il le feit freire ou a autre des freres que laura fait frere ...[37]

Fr. Guglielmo was anxious to emphasize that the Rule had been altered at Margat. He said that he had himself seen the confirmation of the Rule with Lucius III's leaden bull, and also the customs and statutes of 1176 and of later dates which were approved at Margat together with the new statutes enacted there, all in Latin and sealed in 1206 by Master Alfonso. Fr. Guglielmo had the Rule copied in Latin and translated from the Latin into French, which implied that no French version was then available in the Convent at Acre. On leaving the Priory of Lombardy, presumably to go to Cyprus, he left there his copies and translations of the privilege of the sick and of the other *ordenations* of Master Jobert, those of Master Roger of Moulins and the *recordation* of Margat, all in the Latin version sealed by Master Alfonso. Fr. Guglielmo had had these copied in Latin and translated into French; he wrote both that he had left them in Lombardy when he went to Cyprus in or before 1296 but that they were with him in Cyprus when, presumably later, he compiled the *lieure* which formed the second part of his second codex, which did indeed contain these materials in French. The sealed documents of 1185 and 1206 were lost at Acre in 1291. After that the Hospital no longer had a copy of the Rule with a papal seal; Fr. Guglielmo's insistence on that point suggests that he wrote that

---

[36] Or 'B[er]n'. Riley-Smith, *Knights*, p. 273, proposes Fr. Bernard of Chemin, Treasurer in 1299: *Cartulaire*, no. 4469. Delaville, 'Statuts de l'ordre', pp. 350, 351 n. 2, reads 'Brun' and gives him as alive in 1204(!).

[37] There followed (fols 241ᵛ-242ᵛ) further examples of changes to the Rule.

passage before, or just after, the renewed papal confirmation of the Rule which was issued in Italy in 1300 while he was in Cyprus. As witness that he had indeed copied these documents, Fr. Guglielmo cited the Treasurer at Acre who had held them in his custody. The texts bulled at Margat contained an example of the Rule which varied from that confirmed by Lucius III, and these additions and variations were carefully noted in French in the gloss to the French translation in Fr. Guglielmo's first codex. He remarked that these variations had the value of statute but not that of the Rule, since they lacked papal confirmation. In 1184 and 1185 Lucius had confirmed Master Roger of Moulins's hospital *ordenement* but not the other magistral ordinances of 1176 and 1181/2.

Some central records were naturally kept in the Western priories. The Rule and an early version of the Legends were in England probably between about 1181 and 1185, at which time they were turned from Latin into Anglo-Norman verse; the text was copied in a codex compiled in England between 1300 and about 1310.[38] A Latin version of the Rule as amended in 1206 was transcribed in 1253 and sent to the German brethren, who preserved it in a Swiss commandery.[39] One early surviving legislative text is the thirteenth-century fragment in Latin in a mutilated parchment in Provence. The fragment surviving begins with items at least some of which were confirmed at Margat but which were earlier in origin;[40] there followed the hospital *ordenement* probably datable betweeen 1181 and 1185 which was also copied in French in Fr. Guglielmo's first codex; next came variant forms of certain regulations for the reception of brethren and *confratres* and concerning prayers, feasts and fasts which were later considered as *usances*; the rest of the Provençal fragment was lost.[41] Further variant forms of these same texts also followed the *ordenement* concerning the hospital in the French translation which was given in Fr. Guglielmo's first codex but not in the second.[42] Thus, even after 1291, there survived traces of texts and information which had possibly been removed

---

[38] *The Hospitallers' 'Riwle' (Miracula et Regula Hospitalis Sancti Johannis Jerosolimitani)*, ed. K. Sinclair (London, 1984), pp. xxv, xlv-xlviii. The Anglo-Norman Legends were taken from the Latin: K. Sinclair, 'The Anglo-Norman Miracles of the Foundation of the Hospital of St. John in Jerusalem', *Medium Aevum* 55 (1986), p. 103.

[39] *Cartulaire*, no. 70: facsimile in G. Lagleder, *Die Ordensregel der Johanniter/Malteser* (St. Ottilien, 1983), p. 86, showing *plica* and seal. A Latin version in Strasbourg, Archives départementales du Bas-Rhin: H 1363 no. 1, with *plica*, is almost identical in its hand and its text.

[40] Several of these items are similar to those apparently confirmed in 1206: *Cartulaire*, no. 1193/2.36-7).

[41] Cf. *Cartulaire*, no. 2213 ##121-2, 124?.

[42] Klement, 'Alcune osservazioni', pp. 234, 241-2.

from the corpus in or before 1206, and which differed from what were to become the standard codifications which were themselves derived from Fr. Guglielmo's collections in French.

A South German miscellany of Hospitaller documents, probably compiled or copied between 1287 and 1292, included many of the same texts as Fr. Guglielmo's first codex. These began with the Rule in the amended form of 1206 in German translation; also in German were the various customs of Master Jobert of 1176, there wrongly dated to 1181, and of Master Roger of Moulins of 1181/2.[43] The second part of the 1181/2 statutes was twice said to have been 'passed' at Margat under Master 'Arnul' or 'Arnoldes', evidently Master Alfonso of Portugal acting in 1206.[44] These statutes, at one point headed 'Rvgerus' presumably for Master Roger of Moulins, were roughly similar to those later considered as of being of 1206. After the first seventeen items came the heading, 'Diez wart gesezzet ze Akers', perhaps alluding to a chapter general at Acre held before 1206, possibly by Master Roger of Moulins. At the end of this section were passages on the reception of brethren and on prayers which corresponded, as in Fr. Guglielmo's first codex and also in the Latin fragment in Provence, to certain of the later *usances*. There followed some, but not all, of the statutes which were passed before 1262, wrongly given as 1272, in the 'Alberie' – that is the *auberges* – at Jaffa, Acre and Vigne Neuve, but which were approved in 1262 and subsequently ascribed to that year, and then others dating to 1262 and chapters down to 1287. These may have been based on a text earlier than that used by Fr. Guglielmo, since they included some eight statutes of Master Hugues Revel which were not in Fr. Guglielmo's codification of c. 1283 or in any subsequent corpus, while other statutes were omitted, presumably having been lost or suppressed; many were either in garbled form or inaccurately translated.[45]

The German collection next copied many regulations later described as *esgarts*; again the form was garbled and much, including the first twenty so-called *esgarts*, was omitted. These regulations were given not in German but in Latin, perhaps because they came from a different source. There then followed, still in Latin, about twenty of the various statutes approved at Margat,

---

[43] French translations in *Cartulaire*, nos. 494, 504, 627; the dates given here as 1176, 1181/2 and 1206 may be marginally approximate.

[44] Other versions (eg. *Cartulaire*, no. 1193: preamble) recorded a chapter at Caesarea not mentioned in Munich, Bayerische Staatsbibliothek [hereafter Munich]: Clm 4620, fol. 94ᵛ.

[45] Note that the Munich manuscript in German omits statutes ## 24-5, 31, 34-6, 40, 50, of 1262, of which ## 24, 31, 34-6 are also lacking in the Latin version of 1357: cf. *Cartulaire*, no. 1193. Other variations in this manuscript await detailed analysis.

given with many omissions with respect to the standard text established later, and then another seventeen or so statutes which corresponded to no group in the later standard compilations, though some of the items were approximately similar to individual regulations of various dates. This section closed by stating that these regulations were approved in the chapter general at Margat following their attestation by 'old and other' brethren:

> quod adunato capitulo generali apud Margatum omnes iste constitutiones subscripte recitate fuerint coram fratre Al. et fratre Con [sic] Portugali reuerendo magistro Hospitalis et coram antiquis et probis fratribus eiusdem domus unde per testimonium fratrum antiquorum et aliorum predicta statuta inuenta sunt et pro comuni vtilitate aprobata et [uera facta?].

The Master involved was evidently Fr. Alfonso of Portugal; the date was given as 29 September 'm.cc.lij', presumably in error for 'm.cc.uj' or 1206.[46] There followed a selection of papal, royal and imperial privileges dating from 1185 to 1274, a version of the Legends,[47] and a unique Latin treatise on the Jerusalem hospital.[48] Many of the privileges apart, much of this material presumably originated in Syria. It may have been contained on parchments similar to the *chartres* at Acre, one or more of which was in Latin.

---

[46] Munich: Clm 4620, summarily analysed in G. Glauche, *Katalog der lateinischen Handschriften der Bayerischen Staatsbibliothek München Clm 4501-4663*, rev. edn (Wiesbaden, 1994), pp. 210-14. Lagleder, *Die Ordensregel*, pp. 154-81, with facsimiles, gives the regulations of 1176 and 1181/2 in German but breaks off at the end of fol. 84. This codex is being studied by Karl Borchardt who kindly communicated a partial transcription and some preliminary findings, with the suggestion that the language points to a Bavarian origin; nothing is known of the Hospitaller section of this codex before the fifteenth century. The two earliest manuscripts date the '1287' statutes to that year while Munich: Clm 4620, fol. 103^v, gives 1286, but *Cartulaire*, no. 4022, prefers 1288, as given in later manuscripts. The Latin of the *esgarts* is not that of the 1357 translation given in *Cartulaire*, no. 2213. The Margat chapter was most probably held in 1206 (Riley-Smith, *Knights*, p. 120) and 'uj' could easily have become 'lij'. Throughout the so-called *esgarts* there are variations between the versions given in Fr. Guglielmo's two codices, in that of Fr. Daniele of Santo Stefano (BN: ms. fr. 1978) and in BN: ms. fr. 13,531 (datable 1320/30) which contains additional items: *Cartulaire*, no. 2213 and notes. *RHC, Oc.*, 5.cxxiv, notes that the burnt Turin manuscript of the statutes (datable 1344/7) was very close to Fr. Guglielmo's second codex; it may have derived from materials of his available in Lombardy. *Cartulaire*, no. 2213, gives ## 45 ter and quater from Fr. Guglielmo's second codex, and these are also in Munich: Clm 4620, fol. 112^v.

[47] This version of the Legends, published in *RHC, Oc.*, 5.405-10, is also in BN: ms. lat. 5515 and ms. lat. 14,693.

[48] Studied in B. Kedar, 'An Anonymous Twelfth-Century Description of the Jerusalem Hospital', in *The Military Orders, Volume II: Welfare and Warfare*, ed. H. Nicholson (forthcoming).

A roll which survived in Provence contained some of the same texts. The opening section being missing, the portion remaining opened with the end of the Rule as amended at Margat but given in French and in a form varying notably from that of Fr. Guglielmo's French text. It was followed by Lucius III's confirmation of 12 January 1185 given in Latin and thereafter, all in French, by the ordinances of Masters Jobert and Roger of Moulins dating from 1176 onwards, and by the statutes approved in 1206, in 1262 and thereafter down to 1294, with significant variations in content and wording, and with various omissions but including certain statutes for 1292, 1293 and 1294 which were subsequently suppressed and so remained unknown. The so-called *esgarts* and *usances* were not included.[49]

Fr. Guglielmo's second codex was an amalgamation of two separate books, one section called the *Saterian* being completed in Cyprus in September 1296. That involved some repetition of materials in the ensemble, which eventually survived only in a copy made apparently between 1330 and 1332. The first part opened with two versions of the Legends; the Rule and its papal confirmation of 1300 both in French; various punishments, fasts and feast days; many *usances* and statutes down to 1304; a supposed charter of Godfrey of Bouillon; prayers for the sick, the dead and the chapters general; a very brief version of the Chronology of the Deceased Masters; texts concerning the constitutional disputes of 1295 to 1300; a crusade treatise by Charles II of Naples written in 1291/2; a passage on the Hospital's *confratres*; further *usances* and *esgarts* dating between 1301 and 1303; and more on *confratres* and punishments. The second part was more juridical in character, with Fr. Guglielmo's own critical and commonsense account of the Hospital's origins and with a jumble of customs, privileges, statutes, letters and a different version of the Chronology of the Deceased Masters; much of this was arranged chronologically to form an uneven historical account. There followed Fr. Guglielmo's own treatise on the Order's constitution, the *Saterian*. Finally, in the same hand and added after 1319 or more probably after 1330, were three further statutes, a passage on the Order's seals, a list of Hospitaller dignitaries, those statutes of 1311 which were not revoked in 1330, and the statutes and *recordia* of 1330.[50]

---

[49] Marseilles: 56 H 4055 no. 1; e.g., where Fr. Guglielmo (*Cartulaire*, no. 4259 #1) gives *Denamarche*, the Marseilles manuscript has *dosterriche*. The suppressed statutes are not in *Cartulaire*, nos. 4194, 4234, 4259; one is published in Luttrell 'Gli Ospitalieri', p. 81 n. 31.

[50] Various dates have been attributed to this codex (BN: ms. fr. 6049); Delisle's incomplete description indicates only some of the passages published. The final section dates after 1319 since it refers to the Prior of Catalunya, an office only created in that year.

Fr. Guglielmo reproduced, as always in French translation, a charter of Godfrey of Lorraine which was dated 1183 but which, with some lack of scruple, he ascribed to Godfrey of Bouillon in 1099/1100 in order to buttress an argument of his own.[51] His various collections ignored the many other charters and privileges which did survive, including the earliest papal privilege of 1113, perhaps because they had already been sent to the West or possibly because he could not read Latin; indeed his two codices contained virtually nothing in that language. Whether Fr. Guglielmo was a priest or a *miles*,[52] he was interested primarily in juridical and constitutional matters. The legislative tradition established in his corpus, which passed to later codifications, was basically that of 1206. By that time there were already many confusions, some of them further compounded in Fr. Guglielmo's translations and rearrangements.

A papal letter of 1172 mentioned the regulations – 'vestigia et statuta' – of the Hospital's early rulers 'G.' and 'R.', presumably Gerard and Raymond of Puy. The formal written Rule was established by Raymond of Puy, perhaps in the 1130s; and, according to Lucius III in 1184, it was confirmed by Eugenius III, pope from 1145 to 1153.[53] Lucius reconfirmed it in 1184 and 1185 at the request of Master Roger of Moulins who was with the pope in November 1184. Lucius's phrase 'ut accipimus' suggests that he did not at first see Eugenius's confirmation. Indeed Lucius's confirmation, issued and reissued on a number of dates from 4 November 1184 onwards, did not originally include the text of the Rule;[54] only the confirmation of 22 August 1185,[55] as given in

---

[51] Delaville, *De prima origine*, pp. 124-7; Delisle, 'Maître Jean d'Antioche', pp. 29-30.

[52] Folda, *Crusader Manuscript Illumination*, p. 45, claims that he was a lawyer; Riley-Smith, *Knights*, p. 32, that he was a knight.

[53] *Cartulaire*, nos. 434, 690; cf. Hiestand, *Templer und Johanniter*, 1.361, 2.228-30; K. Klement, 'Le prime tre redazioni della Regola Giovannita', *Studi Melitense* 4 (1996). Two versions of the Legends and Fr. Guglielmo held that the Rule was confirmed by Innocent II between 1139 and 1143 (Klement, 'Le prime tre redazioni', p. 51), possibly a confusion with Innocent's privilege in *Cartulaire*, no. 130 (original in Marseilles).

[54] *Cartulaire*, no. 690: facsimile in Lagleder, *Die Ordensregel*, p. 46; further dates noted in Hiestand, *Templer und Johanniter*, 1.361, 363.

[55] Lucius III's privilege of 22 August 1185 in Latin, with *rota* and cardinalate subscriptions but without the text of the Rule, was published by G. Bosio, *Dell'istoria della sacra religione et ill^{ma} militia di San Giovanni Gerosolimitano*, vol. 1 (2nd edn: Rome, 1621), pp. 65-7, from a version then in the Hospital's archives at Paris; this seems to be the version used in Klement, 'Le prime tre redazioni', pp. 237-40. Bosio presumes that when such copies were sent from Syria to the priories the text of the Rule was omitted from it since it would already have been available in the priories: Bosio, *Dell'istoria*, 1.68-71, published the Rule from Boniface VIII's register.

Fr. Guglielmo's French translation,[56] included it, perhaps because only then did the text reach Lucius at Verona. By that time, four extra clauses seem to have been added to the end of the earlier text, since the clause preceding them is clearly a terminating one. Fr. Guglielmo saw and copied at Acre a version of Lucius's confirmation containing the Rule; his copy, which included Lucius's *rota* and its subscriptions, eventually survived only in the French translation. Apparently between 1181 and 1185 the Rule was translated from the Latin into Anglo-Norman verse but with various elaborations and explanations, some of them possibly derived from the later customs of 1181/2.[57] The Provençal roll contained the Rule as amended in 1206 but in French; it was followed by Lucius III's confirmation, in Latin and without the Rule, dated 12 January 1185. At Acre, Fr. Guglielmo also saw a *chartre* with the Latin Rule as amended in 1206 and under the seal of Master Alfonso of Portugal, and in his first codex he annotated the changes there made. He noted: 'Cestes choses que sont escrites en maniere de glose en ce livre tant come la regle tient; aiousta maistre Amfos a la dite regle selonc quel ytient a son escrit fait au Margat'; again he referred to: 'Ce changement que [est] en lescrit fait au Margat de maistre Amphos'.[58]

All other known texts datable before 1300 contained the Rule as amended at Margat in 1206. In 1253 Master Guillaume of Châteauneuf sent a transcription of the Latin Rule, with his own seal attached, to the 'preceptor Alamanie' to be read yearly in chapter and to replace any other text being used in the German province. That copy survived, as did a similar thirteenth-century copy

---

[56] Vat. Lat. 4852, fol. 18; fols 14[r-v], in Klement, 'Le prime tre redazioni', pp. 240-1, shows Lucius III confirming a written text of Roger of Moulin's hospital *ordenement*, though without including the text in his privilege; the *ordenement* dates, therefore, before August 1185.

[57] Riley-Smith, *Knights*, pp. 47-8; *The Hospitallers' 'Riwle'*, pp. xlvi-xlviii; K. Sinclair, 'New Light on Early Hospitaller Practices', *Revue Bénédictine* 96 (1986).

[58] Cited from Klement, 'Alcune osservazioni', pp. 235-7, which lists variations given in the gloss. *Cartulaire*, no. 70, presents Fr. Guglielmo's French translation of the 1185 text of the Rule alongside the Latin copy of 1253 which has various additions. The complete text of Lucius's privilege from Vat. Lat. 4852, with the Rule, *rota* and subscriptions all in French, is in P.A. Paoli, *Dell'origine ed istituto del sacro militar ordine di S. Giovambattista Gerosolimitano* (Rome, 1781), Appendix pp. xvii-xxxi. *Cartulaire*, no. 70, ignores the gloss, but Lagleder, *Die Ordensregel*, pp. 89-115, gives it in text and facsimile. *The Hospitallers' 'Riwle'*, pp. 70-4, gives the 1300 text in a copy datable 1300/10, noting variants with respect to the 1253 copy; Klement, 'Le prime tre redazioni', pp. 254-9, also analyses these changes. E. King, *The Rule, Statutes and Customs of the Hospitallers, 1099-1310* (London, 1934), pp. 3, 20 n. 1, considers that the phrase 'and the defence of the Catholic faith' was probably added to the first clause of the Rule in 1206, but it appeared in no version datable in or before 1300.

at Strasbourg.[59] The 1206 version, in German, was in the Munich codex with the statutes to 1287 which is datable before 1292, and also, in French, in the Provençal roll with the statutes down to 1294; this French translation varied significantly in language and word order from Fr. Guglielmo's French text, and it contained phrases not included in the 1300 confirmation. The copies sealed by Lucius III and by Master Alfonso were lost at Acre in 1291, as Fr. Guglielmo noted.[60]

In 1300, explicitly in view of this loss of 'apostolicas litteras, regule vestre seriem continentes', Pope Boniface VIII confirmed a text of the Rule making certain unspecified changes: 'quibusdam verbis de mandato nostro amotis et correctis, in ea presentibus fecimus annotari'. This confirmation stated that it contained the Rule of Raymond of Puy with that Master's seal which had been provided by the Hospitallers: 'cum vos nonnullas litteras, quondam fratris Raymundi, tunc eiusdem Hospitalis custodis, qui predictam regulam condidit, eius plumbeo sigillo signatas, in quibus ipsa regula continetur expresse, prout asseritis, habeatis'.[61] Raymond of Puy did have a seal,[62] but the phrase 'prout asseritis' suggests that Boniface's chancery did not really see a Rule with Raymond's seal but rather that it accepted something else. The gloss to Fr. Guglielmo's French translation noted certain additions to the Rule, pre-sumably those made in 1206 which he identified by comparing the 1185 and 1206 versions he obtained at Acre, but his French translation contained other phrases which were not noted in the gloss as additions and which were not present in the 1300 text. That suggests that Boniface's chancery had available other unidentified texts which it used to remove additions already made in or before 1185. The resulting text of 1300 became the standard version; precisely how it was established and how it may have differed from that written down by 1153 remains uncertain.[63]

---

[59] *Cartulaire*, no. 2653; supra, p. 143 n. 39.

[60] Supra, pp. 141, 144, 146, 148.

[61] *Cartulaire*, no. 4496.

[62] G. Schlumberger, *Sigillographie de l'Orient latin* (Paris, 1943), p. 232.

[63] However, Klement, 'Le prime tre redazioni', pp. 254-8, argues that Boniface VIII did see a Rule with Raymond's seal which could have been sent to the West before 1283, so that Fr. Guglielmo did not then see it at Acre. Fr. Guglielmo never mentioned a Rule with Raymond's seal, nor did he mention the Latin copy of the Rule contained in Lucius III's confirmation as among the documents left in Lombardy when he went to Cyprus in c. 1296. A detailed collation of all the texts might clarify this problem. The French Rule # 18 in *Cartulaire*, no. 70, concludes: 'il non est frere'. Fr. Guglielmo's gloss, at fol. 14, ends: 'il non est frere bon, et cele paine seuf[r]ir que lautre deurot soufrir se la chose fust prou[e]r'. The 1253 copy reads:

The history of the early statutes is equally complex. Fr. Guglielmo may, in c. 1283, have made the first attempt since 1206 to assemble in a single codex the Hospital's legislation, which had been periodically collected in successive sealed *chartres*. Some earlier statutes not in Fr. Guglielmo's first collection were contained in the South German codex of 1287/92 in which the materials translated into German and those left in Latin were probably taken from sources similar to the *chartres* in existence at Acre in c. 1283. The system involving successive *chartres* created confusions, partly because ongoing legislation required repeated additions to the corpus and the elimination of obsolete items,[64] and partly because scribes continually introduced errors, misunderstandings or variations. By 1206 almost nothing, apart from the Rule itself, seems to have remained in writing which was earlier than the regulations of Masters Jobert and Roger of Moulins; these were added to the statutes in 1206 when all these materials were collected in a new *chartre* under Master Alfonso's seal. An exception was the hospital *ordenement* datable between 1181 and 1185 which survives only in the Provençal fragment in Latin and in Fr. Guglielmo's first codex in French.

The preamble to the *coustumes*, which were apparently already in writing when they were confirmed at Margat in 1206, stated that they were there recognized as 'ancient' by 'old and wise' brethren; they may have included various ordinances going back to 1176.[65] Some element of confusion was thus to be expected. In Fr. Guglielmo's first codex the materials from Margat were followed by the supposed *usances* and the supposed *esgarts*, all given without

---

'ipse frater bonus non est, et eandem penam sustineat quam accusatus, si probari posset, sustineret'. The Provençal roll reads: 'il nen est pas bon frere, et susteigne cele paine que li acusor sousteng[...]'. The German translation, fol. 78ᵛ: 'er ist ain gut pruder nicht und shol die puze leiden die der geruegete pruder leiden sholdt ob er bewert moechte werden'. The 1300 text restores the presumed 1185 reading 'ipse frater non est'. Klement, 'Le prime tre redazioni', pp. 242-53, analyzes the changes made in 1206. Note that Boniface VIII did amend earlier papal decretals when preparing Book VI of the *Corpus juris canonici*. Other problems remain. The Latin version of Lucius III's privilege of 22 August 1185 given in Bosio, *Dell'istoria*, 1.65-7, mentioned four 'medici' and four 'chiurgici' while Fr. Guglielmo's translation of it gave them as five and three. The 1300 version in Bosio, *Dell'istoria*, 1.68-71, included a number of variations given in the 1253 copy (*Cartulaire*, no. 70) but not followed in the Cambridge text of 1300 as given in *The Hospitallers' 'Riwle'*, pp. 70-4.

[64] E.g., a statute of 1297 was annulled in 1300: *Cartulaire*, no. 4515 # 20.

[65] *Cartulaire*, no. 1193: preamble; Latin version, supra, p. 145. Klement, 'Le prime tre redazioni', p. 242 n. 29, suggests a possible oral tradition but without considering the Latin version. Some documents may have been lost at the fall of Jerusalem in 1187.

any date.[66] It is evident from their form that many of the so-called *esgarts* were not judgements derived from judicial cases which had been built up into a cumulative system of case law, but simply regulations, or maybe *usances* or customs, never passed in chapter general as statutes. Many were probably statutes passed at Margat, as the dating in the Latin version in Munich suggested.[67] The first twenty *esgarts* are datable before 1239 at latest[68] and a good many may have been earlier than 1206.[69] Some of the *usances* presumably also preceded 1206 when the Hospital's 'customs' were confirmed. The oldest surviving texts must be those at Munich in Latin, in the mutilated Provençal fragment in Latin, in the Provençal roll in French and, also in French, in Fr. Guglielmo's codices. In subsequent manuscripts, in which they appear in varying order,[70] the so-called *esgarts* and *usances* were accepted as forming an essential part of the Hospital's legislative corpus which was in practice derived from Fr. Guglielmo's compilations.

Equally it was supposed that there was no legislation at any chapter general between 1206 and 1262,[71] even though the preamble to the 1262 statutes explicitly stated that many of them had been passed in earlier chapters general at Caesarea, Jaffa, Acre and the Vigne Neuve.[72] The 1262 chapter general produced a new partial codification contained in a bulled *chartre* seen at Acre, along with subsequent statutes down to 1278, by Fr. Guglielmo. Some further statutes down to 1287 appeared in German translation, much garbled, in the Munich codex, while the Provençal roll with the statutes in French down to 1294 included some which had by 1300 been replaced.

---

[66] *Cartulaire*, no. 2213.

[67] Supra, p. 145. King, *Rule, Statutes and Customs*, pp. 40-1, already made this suggestion, noting that the Latin translation of 1357 described the 1206 statutes as the 'prima pars'. King repeatedly cites the Chronicle of the Deceased Masters in its Latin version of 1357; it is here ignored since its remarks on pre-1291 legislative matters appear to be based merely on the texts available to Fr. Guglielmo in c. 1283.

[68] Riley-Smith, *Knights*, p. 260.

[69] Forey, 'Constitutional Conflict and Change', pp. 18-19.

[70] *Cartulaire*, no. 2213/2.536 n. 1.

[71] This has lead to inflated interpretations of Revel's legislative achievement: eg. C. Humphery-Smith, *Hugh Revel, Master of the Hospital of St. John of Jerusalem, 1258-1277* (Chichester, 1994), pp. 43-5.

[72] *Cartulaire*, no. 3039. The Hospital had a 'vigne neuve' outside Acre in 1261: *RHC, Arm.*, 2.730.

Many subsequent manuscripts with the Rule and statutes contained the *Miracula*, which had been placed in front of the Rule by about 1181/5,[73] and the Chronology of the Deceased Masters, which presumably originated in a prayer list and contained very brief, and often divergent, remarks on successive Masters.[74] Neither item was in Fr. Guglielmo's first codex, but a Latin version of the *Miracula* was in the German codex of c. 1287. Fr. Guglielmo's second codex contained two versions of the Chronology, apparently in their earliest surviving forms; two versions of the *Miracula*; and Fr. Guglielmo's account rejecting the legendary stories of the *Miracula* and giving his own more scientific interpretation of the Hospital's origins. His materials thus constituted a body of records, some of which were of practical value and all of which he had translated and rearranged to create a continuous history of the Hospital in French.

Fr. Guglielmo's first codex of c. 1283 preserved parts of those legislative records lost at Acre in 1291. His second codex added other items, some concerned with events later than 1291. Some of the pre-1291 texts were also available in the West, in the materials surviving in Germany and Provence for example. Meanwhile administrative materials must have been accumulating, first in Cyprus between 1291 and about 1310 and thereafter on Rhodes. The Cyprus archives were lost and so were almost all subsequent chancery materials from Rhodes down to about 1381, except for one register of the chapters general from 1330 to 1344, five magistral registers and other miscellaneous materials.[75] Though the Rhodian chancery was at first organized in very rudimentary form,[76] magistral bulls and other documents were registered[77] and by 1365/6 the chancery had an extremely detailed formulary which included

---

[73] *The Hospitallers' 'Riwle'*, pp. xlv-xlvi; other texts in Delaville, *De prima origine*, pp. 97-128, and *RHC, Oc.*, 5.405-35. See also Sinclair, 'Anglo-Norman Miracles'; A. Calvet, 'Légendes d'Oc de la fondation de l'Hôpital de Saint-Jean-de-Jérusalem', *France latine* 116 (1994); S. Schein, 'The Miracula of the Hospital of St. John and the Carmelite Elianic Tradition — Two Medieval Myths of Foundation?', in *Cross Cultural Convergences in the Crusader Period: Essays Presented to Aryeh Grabois on his Sixty-Fifth Birthday*, ed. M. Goodich, S. Menache and S. Schein (New York, 1995).

[74] References and some texts in Luttrell, *The Hospitallers of Rhodes*, Study IV.

[75] J. Mizzi et al., *Catalogue of the Records of the Order of St. John of Jerusalem in the Royal Malta Library*, vols 1- (Malta, 1964-).

[76] Preliminary study in A. Luttrell, *The Hospitallers in Cyprus, Rhodes, Greece and the West, 1291-1440* (London, 1978), Study XV.

[77] E.g., S. Fiorini and A. Luttrell, 'The Italian Hospitallers at Rhodes, 1437-1462', *Revue Mabillon* 68 (1996), pp. 220-2.

a Latin version of the *Miracula*.[78] The archival materials from 1291 to 1310 could have been lost on Rhodes, or they may have remained on Cyprus and been destroyed, possibly together with the archives of the Cypriot commandery, at any time before or during the Ottoman conquest of Cyprus in 1571 or even later.[79]

Subsequent statutes were added to the corpus, but with considerable further confusion. French was the Hospital's official language.[80] Unlike the Rule, the statutes were not approved by the pope and so did not need to be in Latin. Fr. Guglielmo saw the 1206 statutes in Latin, and they were also in Latin, as were parts of the so-called *esgarts* and *usances* which possibly dated before 1206, in the Munich codex and in the mutilated Provençal fragment. With one minor exception, all other known versions of the statutes were in French or in the *langue d'Oc* until 1357, when the statutes were officially translated into Latin because brethren in the Priory of Lombardy could not understand French;[81]

---

[78] Barcelona, Arxiu de la Corona d'Aragó, Gran Priorato de Catalunya: Armari 24, vol. 13.

[79] The *Cartulaire* shows that at Malta there are, or were, for the years 1278 to 1291 only ten original documents or contemporary copies, all of them papal letters except for two magistral bulls (nos. 3750, 3792, 4012-13, 4030, 4032, 4044, 4050, 4060, 4118), and these were not necessarily ever on Rhodes; and that for 1292 to 1307 there is, excluding papal bulls, only one original, a magistral bull of 1295 addressed to the Prior of Saint-Gilles in Provence (no. 4276) which is quite likely to have reached Malta from Provence rather than from Rhodes. It cannot be said whether the Hospital took pre-1308 documents from Cyprus to Rhodes. Furthermore, there are very few surviving originals for decades following 1308. R. Hiestand, 'Zum Problem des Templerzentralarchivs', *Archivalische Zeitschrift* 76 (1980), considers that the Templars' central archive on Cyprus, whatever it may have contained, passed to the Hospital in 1313 and remained on Cyprus, probably being destroyed in the Ottoman conquest of 1571. The Templar archive could have been lost at Acre in 1291, though other documents would have accumulated thereafter, or Templar documents could have gone to Rhodes and been lost there, as were the Hospital's own archives for the period from 1291 to 1346. It seems unlikely that they would have survived for long without being used or mentioned; very few Templar texts from the East can be shown to have been available after 1307. M. Barber, *The New Knighthood: A History of the Order of the Temple* (Cambridge, 1994), pp. 310-13, also assumes that the central archive disappeared only after 1312, claiming that Templar documents, which he says are conserved in the Hospital's Western archives, are proof of it.

[80] Luttrell, *The Hospitallers in Cyprus*, Study XVII, p. 2, wrongly gives Provençal as the official language.

[81] Text of 1357 in R. Valentini, 'Redazioni italiane quattrocentesche di statuti della religione Gioannita', *Archivum Melitense* 9 (1933), pp. 80-1. The statutes of 1320 are known only in one text which is in Latin: BN: ms. fr. 13,531, fols 59ᵛ-65. Scholars frequently fail to appreciate that the Latin texts of the statutes published alongside the French version in the *Cartulaire* are not the originals but a late, and sometimes anachronistic, translation from the French.

there were other translations into Catalan and Italian.[82] On Rhodes, the registers were kept in the chancery where an inventory of 1447 counted 102 books or registers plus six other books of 'diversarum rerum', 24 'libri veteres' of 'diversarum rerum', and two new registers and a 'formularium foris'. That made at least 135 volumes, about one a year calculating from 1310.[83] Parts of the archive may well have been destroyed before the loss of Rhodes in 1522 and some items were certainly lost in the final siege.[84] A small portion of the original Rhodian archives left Rhodes when it fell and reached Malta in 1530. At Viterbo in Italy in 1527 there were 96 magistral and other registers and 18 registers of council acts, which is almost the number still surviving in Malta. Little was lost thereafter; in fact, almost everything used by the Hospital's official historian Giacomo Bosio in the late sixteenth and early seventeenth century still survives.[85] Bosio did not have access to the Syrian materials sent to safety from Acre to the West shortly before 1291, for these did not reach Malta from Provence until after his death. Only in Bosio's time did the Order begin to arrange effectively for the chronicling of its own history and much still remains to be done. Those early written records which have survived are particularly valuable in defining the Hospital's past and ensuring the continuity of its present activities.[86]

---

[82] Delaville, 'Statuts de l'ordre', lists most manuscripts of the statutes; there seems to be no source for his claim (p. 345) that the ordinances of 1206 prescribed their own translation.

[83] Valletta, National Library of Malta, Archives of the Order of St John [hereafter Malta]: Cod. 359, fol. 96^v (kindly communicated by Jürgen Sarnowsky).

[84] E.g., Malta: Cod. 287, fol. 38; cf. Hiestand, *Templer und Johanniter*, 1.19-23.

[85] A. Luttrell, *Latin Greece, the Hospitallers and the Crusades: 1291-1440* (London, 1982), Study III, pp. 65-7.

[86] Various texts cited here require publication and collation, following which the present hypotheses will need revision. The many registers at Malta and the forthcoming inventory of the pre-1291 documents from Acre await study, while the European priories have preserved numerous unexplored texts. The habitual reliance on the sometimes misleading *Cartulaire* should be abandoned and account taken of new materials. To give just one example, the redating of many statutes should lead to the revision of accepted chronologies for the evolution of knight-brethren and sergeants within the Hospital.

Ehe und Besitz im Jerusalem der Kreuzfahrer

Hans Eberhard Mayer

Die bürgerliche Liebesheirat ist, wie man weiß, eine Erfindung erst der Emp-findsamkeit des frühen 19. Jahrhunderts. Sie wird in der Regel der häuslichen Harmonie förderlich sein. Fördert sie auch die Fortune der Familie, so ist dies allerdings ein Nebenprodukt, das im Mittelalter dagegen im Interesse einer materiell geordneten Aufzucht der Nachkommen, der Sicherung ihres Sozial-status und ihres Lebensstandards die Hauptsache war. Ein solcher Fall aus dem Jerusalem der Kreuzfahrer sei hier nachstehend zu Ehren Bernard Hamiltons, der so viel für die Erforschung des mittelalterlichen Jerusalem getan hat, betrachtet und nachgezeichnet.[1]

Im Chartular des Chorherrenstifts des Hl. Grabs in Jerusalem finden sich eine Reihe von Urkunden, die sich mit einem Haus einer gewissen Maria von St. Lazarus befassen, und auch mit einem Lehen, das ihr erster Mann Petrus vom Stift innegehabt hatte. Die früheste ist *RRH*, n° 128 von 1128 Dezember 25-1129 September 23. Aus ihr läßt sich folgendes entnehmen: Zu einem un-bekannten Zeitpunkt vor der Ausstellung der Urkunde war ein gewisser Petrus von St. Lazarus, ein *confrater* des Hl. Grabes[2], verstorben. Auf dem Totenbett hatte er eine Reihe letztwilliger Verfügungen getroffen:

---

[1] Mit kleineren Teilen dieser Transaktionen hat sich schon J. Prawer, *Crusader Institutions* (Oxford, 1980), S. 311-14 befaßt, aber nicht im Zusammenhang, weil seine Fragestellung eine andere war, nämlich die Jurisdiktionsgewalt des Gerichts des Patriarchen.

[2] Über die männliche Fraternität von Laien am Hl. Grab siehe K. Elm, 'Fratres et Sorores Sanctissimi Sepulcri. Beiträge zu *fraternitas, familia* und weiblichem Religiosentum im Umkreis des Kapitels vom Hlg. Grab', *Frühmittelalterliche Studien* 9 (1975), S. 293-304. Weniger eindringlich Prawer, *Crusader Institutions*, S. 312-14.

1) Er bestellte das Stift zum Vormund seiner minderjährigen Tochter, und diese Vormundschaft sollte das Kapitel gemeinsam mit seiner Frau ausüben, die die Mutter des Mädchens war.
2) Petrus bat das Stift, seiner Tochter das Lehen, das er zu seinen Lebzeiten vom Stift in St. Lazarus (Bethanien) innegehabt hatte, bei ihrer Eheschließung zurückzugeben und den Dienst davon ihrem künftigen Manne aufzuerlegen.
3) Aus den Erträgen des Lehens sollte in der Zwischenzeit bis zur Heirat seiner Tochter seine Witwe unterhalten werden.

Nach Ablauf einer gewissen Zeit ('post multum temporis'), aber immer noch vor dem 24. September 1129[3], beschloß das Stift, das nunmehr heiratsfähig gewordene Mädchen zu verehelichen mit einem gewissen Petrus, 'nostro nutrito famulo'. Nun brach ein Sturm los. Der Mutter drohte der Entzug ihres Unterhalts aus den Erträgen des Lehens. Das hätte sich verschmerzen lassen, wenn ihre Tochter eine gute Partie gemacht hätte, aber *nutritus famulus* deutet wahrhaftig nicht in diese Richtung. Die Mutter griff das Stift frontal und hart an ('post longas obiurgationes et contumelias ab ea nobis illatas') und verweigerte rundheraus die Zustimmung zu der geplanten Ehe. Mutter und Tochter mußten nunmehr im Kapitel vor den Stiftsherren und dem Patriarchen Stephan erscheinen, anwesend waren auch ihr Stiefvater (*victricus* statt klassisch *vitricus*) und ihre Taufpaten. Angesichts dieses massiven Aufmarsches des Familienrats fiel es dem Mädchen, das bisher offenbar nicht gefragt worden war, relativ leicht, energisch zu sein. Auf die Frage des Priors Wilhelm, ob sie dem Vorschlag des Stifts zustimme, entgegnete sie standfest, ohne die Zustimmung ihrer Mutter werde sie den Petrus nicht heiraten, lieber wolle sie um Brot betteln gehen, als ihn zum Mann zu nehmen.

Das Stift hatte diesen Ausgang einkalkuliert. Da man kirchenrechtlich das Mädchen zur Ehe nicht zwingen konnte, regelte man jetzt die materielle Seite der Sache. Das Mädchen hatte bei der Hochzeit das alte Lehen des Vaters erhalten sollen, hatte jetzt aber die Eheschließung verweigert. Das Stift verlangte nun vor Zeugen ihren ewigen Verzicht auf das für sie vorgesehen gewesene Lehen. Das war wohl eher rechtswidrig, denn es konnte ja nicht so sein, daß der Anspruch des Mädchens auf das Lehen sofort obsolet wurde, wenn sie auch nur einen einzigen Kandidaten ablehnte, weil sonst ja eine

---

[3] Jedoch zur Zeit des Patriarchen Stephan, der zwischen dem 27. Juli und dem 19. Oktober 1128 gewählt worden war; siehe R. Hiestand, 'Chronologisches zur Geschichte des Königreiches Jerusalem um 1130', *Deutsches Archiv für Erforschung des Mittelalters* 26 (1970), S. 226–9.

unzulässige Pression auf sie ausgeübt wurde, diesen Kandidaten zu heiraten. In der Praxis jedenfalls mußte sie sich beugen, verzichtete jedoch nur unter der (offenbar bewilligten) Voraussetzung, daß der Nießbrauch ihrer Mutter an den Erträgen dieses Lehens fortdauere, und zwar nunmehr auf längere Zeit als ursprünglich vorgesehen, nämlich auf Lebenszeit der Mutter, ja sogar des Stiefvaters. Die beiden hatten aber aus der zweiten Ehe der Mutter einen gemeinsamen kleinen Sohn, dessen Interessen sie jetzt für den Fall sicherstellten, daß sie beide stürben. Der Nießbrauch an dem Lehen in Bethanien würde dann ja entfallen. Deshalb versprach das Stift jetzt, dem Sohn in diesem Fall vollen Unterhalt ('victum et vestitum') zu gewähren. Hierzu war es nach dem Testament des Petrus von St. Lazarus nicht verpflichtet, denn dieser hatte auf diesem Wege ja nur seine Witwe versorgt. Das Lehen in Bethanien war also vermutlich von respektabler Größe, wenn das Stift mehr als das Notwendige tat, nur um das Lehen nach dem Tode der Eltern des Jungen nunmehr wirklich auf Dauer in die eigene Hand zu bekommen.

Die Mutter hatte mit Klauen und Zähnen die eigenen Interessen und die ihres zweiten Mannes sowie ihres Sohnes aus zweiter Ehe verteidigt. Ihre Tochter aus erster Ehe war scheinbar auf der Strecke geblieben, aber in Wahrheit hatte sie auch deren Interessen im Auge, denn sie arrangierte für sie später eine Ehe, die für sie allemal vorteilhafter war, als es diejenige mit dem *nutritus famulus* Petrus gewesen wäre. Vor dem 24. September 1134 wurde in der Sache nämlich erneut geurkundet (*RRH*, n° 158), und jetzt erfahren wir auch die Namen der Mutter und ihres zweiten Mannes: Maria von St. Lazarus und Roger von St. Lazarus, der ein *cliens* des Stifts war, also wie ihr erster Mann auch zu der großen *familia* der Grabeskirche gehörte. Die beiden nannten sich offenbar nach jenem Lehen in Bethanien (St. Lazarus), dessen Nießbrauch Maria hatte. Sie hatte aber auch wertvollen innerstädtischen Besitz. Sie hatte seit 1129 nunmehr selbst eine Ehe für ihre Tochter arrangiert, die – jetzt mit Zustimmung des Stifts – einen gewissen Bernhard geheiratet hatte. Er gehörte als *cliens* zur *familia* des Patriarchen und war nicht irgendwer, sondern der Bruder des jetzt amtierenden Priors Petrus vom Hl. Grab. Das ebnete in Jerusalem natürlich Wege, nur nicht bei Maria. Bei der Hochzeit hatte diese ihrer Tochter als Mitgift 100 Byzantiner überschrieben, also eine respektable Summe, ferner eine Aussteuer ('vestiens eam, ut ita dicam, in dorso et in lecto') und den Nießbrauch an einem Weinberg, den der Vater des Mädchens angelegt hatte. Das Mädchen war also keine schlechte Partie, doch hatte Bernhard vor der Hochzeit hart verhandelt, denn Maria mußte auch ihm persönlich etwas dafür geben, damit er ihre Tochter heirate. Bei der Hochzeit hatte Maria nämlich ihren Schwiegersohn Bernhard vor Zeugen zum Erben ('post mortem suam') eines Viertels eines von ihr und ihrem zweiten Mann erworbenen Hauses eingesetzt, das in Jerusalem in bevorzugter Lage stand, nämlich auf dem Tempelplatz neben dem Haus eines gewissen Bentulinus. Einen anderen Teil, auch dieser im Umfang eines Viertels, bestimmte sie ihrem Sohn aus zweiter Ehe, doch sollten Bernhard oder seine Erben nach dem Tod dieses Sohnes auch dessen Viertel erhalten. Die restliche Hälfte blieb, ohne daß dies gesagt wird, in Marias oder Rogers vollem Eigentum. Vielleicht gehörte jedem der beiden Ehegatten die Hälfte, weshalb Maria 1134 nur über ihr halbes Haus verfügen konnte.

Noch immer vor dem 24. September 1134 bestritt Maria plötzlich, in dieser Weise über das Haus verfügt zu haben (*RRH*, n° 158). Das zielte auf Bernhard, und Maria handelte sich dessen Klage ein. Diese wurde im Kapitel des Hl. Grabes vor dem Patriarchen Wilhelm und dem Subprior Petrus und anderen Stiftsdignitären verhandelt, obwohl sie 'ratione rei sitae' vor das Gericht des königlichen Stadtherren gehört hätte, denn der Tempelplatz, wo sich das Haus befand, lag ja außerhalb des Quartiers des Patriarchen, wo dessen Jurisdiktion galt. Da alle Beteiligten zur *familia* entweder des Patriarchen oder des Stifts gehörten, muß man wohl annehmen, daß der Patriarch und das Stift in Zivilsachen Jurisdiktion auch außerhalb des Quartiers über ihre Klientel hatten[4]. Des Sachverstandes der königlichen Cour des Bourgeois versicherte man sich durch die Beiziehung des ehemaligen Vizegrafen Anschetin, zu dessen Funktionen ja der Vorsitz in der Cour des Bourgeois gehört hatte[5]. Der Prior Petrus hielt sich zurück und trat nicht als Richter, sondern nur als Zeuge des aus der

---

[4] Das ist letztlich auch die Meinung von Prawer, *Crusader Institutions*, S. 311-14, der aber hinsichtlich dieses Falles nicht sehr klar ist. Er sagt nämlich nirgends, daß das in Frage stehende Haus außerhalb des Patriarchenquartiers lag, aber nur dann ist die Zuständigkeit des Patriarchengerichts bemerkenswert. Ja, Prawer verunklart die Sache, indem er das Haus (S. 311) 'near the Temple area' lokalisiert, was eine Lage im Patriarchenquartier ermöglichen würde, doch lag es auf dem Tempelplatz ('in platea Templi') und damit bestimmt außerhalb des Patriarchenquartiers. An anderer Stelle (S. 312) postuliert er für denselben Fall die Zuständigkeit des Patriarchengerichts über die Bourgeois des Patriarchenquartiers und lokalisiert damit das Haus erneut in demselben. Im Endergebnis (S. 314) kommt er aber zum selben Resultat wie ich, nämlich dem einer patriarchalen Zivilgerichtsbarkeit über die *clientes* des Hl. Grabs unabhängig davon, wo in der Stadt der Besitz lag, um den es jeweils ging.

[5] Der Hinweis in diesem Zusammenhang bei Prawer, *Crusader Institutions*, S. 312 auf die Bestimmung der 'Assises de la Cour des Bourgeois', *RHC Lois*, 2, c. 181/S. 121, daß in gewissen Fällen der Vizegraf ins kirchliche Gericht gehen und dort an der Verhandlung teilnehmen sollte, eignet sich für diesen Fall nicht, weil es sich dort um innereheliche Streitigkeiten handelt und überdies hier gerade nicht der amtierende Vizegraf an der Verhandlung teilnahm, sondern ein früherer.

Verhandlung resultierenden Vergleichs auf, da er des Klägers Bruder war. Gleichwohl hatte vor diesem Gericht Bernhard natürlich die besseren Karten, und man fragt sich, ob Maria nicht gehofft hatte, die Sache werde 'ratione rei sitae' im Königsgericht entschieden werden. Es kam ein Vergleich zustande, nach dem der *status quo ante* wiederhergestellt wurde: Nach Marias Tod sollte Bernhard ein Viertel des Hauses, nach dem Tod ihres Sohnes ein weiteres Viertel erhalten.

Die Datierung des Vergleichs ist problematisch. Man liest 'anno ab incarnatione domini MCXXXV, indictione XII', was nicht zusammenpaßt, denn die 12. Indiktion lief üblicherweise von September 1133 bis September 1134. Hiestand hat den Gebrauch des *stilus Pisanus* (1135 = 25. März 1134-24. März 1135 unserer Rechnung) erwogen, dann aber verworfen[6]. Er hat statt dessen einen Indiktionswechsel erst weit nach dem 1. Januar angenommen, bei dem die 12. Indiktion noch längere Zeit in unser Ziviljahr 1135 hinein gegolten hätte, statt schon am 24. September 1134 zu 13 zu wechseln. Er hat als Parallelen *RRH*, n° 87, 90 angeführt. Das erste ist eindeutig vom 14. Februar 1119, hat aber ind. 11 statt richtig ind. 12. Das zweite, ein Diplom des Königs Balduin I., ist eindeutig vom 31. Januar 1120, hat aber ind. 12 statt richtig ind. 13. Hiestand hat daher *RRH*, n° 158 in den Anfang unseres Ziviljahres 1135 datiert.

So scharfsinnig dies ist, so öffnet es sich doch drei Einwänden:

1) Es kommt häufig vor, daß die Indiktion um 1 zu niedrig ist, weil sie am vorgeschriebenen Tag nicht umgesetzt wird. Viel bedenklicher sind die Fälle, in denen sie um 1 zu hoch liegt.

2) Hiestand unterstellt hier stillschweigend und durchaus im Einklang mit der bisherigen Literatur, daß im ganzen Reich einheitliche Datierungsgebräuche gegolten hätten, während diese tatsächlich im Laufe der Zeiten, aber auch von Institution zu Institution, ja von Konzipient zu Konzipient wechselten. *RRH*, n° 87 ist eine Urkunde des Fürsten von Galilaea, *RRH*, n° 90 ein Diplom aus der Königskanzlei, *RRH*, n° 158 eine Urkunde des Hl. Grabes. Man kann nicht ohne weiteres davon ausgehen, daß alle drei nach denselben Kriterien datiert hätten.

3) Während die *indictio Romana* zwar am 25. Dezember oder am 1. Januar wechselte, ist ein noch späterer Wechsel der Indiktion (nach dem 14.

---

[6] R. Hiestand, 'Zwei unbekannte Diplome der lateinischen Könige von Jerusalem aus Lucca', *Quellen und Forschungen aus italienischen Archiven und Bibliotheken* 50 (1970), S. 16 Anm. 38.

Februar, wie dies Hiestands Theorie voraussetzt), im Abendland so selten, daß er es jedenfalls nicht in die Handbücher gebracht hat. Es kommt zwar gelegentlich eine erst zu Ostern oder am 25. März umsetzende Indiktion vor, wofür ausschlaggebend ist, daß diese Komputisten den Oster- oder den florentinischen Annuntiationsstil für das Inkarnationsjahr benutzten und den Wechsel in beiden Jahreszählungen aus Bequemlichkeit gern am selben Tage hatten. Da dies aber auch den mittelalterlichen komputistischen Handbüchern widersprach, ist die Erscheinung bei der Indiktion selbst bei bestehenden Frühjahrsstilen für das Inkarnationsjahr außerordentlich selten[7].

---

[7] Am besten ist das Problem erforscht für Flandern. C. Callewaert, 'Nouvelles recherches sur la chronologie médiévale en Flandre', *Annales de la Société d'émulation de Bruges* 59 (1909), S. 178, 182 hat überhaupt erklärt, daß Frühjahrsindiktion vor dem 13. Jahrhundert in Flandern unbekannt sei. F. Vercauteren, ed., *Actes des comtes de Flandre, 1071-1128*, *Commission royale d'histoire: Recueil des actes des princes belges* (Brussels, 1938), S. lxxxix, xcf., 216 (n° 96) hat in den gräflichen Urkunden 1071-1128 gerade einen einzigen Fall von Frühjahrsindiktion aufgetan. De Hemptinne und Verhulst haben in den 213 datierten gräflichen Urkunden aus der Zeit 1128-91 festgestellt, daß beim Grafen Dietrich vom Elsaß überwiegend die *indictio Romana* gebraucht wurde, während die Kanzlei seines Sohnes Philipp vom Elsaß in seiner ersten Amtszeit 1158-67 überwiegend die Bedanische Indiktion mit dem Beginn des Indiktionsjahres am 24. September des vorangehenden Inkarnationsjahres benutzte. Bei beiden ist eine Frühjahrsindiktion so gut wie ausgeschlossen. Die Herausgeber haben auch die Möglichkeit der genuesischen Indiktion untersucht, in der bekanntlich bei einem Wechsel am 24. September (erst des laufenden Inkarnationsjahres) die Indiktionszahl um 1 niedriger war als sonst üblich, denn dieser Indiktionsgebrauch, der das hier diskutierte *RRH*, n° 158 erklären würde, wurde auch benutzt von 1113 bis 1138 im Bistum Cambrai. Für die Urkunden der Grafen von Flandern muß dies jedenfalls so gut wie ausgeschlossen werden. Siehe zu all dem E. Van Mingroot, 'Indictio secundum stilum Cameracensem', *Bulletin de la Commission royale d'histoire* 143 (1977), S. 139-205 und T. de Hemptinne und A. Verhulst, edd., *De oorkonden der graven van Vlaanderen (1128-1191) II. uitgave - Band I: Regering van Diederik van de Elzas, Koninklijke Commissie voor Geschiedenis: Verzameling van de akten der belgische vorsten* 6 (Brussels, 1988), S. lxiv-lxix. E. Poncelet, ed., *Actes des princes-évêques de Liège: Hugues de Pierrepont, 1200-1229*, *Commission royale d'histoire: Recueil des actes des princes belges* (Brussels, 1941), S. xcif. hat in den Lütticher Bischofsurkunden Frühjahrsindiktion selbst im 13. Jahrhundert als ganz seltene Ausnahme festgestellt. W. Acht, *Die Entstehung des Jahresanfangs mit Ostern: Eine historisch-chronologische Untersuchung über Entstehung des Osteranfangs und seine Verbreitung vor dem 13. Jahrhundert* (Berlin, 1908), S. 16 hat generell dafür plädiert, daß man bei der Einführung der Frühjahrsstile beim Inkarnationsjahr auch auf die Frühjahrsindiktion umgeschwenkt sei, doch hat er selbst hierfür aus dem ganzen 12. Jahrhundert nur 11 Beispiele beigebracht. Callewaert, 'Nouvelles recherches', S. 42-4, 177-9 hat dies ad absurdum geführt, pikanterweise zum Teil aus Achts eigenen Beispielen. In jedem Falle setzt die Annahme einer Frühjahrsindiktion einen Frühjahrstil beim Inkarnationsjahr voraus, da einzig die Bequemlichkeit für die Vereinheitlichung der Epochen beider Zeitrechnungen sprach. Nun ist man zwar daran gewöhnt, einen

Da bei *RRH*, n° 158 für einen Genueser Gebrauch (siehe Anm. 7) überhaupt kein Indiz vorliegt, ist mit der Vermutung des *stilus Pisanus*, der das Inkarnationsjahr am 25. März unseres heutigen Vorjahres begann und daher mit unserem Ziviljahr die Jahreszahl nur vom 1. Januar bis 24. März gemeinsam hatte, tatsächlich weiterzukommen als mit der Annahme einer Frühjahrsindiktion. Die dann notwendige Umdatierung von *RRH*, n° 158 auf 1134 (März 25-September 23) hat für die Interpretation des Stücks keine unangenehmen Konsequenzen. Die pisanische Zeitrechnung galt am Hl. Grab generell bis zur Wahl des Patriarchen Arnulf 1112, scheint aber dort um 1135 nochmals vorzukommen[8]. Von den Urkunden, die im Chartular des Chorherrenstifts mit diesem Jahr datiert sind, verbinden *RRH*, n° 156, 157, 160 das Jahr 1135 mit der Indiktion 13, sind also mit einem weniger bizarren Jahresanfang als dem pisanischen vor dem 24. September 1135 anzusetzen, und in der Tat ist *RRH*, n° 156 vom 29. Juni, *RRH*, n° 157 vom 2. August datiert. *RRH*, n° 157 ist zwar ein Produkt der Königskanzlei, aber die anderen beiden Stücke stammen aus der Schreibstube des Hl. Grabes. *RRH*, n° 161 hat gar keine Indiktion, stammt aber eher vom Urkundenschreiber des Herrn von Byblos als aus dem Scriptorium des Hl. Grabes. In anderen Stiftsurkunden (*RRH*, n° 154 [März 15], 158) wird 1135 mit der Indiktion 12, in *RRH*, n° 166 wird 1136 am 16. November mit der Indiktion 13 verbunden. Nimmt man *stilus Pisanus* an, so stammen *RRH*, n° 154 vom 15. März 1135, das uns hier interessierende *RRH*, n° 158 von 1134 (März 25-September 23) und *RRH*, n° 166 vom 16. November 1135, wobei allerdings am 24. September vergessen wurde, die Indiktion in *RRH*, n° 154, 166 umzusetzen, was ja oft genug vorkam.

Man wird in der Annahme eines pisanisch berechneten Inkarnationsjahres hier durch den Umstand bestärkt, daß *RRH*, n° 166 von dem Schulmeister des Hl. Grabes Johannes Pisanus geschrieben wurde, den ich für identisch halte mit

---

Frühjahrsanfang beim Inkarnationsjahr als den *mos Gallicus*, also als den klassischen Jahresbeginn in den Kapetingerdiplomen zu unterstellen, was dann auch zu einer Frühjahrsindiktion hätte führen können, aber wirklich sicher ist man beim *mos Gallicus* bei Philipp II. Augustus, also erst seit 1180, während G. Tessier, *Diplomatique royale française* (Paris, 1962), S. 226f. für die beiden Ludwige davor nicht unerhebliche Skepsis ausgedrückt hat. J. Dufour, ed., *Recueil des actes de Louis VI, roi de France, 1108-1137, Chartes et diplômes relatifs à l'histoire de France*, 4 Bände (Paris, 1992-4), 3.176f. rechnet bei Ludwig VI. überwiegend mit dem Weihnachts- oder Circumcisionsstil. Da in Jerusalem bis gegen 1190 der Weihnachtsstil für das Inkarnationsjahr vorherrschend war, ist eine im Frühjahr umsetzende Indiktion dort im 12. Jh. a priori nicht zu erwarten.

[8] Beim Suffragan in Ramla kommt die pisanische Zeitrechnung in den Urkunden, wenn auch nicht durchgehend, sogar bis 1138 vor (*RRH*, n° 165, 190).

dem Subdiakon Johannes, der *RRH*, n° 154 aufsetzte[9]. *RRH*, n° 158 mag ihm dann auch zuzuweisen sein, zumal es mit dem Auftakt 'Breve recordationis conventionis et donationis' ohnehin italienische Urkundensprache aufweist. Ich datiere daher den Vergleich zwischen Maria von St. Lazarus und ihrem Schwiegersohn Bernhard (*RRH*, n° 158) auf 1134 (März 25-September 23).

Als Maria von St. Lazarus bestritt, ihrem Schwiegersohn Bernhard jemals Teile ihres Hauses auf dem Tempelplatz vermacht zu haben, mag sie bereits anderes damit vorgehabt haben. Jedenfalls kam es am 29. Juni 1135 zu einer Einigung mit dem Stift (*RRH*, n° 156). Das Stift erklärte sich bereit, Roger und Maria von St. Lazarus das Lehen zurückzuerstatten, das sie 1129 verloren hatten, als Marias Tochter es – außer für den Nießbrauch durch Maria auf Lebenszeit – an das Hl. Grab zurückgab. Möglicherweise war es also nicht rechtmäßig gewesen, das Mädchen zu dem Verzicht zu zwingen, nur weil sie einen Ehekandidaten ablehnte. Roger und Maria verpflichteten sich im Gegenzuge, innerhalb von zwei Jahren, also bis Ende Juni 1137, ihr Haus in Jerusalem zu verkaufen (an wen auch immer). Da dessen Lage 1135 nicht beschrieben wird, ist anzunehmen, daß sie nur eines in der Hauptstadt hatten, das dann identisch sein muß mit jenem auf dem Tempelplatz, über das sich Maria 1134 mit Bernhard verglichen hatte (siehe dazu auch unten S. 164). Das Interesse, welches das Hl. Grab an dem Verkauf hatte, wird klar, wenn die Urkunde fortfährt, daß Maria und Roger gehalten waren, ihre ganze Habe – also nicht nur das Haus – in Land des Hl. Grabes zu investieren, sei es in Bethanien, sei es in Jerusalem, und hierfür sollten sie liquide gemacht werden. Prawer[10] hat sicherlich recht, daß hier ein Versuch vorlag, das Ehepaar nebst seinem Besitz in das innerstädtische Patriarchenquartier umzusiedeln oder nach Bethanien, was aufs selbe herauskam, da das Hl. Grab hier wie dort die seigneuriale Herrschaft und Gerichtsbarkeit ausübte. Sollten sie diesen Verpflichtungen nicht nachkommen, so würden sie das Lehen nach zwei Jahren unwiderbringlich verlieren, ja sogar aus der Klientel des Hl. Grabes ausgestoßen ('et feodum et amicitiam domus irrecuperabiliter perderent'). Einerseits wird erneut erkennbar, daß das Lehen in Bethanien von erheblichem Ertragswert gewesen sein muß, wenn Roger und Maria hierfür ihr gesamtes Eigengut liquidisierten und beim Hl. Grab investierten, denn vom Hl. Grab würden sie natürlich abhängiges Zinsland kaufen. Andererseits wird deutlich,

---

[9] H.E. Mayer, 'Guillaume de Tyr à l'école', *Mémoires de l'Académie des sciences, arts et belles-lettres de Dijon* 127 (1985-86), S. 262f., dort noch mit den Daten 1135 und 1136 für *RRH*, n° 154, 166.

[10] *Crusader Institutions*, S. 313.

mit welch rüden Methoden das Stift Geld aus seiner Klientel herauspreßte, um den Ausbau des Patriarchenquartiers oder den ja im großen Stil betriebenen Landesausbau um Jerusalem herum zu finanzieren.

Das Haus hatte auf dem Tempelplatz eine sehr gute Lage. Dennoch war sein Ankauf ein zweifelhaftes Geschäft, denn nach dem Tode Marias und ihres Sohnes würde ja ihr Schwiegersohn Bernhard Anspruch auf die Hälfte des Hauses erheben. Zwar wurde das Haus verkauft, aber der Käufer, kein geringerer als der König Fulko, behielt es nicht lange. Im Jahre 1138 schenkte er dem Stift insgesamt zehn Häuser, um die es alle anscheinend irgendeinen Streit gegeben hatte, denn die Schenkung erfolgte 'ad removendam in perpetuum omnem calumpniam vel contradictionem seu quamlibet inquietationem omnium perversorum'. Unter den Häusern war auch dasjenige 'Rogerii fratris eorumdem canonicorum'(*RRH*, n° 181). Daß es sich dabei um Roger von St. Lazarus handelt, erfahren wir aus *RRH*, n° 309 von 1155, als der König Balduin III. es so in einer allgemeinen Besitzbestätigung für das Hl. Grab erwähnte. Weitere königliche Bestätigungen erfolgten 1160 und 1164 (*RRH*, n° 354, 400).

Vermutlich war dieses Haus, als Fulko es dem Hl. Grab schenkte, mit einem neuerlichen Rechtsstreit Bernhards behaftet, wenn Maria es dem König verkauft hatte, ohne Bernhards Rechte zu wahren. Aber es war natürlich eine Sache, wenn der Bruder des Priors vor dem Patriarchen um seine Rechte an dem Haus prozessierte, als wenn er den König in die Schranken fordern mußte. Hier waren seine Chancen wesentlich schlechter als gegen Maria, das Stift konnte ihm hier nicht viel helfen, zumal der Prior, da das Haus jetzt Eigentum des Stifts wurde, von Amts wegen gehalten war, dieses auch gegen Ansprüche seines Bruders zu verteidigen. Vielleicht war der König, der sich dies ja leisten konnte, vom Stift dazu animiert worden, generell in Jerusalem umstrittene Häuser aufzukaufen, um sie dann an das Hl. Grab zu schenken, denn bei den zehn Häusern waren auch drei, die einst Kanonikern gehört hatten, und hierbei handelte es sich offenbar um Häuser, die diese Chorherren noch immer gehabt hatten, obwohl 1114 bei der Reform des Stifts die Individualpfründen aufgelöst worden waren. Zwar hatte schon der Patriarch Arnulf bei der Refom des Stifts 1114 rebellierende Säkularkanoniker vertrieben (*RRH*, n° 75), aber durchgehend erfolgreich war er dabei nicht gewesen, denn noch 1121 nahmen der Kantor und Succentor des Hl. Grabes am gemeinsamen Leben nicht teil, sondern lebten in eigenen Häusern (*RRH*, n° 94).[11]

---

[11] P. Jaffé, *Regesta pontificum Romanorum ab condita ecclesia ad annum post Christum natum MCXCVIII*, 2. Aufl., ed. S Löwenfeld, F. Kaltenbrunner und P. Ewald, 2 Bände (Leipzig, 1885-8), n° 6923.

Nunmehr hatte das Stift das Haus, die königliche Schenkung war nicht so leicht auszuhebeln wie einst die Behauptung Marias, sie habe ihrem Schwiegersohn niemals Teile des Hauses vermacht. Aber Bernhard wird natürlich keine Ruhe gegeben haben, und wenn seine Ansprüche gewahrt wurden, dann bestand das Haus aus zwei Hälften mit ungleichem Rechtsstatus. Diesem Umstand trug das Hl. Grab 1154 Rechnung, als es sich des Hauses entäußerte (*RRH*, n° 295). Es übertrug damals das Haus von Roger und Maria von St. Lazarus, das in Jerusalem gelegen war zwischen dem Haus des Müllers Leodegar und (dem) einer gewissen Goda, 'in dextra parte platee qua itur ad Templum', an einen gewissen Benscelinus, der der Ehemann eben jener Nachbarin Goda war. Damit sollten alle Prozesse als erledigt gelten, die zwischen Goda und Benscelinus einerseits und dem Stift andererseits anhängig waren wegen des Landes und des Weinbergs und des gesamten Lehens, das Goda und ihre Vorfahren in St. Lazarus (Bethanien) innehatten. Hier erfahren wir nun endlich den Namen jenes standhaften Mädchens, das 25 Jahre zuvor den ihr angebotenen Bräutigam zurückwies und lieber auf ihr Lehen verzichtet hatte, ja eher betteln zu gehen gedroht hatte, als die projektierte Ehe einzugehen. Es ist dies keine andere als Goda, die Tochter Marias von St. Lazarus aus deren erster Ehe, die zwischen 1129 und 1134 Bernhard geheiratet hatte. Jetzt, mehr als 20 Jahre später, war dieser Bernhard tot, und Goda war wiederverheiratet mit Benscelinus. Dieser, 1134 Bentulinus geheißen (*RRH*, n° 158), war schon damals der Nachbar von Marias Mutter auf dem Tempelplatz gewesen und dürfte in dieser bevorzugten Lage jetzt zwei Häuser gehabt haben, nämlich seines von 1134 und das seiner Frau von 1154, vielleicht sogar drei, denn in *RRH*, n° 158 ist die Rede von dem Haus des Bentulinus sowie demjenigen von Roger und Maria, also von Godas Eltern, in *RRH*, n° 295 liest man von dem Haus Rogers und Marias, daneben aber auch von einem angrenzenden Haus Godas, das nicht notwendigerweise dasjenige war, das 1134 ihr Mann Bentulinus dort besessen hatte, es sei denn, er habe es ihr bei der Hochzeit als Wittum überschrieben. Letzteres ist allerdings um so wahrscheinlicher, als Goda 1135 auf dem Tempelplatz anscheinend nur ein einziges Haus besessen hatte (siehe oben S. 162).

Goda muß als Bernhards Witwe die ganze Serie von Rechtsgeschäften angefochten haben, mit denen zwischen 1135 und 1138 das Haus erst an den König, dann an das Stift gekommen war (*RRH*, n° 156, 181). Ihre Rechtsbasis mußte dabei der Vergleich *RRH*, n° 158 von 1134 sein, denn dieser hatte ihrem ersten Mann Bernhard das halbe Haus als Erbgut zugesichert, die andere Hälfte hätte Goda beim Tode Marias und Rogers von St. Lazarus geerbt, wenn ihre Mutter und ihr Stiefvater nicht zwischen 1135 und 1137 an den König verkauft hätten. Ihr zweiter Mann konnte Goda bei diesen Prozessen einschlägig beraten, denn 1149-1150 war er Vizegraf von Jerusalem gewesen[12].

In dem neuerlichen Vergleich *RRH*, nᵒ 295 mußte Goda, wie dies in der Natur von Vergleichen liegt, auch Federn lassen. Zunächst ist über das Lehen in Bethanien nichts ausgesagt. Maria hatte 1135 ein Versprechen des Stifts erhalten, daß sie es zurückbekommen würde, wenn sie in Jerusalem ihr Haus verkauft und den Erlös in Land des Hl. Grabs investiert habe, und vor Sommer 1138 war dieser Teil des Handels abgewickelt (*RRH*, nᵒ 156, 181), ja er hatte bis Ende Juni 1137 abgewickelt zu sein, andernfalls Maria das Lehen nicht erhalten werde. Man darf davon ausgehen, daß Maria diese Frist gewahrt hatte.

Aber am 5. Februar 1138 erwarb der König in *RRH*, nᵒ 174 vom Hl. Grab im Tauschwege die Kirche von St. Lazarus (Bethanien), und das bedeutet natürlich auch das zu der Kirche gehörende Land, um damit das Doppelkloster Bethanien zu gründen, was dann 1143 erfolgte[13]. Man muß davon ausgehen, daß ein Lehensland in Bethanien, das einst vom Hl. Grab vergeben worden war, später den dortigen Nonnen gehörte, und so ist es durchaus plausibel, daß 1154 in *RRH*, nᵒ 295 seitens des Hl. Grabs wie auch von Seiten Godas über dieses Lehen nichts mehr bestimmt ist. Goda hatte insoweit nur noch mit dem Kloster Bethanien zu tun, dessen Urkunden verloren sind. Es war natürlich völlig zweifelhaft, ob die dortigen Nonnen in die Abmachungen zwischen Godas Mutter Maria und dem Hl. Grab von 1135 einsteigen würden. Wenn ja, dann hatte Goda ihr Lehen jetzt vom Kloster Bethanien inne, so daß in·*RRH*, nᵒ 295 hierüber nur gesagt werden konnte, daß Goda und ihre Vorfahren es einmal hatten. Weder wird gesagt, daß sie es vom Hl. Grab hatten, noch werden irgendwelche Verfügungen darüber getroffen. Dies alles war jetzt nicht mehr in der Verfügungsgewalt des Hl. Grabs.

Das Lehen war aber, wie ausdrücklich gesagt wird, ein Teil der Klage Godas gegen die Grabeskirche. Man muß daher vermuten, daß die Nonnen es ihr verweigert hatten, schon weil sie von Marias einstiger Gegenleistung von 1135 nicht profitiert hatten, denn diese war einzig an das Chorherrenstift gegangen. In diesem Falle war Goda aber berechtigt, Ersatzansprüche gegen das Hl. Grab zu betreiben. Dazu scheint es nicht gekommen zu sein, weil das Hl. Grab

---

[12] *RRH*, nᵒ 255, 259. Siehe auch H.E. Mayer, 'Die Herrschaftsbildung in Hebron', *Zeitschrift des Deutschen Palästina–Vereins* 101 (1985), S. 70 Anm. 35.
[13] H.E. Mayer, *Bistümer, Klöster und Stifte im Königreich Jerusalem, MGH Schriften* 26 (Stuttgart, 1977), S. 372–402, zu ergänzen durch H.E. Mayer, 'Fontevrault und Bethanien: Kirchliches Leben in Anjou und Jerusalem im 12. Jahrhundert', *Zeitschrift für Kirchengeschichte* 102 (1991), S. 14–41.

durchsetzte, daß Goda alle Klagen, auch die über das Lehen, zurücknahm, dafür aber das wertvolle Haus auf dem Tempelplatz bekam, das seit 1138 dem Hl. Grab gehörte, auf dessen Hälfte aber Godas verstorbener erster Mann Bernhard seit 1134 (*RRH*, n° 158) Ansprüche gehabt hatte, die bei seinem Tode im Erbwege auf Goda übergegangen waren.

Die einst Bernhard zugesichert gewesene Hälfte des Hauses erhielt Goda vom Hl. Grab als freies Eigen. Jene Hälfte, die Maria gehört hatte, ohne mit Ansprüchen Bernhards belastet zu sein, erhielt Goda allerdings nicht zu freiem Eigen, denn dieser Hausteil war ja durchaus rechtmäßig von Maria über den König an die Grabeskirche übergegangen. Hierfür mußte Goda dem Stift deshalb jährlich zu Ostern einen Zins von 4 Byzantinern zahlen[14], und das Stift bekam außerdem ein Vorkaufsrecht und konnte in jeden projektierten zulässigen Verkauf der zinsbelasteten Haushälfte für eine Mark Silber weniger als der prospektive Käufer eintreten. Den Jahreszins mußten Goda und ihre Erben dem Stift auch im Verkaufsfalle weiterentrichten, er ging nicht an den Käufer über. Hinsichtlich der anderen Hälfte des Hauses muß Goda natürlich geltend gemacht haben, daß sie – wären Bernhards Rechte beim Verkauf an den König nicht ignoriert worden – diese Hälfte ererbt hätte, als ihr erster Mann Bernhard starb. Deshalb erhielt sie diese Hälfte jetzt zu freiem Eigen ohne irgendwelche Belastung[15].

Wir stehen jetzt im Jahr 1154 und haben die Geschichte dieses Besitzkomplexes durch ein Vierteljahrhundert verfolgt, seit vor 1129 Petrus von Sankt Lazarus starb, und dies durch zwei Ehen der Mutter Maria sowie ein geplatztes Heiratsprojekt und zwei Ehen der Tochter Goda hindurch. Wir haben gesehen, wie der Besitz von Maria als Altersversorgung eingesetzt wurde und um die Tochter an den Mann zu bringen, und wie Maria, aber auch Goda, immer wieder gegen das Chorherrenstift vom Hl. Grab zu kämpfen hatten, das den Besitz als Druckmittel einsetzte, um eine ihm genehme Heirat innerhalb der eigenen Klientel zustandezubringen und auch, um diese in seiner eigenen Grundherrschaft anzusiedeln, sei es im innerstädtischen Patriarchenquartier, sei es in Bethanien vor der Gründung des dortigen Doppelklosters. Es ist ein

---

[14] In einem Zinsverzeichnis von Häusern in Jerusalem aus der zweiten Hälfte des 12. Jahrhunderts wird dieser Zins erwähnt: 'In vico Templi ... dame Gode IV b'; *RRH*, n° 421.

[15] Ob und wie die Angelegenheit sich weiterentwickelte, wissen wir nicht, denn Benscelinus ist nach 1154 gar nicht, Goda nur in dem Zinsverzeichnis aus der zweiten Hälfte des 12. Jahrhunderts erwähnt, das den Rechtsstand von 1154 widerspiegelt, und von gemeinsamen Kindern Godas mit ihren beiden Ehemännern verlautet nichts. Um 1165 endet dann auch, von wenigen Nachträgen abgesehen, das Kopialbuch des Chorherrenstifts, in dem ein Fortgang hätte verzeichnet sein müssen.

interessanter Fall, der tiefe Einblicke in die Fortune einer bourgeoisen Familie von Jerusalem ermöglicht. So war das tägliche Leben, denn um einen Ausnahmefall handelte es sich gewiß nicht.

The *Livre des Assises* by John of Jaffa: The Development and Transmission of the Text

Peter W. Edbury

John of Ibelin, count of Jaffa, was one of the greatest noblemen in the Latin East in the mid-thirteenth century. Indeed, during the two decades which preceded his death in 1266 he was part of the small coterie of closely related aristocrats that dominated the truncated kingdom of Jerusalem. John's father, Philip of Ibelin, had acted as regent of Cyprus for most of the 1220s, and his uncle, John of Ibelin, lord of Beirut, had led the opposition to the emperor, Frederick II, and his supporters in Cyprus and Latin Syria between 1228 and 1236. The Ibelins were closely related by marriage to the royal houses of both Cyprus and Jerusalem, and John of Jaffa, who was born c. 1215, inherited property in both kingdoms. In the years 1232-33 he was just old enough to be a participant in the closing stages of the civil war in Cyprus against the emperor's partisans, but his greatest prominence began in about 1246 when he acquired the county of Jaffa. It has been suggested that he obtained it as part of a deal which opened the way for the then king of Cyprus, Henry I, to take control in Acre — at that time by far the wealthiest city in Christian hands in the Levant. As count of Jaffa, John was responsible for the most southerly Christian-held territory in the Latin East. He himself briefly held the regency of the kingdom of Jerusalem (1254-56), and in 1258 he intervened decisively in the War of St Sabas, fought between the Genoese and the Venetians in and around Acre, by bringing the authorities there firmly over to the side of the Venetians. His marriage to an Armenian princess also involved him in the politics of Cilician Armenia, and his illicit relationship with the widowed queen of Cyprus around 1260 was sufficiently notorious to earn him a rebuke from Pope Urban IV. There is some reason to suppose that his pre-eminence faded in the last few years of his life. Jaffa itself fell to the Muslims in 1268, two years after his death.[1]

In the mid-1260s, not long before he died, John composed a treatise on the procedures of the High Court of Jerusalem and the customary law of the kingdom.[2] He wrote in French, and his treatise together with some other similar though shorter works by his contemporaries, Philip of Novara and Geoffrey Le Tor, and by his son, James of Ibelin, comprise a major source for our understanding of the social and legal fabric of the Latin East. Rather misleadingly these works are usually known collectively as the '*Assises* of Jerusalem'. John's treatise continued to be copied and modified in Cyprus after the fall of Latin Syria in 1291, and in 1369 a version of his work was adopted as an official work of reference in the Cypriot High Court. It retained its importance long after, and in 1531 the Venetian authorities in Cyprus had it translated into Italian.[3]

The text of John's treatise has been published twice. The earlier edition by G. Thaumas de la Thaumasière appeared in 1690 and was taken from a late and very corrupt manuscript copy.[4] The edition still used by modern scholars was prepared for publication by Comte A. Beugnot and appeared in 1841 in the first volume of the *Recueil des historiens des croisades: Lois*. The manuscript tradition was elucidated by Maurice Grandclaude in an article published in 1926.[5] In this article Grandclaude exposed the inadequacies of Beugnot's edition, but until now no one has taken up the challenge to examine the manuscripts further and set about preparing a critical edition.

---

[1] J. Riley-Smith, *The Feudal Nobility and the Kingdom of Jerusalem, 1174-1277* (London, 1973), chapters 7-8 passim. For a debate over particular aspects of his career, see P.W. Edbury, 'John of Ibelin's Title to the County of Jaffa and Ascalon', *English Historical Review* 98 (1983), pp. 115-22; H.E. Mayer, 'John of Jaffa, his Opponents and his Fiefs', *Proceedings of the American Philosophical Society* 128 (1984), pp. 134-63.

[2] For the date, M. Grandclaude, *Étude critique sur les livres des assises de Jérusalem* (Paris, 1923), p. 88.

[3] Grandclaude, *Étude critique*, pp. 82-3.

[4] G. Thaumas de la Thaumasière, ed., *Coustumes de Beauvoisis, par Messire Philippes de Beaumanoir Bailly de Clermont en Beauvoisis. Assises et bons usages du royaume de Jerusalem, par Messire Jean d'Ibelin Comte de Japhe et de Ascalon, S. de Rames et de Baruth* (Bourges, 1690). For the inadequacies of the text as published in 1690, see P.W. Edbury, 'The Disputed Regency of the Kingdom of Jerusalem, 1264/6 and 1268', in *Camden Miscellany* 27, *Camden Fourth Series* 22 (London, 1979), pp. 2-3.

[5] M. Grandclaude, 'Classement sommaire des manuscrits des principaux livres des assises de Jérusalem', *Revue historique de droit français et étranger*, sér. 4, 5 (1926), pp. 418-75.

Five medieval manuscripts of John's treatise survive, and these five manuscripts will form the basis for a modern edition:

(1) Paris, Bibliothèque Nationale (BN): ms. fr. 19025 (= Beugnot's manuscript C)

(2) Oxford, Bodleian: Selden Supra 69 (not used by Beugnot)

(3) Venice, Marciana: fr. app. 20 (= 265) (not used by Beugnot who used an eighteenth-century copy as his manuscript A)

(4) Paris, Bibliothèque Nationale (BN): ms. fr. 19026 (= Beugnot's manuscript B)

(5) Rome, Vatican: Codex Vaticanus latinus 4789 (not used by Beugnot who used corrupt seventeenth-century derivatives as his manuscripts D and E).

Each manuscript is unique, with no two preserving an identical text. All contain material added after John of Jaffa had laid down his pen. Beugnot's printed edition reproduces more or less the text as found in the Marciana manuscript, but, as will be seen, that manuscript contains a version of the text that stands mid-way in its development.

The oldest manuscript is the BN 19025, which was copied in Acre in the 1280s.[6] The manuscript contains solely John's treatise, and the text would seem to be the closest we can get to his original. But even this manuscript, copied perhaps no more than a decade and a half after his death, contains at least one interpolation. Sandwiched between the chapters which in Beugnot's edition are numbered 143 and 144 there is a passage lifted from Philip of Novara's treatise. It appears in no other John of Jaffa manuscript, but is of considerable interest.[7] In Philip's version of this passage there is mention of John of Jaffa himself, and in the BN 19025 the phrase is recast into the first person: it reads 'je meismes m'en entremis moult' for 'moult s'en entremist le conte de Jaffe'. This immediately raises the question of whether John himself was responsible for this insertion. It is quite likely that he was. Elsewhere there is another chapter taken from Philip of Novara which appears in a modified

---

[6] P.W. Edbury and J. Folda, 'Two Thirteenth-Century Manuscripts of Crusader Legal Texts from Saint-Jean d'Acre', *Journal of the Warburg and Courtauld Institutes* 57 (1994), pp. 250, 253-4 and plate 32.

[7] BN 19025, chapter 129/fol. 105ᵛ. This chapter consists of approximately three-quarters of Philip of Novara's chapter 73 ('Livre de forme de plait', *RHC Lois*, 1.543-4 [hereafter Philip of Novara]). One manuscript of Philip's treatise has a chapter-break where the chapter ends in John of Jaffa. Munich, Bayerische Staatsbibliothek: ms. cod. gall. 771, fols 133ᵛ-135ᵛ.

form in all the manuscripts of John of Jaffa's law book.[8] It must therefore
have been inserted at a very early stage in the transmission of the text and
indeed was probably part of John's original version.

The Selden manuscript in the Bodleian Library in Oxford is datable to the
fourteenth century and is of Cypriot provenance. In the sixteenth century it
belonged to Francesco Attar, a member of the commission set up by the
Venetian authorities in Cyprus to arrange the translation of John's treatise into
Italian.[9] The text is very close to that in the BN 19025; indeed, of all the
medieval manuscripts, these two are by far the closest. It lacks the chapter
from Philip of Novara found in the BN 19025 that refers to John of Jaffa, but
instead it contains another chapter from Philip's work which is not found
elsewhere in the manuscripts of John's law book.[10] Incidentally there is one
other chapter common to both these first two manuscripts, but not found in any
of the others. It concerns trial by battle in disputes over debt.[11]

The Marciana manuscript is really rather special. This is a large and lavishly
produced codex which consists of two separate sections. The first, which starts
with John of Jaffa's treatise, contains a fine miniature which is undoubtedly the
work of the artist Professor Folda rather unhelpfully dubbed the 'Hospitaller
Master' and who was probably at work in Acre from around 1276 until its fall
in 1291.[12] This manuscript — or rather this section of the manuscript — seems
to date to c. 1290, and it contains besides John's treatise, his discourse on the

---

[8] John of Ibelin, 'Livre des Assises de la Haute Cour', *RHC Lois*, 1, chapter 155/pp. 232-5
[hereafter John of Ibelin]; Philip of Novara, chapter 29/pp. 503-6.

[9] Grandclaude, 'Classement sommaire', pp. 456-8. There are various reports on population
and other information about Cyprus in the sixteenth century attributed to Francesco Attar. See
B. Arbel, 'Cypriot Population under Venetian Rule (1473-1571): A Demographic Study',
Meletai kai Ipomnimata 1 (1984), pp. 194-5.

[10] Selden Supra 69, fol. 30^{r-v}. It is placed between chapters 44 and 45 of Beugnot's edition
of John's text, and is Philip of Novara, chapter 48/p. 523.

[11] BN 19025, fols 207^v-209^r; Selden Supra 69, fols 289^r-291^v. It is not published by Beugnot.
Grandclaude ('Classement sommaire', p. 441 n. 5) errs in claiming that it is John of Ibelin,
chapter 250 *bis*/pp. 401-2, although the rubric is very similar. A marginal note in the Selden
ms. asserts that it is taken from Philip of Novara, but I have not found it there.

[12] Edbury and Folda, 'Two Thirteenth-Century Manuscripts', pp. 243-9, 250-3 and plate 31
which reproduces the miniature which shows Godfrey of Bouillon standing in the city of
Jerusalem presenting the laws of the kingdom to the assembled notables. For the 'Hospitaller
Master', see J. Folda, *Crusader Manuscript Illumination at Saint-Jean d'Acre, 1275-1291*
(Princeton, 1976), chapters 3-4.

regency of Jerusalem, the 'A' text of Geoffrey Le Tor,[13] the treatise by John's son, James of Ibelin, which was written in 1276, the earlier recension of the *Lignages d'Outremer* which appears to have been compiled in the 1270s, a short treatise on trial by battle which until recently was believed to belong to the mid-fourteenth century, and the pleading between King Hugh III of Cyprus and James of Ibelin in the dispute of 1271 as to whether the knights of Cyprus owed service outside the island. The second part of the Marciana manuscript would appear to have been copied in Cyprus towards the middle of the fourteenth century and contains five other texts including Philip of Novara's law book and the so called *Abrégé du livre des assises de la cour des bourgeois*. The text of John's treatise in this manuscript contains a substantial number of interpolations scattered through it. The most obvious category of these additions comprises passages copied or adapted from Philip of Novara, including much of the material which makes up the final chapter in Beugnot's edition of John of Jaffa, a chapter which is absent from both the manuscripts discussed in the previous paragraphs. In all there are about a dozen chapters as well as shorter extracts taken from Philip of Novara. In other words, the phenomenon that we have seen already in the earlier versions is here continued on a much larger scale.[14] Two particular aspects of this material are worth noting. The sole reference in Beugnot's edition of John of Jaffa to the *Letres dou Sepulcre* is introduced at this stage from Philip of Novara's treatise with the result that the apparent unanimity of the two writers on this question proves to be a chimera. I have argued elsewhere that the *Letres dou Sepulcre* were a piece of mid-thirteenth-century legal fiction designed to protect Latin Syrian

---

[13] For Geoffrey Le Tor and his writings, see P.W. Edbury, 'The *Livre* of Geoffrey Le Tor and the *Assises* of Jerusalem', in *Historia administrativa y ciencia de la administración comparada*, ed. M.J. Pelaez, *Trabaios en homenaje a Ferran Valls i Taberner* 15 (Barcelona, 1990), pp. 4291-8.

[14] In the following list the chapters in the text of John of Jaffa's treatise either copy the chapters from Philip of Novara's treatise or employ material adapted from it. John, chapter 4 = Philip, chapter 47; John, chapters 38-40 = Philip, chapter 11; John, chapter 69 = Philip, chapter 18 (the text of Philip of Novara in the Munich, Bayerische Staatsbibliothek: ms. cod. gall. 771, fols 83ᵛ-84ᵛ gives the entire chapter as it appears in John's treatise, whereas the published edition of Philip of Novara (at pp. 492-3) has only about half); John, chapter 158 = Philip, chapter 30; John, chapter 170 = Philip, chapters 20-2; John, chapter 199 = Philip, chapter 51; John, chapter 209 = Philip, chapter 37; John, chapter 210 = Philip, chapter 39; John, chapter 238 = Philip, chapter 35; John, chapter 239 = Philip, chapter 38; John, chapter 247 = Philip, chapter 62; John, chapter 273 = Philip, chapter 94.

practice from being overridden by arguments from French customary law.[15] Secondly, in one of these passages where Philip refers to John of Ibelin, the Old Lord of Beirut (died 1236), the John of Jaffa text refers to him in the way John normally does – as 'my uncle, the Old Lord of Beirut' – and the author alludes to himself in the first person.[16] This raises various questions: was John of Jaffa himself responsible for including this passage in this version of his treatise? If so, had he revised his work so as to include all the other passages and extracts that are in the Marciana manuscript but not in the BN 19025 or the Selden Supra 69? Alternatively, has a later redactor inserted these passages and been rather clever in adapting the allusion to John of Beirut to bring it into line with the other instances in which he appears in the treatise? If John himself revised the work to include this new material, he must have done so very soon after the completion of the first version as represented by the BN 19025 and the Selden Supra 69. The Marciana manuscript, though copied c. 1290, would thus contain a text that had been in existence since the mid-1260s. On the other hand, if the new material was added by someone else, then there are two and half decades in which this could have happened. As has been noted, several of the other texts in this part of the manuscript date from the 1270s. Maybe these revisions date from that period too, in which case we might wonder whether John's son, James of Ibelin, had some part in them.

But there are other additions in the Marciana version of John of Jaffa's treatise that are not from Philip of Novara and which I have not been able to identify. Chapter 130 deals with debt; chapters 193-4 deal with oaths due to the king or regent; chapter 228 discusses aspects of *servise de mariage* – the lord's rights to oblige heiresses to marry; and chapters 251-5 consider the subject of serfs. Clearly there was an awareness that, long though it was, John's original treatise had not discussed everything, and so someone – perhaps John himself, perhaps his son James, perhaps another person altogether – felt free to add texts culled from elsewhere, in particular from the treatise by Philip of Novara, or to include new material. Perhaps these interpolations warrant special attention as concerning matters that people may have considered important. But in connection with Philip of Novara, there is another point that is worth making. The BN 19025 and the Marciana manuscript both date from the closing decades of the thirteenth century; they are thus

---

[15] P.W. Edbury, 'Law and Custom in the Latin East: *Les Letres dou Sepulcre*', *Mediterranean Historical Review* 10 (1995), pp. 71-9.

[16] John of Ibelin, chapter 239/pp. 383-4 left-hand column; Philip of Novara, chapter 38/pp. 515-16. For John of Beirut as the author's uncle, John of Ibelin, pp. 112, 325, 327.

appreciably older than any manuscript copy of Philip of Novara's work (two mid-fourteenth-century manuscripts and one early seventeenth-century manuscript),[17] and so the interpolations drawn from there would be of the utmost importance in the preparation of any new edition of Philip's treatise – itself a subject that is both strewn with difficulties and at the same time a major desideratum.

Like the Marciana manuscript, the BN 19026 contains several works: part of the *Livre des assises de la cour des bourgeois*, the *Lignages d'Outremer*, James of Ibelin, the 'B' text of Geoffrey Le Tor, Philip of Novara and the *Livre au Roi*. It appears to date from the mid-fourteenth century and is probably from Cyprus.[18] The text it gives of John of Jaffa's treatise is best thought of as a development from the text found in the Marciana manuscript. It has grown even longer, with eleven more chapters, of which six were not printed by Beugnot in his edition of John of Jaffa.[19] Some are lifted from other extant writings: Philip of Novara yet again, Geoffrey Le Tor and the *Assises de la cour de bourgeois*.[20] Others I am unable to identify. Maybe they were composed by the redactor of the version preserved in this manuscript. Perhaps the most interesting are two chapters outlining the moral qualities that are expected of a ruler with references to Aristotle and Cicero.[21] But despite their intrinsic interest, these chapters seem far removed from the twin subjects of John's treatise: the law and procedures of the High Court.

Finally we come to the text preserved in the Vatican manuscript. This is a fifteenth-century codex containing John's law book together with an early fourteenth-century version of the *Lignages d'Outremer* and some other, later accretions. It starts with a prologue explaining how John's treatise was revised

---

[17] Grandclaude, 'Classement sommaire', pp. 459-60, 467-71; Edbury and Folda, 'Two Thirteenth-Century Manuscripts', p. 244.

[18] Grandclaude, 'Classement sommaire', pp. 459-60.

[19] Published by Beugnot: John of Ibelin, chapters 176 *bis*, 226 *bis* (where 'manuscrit C' is an error for 'manuscrit B'), 234 *bis*, 250 *bis*, 250 *ter*/pp. 277-9, 358-9, 372, 401-3. Not published by Beugnot: BN 19026, chapters 9, 240, 254, 257, 265, 266.

[20] BN 19026, chapter 9 = 'Livre des assises de la cour des bourgeois', *RHC Lois*, 2, chapter 2/p. 20; BN 19026, chapter 240 = Philip of Novara, chapters 32-4 and the beginning of 35/pp. 508-12; BN 19026, chapter 257 = Geoffrey Le Tor, 'Livre', *RHC Lois*, 1, chapter 16/p. 449; BN 19026, chapter 258 = Philip of Novara, chapter 92/pp. 564-7. The BN 19026 also has a fuller version of Philip of Novara, chapters 20-22 than in the printed text at chapter 170/pp. 261-2.

[21] BN 19026, chapters 125-6/fols 206ʳ-207ʳ. These chapters were printed by G. Thaumas de la Thaumasière (above note 4) from a manuscript derived from the Vaticanus latinus 4789 at pp. 187-8.

and established as a work of reference in the High Court of Cyprus following the murder of King Peter I in January 1369. The clear implication is that this is a copy of that revision. It contains embedded within it the text of the *bailliage* pleading from the 1260s and the formal claim for the throne advanced by King Hugh IV of Cyprus in 1324.[22] The *Lignages d'Outremer* is similarly treated as an integral part of the text. Comparing the text with that of the Marciana and BN 19026 manuscripts we find that, while it is broadly similar, there are some new additions, several of which can be identified as coming from Philip of Novara, James of Ibelin, Geoffrey Le Tor or the *Livre au Roi*.[23] Three of the eleven chapters found in the BN 19026 but not in the Marciana manuscript are omitted.[24] How many of these additional chapters were introduced in 1369 and how many were already in the text or texts that were being employed at that time is unknowable. Of the unidentified additions, there is one that is of especial interest in the light of an earlier aspect of this discussion: a chapter that is unique to this version of John of Jaffa's treatise again refers to John of Ibelin, lord of Beirut, as 'my uncle'.[25] It is impossible to know what to make of this addition or when it first appeared in a text of the treatise: there is no particular reason to believe that it was new in 1369. The genealogical information in the *Lignages* stops dead in the first decade of the fourteenth century, and it may be wondered whether some of the other additions or modifications belong rather to that period than to 1369. How the text as preserved in the Vaticanus latinus 4789 fared as an official work of reference is not at all clear: when, in 1531, the Venetians decided that they wanted an Italian translation prepared they appear to have been unaware of this version and relied instead on the manuscript now in Venice.

Perhaps the most obvious point to be made by way of conclusion is that in its original form John of Jaffa's law book was not nearly as similar in content

---

[22] The 1260s *bailliage* pleading has been re-edited from the Vaticanus latinus 4789 in Edbury, 'Disputed Regency' (see note 4). For Hugh IV's accession, see *RHC Lois*, 2.419-22. The Vaticanus latinus 4789 also includes the texts published as 'Bans et Ordonnances des rois de Chypre', *RHC Lois*, 2, nos. 25, 31, 33/pp. 368-70, 373-7, 378-9 [hereafter 'Bans et Ordonnances']. No. 33 should be dated 16 January 1368 (i.e. 1369 n.s.).

[23] Vaticanus latinus 4789, chapter 265 is adapted from James of Ibelin, 'Livre', *RHC Lois*, 1, chapter 62/p. 467; the opening of chapter 266 comes from Philip of Novara, chapter 30/p. 507; chapter 273 = 'Livre au Roi', *RHC Lois*, 1, chapter 21/p. 620; chapters 283-4 = James of Ibelin, chapter 1/pp. 453-4.

[24] BN 19026, chapters 9, 177 (= John of Ibelin, chapter 176 *bis*/pp. 277-9), 237 (= John of Ibelin, chapter 234 *bis*/p. 372).

[25] John of Ibelin, chapter 63 *bis*/p. 103.

and style to Philip of Novara's as is usually assumed. It should also be realized that John of Jaffa wrote appreciably less than might be imagined from using the standard edition of his work. The text as given in the Vaticanus latinus is around 25-30% longer than in the earliest manuscript, the BN 19025. After the original version had been composed, the work was modified, largely by inter-polations from other works. Where there is new material which cannot be identified, it could be that we are seeing fragments of a lost treatise or treatises, or it may be that the redactor has written something new. The additions, and also the changes in chapter divisions – not a subject which is necessary to discuss here – and the chapters which only appear in one or perhaps two manuscripts and are then lost to view suggest that the five manuscripts that survive from the middle ages represent only a tiny proportion of the whole and a plethora of different texts had once existed. Were another manuscript to come to light, it might well have a version that is different again. Identifying the provenance of the interpolations is all very well, but there is another, as yet unexplored, dimension to the problem: how far do the modifications to the text represent changes in the law or the customary procedures? As with modern law text-books that go through numerous editions, so changes to the text may, in certain instances, reflect changes to the law. Law is not static, and, in the absence of other evidence, a line-by-line, chapter-by-chapter analysis may produce indications of legislation and changes to legal custom in the century between the mid-1260s and the death of Peter I of Cyprus in 1369. This is a matter for future study. If the book was to be of practical use to lawyers, then we might expect to find it brought up to date by subsequent generations. But was it? The decision to make it an official work of reference in Cyprus in 1369, and the decision to have it translated into Italian in 1531 suggest that the answer is yes. On the other hand, the manu-scripts do not have the sort of marginal annotations we might expect to find if practitioners in the courts were utilizing them in preparing their pleas. Moreover, some of the accretions seem to betray an interest in constitutional and genealogical rather than legal matters and so add an antiquarian flavour to the work. Antiquaries in France in the seventeenth century such as Peiresc sought out copies of the work; maybe even earlier it was valued more for its intellectual stimulus and historical information than for its utility in the courts – but that is another topic for another occasion.

Appendix

This discussion has highlighted the need for a new edition of John of Jaffa's treatise, but until such time as one is forthcoming historians will have to continue using Beugnot's text in the *Recueil des historiens des croisades: Lois*. These notes are designed to help readers find their way round that edition in the light of what has been said.

There are some variations in the order the chapters appear in the manuscripts, and in some instances chapters have been divided or run together. I shall not attempt to list these variants, and in any case they are probably of little significance.

1) Beugnot used a copy made from the Marciana manuscript as his base (ms. A). This means that his edition, excluding the chapters that he numbered *bis* or *ter* (e.g. 63 *bis,* 250 *ter*), gives a close representation of the Marciana text.

2) The earlier form of John's treatise is represented by the BN 19025 and the Selden manuscripts. These two manuscripts give an almost identical text except for the two single additions from Philip of Novara described above (notes 7 and 10). Neither of these chapters is included in Beugnot's edition of John's treatise. Beugnot used the BN 19025 as his ms. C, and the chapters that were added subsequently are usually indicated by the .words 'manque dans C' in the apparatus. They are Beugnot's chapters 38-40, 69, 130, 158, 165, 170, 193-4, 199, 209-10, 228, 238-9, 247, 251-5, 273 together with all the chapters numbered *bis* or *ter*. For an example of a shorter omitted passage (dealing with the *Letres dou Sepulcre*), see John of Ibelin, p. 25 n. 42. There is one chapter in these two manuscripts that is not published by Beugnot and is not found in the other manuscripts (above note 11).

3) The version in the BN 19026 (Beugnot's ms. B) marks a development of the Marciana text though lacks Beugnot's chapter 69. It does however contain chapter 2 of the *Assises de la cour des bourgeois* sandwiched between Beugnot's chapters 8 and 9; chapters 32-4 and the beginning of chapter 35 of Philip of Novara (between chapters 236 and 237); chapter 16 of the 'B' text of Geoffrey Le Tor and chapter 92 of Philip of Novara (immediately before chapter 251). In addition it contains the chapters numbered by Beugnot as 176 *bis,* 226 *bis,* 234 *bis,* 250 *bis* and 250 *ter*. Two chapters which appear immediately before Beugnot's chapter 256 are not printed by

Beugnot, but are to be found in la Thaumasière's edition (see above note 21).

4) Beugnot did not use the Vaticanus latinus 4789, but he did have two manuscripts (D and E) as well as la Thaumasière's edition (T) which were derived from it. Those texts are seriously defective, with substantial omissions; in consequence, the words in Beugnot's apparatus, 'manque dans DET', are of no help in establishing what the Vaticanus latinus 4789 contains or does not contain. The Vaticanus latinus 4789 lacks Beugnot's chapters 130, 176 *bis*, 193, 234 *bis*, as well as the chapter from the *Assises de la cour des bourgeois* found in the BN 19026. Otherwise it contains all the material in the BN 19026. It alone of the medieval manuscripts contains the following chapters: 63 *bis*, 127 *bis*, 170 *bis*, 172 *bis*. There is also a short chapter printed by Beugnot in his apparatus (John of Ibelin, p. 128). Sandwiched between Beugnot's chapters 225 and 226 there is an unpublished chapter on the subject of summonses to court. Between Beugnot's chapters 247 and 248 there is a chapter taken from James of Ibelin (chapter 62) and a much expanded version of Philip of Novara (chapter 30). After Beugnot's chapter 249 there is a chapter from the *Livre au Roi* (chapter 21). Immediately before Beugnot's chapter 194 (itself re-positioned later in the text) there are two chapters derived from the first chapter of James of Ibelin's treatise. There is a substantial body of material inserted between Beugnot's chapters 259 (the office of the chamberlain) and 260 (the start of the account of the ecclesiastical hierarchy in Jerusalem). This consists of: (i) the texts from the 1260s edited by Beugnot as 'Documents relatifs à la successibilité au trône et à la régence', *RHC Lois*, 2, chapters 3-17/pp. 401-19 and for which a modern edition exists (see above note 22); (ii) an ordinance of 1311 (1310 o.s.) from Cyprus published as 'Bans et Ordonnances', no. 25/pp. 368-70; (iii) Hugh IV's claim to the throne of Cyprus, 1324: 'Documents relatifs à la successibilité', chapter 18/pp. 419-22; (iv) ordinances of 1355 and 1369, also from Cyprus: 'Bans et Ordonnances', nos. 31, 33/pp. 373-7, 378-9. At the end of the text the recension of the *Lignages d'Outremer* dating from the 1300s follows without a break and with continuous chapter numbers (chapters 331-61).

Les évêques de Chypre et la Chambre apostolique: un arrêt de compte de 1369

Jean Richard

L'Archivio segreto Vaticano conserve, sous la cote *Instrumenta miscellanea* 2469, un cahier de papier qui n'est sans doute que la dernière partie d'un document plus étendu, lequel serait le compte de la collectorie de Chypre pour les années 1364-68. Il fait suite à celui rendu par le collecteur Pierre *Domandi*, couvrant les années 1357-63, que nous avons eu l'occasion d'éditer.[1] Pierre, qui avait quitté Chypre, avait été remplacé en qualité de nonce et collecteur par Bérenger Grégoire, associé comme son prédécesseur à Thomas Foscarini: le premier, alors doyen du chapitre de Nicosie, devait devenir archevêque de ce siège en 1376, et le second, archidiacre de Nicosie, mourut en 1372. Ce document constitue l'arrêt de leur compte, présentant l'état des sommes dont ils étaient redevables envers la Chambre apostolique, et son intérêt est de nous révéler quelles difficultés rencontraient les agents de la fiscalité pontificale dans le petit royaume insulaire au moment où celui-ci venait d'être engagé par la politique du roi Pierre Ier dans une guerre avec le sultan mamelûk du Caire.[2]

Le document commence ainsi:

---

[1] J. Richard, 'Les comptes du collecteur de la Chambre apostolique dans le royaume de Chypre (1357-1363)', dans *Epeteris* du Centre de recherche scientifique de Chypre 13-16 (1983-87), pp. 61-75, reprint. J. Richard, *Croisades et états latins d'Orient* (Aldershot, 1992), art. XV. Le mot *supradictus* qui revient plusieurs fois dans ce texte indique que celui-ci faisait suite à une partie disparue. Selon toute apparence le document en question daterait de 1369, du fait qu'il est fait état de ce que Pierre de Soller avait été au service de la Chambre pendant sept ans; or il avait été institué sous-collecteur en 1363/64, d'après *Instr. Misc.* 4600, où figurent des informations complémentaires et une copie de notre document (f° 9-11^v).

[2] Cf. P.W. Edbury, *The Kingdom of Cyprus and the Crusades, 1191-1374* (Cambridge, 1991), pp. 165-77; K. M. Setton, *The Papacy and the Levant, 1204-1571*, 4 vol. (Philadelphia, 1976), 1.224-84.

Sequuntur illa que debentur adhuc camere apostolice in collectoria regni Cipri prout per cameram scriptum fuit.

Primo computaverunt et dixerunt nuncii et collectores apostolici adhuc penes se habere de summa levata et per eos recepta   1300 B.

Respondetur quod P. de Solerio fuit hic per septennum in servicio camere cum modica utilitate, quare supplicat et requirit quod istud debitum sibi remittatur.

Le reliquat dont il s'agit ici n'apparaît pas nettement dans le compte rendu en 1363, dont nous ne possédons pas l'arrêt. Mais les collecteurs demandaient à la Chambre de l'abandonner, en raison de son peu d'importance (1300 besants correspondent à peu près à 300 florins), à leur sous-collecteur, maître Pierre de Soller, clerc d'origine catalane, *scriptor* de lettres apostoliques, qui ne détenait qu'un bénéfice mineur (une 'assise' de diacre en l'église de Famagouste) et qui, selon eux, ne percevait qu'une faible rétribution, pour le dédommager. Maître Pierre, qui avait été procureur du roi Pierre en cour de Rome, devait en effet attendre le 22 juin 1371 pour échanger son 'assise' contre une prébende de chanoine et la dignité de trésorier de l'église de Nicosie qu'abandonnait alors Aymeri de Laval.[3]

Le second article concerne le revenu de la décime instituée pour la croisade par le pape Urbain V, lorsque celui-ci avait accédé à la demande de Pierre Ier, alors en guerre avec le sultan, et décidé de lancer une croisade générale dont le roi de France Jean II était désigné pour prendre la tête (avril 1363). La levée était prévue pour six années (on l'appelle *decima sexennalis*). Le 'passage général' ne s'était pas déclenché, et Jean II était mort avant d'avoir donné suite à son projet. Pierre Ier n'avait donc emmené qu'un 'passage particulier' qui lui donna occasion d'occuper un moment Alexandrie et de mettre la ville à sac. Mais notre document nous révèle un désaccord entre la Chambre et les collecteurs:

Item computaverunt et dixerunt quod prefatus dominus noster papa IIII° pontificatus sui anno imposuit et indixit in dicto regni Cipri decimam sexennalem in subsidium generalis passagii faciendi, quod factum non fuit. Ideo prefatus dominus noster papa postmodum ordinavit et mandavit quod levaretur per collectores predictos decima supradicta que ascendit ad summam   108.000 B.

---

[3] Pierre de *Solerio*, 'Piere dou Soulier' en français de Chypre, du diocèse de Gérone, avait reçu son canonicat et sa dignité à charge de renoncer à son assise de diacre. Cf. W.-H. Rudt de Collenberg, 'Etat et origine du haut clergé de Chypre d'après les registres des papes des 13e et 14e siècles', *Mélanges de l'ecole française de Rome: Moyen Age* 91 (1979), pp. 259, 284, 298.

Nichil fuit receptum, quia rex non curavit ac eciam quod collectores levaverunt decimam virtute alterius mandati quod fuit factum per dominum anno suo primo ad terminum, et postea anno suo sexto renovavit mandatum ad terminum, et durat adhuc usque in festo sancti Johannis Baptiste veniente, et erit tunc ultimum terminum.

Il semble que se soit introduite une confusion entre la *decima sexennalis* déjà mentionnée, Urbain V ayant assigné à Pierre Ier les *subsidia fidelium* en provenance de plusieurs provinces ecclésiastiques dont celle de Nicosie (24 mai 1363), et la *decima triennalis* destinée au financement de la défense de Smyrne: c'est celle-ci dont le pape avait prescrit la levée en novembre 1362 et les collecteurs en poursuivirent le recouvrement jusqu'en octobre 1365.[4] Selon eux, le roi Pierre ne se serait pas préoccupé de la levée de cette 'décime sexennale' destinée au 'passage général', ce qui peut surprendre en raison des difficultés financières où se débattait le roi de Chypre. Ils ajoutent qu'aucune décime n'avait été levée entre 1365 et 1369, ce qui surprend aussi, parce que le pape avait ordonné en septembre 1367 la levée d'une décime pour la défense du royaume contre les Turcs, et renouvelé cette imposition le 5 décembre 1370 – et que nous savons d'autre part que le diocèse de Limassol avait payé sa part de la décime en décembre 1367.[5] Mais la date de notre document explique peut-être pourquoi on ne tint pas alors encore compte de cette rentrée; et le fait que Bérenger Grégoire se fût déclaré incapable de verser en 1367 la somme destinée au capitaine de Smyrne tient peut-être à ce que la décime que l'on levait alors était destinée à contribuer à la défense du royaume et non au paiement de la garnison de Smyrne.[6]

L'article suivant envisage une autre rentrée attendue par la Chambre:

Item debentur adhuc camere predicte, ut dixerunt, de debitis ecclesie Nicossiensis supradicte de anno LX° quo vacavit, prout in eorum racionibus continetur, et in libris secrete sive thesaurarie dicte Nicossiensis ecclesie dixerunt contineri

4.414 B. et 4 d.

---

[4] J. Richard, 'Les marchands génois de Famagouste et la défense de Smyrne', dans *Oriente e Ocidente fra medioevo ed età moderna: Studi in onore di G. Pistarino*, éd. L. Balletto (Gênes, 1997).

[5] Cf. C. Baronio et al., *Annales ecclesiastici*, éd. A. Theiner, 37 vol. (Paris, 1864-83), 27.82-7; la lettre du pape à l'archevêque et aux évêques prolongeant la levée de décime, le 5 février 1370: Arch. Vat. Reg. Av. 171, f°. 405 v°. L'*annus sextus* d'Urbain V correspond à la période allant de septembre 1367 à septembre 1368.

[6] Sur la levée de cette décime pour une demi-année dans ce diocèse, cf. J. Richard, *Documents chypriotes des Archives du Vatican (XIVe-XVe s.)*, Bibliothèque archéologique et historique 73 (Paris, 1962), pp. 87, 101.

De istis lapidariis[7] collectores ipsi posuerunt procuratores duos et unum scriptorem, et in qualibet diocesi unum procuratorem, quibus debentur certa stipendia; et quia dominus temporalis non poterat, secundum eorum statuta, dare vel facere exequtionem realem, ideo fuit obmissum. Et requisivimus dominos prelatos quod exigerent et responderent camere, et de his fecimus instrumenta publica, et misimus vobis copias sepe, specialiter per dominum Famagustanum, et etiam quia domini prelati exhigebant partes suas et restabat pars camere in debito, et sic pro meliori dimisimus totum eis.

La question des fruits de la vacance de l'église de Nicosie lors du transfert de Philippe de Chamberlhac à Bordeaux avait déjà été évoquée dans le compte rendu en 1363.[8] Elle n'avait pas progressé depuis et la Chambre attendait toujours le règlement des 4.414 besants qu'elle estimait lui être dûs. Les collecteurs se retranchent derrière les frais de recouvrement (la désignation de procureurs dans chaque diocèse entraînait le paiement de gages); derrière l'impossibilité où, selon eux, ils se trouvaient de faire appel au roi pour obtenir la saisie des biens des débiteurs,[9] et sur ce que les prélats qui devaient réserver au Saint-Siège une part des fruits de la vacance s'estimaient en droit de prélever d'abord la part qui leur en revenait. Et les collecteurs leur avaient finalement abandonné cette créance.

L'article suivant concerne les sommes restant à recouvrer de la 'décime triennale' déjà mentionnée dont Bérenger Grégoire avait rendu compte en 1366. Ici la réponse est brève et éloquente; c'est la pauvreté du royaume, et partant celle des églises qui justifie l'absence de toute rentrée:

Item debentur adhuc dicte camere de decimis triennalibus supradictis restantibus adhus ad solvendum, ut dixerunt, in summa   1.963 B. 38 d.

Nichil fuit exactum propter paupertatem.

Nous avons évoqué ailleurs ce que furent les conséquences de la défaillance des Chypriotes à s'acquitter de cette imposition: la défense du château de mer

---

[7] Le mot rare de *lapidaria* paraît désigner les biens meubles de l'actif successoral, peut-être en y incluant les créances à recouvrer.

[8] Richard, 'Les comptes' (cité n. 1), p. 47.

[9] Il faut comprendre que le rois se voyait interdire les Assises de procéder à la saisie des biens des hommes liges; par contre il pouvait le faire à l'encontre d'autres personnes: on voit la connétablie du royaume faire procéder à une vente des biens meubles de l'évêque de Limassol pour le paiement de ses serviteurs et de ses familiers: J. Richard, 'Guy d'Ibelin, O.P., évêque de Limassol, et l'inventaire de ses biens', *Bulletin de correspondance hellénique* 74 (1950), pp. 131-3, reprint. J. Richard, *Les relations entre l'Orient et l'Occident au Moyen Age* (London, 1977), art. V.

de Smyrne allait passer de la Papauté et du capitaine désigné par elle aux Hospitaliers.[10]

La Chambre allait-elle avoir moins de déconvenues en matière de fiscalité bénéficiale?

Item de beneficiis vacantibus debentur adhuc dicte camere, ut dixerunt,
8.772 B. et 2 s.

Super quibus vacantibus respondemus in hunc modum, et de eisdem fuerunt exacta ea que infra secuntur:

A domino Seguino de Altigiis pro archidiaconatu et prebenda ecclesie Paphensi	900 B.
Item de prebenda domini P. de Sermesiis	600 B.
Item de thesauraria et prebenda ecclesie Nicossiensis, a domino Aimerico de Laval	900 B.
Item de prebenda domini Nicholai de Auximo	600 B.
Item de domino Bertholomeo Scafasii	600 B.
Item de domino Guidoni de Neffino	135 B.

Summa 3.735 B. recepta

Item de decanatu Nicossiensi repertum est per secretam quod dominus Nicossiensis habet penes se fructus primi anni decanatus Nicossiensis, et decanus Nicossiensis etiam fuit factus collector eodem tempore, quare requisivimus sepe dominum Nicossiensem super hoc et ipse respondit quod libenter fecebit juri coram dominis de camera, et dominus noster papa mandavit hoc quod exigantur fructus primi anni a tempore quo fuit collatum penes quocumque sint dicti fructus.

Item dominus Nimociensis respondit quod non habet prebendam aliquam in ecclesia sua, videlicet de illis de domino Bertholomeo Scaffasa nec de aliquo alio; ideo nichil solverit quia nullus eorum portavit sibi aliquam bullam.

Item etiam de beneficiis vacantibus in ecclesia Famagustana, de prebenda domini Berengarii Gregorii fuit repertum quod fructus primi anni fuerunt penes Leodegarium tunc episcopum; ideo super bonis suis devolutis ad cameram debet vacans illa exigi.

Item Belfarach dixit quod fructus sue scriptorie sunt penes dominum Nicossiensem et quod ipse solvat, et dominus Nicossiensis dicit quod non habet nec habuit ipsum pro scriptore, quia tale officium est ad suam voluntatem et non potest conferri per alium quam per ipsum.

---

[10] C'est seulement en 1370 que reprirent les versements faits au capitaine de Smyrne, Pietro Recanelli (*Instr. Misc.* 4603); celui-ci ne fut donc remboursé que très tardivement de ses avances et il aurait négligé le paiement de ses mercenaires. Cf. 'Les marchands' (n. 4).

Johannes de Leonis dicit quod pro illo beneficio semel solvit domino P. Demandi
et quod pro eodem beneficio non debet solvere bis.

(en marge: et ita est repertum in secreta domini Nicossiensis)

De aliis faciemus et exigemus prout melius poterimus.

L'intérêt de ce débat est de nous révéler la réalité qui se dissimule derrière
les collations de bénéfices figurant dans les registres de la chancellerie pontificale, et qui donnaient droit à la Chambre à réclamer la perception du revenu
de la première année de chaque bénéfice. Elle nous montre qu'il faut tenir
compte d'une certaine distortion entre les informations dont disposait la Curie
et la situation locale, en même temps que des interventions des ordinaires de
chaque diocèse, tant pour les nominations des bénéficiers eux-mêmes que de
la perception des revenus de la première année, qui revenait au pape en vertu
du jeu des réserves pontificales.

Nous retrouvons bien ici les noms de chanoines et de dignitaires qui ont
bénéficié de collations émanant du Siège apostolique: Raymond Seguin de
Altigiis (21 septembre 1363);[11] Pierre de Sermaises (même date);[12] Nicolas
de Romanis d'Osimo (19 juin 1362);[13] Barthélemy Escaface pour son canonicat à Nicosie (23 avril 1365);[14] Guy de Nephin (12 octobre 1363);[15]
Bérenger Grégoire lui-même (14 avril et 13 septembre 1363);[16] Aymeri de
Laval (16 juillet 1364).[17] D'autres noms sont absents, et l'évêque de Limassol
affirme ne pas avoir de prébendes disponibles, même pour Barthélemy

---

[11] Sur ces collations de bénéfices, cf. l'article de M. de Collenberg, cité note 3. Raymond
Seguin, curialiste bien pourvu de bénéfices, notamment chanoine d'Agen, succédait à Pierre
de Lascoutz, devenu archidiacre de Limassol: M. et A.-M. Hayez, *Urbain V, 1362-1370:
Lettres communes*, 12 vol. (Paris, 1954-89), n° 4939. Il devait, pour justifier sa non-résidence
et obtenir le droit de percevoir ses revenus malgré celle-ci, invoquer un motif original (15
octobre 1373): le climat malsain de Paphos et la fréquence des tremblements de terre!

[12] Hayez, *Urbain V*, n° 7852; cf. n° 22679.

[13] Ce personnage occupait un poste important à la Curie et cumulait les bénéfices; il n'est
sans doute jamais venu en Chypre.

[14] Hayez, *Urbain V*, n° 13427. Barthélemy, un chypriote, avait d'abord reçu des prébendes
à Coron et à Modon, en Grèce vénitienne; il échangea cette dernière contre son canonicat de
Nicosie.

[15] Hayez, *Urbain V*, n° 4266. Autre chypriote, apparenté aux Lusignan, Guy détenait une
'assise' au grand autel de Nicosie: Hayez, *Urbain V*, n° 14945.

[16] Hayez, *Urbain V*, n° 2551 (décanat de Nicosie) et 2769 (canonicat de Famagouste).

[17] En contrepartie de l'attribution d'un canonicat et de la trésorerie de Nicosie, Aimery
renonçait à une prébende canoniale en la même église, à 'une autre au chapitre de Tortose et
à une "assise perpétuelle"' à Famagouste. Il conservait la chapelle Saint-Michel au grand
cimetière de Famagouste (*lire*: Nicosie): Hayez, *Urbain V*, n° 9640.

Escaface qui avait reçu collation d'un canonicat en cette église le 24 avril 1365.[18] On peut se demander si Guillaume Galiot, Jean *Cassaguerra* de Parme et Raymond Robert, désignés respectivement comme chantre de Nicosie (28 avril 1363), chanoine de Limassol (18 avril 1366) et chanoine et archidiacre de Famagouste (5 juillet 1366), tous bien introduits à la cour royale, et dont le second avait bien pris possession de sa stalle en 1367,[19] n'ont pas été recommandés au choix des chapitres par le roi, ce qui les aurait dispensés de l'obligation de présenter leur bulles.

C'est en tout cas très régulièrement que Guy de Nephin a été coopté par l'évêque et le chapitre de Famagouste à la faveur d'une vacance, non sans s'assurer ensuite que cette prébende ne faisait pas l'objet d'une réserve pontificale (31 janvier 1365).[20]

En ce qui concerne Bérenger Grégoire, le fait que les 'fruits' de ses bénéfices soient aux mains de l'archevêque et de l'évêque de Famagouste ne doit pas surprendre: dans les églises de Chypre, la mense épiscopale n'est pas séparée de la mense capitulaire et la 'paye' des dignitaires, chanoines et autres 'assis' est prélevée sur la masse des revenus de l'église.[21]

Mais en ce qui concerne *Belfarach* - c'est-à-dire Thibaut Abu'l Faraj, ce clerc, Syrien melkite passé au rite latin, qui était familier du roi Pierre Ier, chargé de missions par ce dernier et qui, lors de l'invasion gênoise, leva une compagnie de mercenaires, ce qui lui permit d'accéder à la chevalerie et au rang de turcoplier du royaume avant d'être mis à mort pour avoir assassiné un chapelain du roi,[22] la Chambre paraît avoir réclamé le paiement des 'fruits' de son office d'écrivain de l'église de Nicosie tandis que l'archevêque revendiquait vigoureusement son droit exclusif de pourvoir cet office. On découvrit après enquête auprès de la 'secrète' (le service financier) de l'église que

---

[18] En fait, Barthélemy se titrait chanoine de Limassol parce qui'il avait reçu une 'grâce expectative' en 1352; il avait présenté en 1363 une supplique pour obtenir une collation effective, et celle-ci avait été acceptée, mais ne donna pas lieu à l'établissement d'une bulle (Collenberg, 'Etat et origine' (cité n. 3), pp. 298 et 307).

[19] Il est cité au nombre des chanoines qui bénéficient de distributions dans le compte de l'église.

[20] Hayez, *Urbain V*, n° 14945.

[21] Le compte de l'église de Limassol pour 1367 ne laisse aucun doute à ce sujet; c'est même l'église cathédrale qui rétribue les 'prieurs paroissiens' desservant les paroisses.

[22] La pittoresque carrière de ce personnage, qui devait bénéficier de nombreux indults pontificaux au temps de sa fortune, et qui accompagnait Pierre Ier à Rome en 1367, a été racontée par Leontios Makhairas, *Recital concerning the Sweet Land of Cyprus entitled 'Chronicle'*, éd. et trad. R.M. Dawkins, 2 vol. (Oxford, 1932), 1.214, 403-4, 556-79; 2.191.

Thibaut avait bien versé les 'fruits' au collecteur d'alors, Pierre *Domandi*.[23] En fait ce personnage fort intrigant aurait pu profiter de la faveur royale pour se faire accorder par le pape un office qu'il convoitait en passant outre aux droits du prélat.

Néanmoins tous les noms que nous venons de citer allaient se retrouver dans les comptes postérieurs, nous montrant ainsi que la Chambre apostolique n'avait pas accepté les échappatoires par lesquelles on aurait pu essayer d'éviter de s'acquitter du paiement des 'vacants'. Certains d'ailleurs n'avaient sans doute pas encore pris possession de leur bénéfice depuis assez longtemps pour avoir été astreints à s'acquitter de ce paiement.

Du chapitre des bénéfices vacants, on passe à celui du revenu des droits de dépouilles dont jouit la Papauté. Et le premier article nous est bien connu: c'est celui de la succession de Guy d'Ibelin, évêque de Limassol:[24]

> Item de spoliis domini Guidonis quondam episcopi Nimociensis, deductis expensis funeralium et familie ac aliorum debitorum   400 B. 12 d.
>
> Item habet dominus episcopus, ut dicunt canonici, et sepe requisivimus eum super hiis et aliis, et ipse dicit quod bene concordavit cum dominis camere quia predecessor suus in multis tenebatur ecclesie sue.
>
> Item debentur adhuc dicte camere de lapidariis sive debitis que dictus dominus Nimociensis quondam ante obitum suum debebantur, prout dixerunt et a scriba secrete sive thesaurarie dicti (?) quondam domini episcopi habuerant.   10.136 B.
>
> Responsum est quod requisivimus dominos prelatos cum instrumento sepe quód exigant et mittant camere, quia ita est fieri consuetum, et responderunt quod non habent in mandatis quare mandetur vel quod ipsi levant vel componant cum camera, quia dominum temporalem non potest, ut dicit, super his facere exequtionem.

Si nous possédons bien l'inventaire, avec l'indication, pour chaque article, de ce qu'avait rapporté la vente des biens meubles de l'évêque, la somme totale qui en était ressortie reste très incertaine. La secrète royale évaluait le montant de la succession à 6.494 besants 21 deniers et affirmait que tout avait été absorbé par le règlement des dettes de l'évêque.[25] La Chambre estime à 400 besants 1/4 la somme qui lui revient en argent liquide; mais l'évêque Aymar de la Voute, qui avait succédé à Guy, n'avait rien versé en arguant que la dette

---

[23] Profitant de son passage à Rome, il se fit accorder le droit de percevoir les fruits de son bénéfice sans l'exercer pendant deux ans et il rappela à cette occasion qu'il l'avait obtenu du Siège apostolique: Hayez, *Urbain V*, n° 21584 (3 juin 1368). Jean de Leonis, cité dans l'enquête, est un chanoine de Nicosie.

[24] Richard, 'Guy d'Ibelin', cité note 9.

[25] Richard, 'Guy d'Ibelin', p. 103.

de Guy envers son église excédait cette somme. Quant aux créances de l'évêque, généreusement estimées à 10.136 besants, le texte, d'interprétation difficile en raison de l'incertitude grammaticale qui y règne, laisse supposer que rien n'en avait été recouvré. Ici les collecteurs se plaignent de n'avoir pu obtenir des évêques, cependant mis en demeure par instrument notarié, que ceux-ci recouvrent ces arriérés et les envoient à la Chambre; les évêques se disculpent en excipant de ce que ceci n'est pas de leur compétence et affirment à nouveau ne pas pouvoir recourir au bras séculier pour faire procéder à des saisies, qui permettraient de contraindre les débiteurs à rembourser leurs dettes.

Item debentur adhuc dicte camere, ut dixerunt, de fructibus ecclesie Nimociensis anni Domini MCCCLXVII quo vacavit, de quatuor mensibus et XV diebus
                                                                      6.101 B. 2 s. 6 d.

Item debentur adhuc de fructibus dicte Nimociensis ecclesie dictorum IV mensium et XV dierum quibus vacavit dicta ecclesia de frumento 74 modii et 2 caffisia, de quibus caffisiis 8 faciunt modium et 5 modia faciunt unam saumatam grossam, et potet valere quodlibet modium unum bisantium, et sic ascendit ad summam cum
                                                                      74 B. 12d.

Item de ordeo, 107 modia 2 caffisia

Item de avena, 18 modia 4 caffisia; possunt valere communiter, ut dixerunt, ad rationem una cum ordeo, 2 modia pro bisantio   62 B. 3 s. 6 d.

Item de vino 19 metretas, quarum 4 faciunt saumatam grossam; possunt valere communiter, ad rationem unius bisantii pro qualibet metra, et sic ascendit ad summam   19 B.

Summa   16.706 B. 6 d.[26]

Le compte fourni par le chanoine Bernard Anselme, qui administrait l'église pendant la vacance, concorde avec notre document en ce qui concerne les recettes en nature, mais non pour les recettes en argent, qui montent selon lui à 1.018 besants pour l'année entière, sur lesquels la part du pape n'était que de 381 besants 3/4.[27] Nous avons supposé que le bailli de l'église n'avait pas tenu compte des dîmes non encore payées à la date de son compte; mais cette explication n'est sans doute pas suffisante. Ici encore, il nous faut constater ces discordances sans prétendre les expliquer; mais la mauvaise volonté des prélats

---

[26] Cette somme correspond à peu près à celle que réclamait la Chambre au titre de la sucession de l'évêque Guy, vacance de l'église et dépouilles confondues. Mais, dans le manuscrit, elle est portée au milieu du paragraphe consacré à l'orge. Les équivalences des mesures sont données par rapport à la saumée d'Avignon: cf. Richard, *Documents chypriotes* (cité note 6), pp. 19-20.

[27] Richard, *Documents chypriotes*, p. 109.

à admettre les prétentions sans doute excessives de la Chambre paraissent évidentes.

Le dernier chapitre de l'arrêt de compte est consacré à une autre succession: celle de Léger de Nabinaud,[28] mort sans doute à Avignon dans le courant de 1365, qui avait été depuis 1348 titulaire du siège épiscopal de Famagouste auquel était uni celui, *in partibus infidelium*, de Tortose (Antarados).

> Item debentur adhuc dicte camere, ut dixerunt, de lapidariis, arreragiis et debitis que domino quondam Leodegario episcopo Famagustano supradicto ante ipsius obitum debebantur   15.000 B.
>
> Hic responsum est per supradicta competenter.
>
> Item debentur adhuc dicte camere de fructibus dicte ecclesie Famagustane anni LXV quo vacavit.   17.418 B. 42 d.
>
> Item dixerunt quod debebantur dicto domino Leodegario quondam Famagustano episcopo, nomine ecclesie Antheradensis, in Venetiis, quedam debita de quibus nondum potuerunt scire veritatem ad plenum, ut dixerunt.
>
> Summa   33.910 B. 3 s.[29]
>
> Item dixerunt quod dominus Leodegarius, quondam episcopus Famagustanus, habebat in Venetiis etiam quandam mitram pulcram quam ibidem fieri seu reparari fecerat, que debet ad cameram apostolicam pertinere. (*Note en marge*: Est in ecclesia Famagustana. Mandatis si vultis quod recipiatur videlicet 500 florenos, ut dicitur.)

La succession de l'evêque Léger avait sans doute déjà été réglée en ce qui concerne le droit de dépouille: il ne restait plus à ce titre que cette mitre, qui avait sans doute échappé lorsqu'on avait dressé l'inventaire de ses biens, parce qu'elle se trouvait alors à Venise – et, selon les informations que la Chambre avait recueillies, chez l'orfèvre qui l'avait confectionnée ou réparée. Elle était entre temps revenue à Famagouste, et les collecteurs paraissent suggérer de la laisser à cette église qui la rachèterait pour 500 florins, soit plus de 4.000 besants.

Au titre des 'vacants', une somme de 17.418 besants devait revenir au pape; elle n'avait donc pas encore été versée.

La Chambre réclame le montant des sommes qui étaient dues à l'évêque – la réponse des collecteurs se trouvait dans les pages perdues. Mais elle s'est

---

[28] *De Nabinaliis*. Il s'agit de Nabinaud, Charente, canton Aubeterre. Sur cette famille, qui donna plusieurs dignitaires et prélats aux églises de Chypre grâce à la protection du cardinal Hélie Talleyrand de Périgord, cf. Collenberg, 'Etat et origine' (cité note 3), pp. 248-51.

[29] Faute de connaître les sommes attendues des biens vénitiens, l'addition des créances de l'évêque Léger et des fruits de la vacance de son église ne donne qu'une somme de 32.418 besants.

avisée qu'en qualité d'évêque de Tortose, l'évêque de Famagouste percevait à Venise, et dans la région vénitienne, d'autres revenus (sans doute des rentes) qui n'avaient pas précédemment été pris en compte. Un document ultérieur précise que ces créances portent sur les diocèses de Castello (Venise), Padoue et Trévise.[30] Nous comprenons ainsi pourquoi, le 13 juillet 1295, Boniface VIII avait décidé d'unir les sièges de Famagouste et de Tortose, au moment où le roi Henri II donnait à Famagouste un nouvel essor.[31] C'est que l'église de Tortose, lieu d'un pèlerinage important, jouissait en Occident d'un patrimoine qui permettait, malgré la perte de son domaine au comté de Tripoli, de continuer à entretenir un petit chapitre cathédral qui ne se confondit pas avec celui de Famagouste et un évêque dont les moyens de vivre paraissaient sans doute insuffisants, mais pouvaient étoffer les revenus de celui de Famagouste.

En mai 1371, Grégoire XI devait renouveler l'invite aux évêques vénitiens de faire payer au nouvel évêque, Arnaud, les sommes qui lui étaient dues. Mais nous apprenons aussi qu'un accord avait été passé entre la Chambre et Arnaud, par lequel ce dernier s'était engagé à verser 2.000 florins, sur quatre ans, en contrepartie de l'abandon des revendications de la Chambre sur la succession de son prédécesseur - à l'exclusion de la fameuse mitre.[32] Cet accord portait aussi sur un dernier point qu'envisage notre document:

Item dixerunt quod debentur adhuc dicte camere de bonis que quondam fuerunt domini Gauffredi, quondam archidiaconi Famagustani, reservatis que habebat tempore mortis sue in quadam prestaria seu grangia, Couboucle vulgariter nuncupata, in diocesi Famagustano scituata   2.000 B.

Ista habet dominus Famagustanus, dicens quod ad eum pertinet, et concordabit cum camera; fuit tamen repertum quod dominus P. de Luges receperat in vacatione ecclesie 900 bisantios de quibus dicit se redemisse mitram que est nunc in ecclesia, et residuum tradidisse domino Famagustano episcopo, prout est contentum in cedula

---

[30] A.-M. Hayez, *Grégoire XI, (1370-1378): Lettres communes*, 3 vol. (Paris, 1992), n° 12032 (29 juillet 1371).

[31] J. Richard, 'La situation juridique de Famagouste dans le royaume des Lusignans', *Praktikon tou protou diethnous Kyprologikou Synedriou* 2 (1972), pp. 221-9, reprint. J. Richard, *Orient et Occident au Moyen Age: contacts et relations* (London, 1976), art. XVII. C'est à l'évêque de Tortose, Mansel, privé de son siège épiscopal, que fut attribué celui de Famagouste.

[32] Hayez, *Grégoire XI*, n° 11751-2. L'évêque demandait aussi qu'on lui restituât la 'presterie' de Couvoucle, qui avait été distraite des biens de son église du fait qu'au temps de la vacance elle était aux mains de l'archidiacre. Pierre de Luges, dont il est question ci-après, était un 'assis' de l'église de Famagouste (un des clercs exerçant une fonction subalterne dans celle-ci); c'est lui qui avait administré le temporel de celle-ci durant la vacance du siège épiscopal.

que fuit facta inter collectores et dictum dominum episcopum coram domino Nicossiensi archiepiscopo; et mandetis si vultis quod recipiamus mitram qui valet bene 500 florenos (*Note*: de 535 B. residuum dedit procuratoribus domini Famagustani).

Item quedam alia bona ipsius domini archidiaconi quondam, de quibus, ut dixerunt, non potuerunt se adhuc plene informare, que sunt penes dominum archiepiscopum Nicossiensem, exequtorem ultime voluntatis seu testamenti dicti quondam archidiaconi, qui in suis racionibus declarabuntur pariter et distincte.

Summa   2.000 B.

De his habuerunt 1.000 B. a domino Nicossiensi, quia alia que ipse habuerat fuerunt expensa tam pro funeralibus quam pro debitis suis, ut respondit dominus archiepiscopus sepedictus.

La succession dont il s'agit était celle de Goffredo Spanzota de Novare, dit de Milan, chanoine de Nicosie et archidiacre de Famagouste depuis 1333, qui était mort quelque temps avant le mois de juillet 1366. Ce dignitaire paraît avoir détenu un des principaux domaines de l'église, celui de Kouklia (aujourd'hui ennoyé dans une retenue d'eau de ce nom, au sud-ouest de la ville); c'est sans doute pourquoi l'évêque avait mis la main sur sa succession avant de s'entendre avec la Chambre à ce sujet. Mais une partie du revenu était échue à l'administrateur de l'évêché vacant, qui l'avait utilisée pour dégager la mitre déjà mentionnée. Les autres biens de Goffredo avaient été remis à son exécuteur testamentaire,[33] l'archevêque Raymond de Pradella, auquel il revenait d'acquitter les dettes du défunt et de payer ses frais funéraux; il ne pouvait donc pas effectuer un règlement définitif avant de s'en être exécuté, et il se borna à verser aux collecteurs une somme de mille besants.

Notre arrêt de compte s'achève triomphalement sur le montant des sommes réclamées par le Chambre apostolique:

Summa summarum omnium precedentium apostolice camere debitorum ut superius continetur: 177.067 B. 12 d.,

qui, deducti ad florenos, valent 41.262 floreni, 15 s. monete Cipri, qui valent 3 B. 3 quars, singulo floreno computato pro 4 bisantiis et quarto.

Responsum est de omnibus particulariter.

L'ensemble de ces réponses 'particulières' laissait bien peu d'espoir aux agents de la Chambre de recouvrer la somme attendue.

---

[33] Goffredo avait en effet obtenu d'Innocent VI la permission de disposer de ses biens par testament, ce qui limitait la revendication que pouvait émettre la Chambre sur ses biens mobiliers. Il était depuis de longues années en Chypre, ayant reçu dès 1327 un canonicat à Nicosie, et il avait exercé les fonctions de collecteur.

Cette reddition de compte paraît témoigner d'un moment difficile dans les relations de l'église de Chypre avec la Chambre. Les collecteurs paraissent surtout soucieux de justifier les retards ou l'absence de leurs versements. Ils cherchent à faire renoncer la Chambre à des rentrées de faible importance; ils acceptent les dires des évêques se déclarant incapables de recouvrer des créances du fait de l'impossibilité de recourir à des saisies réelles. Et Bérenger Grégoire s'est déclaré incapable de répondre aux demandes des marchands gênois, agents du capitaine de Smyrne, Pietro Recanelli, parce qui'il n'avait pas d'argent en caisse.[34] Les évêques qui doivent s'acquitter du paiement des sommes dues à la Papauté au titre de la vacance de leur siège se dérobent en invoquant les dettes de leurs prédécesseurs envers leurs églises. Le système fiscal mis en oeuvre dans le royaume de Chypre paraît ainsi devenu inefficace.

Ceci s'explique par leur situation; on les voit eux-mêmes chargés de dettes; il leur a fallu en prenant leur charge s'acquitter du paiement des communs services, directement encaissés par la Chambre.[35] Ils ont trouvé leur église endettée, et il leur a fallu recourir aux emprunts.[36] Avignon s'est réservé la nomination de beaucoup de chanoines, et les évêques diocésains ne peuvent profiter des collations pour demander à ceux-ci les habituels présents.[37] Or le compte de la succession de Guy d'Ibelin et l'inventaire des biens de celui-ci révèlent que leur revenu reste relativement modeste, le cas de l'archevêque sans doute mis à part.

Les collecteurs eux-mêmes, deux dignitaires du clergé de Chypre, paraissent portés à ménager prélats et chanoines dont ils partagent les difficultés. On ne s'étonnera pas de voir le chapitre cathédral de Nicosie, en 1376, demander Bérenger Grégoire comme archevêque: il n'avait sans doute pas pressuré ses confrères.

La situation du royaume dans son ensemble est d'ailleurs difficile. Pierre Ier, après le succès de son coup de main sur Alexandrie, a bien tenté quelques autres descentes sur la côte syrienne; mais en fait il cherche à rétablir ses

---

[34] Richard, 'Les marchands' (cité note 4).

[35] A titre d'exemple, citons l'engagement pris par Philippe de Chamberlhac lors de sa promotion à l'archevêché de Nicosie (Arch. Vat., Obl. et Sol., 6, f° 187) de payer 'pro suo communi servitio quinque milia florenos auri et quinque servicia familie consueta', moitié pour la Saint-Michel, moitié pour la Saint-Jean suivante (1342).

[36] Le pape Clément VI avait accordé à l'évêque Léger, le 7 octobre 1346, la faculté d'emprunter jusqu'à 3.000 florins.

[37] C'est à titre de privilège que Grégoire XI accorde à l'évêque Arnaud (15 octobre 1373) le droit de conférer l'expectative d'une prébende de chanoine dans son chapitre à une personne de son choix.

relations avec le sultan et il négocie avec celui-ci.[38] Il est à court d'argent et son second voyage l'a mené à Rome où Urbain V lui a montré les difficultés où se débat l'Occident, en proie aux ravages des Grandes Compagnies. Il mutiplie les expédients, pressure les nobles et les bourgeois au point de s'aliéner ses barons.[39] L'Eglise n'est certainement pas restée en dehors de ses sollicitations.

La Papauté a vigoureusement réagi. Si les archives de la Chambre ont conservé un nombre exceptionnellement élevé de documents concernant Chypre au temps de Pierre Ier et de Pierre II, c'est en raison de la remise en ordre à laquelle se sont livrés Urbain V et Grégoire XI. Le premier a assigné sur l'île le paiement de 10,000 besants en faveur des Hospitaliers, et d'autres assignations ont suivi; un compte des décimes, arrérages compris, a dû être fourni pour 1369-71; une information a été ouverte en 1372 sur l'exercice du droit de dépouille dans le royaume, et Bérenger Grégoire a été relevé de ses fonctions de collecteur, en 1373, en raison de sa négligence à lever la *decima triennalis*.[40] La paix rétablie avec l'Egypte permettait d'envisager le retour à une situation plus normale; la crise de 1373-74 allait à nouveau ébranler le royaume chypriote.

---

[38] Dans cette perspective, le pape accorde au roi et aux habitants du royaume la faculté d'envoyer dix coques et dix galées chargées de marchandises aux pays du sultan, le 29 mai 1368 (Hayez, *Urbain V*, n° 22337).

[39] Edbury, *The Kingdom* (cité n. 2,), p. 175. Des mesures sont prises à l'occasion des expéditions, qui ont pu apporter une gêne à l'économie: ainsi l'interdiction de vendre les chevaux citée dans le compte de l'église de Limassol.

[40] Les documents constitutifs de ce dossier: *Instr. Misc.*, 4600, 4602-4. La révocation de Bérenger: G. Mollat, *Grégoire XI (1370-1378): Lettres secrètes et curiales du intéressant les pays autres que la France*, 3 vol. (Paris, 1962-65), n° 2697, 2702. Il semble toutefois avoir continué ses fonctions.

Picturing the Crusades: The Uses of Visual Propaganda, c. 1095-1250

Colin Morris

Pictures, commented Gratian, are the 'literature of the laity'.[1] The idea had received its classic statement long before, in Gregory the Great's ruling to Bishop Serenus of Marseilles: 'pictures of images ... were made for the instruction of the simple people, that those who do not know letters may understand the history'. Gregory's words provided the starting-point of medieval discussion of the use of images, and much modern commentary has followed the supposition that religious art was designed as a simple language for the laity.[2] Crusading was not a legal obligation, but depended on the ability to persuade. The popes were well aware of the power of visual imagery: the Romans, as Gerhoh of Reichersberg wrote, 'paint, speak and write, indoors and out' to communicate their message.[3] The use of images naturally took its place alongside sermons, songs and liturgy in the dissemination of crusading ideology.[4]

---

[1] Gratian, 'Decretum', D. 3 de cons. c. 27, in E. Friedberg, ed., *Corpus iuris canonici*, 2nd edn, 2 vols (Leipzig, 1879), 1, col. 1360.

[2] For abundant references to medieval statements based on Gregory, and their influence on modern thinkers, see the important article by L.G. Duggan, 'Was Art Really "the Book of the Illiterate"?', *Word and Image* 5 (1989), pp. 227-51.

[3] Gerhoh, 'De investigatione Antichristi', *MGH Libelli*, 3.393.

[4] For observations about crusading propaganda as a whole, see S. Menache, *The Vox Dei: Communication in the Middle Ages* (Oxford, 1990), chapters 5 and 8. Recent studies of crusade preaching include P.J. Cole, *The Preaching of the Crusades to the Holy Land, 1095-1270* (Cambridge, Mass., 1991), and C.T. Maier, *Preaching the Crusades: Mendicant Friars and the Cross in the Thirteenth Century* (Cambridge, 1994). For crusading songs, see the references in C. Morris, 'Propaganda for War: The Dissemination of the Crusading Ideal in the Twelfth Century', in *The Church and War*, ed. W.J. Sheils, *Studies in Church History* 21 (Oxford, 1983), pp. 79-101, and M. Routledge, 'Songs', in *The Oxford Illustrated History of the*

There are, however, complications in tracing the development of crusading propaganda in art and architecture. Much of the material survives only in copies, or has recently been uncovered in very imperfect form. There is every reason to suppose that a great deal has been lost without trace. More fundamentally, it is a mistake to assume that, in medieval art, every picture tells a story. The precept of Gregory must not be accepted in too uncritical a fashion.[5] It was quoted because of authority and because it conveniently allowed the use of images while side-stepping any suggestion that they were objects of worship in themselves, and not because his words really shaped the medieval attitude to symbolism. Christian images had never provided a simple narrative, but had from the beginning expressed levels of theological meaning: 'little medieval art is merely instructive'.[6] Images are ambiguous. Their power consists in their ability to present the viewer with several references at the same time, and it appears that artists and patrons were not rigidly controlled in the way they presented their themes. The idea of images as the direct translation of verbal teaching was based on belief in an 'all-powerful, encyclopedic, Christian intellectual atmosphere' dominating the Middle Ages. Few people would now see medieval culture in such a hierocratic way.[7]

It is true that the survival of illustrated vernacular manuscripts, including copies of the French translation of William of Tyre's history of Outremer, gives more confidence that we know what the higher aristocracy was reading. Such manuscripts become numerous from about 1250 onwards. Questions still remain about the true purpose of these luxurious books and the relationship of the images with the text which they supposedly clarify.[8] Still, the survival of vernacular manuscript evidence does open a new propaganda period. This is

---

Crusades, ed. J. Riley-Smith (Oxford, 1995), pp. 91-111. There is a discussion of liturgy as propaganda by A. Linder, '*Deus venerunt gentes*: Psalm 78 (79) in the Liturgical Commemoration of the Destruction of Latin Jerusalem', in *Medieval Studies in Honour of Avrom Saltman*, ed. B. Albert, Y. Friedman and S. Schwarzfuchs (Ramat-Gan, 1995), pp. 145-72.

[5] See the introduction to *Iconography at the Crossroads*, ed. B. Cassidy (Princeton, 1993). There is an important analysis of the relation of text, image and orality by M. Camille, 'Seeing and Reading: Some Visual Implications of Medieval Literacy and Illiteracy', *Art History* 8 (1985), pp. 26-49.

[6] A. Henry, ed., *Biblia pauperum* (Aldershot, 1987), pp. 17-18.

[7] See, for this whole subject, J. Baschet, 'Inventivité et sérialité des images médiévales', *Annales: histoire, sciences sociales* 51 (1996), pp. 93-133.

[8] There is a valuable summary of the discussion about the purpose of the miniatures, and their relation to the text, by L. Lawton, 'The Illustration of Late Medieval Secular Texts', in *Manuscripts and Readers in Fifteenth-Century England*, ed. D. Pearsall (Cambridge, 1983), pp. 41-69.

marked, too, by the loss of Latin Syria, and the dominance within the crusading movement of a new type of national state, especially France. In spite of the limitations in the earlier evidence, I shall concentrate here on what we know about visual propaganda during the twelfth and early thirteenth centuries.

It is difficult to find examples of art designed to advertise a particular expedition in the same way as the song, *Chevalier, mult estes guariz*, was written for the Second Crusade. Rather surprisingly, we hear from Muslim sources of placards carried around to advertise a crusade. Baha' al-Din reports that Conrad of Montferrat used one in the West:

> He had a picture of Jerusalem painted showing the komama ... Above the tomb the marquis had a horse painted, and mounted on it a Muslim knight who was trampling the tomb, over which his horse was urinating. This picture was sent abroad to the markets and meeting-places; priests carried it about, clothed in their habits, their heads covered, groaning, 'O the shame!'.[9]

Ibn al-Athir has a similar account of recruiting by Patriarch Eraclius, who led a group of clergy and knights, wearing mourning, and 'made a picture showing the Messiah, and an Arab striking him, showing blood on the face of Christ – blessings on him! – and they said to the crowds, "This is the Messiah, struck by Mahomet the prophet of the Muslims, who has wounded and killed him"'.[10] The themes are plausible ones for Christian propaganda, and placards of this sort may have been made familiar by the 'props' used in plays such as the *Jeu de St Nicholas* (c. 1202), itself possibly directed to recruiting for the Fourth Crusade. It would be unreasonable to hope for the survival of such transient objects, but there is also a lack of clear references to their use by preachers. When a Welsh prince joined the Third Crusade in 1188 with the words, 'I hasten to avenge the injury done to God the Father Almighty', he could indeed have been responding to such a placard, but there is no secure evidence that he was.[11]

There is, in fact, little proof of the use of any sort of visual aid by preachers, with the important exception of the Cross. This was regularly carried by crusade and other preachers, and of course the sign of the Cross was adopted by

---

[9] English translation in F. Gabrieli, *Arab Historians of the Crusades*, trans. E.J. Costello (Berkeley, 1969), pp. 208-9.

[10] Gabrieli, *Arab Historians*, pp. 182-3. The Winchester Psalter of c. 1150 has precisely such a picture, with Jews and (seemingly) Muslims tormenting Christ: *The Oxford Illustrated History of Christianity*, ed. J. McManners (Oxford, 1990), p. 183.

[11] Gerald of Wales, *The Journey through Wales and the Description of Wales*, trans. L. Thorpe (Harmondsworth, 1978), p. 76.

crusaders and became the badge of the movement. Taking the Cross became the standard expression for enlisting: 'A man should receive on his shoulder the sign of the holy Cross and say in his heart, "Lord, as you call upon me, I commend myself to you"'. The *Brevis ordinacio*, a collection of notes for the use of crusade preachers in England in 1216, strongly suggests that preachers were expected to use the Crucifix as a visual aid.[12]

Although it is hard to find works of art directly designed to recruit for a specific expedition, a few can plausibly be attached to its ceremonial departure. One of the ambulatory chapels in Suger's new church at St-Denis contained a set of panes devoted to the celebration of the glories of the First Crusade. They provided a narrative of its history, clearly based on chronicle accounts: the captures of Antioch and Jerusalem reflect a good knowledge of what actually happened, and the designer realized that the Saldjuks and Egyptians were different powers, indicated in the titles by *Parti* and *Arabes*. Charlemagne's legendary expedition to the East was celebrated in a second window, or in some panes within the Crusade window.[13] The occasion for which it was intended was perhaps the solemn departure of King Louis VII from St-Denis on 8 June 1147. The St-Denis glass does look like a special design for a unique occasion.

Another major artistic composition whose links with specific crusades are more obscure was the tympanum in the narthex at Vézelay. This was a great sculpture of the glorified Christ sending his power upon the apostles. In the outer bands of the composition are representations of the peoples of the world, including the distant dog-headed races of whom geographers had told them. The carving is a confident statement of the universal mission of the church, due, it has been suggested, to the influence of Abbot Peter the Venerable of Cluny. Vézelay was the site of Saint Bernard's preaching of the Second Crusade, and of the joint departure of the kings of France and England for the Third Crusade on 4 July 1190. It is more difficult to be sure that tympanum and crusade were genuinely connected. The tympanum looks like a depiction of the *divisio apostolorum*, when the apostles separated to take the gospel

[12] R. Röhricht, ed., *Quinti belli sacri scriptores minores, Société de l'Orient latin, série historique* 2 (Geneva, 1879), pp. 11-13, 19.

[13] See Plates 1-2. The glass was lost at the time of the French Revolution, but had been copied by B. de Montfaucon, *Les monumens de la monarchie française*, 5 vols (Paris, 1729-33), 1.384-97. See also L. Grodecki, *Les vitraux de St-Denis* (Paris, 1976), pp. 115-21, and E.A.R. Brown and M.W. Cothren, 'The Twelfth-Century Crusading Window of the Abbey of St-Denis', *Journal of the Warburg and Courtauld Institutes* 49 (1986), pp. 1-40. This article suggests a possible date after the Second Crusade, which I do not myself find convincing.

throughout the world, and does not contain overt references to crusading. On the other hand, the feast day of the *divisio* (15 July) was notable as being the very day when Jerusalem was liberated by the First Crusade, and contemporaries may have discerned a hidden pattern of references here. At all events, it was not a work of crusade propaganda in as obvious a sense as the St-Denis window.[14]

In the first 150 years of the movement we are able to find few single artistic compositions designed for raising troops for individual crusades. Almost every crusade produced a chronicle, or several chronicles, and it is tempting to look for narrative accounts on the walls of churches, designed for the glory of God and the encouragement of pilgrims. Here again, we almost draw a blank. Apart from the St-Denis window, there was a record of the history of the Fourth Crusade in the mosaic floor of the church of San Giovanni Evangelista at Ravenna. The floor was destroyed in the sixteenth century, but the few remaining panels can be best understood as part of a longer sequence. Unlike the glass at St-Denis, it would be readily accessible to the public, and is a very simple piece of work: crude representations in relatively cheap materials, and accompanied by other panels of popular proverbs, such as the story of the fox and goose.[15] Seen from our standpoint, it is difficult to believe that there were other major memorials which have disappeared without trace; but when we remember that there is no medieval mention of those at St-Denis and Ravenna, and that they survive only in copies or fragments, it is clear that nothing excludes the total disappearance of similar works at other major centres. We know, indeed, that in the 1250s the commitment of Henry III of England to the crusades, if it did not extend as far as a journey to the Holy Land, led him to have wall paintings made of their history on the walls of royal residences.[16]

Whatever may be the truth about extended historical narratives, there is little doubt that by 1200 the churches and great halls of the West had acquired allusions to the crusades, which would keep the fate of the Holy Land in the minds of the military classes, and, indeed, of the people as a whole. Enough

---

[14] See A. Katzenellenbogen, 'The Central Tympanum at Vézelay', *Art Bulletin* 26 (1944), pp. 141-51, and M.D. Taylor, 'The Pentecost at Vézelay', *Gesta* 19 (1980), pp. 9-15. There are photographs in these articles, and in M.F. Hearn, *Romanesque Sculpture* (Oxford, 1981), p. 168.

[15] Plate 3. The date 1213 has been suggested for this pavement (G. Bovini, *Ravenna* [Ravenna, 1979]): under Innocent III the Latin conquest of Constantinople was being seen as an unambiguous victory and a great step towards the reunion of the Catholic church.

[16] Two favourite themes were the capture of Antioch, and the legendary duel of Richard I and Saladin. See *The History of the King's Works*, gen. ed. H.M. Colvin, 6 vols (London, 1963-82), 1.128-9.

remains to suggest that such paintings were once common. They were originally designed to fulfil a wide range of purposes: to give thanks for a victory or a safe return; to obtain the blessing of God on departure by an *ex voto* offering; to honour a king by displaying him as a warrior for Christendom; to celebrate the prowess of a Military Order and drum up support for its activities. A sequence of wall paintings was discovered after long obscurity in the little Templar chapel of Cressac in Charente where the whole chapel was once decorated. On the north wall we see a group of knights riding out from a Christian town to defeat a group of Saracen horsemen. The presence of a crowned Saracen has suggested that the decoration of the chapel commemorated a specific episode, the defeat of Nur al-Din in the battle of the Homs gap in September 1163. He was attacking Krak des Chevaliers, and in the Christian forces were a Templar contingent and two great nobles of western France — Hugh, count of Lusignan, and the brother of the count of Angoulême — who were returning from pilgrimage to Jerusalem. The decoration on the other walls is difficult or impossible to decipher, but it appears to include St George killing his dragon and a 'Romanesque rider' — two symbolic themes which I will discuss in a moment.[17] There are other sieges and battle scenes which may well have a crusade reference, but which cannot be firmly attributed. A bas-relief in the church of St-Nazaire, Carcassonne seems to commemorate the death of Simon of Montfort at Toulouse in 1218 during the Albigensian Crusade, although its purpose is obscure.[18] Often, we are left unsure of the exact subject which the designers had commissioned. It is natural to think that the scenes of battle on the Porta dei Leoni at San Nicola, Bari and the siege in the Salle d'Armes at Le Puy tell a crusade story, but there is no way of being certain.[19]

The rarity of funeral statues of the nobility in the twelfth century means that there are few commemorative portraits of crusaders. It is likely that a famous statue, formerly in the monastery of Belval, Lorraine, was an *ex voto*, an act of thanksgiving for a safe, if very delayed, return. It appears to show Count

---

[17] *Oxford Illustrated History of the Crusades*, p. 196 shows a Templar knight at Cressac, with motif on his shield and banner. See also P. Deschamps, 'Combats de cavalerie et épisodes de croisades dans les peintures murales du XIIᵉ et du XIIIᵉ siècle', *Orientalia christiana periodica* 13 (1947), pp. 454-74.

[18] Photograph in H. Kraus, *The Living Theatre of Medieval Art* (London, 1967), p. 135.

[19] There is a good account of the progressive investigation of this painting by F. Énaud, 'Peintures murales découvertes dans une dépendance de la cathédrale du Puy-en-Velay: problèmes d'interprétation', *Monuments historiques* 14/4 (1968), pp. 30-76, although the final interpretation is so complex that one wonders if viewers could understand it.

Hugh of Vaudémont, who came home from the Second Crusade after some fifteen years. His wife embraces her elderly husband, who has a cross on his breast and supports himself on a pilgrim staff.[20] Royal propaganda was beginning to present the ruler as a crusading hero. Frederick Barbarossa appears as a champion of the Cross and as a martyr, and a splendid English manuscript drawing of about 1250 shows a knight doing homage, conceivably Henry III making a commitment to a crusade.[21] A statue of St Louis and his wife, Marguerite of Provence, is a forceful statement of crusade ideology: Louis wears a robe with a cross, a sword and mail gauntlets, and carries a shield with the fleur-de-lys symbol. In his left hand, he holds a copy of the Holy Sepulchre.[22] Nobles, as well as kings, wanted to record their enthusiasm. It has been plausibly suggested that a group of knights on the wall at St-Jacques des Guérets in Loir et Cher is an *ex voto* for the departure of Count Peter I of Vendôme on crusade in 1248.[23] Problems of the survival and identification of works of art do not leave us with many specific references to crusades and crusaders before the middle of the thirteenth century. We can trace with more confidence the use of iconography to define the ideals of holy war, and conversely the invasion of Christian imagery by crusading themes. In art, as well as in its other expressions, crusading ideology cannot be isolated as a distinctive area within medieval culture. The word 'crusade' and its equivalents were slow to emerge, and were not much used. In canon law, Gratian was unaware of crusades as a distinct entity: crusading privileges were only defined legally in the thirteenth century, and then they were applied to a wide range of activities in the service of the church. Crusading settled like a cancer inside the body of medieval Christendom, adapting itself to its host in ways which the science of the time could not discern, and being carried to every part of the organism.

The image of the Christian life as a battle goes back at least to the injunction of Ephesians 6:10-20: 'Put on the whole armour of God'. In the visual arts, it was mediated to the West specially through the battle poem of Prudentius, the *Psychomachia*, composed about 400.[24] The warfare between individual virtues

---

[20] Illustration in *Oxford Illustrated History of the Crusades*, p. 69. It seems that Hugh returned about 1163 and died in 1165. See P. Deschamps, *Au temps des croisades* (Paris, 1972), pp. 81-3, and M. François, *Histoire des comtes et du comté de Vaudémont* (Nancy, 1935).

[21] *Oxford Illustrated History of the Crusades*, pp. 38, 79 (for Barbarossa); 51 (Henry III?).

[22] Illustrated in R. Delort, *Life in the Middle Ages* (London, 1974), p. 115.

[23] Deschamps, 'Combats de cavalerie', p. 463.

[24] See A. Katzenellenbogen, *Allegories of the Virtues and Vices in Medieval Art* (London, 1939), and J.S. Norman, *Metamorphoses of an Allegory: The Iconography of the Psychomachia in Medieval Art* (New York, 1988).

and their opposing vices, such as *largitas* and *avaritia*, was described there in very visual images, which tempted copyists to produce illuminated manuscripts. The first survives from the ninth century, but the archetype may well be much older than that. Prudentius was writing a psychological allegory about the triumph within the Christian soul of holiness over temptation, but once the imagery emerged into public life, the simplicity of his division between vice and virtue had drastic effects. It gave visual expression to the contemporary belief that, as *The Song of Roland* incisively put it, 'Christians are right and pagans are wrong'.

From the eleventh century onwards, there was a growing intensity in contemporary interest in the imagery of the *Psychomachia*. Illustrations were up-dated to show battles between modern knights. Single battles between a vice and a virtue were taken as subjects in the emerging art of figural sculpture. Joanne Norman has pointed to the capitals at Notre-Dame-du-Port, Clermont, as being 'an important example of the transition of the allegorical theme from manuscript to sculpture'.[25]

Given the probable use of model books in design, it was possible for images to travel both ways between Prudentius's battles of virtue versus vice and pictures of contemporary warfare. 'Affronted knights' engaged in battle were a favourite theme in Saintonge, Poitou and south-western France generally, as well as in northern Spain, in the years around 1100. The purpose of these images varied. Some of the earliest ones have plausibly been interpreted as advertising the Peace of God or expressing the reliability of judicial combat.[26] These regions had a history marked by conflict with Muslim invaders, but it is difficult to be sure when 'affronted knights' first represented the battle between Christian and Muslim. There seems to be a convincing example on the 'screen' west front of Angoulême cathedral about 1130. On a capital at Cunault in Anjou, perhaps a few years later, a Christian knight is unquestionably confronted by a devilish Saracen.[27] The struggle of virtue against vice,

---

[25] Norman, *Metamorphoses of an Allegory*, pp. 29-32. Unfortunately, it is impossible to date the capitals at Clermont, beyond saying that they must be roughly 1075/1125.

[26] R. Lejeune and J. Stiennon, *La légende de Roland dans l'art du moyen âge*, 2nd edn (Brussels, 1967), pp. 19-25, on 'Peace of God' capitals. For the judicial combat theme at Cluny, see F. Cardini, *Le crociate tra il mito e la storia* (Rome, 1971), tav. XIIa; the correct text for this is under tav. XV.

[27] Lejeune and Stiennon, *Roland*, pp. 29-30 and 88, and Hearn, *Romanesque Sculpture*, pp. 181-5. D.J.A. Ross, 'The Iconography of Roland', *Medium Aevum* 37 (1968), pp. 46-65, is sceptical about suggestions of earlier instances of warfare with Islam, but agrees that this is portrayed at Angoulême and Cunault. For the capital at Cunault, see Plate 4. Anjou had very

having absorbed into itself the elements of war against the unbeliever, was further enriched by one of the great medieval epics, *The Song of Roland*, which began to be depicted all over Europe. Important examples are: the two knights (1139?) on the west front of Verona cathedral, one of them bearing the sword 'Durindarda'; the mosaic floor of Brindisi (1168?), which had the story of Roland at its margins; and the German manuscript of the *Ruolantes Liet*, illustrated perhaps about 1175. The wide dissemination of the theme suggests that there must have been earlier examples, but they are lost or cannot be conclusively identified.[28]

It was important to represent not only the conflict of faith with unbelief, but also its victory. In Saintonge and Poitou a clearly triumphant horseman, the 'Romanesque rider' as he is sometimes called, was a frequent figure. His majestic air has led to his identification with Constantine, himself a historic symbol of the triumph of the church over paganism.[29] Porches and west fronts began to incorporate another classical expression of triumph by adopting themes from Roman arches of victory. True, triumphalism is not necessarily directed against Islam, but at Moissac a carving showing the fall of the idols, and perhaps the entry into Jerusalem, underlines the crusade reference.

The first half of the twelfth century saw the abundant entrance of Islamic motifs, derived from buildings in the East and precious cloths brought back from the crusades, into the art of southern Europe. They were no doubt attractive as artistic novelties, but their presence was also part of the triumphal theme. Linda Seidel has suggested that façades were designed to celebrate the 'artistic piracy' practised in Spain and Syria by the lords who financed the building of the churches.[30] This view is confirmed by the presence of the

---

strong links with the kingdom of Jerusalem from 1129 onwards.

[28] See Lejeune and Stiennon, *Roland*, passim, for possible earlier occurrences.

[29] The most careful discussion of the 'Constantine thesis' is to be found in R. Crozet, 'Nouvelles remarques sur les cavaliers sculptés ou peints dans les églises romanes', *Cahiers de civilisation médiévale* 1 (1958), pp. 27-36. There are other studies of the teasing iconography of these façades in Saintonge and elsewhere by H. Le Roux, 'Figures équestres et personnages du nom de Constantin aux XIᵉ et XIIᵉ siècles', *Bulletin de la société des antiquaires de l'Ouest et des musées de Poitiers*, sér. 4, 12 (1974), pp. 379-94; L. Seidel, 'Holy Warriors: The Romanesque Rider and the Fight against Islam', in *The Holy War*, ed. T.P. Murphy (Columbus, 1976), pp. 33-54; and especially her *Songs of Glory: The Romanesque Façades of Aquitaine* (Chicago, 1981). See also A. Tcherikover, 'Une invention de XIXᵉ siècle: les prétendus cavaliers de la cathédrale d'Angoulême', *Cahiers de civilisation médiévale* 38 (1995), pp. 275-8.

[30] Seidel, *Songs of Glory*, pp. 79-82.

themes in churches with special crusade associations, such as Le Puy, or Le Wast, near Boulogne, which was founded by Ida, the mother of Godfrey of Bouillon. The cathedral at Pisa seems to be an early example of this motif: an Islamic griffon, apparently captured in a raid on Palermo, was displayed prominently on its east end.[31] At San Nicola, Bari, the victory motif takes a rather different form in a splendid throne designed for Archbishop Elia (1098-1105), just after the victory of the First Crusade. The massive seat is upheld by distorted and exotic figures, which probably represent the pagan races who were being brought into obedience to Christendom.[32]

The artistic identification of Prudentius's virtues with crusaders is vividly illustrated in a carving at Civray (Vienne), where one of the virtues has a crusader cross on his sword.[33] It was confirmed by one of the most important steps towards an iconography of the crusades: the saints became Christian warriors. In all probability it was an irresistible tendency, but it had a historical basis. In the battle outside Antioch in June 1098 the Franks had been assisted by 'a countless host of men on white horses, whose banners were all white', led by Saints George, Mercurius and Demetrius.[34] The event is commemorated on the south doorway of the church at Fordington, near Dorchester, where the style of the figures suggests a date very shortly after 1100. George, with banner and lance, is overcoming the enemies of the faith, at the intercession of the knights kneeling behind him. The same episode is recorded in a painting at Poncé-sur-le-Loir, where Saracen soldiers are put to flight by white knights.[35] More commonly, artists loved to depict the victory of St George over the dragon, a theme which appeared in the West early in the twelfth century. There is a particularly triumphant one over the portal of the cathedral of St George at Ferrara, where George has already thrust his lance down the dragon's throat and is now brandishing his sword for the *coup de grâce*. The carving was designed by one of the greatest of the north Italian sculptors,

---

[31] The cathedral was begun in 1063, financed by spoil from the raid on Palermo. We do not know when the decision was taken to put the captured article in its prominent position. The most striking example of display of booty is at San Marco, Venice, where the Pala d'Oro, the façade and the treasury proclaim victory over Byzantium rather than over Islam.

[32] Hearn, *Romanesque Sculpture*, pp. 80-1. The statement by a later chronicler that the throne was a gift of Urban II in 1098 was probably a misunderstanding of the inscription.

[33] Cardini, *Le crociate*, tav. XI.

[34] *GF*, p. 69.

[35] For the Fordington sculpture, see *Oxford Illustrated History of the Crusades*, p. 80. On Poncé see P. Deschamps, 'Combats de cavalerie', pp. 454-74. The St George wall paintings at Hardham in Sussex do not seem to allude to his appearance at the Battle of Antioch.

Nicolà, about 1135.[36] By that time, George and the dragon had already appeared in another superb artwork, the Ganagobie mosaic (c. 1125) (Plate 5). The presence of George and the dragon among the holy war symbols at Cressac confirms that the legend was seen in a crusading context: in literature, it was located in Syria and linked to the conversion of a pagan king. By the 1160s, St Maurice too, on his home ground on a great reliquary in the treasury of Agaune in Switzerland, was bearing a cross on his shield and banner (Plate 7).

Chroniclers of the First Crusade readily adapted Biblical ideas to clarify God's work in the liberation of the Holy Land. Painters and sculptors did the same thing. Some of their devices were straightforward ones. On the central doorway of Autun cathedral, the last judgement (itself a new theme for grandiose sculpture) calls to their eternal reward two pilgrims, whose bags are marked with the cockleshell of Compostella and the cross of Jerusalem.[37] Other designs were more ambitious and original. The decoration of the south transept of Le Puy cathedral incorporates Biblical motifs quite rare in medieval churches: the life of Moses; three scenes from the life of Solomon, including his entry into Jerusalem; the building of the Temple after the return from exile(?); the entry of Christ into Jerusalem; and a scroll from Zephaniah 3:14: 'Rejoice and exult with all your heart, O daughter of Jerusalem!' Unfortunately the paintings are only recorded in a nineteenth-century copy, and are consequently difficult to date, but Anne Derbes has argued that they are best understood as a commemoration of the delivery of Jerusalem in 1099, and a memorial to the great bishop Adhémar, who was the spiritual leader of the expedition until his death at Antioch.[38]

In Auxerre cathedral, the vaults of the apsidal crypt chapel are decorated with paintings of Christ, mounted on a white horse and carrying a jewelled cross, accompanied by four mounted angels. The reference is to Revelation 19:11-16, but the treatment is unusual. The design has been ascribed to Bishop Humbald (1092-1114), an assiduous decorator of the cathedral and enthusiast of the Holy Land; the suggestion is plausible, although less conclusive than the case of Le Puy.[39] Shortly after the Second Crusade, in 1151, the church of Schwarzrheindorf was consecrated. It was built by the archbishop of Cologne,

---

[36] Plate 6. The statue is attributed to him by the inscription surrounding the tympanum. See S. Stocchi, *Italia Romanica 6: L'Emilia-Romagna* (Milan, 1984), pp. 342-50.

[37] Cardini, *Le crociate*, tav. VIII.

[38] A. Derbes, 'A Crusading Fresco Cycle at the Cathedral of Le Puy', *Art Bulletin* 73/4 (1991), pp. 561-76.

[39] D. Denny, 'A Romanesque Fresco in Auxerre Cathedral', *Gesta* 25 (1986), pp. 197-202.

Arnold of Wied, who had accompanied Conrad III to the Holy Land. The decorative scheme is very unusual indeed: twenty scenes from Ezekiel's visions of Jerusalem, concentrating mostly on the destruction of the city. Christ's purification of the Temple (itself, perhaps surprisingly, a very rare subject in Romanesque art) is prominent at the west end of the church. This concentration on Jerusalem must, one supposes, say something about expectations for the city in the aftermath of the failure in Palestine, but it is impossible for us to read the message: there may well be a strongly anti-Jewish element in this concentration on judgement. Perhaps the designer saw in the punishment of unfaithful Jerusalem a guarantee for the safety of the Christian city, in spite of the devastating setback which the Western armies had experienced.[40]

It was of course not necessary to find new Biblical iconography to express the holy war against Islam: ideas already established could be developed. The apocryphal gospel according to Matthew had told how, when the Holy Family fled to Egypt from Herod and entered a temple, 'all the idols fell to the ground so that all lay on their faces completely overturned and shattered'. It had long been believed, in defiance of reality, that Islam was idolatrous, and in the medieval mind its worship was not clearly distinguished from the paganism of the Greco-Roman world. This reputation was confirmed by the widely reported image of Antichrist discovered in the Temple by Tancred at the fall of Jerusalem.[41] One of the most dramatic presentations of the fall of the idols in face of the power of the Holy Family was on the portal at Moissac about 1125, as part of a rendering of the nativity stories from the Annunciation to the Flight into Egypt. Given the links between Moissac and Urban II, and imitation of classical triumphal architecture in its portal, one must agree with Michael Camille that 'the meaning of the Moissac image in its particular site has obvious bearings on the current concerns with Christian reconquest of the Holy Land'.[42] A few years before, the west front at Angoulême had shown a Saracen defeat in front, it seems, of an idol in a temple. The *Psychomachia* motif of the conflict of faith and idolatry obtains a full application to holy war in a

---

[40] A. Derbes, 'The Frescoes of Schwarzrheindorf, Arnold of Wied and the Second Crusade', in *The Second Crusade and the Cistercians*, ed. M. Gervers (New York, 1992), pp. 141-54.

[41] R.C. Schwinges, *Kreuzzugsideologie und Toleranz: Studien zu Wilhelm von Tyrus* (Stuttgart, 1977), Part II; M. Camille, *The Gothic Idol: Ideology and Image-Making in Medieval Art* (Cambridge, 1989), pp. 140ff.

[42] Hearn, *Romanesque Sculpture*, with illustration at p. 175; Camille, *The Gothic Idol*, pp. 4-9; L. Seidel, 'Images of the Crusades in Western Art: Models and Metaphors', in *The Meeting of Two Worlds: Cultural Exchange between East and West during the Period of the Crusades*, ed. V.P. Goss and C.V. Bornstein (Kalamazoo, 1986), pp. 377-91.

poem written for the Second Crusade: *Fides cum idolatria pugnavit, teste gratia.* In Jean Bodin's play, the *Jeu de St Nicholas*, composed for performance at Amiens in 1202, a great deal of the action turns on the power struggle between the true image of St Nicholas and the false idol, and the action of the play suggests that the theme may have been far more familiar visually to contemporaries, from scenery and stage properties, than we would deduce from the surviving architectural fragments. Although there were Christian scholars who realized that Muslims did not worship idols, the obsession with the supposed idolatry of the enemy grew during the thirteenth century. A Parisian manuscript of William of Tyre, now in Baltimore, summarized the crusading movement in a diagram which consisted of the preaching of Urban II, the Crucifixion, a pilgrim at the Holy Sepulchre, and Muslims worshipping a naked idol on a column.[43]

It is increasingly accepted by historians that the primary and original purpose of Urban II in 1095 was the recovery of the Holy Sepulchre for Christendom. It is no accident that the crusades developed at a time when Western spirituality was placing increasing stress on the human life of Jesus, his suffering and death on the cross, and the apostolic life as a model of monastic discipline. This quest for the historical Jesus (if hardly in Albert Schweizer's sense of the words) was an authentic expression of contemporary attitudes, and involved an increased reverence for the sacred sites 'where his feet have trod'. Nativity sequences, 'majesties' of Mary and child, crucifixes, these and many other works of art could stimulate the imaginations of contemporaries and their love of the Holy Land, without the need to incorporate any specific allusion to the crusades. So, pre-eminently, could the arrival in the West of relics, of fragments of the True Cross and even soil from the Holy Sepulchre. The swelling pilgrimages of the eleventh and twelfth century brought such relics to parts of Europe which had not previously possessed them.

One aspect of this reverence for the Holy Places was the long-standing fascination of Christians with the actual form of the Holy Sepulchre. Its architecture seems to have been depicted, shortly after 400, in the great mosaic at Santa Pudenziana in Rome; just after 600 A.D. flasks designed for holy oil or earth were brought to the Lombard court, with diagrams of the Holy Places on them. Carolingian liturgy adopted Jerusalem ceremonial; the great churches incorporated areas which (symbolically at least) represented the Sepulchre; and manuscripts of the descriptions by Adomnan and Bede, which incorporated

---

[43] *Oxford Illustrated History of the Crusades*, p. 44.

plans of the major Jerusalem churches, were widely distributed.[44] Attempts at a precise reproduction of the aedicule (or Sepulchre itself) or of the great fourth-century dome which overshadowed it, the Anastasis, preceded the crusades by more than a century. A diploma of Charles the Bald in 887 described the complex of churches at Santo Stefano, Bologna, as 'Jerusalem', although the significance of this is far from clear.[45] Bishop Konrad of Konstanz (935-75), assiduous pilgrim to the Holy Land and confidant of the Ottonian court, built a copy of the Sepulchre at his cathedral. It was entirely rebuilt *in situ* in the thirteenth century. The oldest such copy which survives intact is at Aquileia, built before 1077.

It is scarcely surprising that returning crusaders wanted to provide themselves with copies of the Sepulchre. The unusually fine version of the Anastasis at Holy Sepulchre, Northampton, was built by Simon of Senlis on his return from the First Crusade (Plate 8). The church of the Holy Sepulchre at Asti in Piemonte, long supposed to be a baptistery, is most naturally ascribed to Bishop Landulf after his return from the Holy Land in 1103.[46] In the distant Orkneys, the Jerusalem pilgrim Earl Hakon Paulsson (died 1122) built a small round church, of which the apse still remains, at his seat at Orphir (Plate 9). The site of the Round Church at Cambridge was granted by Abbot Reinald of Ramsey (1114-30) to the 'fraternity of the Holy Sepulchre' (probably an association of pilgrims) to build there 'in honour of God and the Holy Sepulchre'. At Pisa, which had close links with Jerusalem in the middle years of the twelfth century, the architect Diotisalvi produced two buildings inspired by the Anastasis: the delicate little church of Santo Sepolcro on the left bank of the Arno, and the majestic baptistery beside the cathedral, which

---

[44] A twelfth-century ground plan of the Holy Sepulchre still clearly reflects the influence of the Adomnan/Bede plans: *Oxford Illustrated History of the Crusades*, p. 115. The source and extent of the Jerusalem influence on Carolingian liturgy is disputed, but for a persuasive survey see C. Heitz, *Recherches sur les rapports entre architecture et liturgie à l'époque carolingienne* (Paris, 1963).

[45] The Leverhulme Trust generously made it possible for me to visit some of the important sites in Italy and southern Germany. The issue of 'Jerusalem in the West' will be discussed in an article, 'Bringing Jerusalem to the West: S. Stefano, Bologna, from the Fifth to the Twentieth Century', in *Church Retrospective*, ed. R.N. Swanson, *Studies in Church History* 33. The cemetery chapel consecrated in 822 under Abbot Eigil at Fulda is sometimes listed as the first precise copy, but the inscription by Hrabanus Maurus probably meant simply that there was earth from the Holy Sepulchre there. See O. Ellger, *Die Michaelskirche zu Fulda als Zeugnis des Totensorge* (Fulda, 1988).

[46] S. Casartelli-Novelli, 'L'église du St-Sépulchre ou le baptistère St-Pierre-Consavia', *Congrès archéologique* 129 (1977), pp. 358-63.

was similarly designed as an imitation of the great rotunda at Jerusalem.[47] Bologna acquired a rather remarkable version of the Holy Sepulchre, and the Templars favoured round or polygonal buildings for some of their chapels. Along the same line of thinking, churches and chapels with crusading links were decorated with themes reminiscent of the Holy Sepulchre, such as the entombment of Christ.[48]

All these, and other such memorials, pointed to Jerusalem. Joshua Prawer commented that the Frankish rebuilding of the city was more ambitious than any other before the twentieth century. Logically, this survey should end with an examination of their work there, which in some senses was the supreme expression of the iconography of crusading. It is appropriate, however, that Bernard Hamilton himself has spared us the necessity, by illustrating in one of his most impressive articles how Jerusalem was rebuilt by its Latin rulers, not simply to provide pictures for the illiterate, but to form 'a visual expression of the faith of the crusaders, and indeed of that of the whole Christian west, and a symbol of their deep devotion to the humanity of Christ'.[49]

---

[47] The photograph in *Oxford Illustrated History of Christianity*, p. 207, shows the baptistery at Pisa, to the front of the Piazza dei Miracoli. The gallery is a later substitution.

[48] *Oxford Illustrated History of the Crusades*, p. 89, for the Holy Sepulchre chapel at Winchester cathedral, which was perhaps painted on the occasion of Bishop Peter des Roches' crusade of 1227.

[49] B. Hamilton, 'Rebuilding Zion: The Holy Places of Jerusalem in the Twelfth Century', in *Renaissance and Renewal in Christian History*, ed. D. Baker, *Studies in Church History* 14 (Oxford, 1977), pp. 105-16. More recently, the ideology of crusading art in the Holy Land itself has been magnificently examined by J. Folda, *The Art of the Crusaders in the Holy Land, 1098-1187* (Cambridge, 1995). The crusader buildings at the church of the Holy Sepulchre are illustrated in detail there, and much more briefly in *Oxford Illustrated History of the Crusades*, pp. 163, 212-13.

Plates 1-2. Two panes from the First Crusade window, abbey of St-Denis, nea
Paris: the battle with Corbaram (Kerbogha) outside Antioch and the entry int
Jerusalem. Copies from Bernard de Mountfaucon, *Les monumens de la monar*
chie française (Paris, 1729-33).

Plate 3. The Fourth Crusade at the gates of Constantinople. Panel from an original floor mosaic at San Giovanni Evangelista, Ravenna, perhaps 1213.

Plate 4. In this capital from Cunault (Anjou), dating from the 1130s, a Christian knight confronts a devilish Saracen.

Plate 5. In this floor mosaic at Ganagobie (Provence), c. 1125, is an early, but fine, depiction of St George slaying the dragon.

Plate 6. A triumphal St George on the tympanum of the cathedral at Ferrara, c. 1135.

Plate 7. By the 1160s, St Maurice, on a reliquary casket at Agaune (Switzerland), has acquired a cross on his shield and banner.

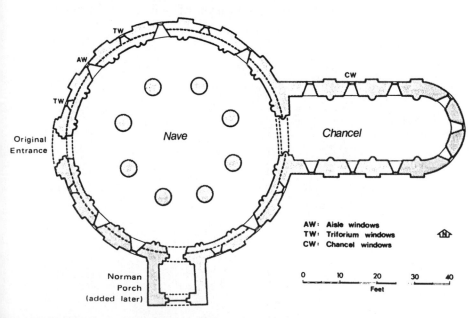

Plate 8. The church of the Holy Sepulchre, Northampton, was built by Simon of Senlis on his return from the First Crusade. It has been greatly altered in later centuries, but its original appearance and plan can be reconstructed with some confidence.

Colin Morris

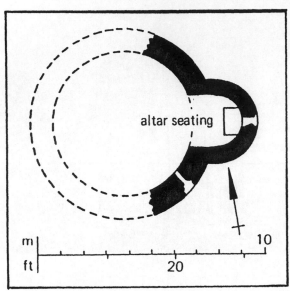

altar seating

m

ft

10

20

Plate 9. Earl Hakon Paulsson, a pilgrim to Jerusalem (died 1122), built a round church near his seat at Orphir in the Orkneys, of which the foundations and some fragments remain.

'Mighty Against the Enemies of Christ': The Relic of the True Cross in the Armies of the Kingdom of Jerusalem

Alan V. Murray

In the lives of medieval states, there were few caesuras as definitive as the events of the summer of 1187 proved to be for the Latin kingdom of Jerusalem. On 4 July the Franks of Jerusalem under their king, Guy of Lusignan, accompanied by contingents from Antioch and Tripoli, suffered a disastrous defeat at the hands of Saladin, king of Egypt, who had managed to unite most of the Muslim Middle East against the European occupiers of Palestine and Syria. The Frankish mobilization had been so comprehensive that only skeleton garrisons remained to defend most of Outremer, and Saladin proceeded to overrun the entire Christian territory with the exception of a few coastal cities. Despite the efforts of the Third Crusade which was the response of the West to this great defeat, the kingdom never regained its former extent.

For contemporaries both in Outremer and the Christian West, one of the most traumatic aspects of the disaster of Hattin was the loss of a relic which was believed to have been part of the Cross of Christ. It had been the custom for this relic to be carried into battle along with the army of the kingdom, normally by the patriarch of Jerusalem or his representative, but on this occasion Patriarch Eraclius had refused to join the army, and sent the True Cross in the charge of the prior of the Holy Sepulchre. The loss of the Cross was disastrous enough in itself, but in addition it threatened the whole belief system of those who had previously trusted to its powers; how was it possible for such a powerful relic to be captured, and its followers killed or imprisoned? The author of the Old French continuation of William of Tyre judged that the king 'had trusted more in his own power and in his men than in the virtue of Jesus Christ and the Holy Cross',[1] and indeed the sins of the Christians came

---

[1] P.W. Edbury, ed. and trans., *The Conquest of Jerusalem and the Third Crusade: Sources in Translation* (Aldershot, 1996), p. 37.

to be advanced as one of the most frequent explanations of the defeat by writers in East and West. At the same time there was a desperate need to believe that the Cross had survived, which can be seen in legends which rapidly grew up about its fate. According to a letter sent by unknown writers – possibly from Outremer – to the Emperor Frederick Barbarossa after the battle, Saladin threw the relic into a fire, but it jumped out of the flames, with no apparent damage. During the Third Crusade, a Templar apparently managed to convince Henry, count of Troyes, that the Cross had not been secured by Saladin, but was actually still near to where it had fallen. Even though this was now three whole years after the battle, Henry spent three nights searching the battlefield, in a touching but quite desperately hopeless effort to recover the Cross.[2]

In his wide-ranging study of the cult of the True Cross Anatole Frolow remarked on the habit of the Franks of Outremer of taking the relic into battle, but did not analyse this phenomenon beyond collecting a significant number of references.[3] More recently, Penny Cole has discussed the significance of the loss of the relic in 1187 for Christendom as a whole, while in a forthcoming article Deborah Gerish examines the role of the True Cross in the legitimation of both monarchy and patriarchate of Jerusalem.[4] Given Bernard Hamilton's interests in and major contributions to both the political and ecclesiastical history of Outremer, it seems appropriate in a volume dedicated to him to discuss a relic which played a central role in both the religious and military life of the kingdom of Jerusalem. In this article I would like to explore how this particular relic of the True Cross functioned as a military artefact (avoiding as far as possible the themes of Cole and Gerish), and to establish as complete as possible a catalogue of its use.

As will become clear below, the main purpose of the Cross in battle was a morale-raising one, and in this respect it stood in a long tradition of relics and other sacred objects being used in warfare in Christian Europe to encourage the

---

[2] P. Cole, 'Christian Perceptions of the Battle of Hattin (583-1187)', *Al-Masaq* 6 (1993), pp. 9-39.

[3] A. Frolow, *La Relique de la Vraie Croix: recherches sur le développement d'un culte* (Paris, 1961).

[4] Cole, 'Christian Perceptions of the Battle of Hattin'; D. Gerish, 'The True Cross and the Kings of Jerusalem', *The Haskins Society Journal* (forthcoming). The propagandistic use of the Cross in connection with a diplomatic mission to Henry II of England is treated by G. Ligato, 'The Political Meanings of the Relic of the Holy Cross among the Crusaders and in the Latin Kingdom of Jerusalem: An Example of 1185', in *Autour de la Première Croisade*, ed. M. Balard (Paris 1996), pp. 315-30, although much of the argumentation is less than clear.

spirits of the troops fighting alongside them. The best-known example of this may be the banner of St Denis. Originally a purely secular object – the standard of the Vexin – it came to be identified with the *oriflamme*, the red banner of Charlemagne. It was kept in the abbey of Saint-Denis near Paris, and was used by the Capetian monarchs in cases of military emergency, even going on crusade with St Louis.[5] A similar role was played by the Holy Lance acquired by Henry I of Germany from Rudolf II of Burgundy in 926, which was believed to be the weapon which had pierced Christ's side at the Crucifixion and which was also thought to contain the nails from the Cross. It became part of the coronation insignia of the German emperors and was taken into battle on several occasions by the Ottonians.[6] Possibly the most sophisticated example of the military sacred object was the *carroccio* used by several of the Lombard towns, and first mentioned in the case of Milan in 1039. The *carroccio* was a battle-wagon, sometimes consecrated, which was kept in the cathedral in times of peace, but which in wartime was wheeled forth bearing banners, often accompanied by priests bearing monstrances. The chronicler Salimbene of Parma even compared the *carroccio* of Milan to the *oriflamme*.[7] Such wagons served as a very concrete rallying and re-grouping point, and at a pinch a number of wounded could be hauled on board and kept in safety. This kind of object was of course far more suitable for infantry forces such as the urban militias of Lombardy, than for the armies of knights which were the fighting forces of the northern kingdoms.

Nevertheless, in the cases of actual relics of Christ and the saints, rather than banners, their use in battle seems to have been restricted, occurring only in cases of great necessity. This is clearly illustrated in Claude Gaier's study of the banner and relics of St Lambert in the ecclesiastical principality of Liège. From the twelfth to the fifteenth centuries the army of the bishopric regularly carried the gonfalon or banner of St Lambert, the patron saint of the diocese. By contrast there only seem to have been two occasions (1141 and 1151) when the actual bones of the saint in their reliquary were taken into battle, and even these were permitted only with great reluctance by the clerics responsible for

---

[5] G.M. Spiegel, 'The Cult of Saint Denis and Capetian Kingship', *Journal of Medieval History* 1 (1975), pp. 43-69.

[6] P.E. Schramm, *Herrschaftszeichen und Staatssymbolik*, 3 vols (Stuttgart, 1954-6), 2.492-6; M. Zufferey, 'Der Mauritiuskult im Früh- und Hochmittelalter', *Historisches Jahrbuch* 106 (1986), pp. 23-58; Gerish, 'True Cross'.

[7] T. Struve, 'Bischof Milo von Padua und der Paduaner Fahnenwagen', *Frühmittelalterliche Studien* 30 (1996), pp. 294-314.

them.[8] Even the Capetian kings had to ask permission to carry the banner of St Denis, although this normally seems to have been given. The Holy Lance of the German monarchs was something of an exception to the general trend in that this relic was recognized as the property of the monarchy, rather than as belonging to an ecclesiastical institution, which was the case with the great majority of sacred objects.

During the First Crusade, the combination of religious fervour and military tribulation produced an evident need for miraculous assistance for the Christian army, which was met during the siege of Antioch by the discovery of a piece of metal in the cathedral by a poor Provençal pilgrim called Peter Bartholomew. This object was readily accepted by most of the crusaders as the Holy Lance which had pierced the side of Christ at the Crucifixion, although there were far better authenticated Holy Lances in the possession of the Salian monarchs and at Constantinople. The lance of Antioch inspired the army during its time of greatest privation, but in the course of the march it came to be increasingly discredited, not least by the higher clergy in the army. On 8 April 1099 Peter Bartholomew perished while undergoing an ordeal by fire in a final, vain attempt to prove its authenticity by divine witness.[9]

Despite this cautionary example of the transitory success of such an important relic, a need for effective holy objects evidently remained, and surfaced soon after Jerusalem was captured on 15 July 1099. Some time after the army had elected a ruler and a patriarch – and thus probably in early August – a piece of the Lord's Cross was discovered, which became the military talisman *par excellence* of the Franks of Outremer. The accounts of the circumstances and even the place of its discovery are vague and contradictory. It is, of course, pointless to speculate as to the authenticity of the relic. What is important is what contemporaries believed it to be, and what purposes it served in the society which venerated it. To the Latin Christians of Outremer and many people in the West, it was believed to be a piece of the wood of the Crucifixion, discovered by St Helena, the mother of the Emperor Constantine, who had split the relic into two pieces which were awarded to Constantinople and Jerusalem. The piece belonging to Jerusalem had been taken by the

---

[8] C. Gaier, 'Le rôle militaire des reliques et de l'étendard de saint Lambert dans la principauté de Liège', *Le Moyen Âge* 72 (1966), pp. 235-49.

[9] C. Morris, 'Policy and Visions: The Case of the Holy Lance at Antioch', in *War and Government in the Middle Ages: Essays in Honour of J.O. Prestwich*, ed. J. Gillingham and J.C. Holt (Woodbridge, 1984), pp. 33-45; W. Giese, 'Die lancea domini von Antiochia (1098/99)', in *Fälschungen im Mittelalter*, ed. W. Setz, 6 vols (Hannover, 1988-90), 5.485-504.

Persians and recovered by the Emperor Heraclius in the seventh century. In the face of the Arab invasions the Jerusalem piece was further divided, and it was one of these fragments – so the Franks believed – which had re-emerged after the capture of the Holy City.[10] However, one must remember that, just as in the case of the Holy Lance at Antioch, the True Cross was a case of the right relic at the right time. The newly elected Latin patriarch, Arnulf of Chocques, had not been the unanimous choice of the entire army for the post.[11] The discovery of such a precious relic at this time could be represented as a sign of divine legitimation far more significant than the approbation of part of the crusading army. It is likely that it was the patriarch's initiative which led to the discovery, since it was his church, the Holy Sepulchre, which housed the relic forthwith.

As early as 1109 a canon of the Holy Sepulchre named Anselm wrote that there were no fewer than twenty known pieces of the True Cross in existence in both East and West. From evidence collected by Frolow it also seems that further fragments were sent from Palestine to various highly placed individuals and religious houses in the West in the course of the twelfth century; they, too, may have been discovered in the aftermath of the successful crusade.[12] Yet none of the other fragments originating in Outremer ever attained the renown of the relic discovered in August 1099. It is possible that, however contradictory the evidence may seem today, the circumstances of its discovery were a sufficient guarantee of authenticity to the Franks. What is probably more important, though, is the reputation which the relic rapidly acquired. Only a few days after its discovery the Cross was taken into battle at Ascalon, and by August 1105 it had been present at four major victories over numerically superior Fatimid forces.[13]

In physical form, the actual fragment seems to have been set in precious metals, and was embedded in a larger piece of wood fashioned in the shape of a cross. Although modern scholarship seems to prefer the term 'True Cross', the Latin sources refer to it as 'the wood of the Lord' and 'the Cross of the Lord', as well as by other formulations, and the imprecision of terminology may derive from the fact that the actual relic (i.e. the sacred wood) was merely

---

[10] For the different accounts see Frolow, *Relique*, pp. 286-7 and Hagenmeyer in FC, pp. 309-10.

[11] B. Hamilton, *The Latin Church in the Crusader States: The Secular Church* (London, 1980), pp. 12-14.

[12] 'Anselmi cantoris S. Sepulcri epistula ad canonicos ecclesiae Parisiensis de S. Cruce', *PL*, 162.731-2.

[13] Appendix, nos. 1099, 1101(b), 1102, 1105.

part of the larger object.[14] The Cross was kept in the Holy Sepulchre, where it was an object of devotion for pilgrims, and consequently a source of revenue. A charter of Baldwin I in 1114 reveals that offerings made to the Cross were to be kept by the canons of the Holy Sepulchre, except for those given on Good Friday and those made when the patriarch carried the Cross in case of necessity (i.e. military campaign).[15] As we might expect, the relic figured prominently in the great festivals of the Latin church, particularly in the ceremonies held on Palm Sunday, Good Friday and Easter Sunday. What is remarkable is that a relic which had such a central and regular place in the religious life of the kingdom should have been so often sent out of its normal liturgical orbit to accompany the Frankish armies into battle.

Between its discovery in August 1099 and its final loss in July 1187 the True Cross was carried on no fewer than thirty-one military (or primarily military) actions, accompanying the king of Jerusalem or his representative.[16] This means that on average the relic was deployed in the field once every 2.8 years at the very least. It is possible that the actual frequency was much higher. It is striking that we know of only three military actions involving the Cross in the 1130s and 1140s. This of course was a time of relative security for the kingdom compared to the reigns of Baldwin I, Baldwin II and Baldwin IV which show a frequent use of the relic. The history of Fulcher of Chartres ends

----

[14] For reasons of space it is impractical to list the full range of terms used. The descriptions used of the relic at the first battle of Ramla give an impression of the variation in terminology: 'crucem dominicam', 'lignum sanctae crucis' (AA, VII:66-7/p. 550), 'crux dominica' (FC, p. 414), 'dominicae crucis lignum' (FC, p. 409), 'ligno crucis dominice' (WT, p. 473).

[15] *Le cartulaire du Saint-Sépulcre de Jérusalem*, ed. G. Bresc-Bautier (Paris, 1984), no. 20: 'de Cruce vero Domini, quam canonici custodiunt, omni tempore oblationes habebunt, nisi in sola die sancti Parascheve, aut si patriarcha eam secum detulerit pro aliqua necessitate'; Hamilton, *Latin Church*, pp. 150-1. A canon, Baldwin, was referred to by William of Tyre as treasurer of the Holy Sepulchre and 'vivifice crucis baiulus' (WT, p. 1032).

[16] These are set out in the Appendix below, identified by the year of each action, with lower-case letters to distinguish actions in the same year. Frolow, *Relique*, pp. 287-90 listed 22 occasions prior to the battle of Hattin at which the Cross was carried. B.Z. Kedar, 'The Patriarch Eraclius', in *Outremer: Studies in the History of the Crusading Kingdom of Jerusalem presented to Joshua Prawer*, ed. B.Z. Kedar, H.E. Mayer and R.C. Smail (Jerusalem, 1982), pp. 177-204, mentions 18 instances from the years 1101-79 'in which the Cross was carried into a battle or siege' (p. 181). I therefore believe that the Appendix to this article represents the most complete listing to date of the military use of the True Cross during the existence of the first kingdom of Jerusalem (1099-1187). The 31 actions can be broken down by reign as follows: Godfrey (1099-1100) - 1, Baldwin I (1100-18) - 6, Baldwin II (1118-31) - 8, Fulk (1131-43) - 1, Baldwin III (1143-63) - 4, Amalric (1163-74) - 3, Baldwin IV (1174-85) - 7, Guy (1186-92) - 1.

at 1127, and from then on we are dependent on William of Tyre. Although William made use of Fulcher's work he did not always record the presence of the Cross in the pre-1127 period even where this is attested by Fulcher, and so there may have been other relevant occasions from the central part of the twelfth century which William failed to record.[17]

In the majority of cases, the Cross was deployed when the kingdom's security was seriously threatened by a major invasion requiring the mobilization of the largest part of the kingdom's forces, which were obliged to march to the relief of a threatened strongpoint or district, or to meet the enemy in the field. Most of these engagements took place within, or on the borders of the territory of the kingdom.[18] Yet the relic was not only used *in extremis*, as it were. On nine occasions it was carried on offensive expeditions or sieges.[19] In these cases it could normally be expected that the campaigns in question would lead to the acquisition of territory which would be incorporated into the kingdom, or to other benefits in the form of booty or captives.

It was only rarely that the relic was allowed to go beyond the kingdom or its immediate frontier zones. In two of these cases the army went to the relief of the king of Jerusalem, who was either in captivity or under siege, so that one could argue that the Cross was still being used in the interests of the kingdom.[20] The relic also left the kingdom in cases where the principality of Antioch came under major threat, a feature of the reign of Baldwin II.[21] The battle of Zerdana or Hab in northern Syria in 1119 was a case of extreme emergency, since in that year Prince Roger of Antioch and most of his army had been slain in a disastrous battle against the Turks, known afterward as the *Ager Sanguinis*, the Field of Blood. Thus the security of the entire Latin settlements was in question, which explains why Baldwin II took the relic well beyond the confines of the kingdom. Fulcher of Chartres reports that the armies of Jerusalem and Tripoli carried the Cross to battle as servants of the Lord, 'whom Almighty God, by the power of that same most holy and precious cross, had mightily snatched from the grasp of the abominable race

---

[17] For example, Appendix, nos. 1102, 1122(b).

[18] Appendix, nos. 1099, 1101(b), 1102, 1105, 1113, 1119(a), 1123(a), 1158, 1169/71, 1170, 1171, 1177, 1179, 1182(a), 1183(a), 1183(b), 1187.

[19] Appendix, nos. 1101(a), 1108, 1122(a), 1124, 1147, 1148, 1153, 1182(b), 1182(c).

[20] Appendix, nos. 1123(b), 1137.

[21] Appendix, nos. 1119(b), 1120, 1122(b).

of Turks and preserved for some future mission'.[22] This occasion was also important in constituting a precedent. Despite the victory gained by Baldwin, Antioch continued to be threatened by the Artukids, a Turkish dynasty of northern Syria. In 1120 Baldwin II proposed to march north again, and in doing so gave rise to a debate among the the Frankish nobility and clergy, which reveals much about the status of the relic in the kingdom, as well as the proprietorial claims on it. A faction among the nobility opposed the policies of the king, who, they thought, was spending too much time outside the kingdom. The patriarch aligned himself with this faction, and started a campaign to prevent the relic from leaving, speculating that the army would be unwilling to leave without it, so that the whole expedition could be sabotaged. The debate is reported by Fulcher of Chartres:

> ... there arose a strong difference of opinion between those going to war and those to remain in Jerusalem, whether in such a crisis for Christianity the Cross ought to be carried off to Antioch and whether the Church of Jerusalem ought to be deprived of such a treasure. And we said, 'Alas, what will we do if God permits us to lose the Cross in battle as the Israelites once lost the Ark of the Covenant?'[23]

The king had precedent on his side. The patriarch refused to accompany the relic, but it seems that he had no recognized right to refuse the king access to it in such an obvious case of necessity, and the Cross went north with the army.[24] The term 'Ark of the Covenant' is revealing of the political and religious status of the relic. One of the major themes of Frankish writers such as Fulcher of Chartres and William of Tyre was how the Franks had journeyed through adversity like the Israelites, and regained the Holy Land for Christendom. Even after large numbers of crusaders returned to the West, the remaining Franks survived against overwhelming hostile numbers thanks to the

---

[22] My translation. FC, p. 630: ' ... quos Deus omnipotens per virtutem eiusdem sanctissimae et pretiossimae crucis de manu nefandae gentis potenter eripuit et ad aliud suum negotium quandoque futurum reservavit'.

[23] FC, p. 639: 'unde ibi ratio bipertita inter euntes ad bellum et remanentes in Hierusalem satis decens habita est: sive debeat pro tanta necessitate Christianitatis Antiochiam crux deferri, sive Hierosolymitana ecclesia de tanto thesauro suo non privari. Dicebamusque: "heu miseri! Quid faciemus, si permittente Deo perdideramus in bello crucem, sicut perdiderunt Israelite olim foederis arcam?"'; translation: Fulcher of Chartres, *A History of the Expedition to Jerusalem*, trans. F.R. Ryan (Knoxville, 1969), p. 233 [hereafter to be cited as Fulcher, *History*].

[24] A.V. Murray, 'Baldwin II and his Nobles: Baronial Factionalism and Dissent in the Kingdom of Jerusalem, 1118-1134', *Nottingham Medieval Studies* 38 (1994), pp. 60-85.

special protection of the Lord.[25] Thus the True Cross was indeed a kind of Ark of the Covenant, since it was through this relic, on the field of battle, that the divine favour was most tangibly demonstrated.

It is equally illuminating to consider those occasions when the Cross was not carried. One must of course be wary of negative evidence, but at least in the first two decades of the kingdom's existence it seems reasonably safe to infer an absence of the relic when not mentioned by either Albert of Aachen or Fulcher of Chartres, who are normally punctilious in mentioning its presence. It was present at several sieges during the entire period. However, the two such occasions in the reign of Baldwin I are few indeed, given the amount of time and effort he devoted to the reduction of the Muslim-held cities of the coast.[26] This discrepancy would seem to indicate that in offensive actions the presence of the relic was not considered so necessary as during defensive ones. In a potentially long, drawn-out siege it was less easy to bring religious fervour to a peak than it was in a single battlefield encounter, and there may have been a basic psychology at work which tried to prevent the efficacy of the relic being diluted through use in cases where it was not absolutely necessary. One possible explanation for the sieges where the Cross *was* utilized may be the presence of numbers of pilgrims or other Europeans, such as the Franks' Venetian allies at the capture of Tyre, whom it was felt advisable to impress.

It seems – again subject to the caveats of negative evidence – that the Cross was not carried on purely offensive long-distance expeditions where there were no Latin settlements to defend. This applied to Baldwin I's exploration of Arabia in 1116 and to the expedition to Egypt in 1118 during which he died. The relic does not appear to have been present during the invasions of Egypt mounted by King Amalric in 1164, 1167 and 1168. This could be explained by the consideration that expeditions to Egypt meant that the relic would be outside the kingdom for too long, with a consequent increased risk of capture. Yet the king did not go unprotected. In 1164 Amalric is known to have had with him another, smaller fragment of the Cross, which he wore around his neck, and in battle against the Zankid general, Shirkuh, he made a vow to send it to the abbey of Clairvaux, where it seems to have ended up.[27]

---

[25] A.V. Murray, 'Ethnic Identity in the Crusader States: The Frankish Race and the Settlement of Outremer', in *Concepts of National Identity in the Middle Ages*, ed. S. Forde, L. Johnson and A.V. Murray (Leeds, 1995), pp. 59-73.

[26] Appendix, nos. 1101(a), 1108.

[27] Frolow, *Relique*, p. 338.

Of all the sources, it is Fulcher of Chartres who most clearly reveals how the Franks believed that the Cross brought divine favour and protection. In almost every case where he reports that the Cross was carried, he states explicitly that it was this relic which had brought victory. William of Tyre was less explicit on the qualities of the Cross. Nevertheless, the relic was clearly important to him. After all, he began his history with an account of how the Roman Emperor Heraclius had brought the Cross back from Persian captivity; it is also noticeable that he frequently describes it as *vivifice* ('life-giving').[28] The fact that William was less effusive could be explained by the fact that the military use of the relic had become much more commonplace by the time he was writing, or because the kingdom was not – yet – again in such dire straits as had been personally experienced by Fulcher, who on several occasions feared that the Frankish army would be wiped out and the Latin settlements overrun. His account of the first battle of Ramla reveals his faith in the power of the relic:

> There was present with us the Cross of the Saviour, mighty against the enemies of Christ. Against it, by the grace of God, the pomp of the pagans could not prevail. As if confounded by the presence of the Cross not only did they cease from attacking us but, struck with shame, all thought of precipitate flight.[29]

Fulcher is even more specific in his judgement of the second battle of Ramla and the battle of Jaffa, both fought in rapid succession a year later. In the first engagement the Franks were initially put to flight. The king escaped to Arsuf and summoned help. Reinforcements were brought up by Hugh, lord of Tiberias, while the patriarch arrived with the Cross, and the Frankish forces regrouped, and gave battle again. Fulcher not only attributed victory to the Cross, but states quite explicitly that:

> Truly it was right and just that they who were protected by the wood of the Lord's Cross should emerge as the victors over the enemies of that Cross. If indeed this benevolent Cross had been carried with the king in the previous battle, it cannot be doubted that the Lord would have favoured his people.[30]

---

[28] WT, p. 105.

[29] FC, p. 414: 'Aderat ibi crux dominica, inimicis Christi valde contraria, contra quam gratia Dei pompa eorum praevalere non potuit. Sed ac si praesentia eius verecundi effecti, non solum nos invadere cessaverunt, verum etiam pavore caelitus percussi, omnes in fugam celerem suam verterunt sententiam'; Fulcher, *History*, pp. 158-9.

[30] FC, p. 543-4: 'Vere dignum erat et iustum, ut qui ligno dominicae crucis muniti erant, super inimicos eiusdem crucis victores exsisterent. Quod si in anteriore bello eadem crux alma cum rege deferretur, non est haesitandum, quod populo suo Dominus propitiaretur'; Fulcher,

The majority of actions in which the Cross figured were either Frankish victories, or indecisive encounters. William of Tyre soberly records the presence of the relic at Marj Ayun in 1179, but makes no attempt to explain why it failed to prevent a defeat on Frankish territory by Saladin. Fulcher of Chartres may have been less confident in the case of defeat. William of Malmesbury reveals that at the battle of al-Sinnabrah in 1113 the Franks not only lost the battle, but even temporarily lost possession of the Cross itself. It would seem that Fulcher tried to deal with this problem by simply omitting to mention the presence of the relic in this engagement altogether.[31] Nevertheless, by and large the success of Frankish arms meant that it was not until the disaster of Hattin that Christian writers were confronted with the major theological problem of why God had not only permitted his people to be defeated, but also allowed the most precious relic to fall into infidel hands.

In general then, the relic was used defensively, in cases of great danger, usually with a field army which comprised the near totality of the military levy of the kingdom. It was normally the patriarch of Jerusalem who actually carried the relic when it went to war. In cases where the patriarch was unable (or in some cases, unwilling), it was carried by another senior ecclesiastic, most often an archbishop or bishop. Even where the patriarch was opposed to the action, as in 1120, he never seems to have had a recognized right to prevent the Cross going to war. Although the relic was in the care of an ecclesiastic, military command over the entire army was exercised by the king or his representative: this was the constable of the kingdom during the captivity of Baldwin II (Eustace Granarius and William of Bures), and the regent during the incapacity of the leper-king Baldwin IV (Guy of Lusignan and Raymond of Tripoli). Only in one case (1137) did the patriarch himself command the army. Another important distinction to be made is that between tactics and morale. In the armies of Jerusalem it was the royal banner, usually carried by

---

History, p. 173.

[31] Appendix, no. 1113. William of Malmesbury, *De gestis regum Anglorum*, ed. W. Stubbs, 2 vols, *RS* 90 (London, 1887-9), 2.451: 'Altera illi pugna posterioribus annis fuit, in qua milites nostri, Turcorum copia pressi et in fugam acti, etiam salutare vexillum amisere: sed cum longiuscule fugisset, reversi; pudor famae trepidos animavit ut ignominiam propulsarent. Ingens ibi pugna virorum fuit, collato pede et adverso pectore rem agentium. Nostri crucem reportarunt, fusis adversariis campum vindicantes.' See A.V. Murray, 'A Little-Known Member of the Royal Family of Crusader Jerusalem in William of Malmesbury's *Gesta regum Anglorum*', *Notes and Queries* 241 (1996), pp. 397-9.

one of the king's knights, which had the greater tactical significance.[32] In medieval warfare a banner served both as a rallying point and a signal of unbroken resistance, an important disciplinary function. The latter role of banners is detailed most clearly in the Rule of the Templars, which specified that no Templars might leave the field of battle as long as the black-and-white banner of the order could be seen. If it went down, the Templars were obliged to rally to the banner of the Hospitallers, and then, to any other banner still flying on the Christian side. Only when no more banners were visible did the Templar knights have permission to retreat.[33]

The function of the True Cross, by contrast, was to raise or maintain morale and to inspire courage, and in this respect it may have been more important before battle than during the actual fighting. The powers of the relic were presumably well-known throughout the Frankish population, and so the knowledge that it was with the army was in itself a reassurance of divine protection. In this respect it was much more precious than the royal banner, which of course could be replaced if lost. The Rule of the Templars specified that when the True Cross was transported by horse, it was to be guarded by the Commander of Jerusalem and ten knights, who were to camp as near to the relic as possible for the duration of the journey.[34]

Most mentions of the relic, especially those made by William of Tyre, simply attest to its presence with the army, but there is enough detail given on a few occasions for us to piece together a picture of how the relic was employed. The favourable psychological starting point established by its presence was reinforced by other liturgical or quasi-liturgical activities which were designed to prepare the troops for battle, reinforce their faith and convince them that God would assist them. When the army had been drawn up in battle array, the Cross was taken to a prominent position where it could be seen by the troops. At the third battle of Ramla the Patriarch Evremar rode up and down the lines displaying the relic at close quarters. He also delivered an

---

[32] Some authorities refer to the Cross as the banner of the kingdom, but it was distinct from the royal banner. Cf. FC, p. 498: 'signum suum album'; WT, p. 1051: 'Nostri ... vivifice crucis lignum regiaque vexilla sequuti'.

[33] *The Rule of the Templars: The French Text of the Rule of the Order of the Knights Templar*, trans. J.M. Upton-Ward (Woodbridge, 1992), p. 60.

[34] *Rule of the Templars*, p. 49. In her translation of the *Rule*, Upton-Ward recognises that this ordinance refers to the relic lost at Hattin, but claims that it was a portion of the Cross in the possession of the Order. However, it seems quite unlikely that any piece other than that discussed here would simply be described as the True Cross, particularly since this was the only piece that was regularly taken into battle.

exhortation to fight valiantly, and promised them remission of sins.[35] Before the capture of Caesarea, the patriarch gave absolution and communion to the army before it made the assault.[36] In some cases, an oration was given by the commander, usually the king.[37] It is difficult to tell how much the speeches of the commander and the senior ecclesiastic differed from each other, since few reports have survived, and of course those which do survive have clearly been elaborated on by the chroniclers. Since in 1105 the patriarch promised remission of sins, we might regard the ecclesiastics' exhortations as having the character of sermons.

In their intention, the speeches of the field commanders and ecclesiastics probably had similar content, especially in the case of Baldwin I who had originally trained for the priesthood. Fulcher of Chartres purports to give the words addressed by him to his men at the first battle of Ramla. While obviously a reconstruction rather than a verbatim report, the combination of pious reassurance and hard-headed realism may well derive from the kind of pep-talk given by a monarch like Baldwin I, who by this time was an experienced field commander, but evidently retained something of his theological training:

> Come then, soldiers of Christ, be of good cheer and fear nothing! Conduct yourselves manfully and ye shall be mighty in this battle. Fight, I beseech you, for the salvation of your souls; exalt everywhere the name of Christ whom these degenerate ones always vigorously revile and reproach, believing in neither His Nativity nor Resurrection. If you should be slain here, you will surely be among the blessed. Already the gate of the Kingdom of Heaven is open to you. If you survive as victors you will shine in glory among all Christians. If, however, you wish to flee remember that France is indeed a long distance away.[38]

The third battle of Ramla in 1105 illustrates further morale-building elements. On this occasion Baldwin employed a tactic which was probably not always practicable, but which in this case evidently raised morale: he managed to delay battle until a Sunday. This meant that there was time to summon the

---

[35] Appendix, no. 1105.

[36] Appendix, no. 1101(a).

[37] For instance Appendix, nos. 1101(b), 1105.

[38] FC, pp. 411-12: 'Eia Christi milites, confortamini, nihil metuentes. Viriliter agite et in proelio fortes estote et pro animabus vestris, quaeso, pugnate et nomen Christi omnino exaltate, cui degeneres isti semper exprobrant et viriliter conviciantur, nativitatem eius non credentes neque resurrectionem. Quod si hic interieritis, beati nimirum eritis. Iamiamque est vobis ianua regni caelestis. Si vivi victores remanseritis, inter omnes Christianos gloriosi fulgebitis, si autem fugere volueritis, Francia equidem longe est a vobis'; Fulcher, *History*, pp. 157-8.

patriarch from Jerusalem with the Cross, for it was thought that the relic would be particularly effective on the day of the Resurrection. The king also ordered processions, prayers and almsgiving for victory in the city of Jerusalem. Thus the Frankish population, both combatant and non-combatant, was united in its devotion in a manner that was designed to maximize the efficacy of divine intervention.[39] When battle was joined, the Frankish knights charged the enemy with the war-cry: 'Christus vincit, Christus regnat, Christus imperat.' At the first battle of Ramla the war-cry was 'Adiuva Deus'. Both of these, particularly the former, have a much more liturgical ring to them than the 'Deus lo volt' of the First Crusade.

The relic's efficacy was not confined to the pitched battle. During the retreat from an abortive expedition into the territory of Damascus in 1147, the army was being harried by Nur al-Din's superior Turkish forces who had set the brush on fire. The Frankish soldiers implored the bearer of the Cross, the archbishop of Nazareth, to pray for intercession through the Life-Giving Cross. Robert of Nazareth raised the Cross towards the flames, and called for divine assistance. Straightaway the wind changed, driving the flames and smoke towards the enemy, and the army was able to withdraw unimpeded. The relic provided inspiration as well as protection. At the siege of Ascalon in 1153, certain reverses had caused opinion to divide as to whether the investment should be continued. Baldwin III summoned a council of war of his leading nobles and clerics, and had the Life-Giving Cross placed before them both to concentrate their minds and evidently to ensure that they would be inspired to arrive at the correct decision. The council agreed to continue the siege, and when Ascalon eventually surrendered, the Cross was triumphantly born into the city and taken into the mosque, in an act which clearly demonstrated the victory of the Christian faith over Islam.

When the army of Jerusalem returned after the victory of Zerdana in 1119, it reached Jerusalem on 14 September, the same day that the Roman Emperor Heraclius had brought back the Cross from Persia in 629. This day was kept as a special feast in the Latin kingdom, and so the return of the relic on this date was regarded as particularly auspicious, and it was met at Jerusalem with great rejoicing. Yet it seems that on many occasions, even on less auspicious

---

[39] It is surely significant that Prince Roger and the army of Antioch fought the victorious battle of Tell Danith on Holy Cross day, 14 September 1115. It is thus likely that the church of Antioch had its own relic of the Cross, and in this matter I am convinced by the arguments deployed by Gerish, 'True Cross'.

days, the Cross was received in Jerusalem with elaborate ceremony.[40] Fulcher describes how, after the battle of Ashdod in 1123, the patriarch returned with the Cross: 'It was received outside the Gate of David [i.e. the Jaffa Gate] by a glorious procession and conducted with the highest honour into the Basilica of the Lord's Sepulchre. Chanting *Te Deum laudamus*, we rendered praises to the Almighty for his blessings.'[41] These ceremonies demonstrate how the military use of the Cross was integrated into the liturgical life of the Latin church. In fact, in twelfth-century terms it may be misleading to attempt to make a distinction between the military functions of the relic and its role in what we might think of as the 'normal' life of the church. The frequency with which the relic was sent into battle, and the liturgical ambience in which this was done, suggest that the function I have discussed here was not something exceptional, but rather fundamental to its place within the Frankish community. Indeed, one could argue that the defence of the Holy Land was a liturgical act *par excellence*.

In his study of the society of crusader Jerusalem, Joshua Prawer raised the question whether settlers who were in daily contact with the shrines and relics of the Holy Land had a less devoted attitude to them than did those, such as pilgrims, who came from afar in quest of such sites and objects.[42] The study of the military use of the True Cross suggests that this was not the case at least as far as this particular relic was concerned. Within a few years of its discovery, the Cross had acquired a reputation as a powerful vehicle of divine favour and assistance, which eclipsed all other holy objects in Palestine, so that it became a talisman which the Franks of Jerusalem regarded as essential to military success whenever the security of the realm was threatened. Within the eighty-eight year existence of the first kingdom of Jerusalem, the True Cross had a military function which was both regular and systematic, perhaps more so than any other comparable relic in medieval Christendom.

---

[40] Appendix, nos. 1119(b), 1120, 1122(b), 1123(a), 1123(b), 1124.

[41] FC, p. 668: 'qua extra portam Daviticam cum glorifica processione suscepta et usque in basilicam dominici Sepulcri honorifice deducta: te Deum laudamus cantantes, Omnipotenti de beneficiis universi laudes reddidimus'; Fulcher, *History*, p. 243.

[42] J. Prawer, *The Latin Kingdom of Jerusalem: European Colonialism in the Middle Ages* (London, 1972), p. 184.

Appendix

The Military Deployment of the Relic of the True Cross in the Armies of the Kingdom of Jerusalem, 1099-1187

This catalogue is an attempt to list all known occasions on which the relic of the True Cross accompanied the armies of the kingdom of Jerusalem in the field, in particular to correct and supplement the references collected by Frolow. The sources listed below are not meant as exhaustive references, but are restricted to those necessary to document the presence and use of the True Cross in each engagement as well as, in some cases, to refer to pertinent discussion in the secondary literature. Wherever possible the names of the field commander and the bearer of the Cross are given. The headings for each item are chosen to give a rough indication of the character of the action. *Defence* denotes a move to counter an enemy invasion of Frankish territory, and *relief* means specifically an expedition to assist friendly forces threatened by the enemy, while *invasion* denotes an incursion into enemy territory; in all three cases without a pitched battle having been fought. *Battle* denotes a major engagement with the enemy, irrespective whether this was offensive or defensive in nature. *Capture* refers to the successful investment of an enemy town, *siege* an unsuccessful one. It should be noted that names of some battles vary considerably in the scholarly literature, and so in some cases alternative names are given. Items 1119(a) and 1119(b), and likewise 1122(a) and 1122(b) are treated as separate engagements, although in both cases the Cross was present on the first action and taken on to the second without returning to Jerusalem in between. Nevertheless, in both cases the purpose of each action was quite different. The distinctiveness of the two actions in 1119 can be seen from the change in personnel; in the first action the Cross was carried by the patriarch, who then returned to Jerusalem, while the Cross went north in the charge of the archbishop of Caesarea. Potentially, at least, the king had the possibility of having the relic sent home with the patriarch, although he chose not to exercise this option.

1099   12 August   **Battle of Ascalon**
Godfrey of Bouillon and the other leaders of the First Crusade defeated a Fatimid army from Egypt commanded by the vizier al-Afdal. Cross carried by the patriarch, Arnulf of Chocques.
    Sources: Peter Tudebode, *Historia de Hierosolymitano itinere*, ed. J.H. and L.L. Hill (Paris, 1977), p. 145; FC, pp. 311-18; AA, VI:41-4/pp. 491-3; 'Balduini III historia Nicaena vel Antiochena', *RHC Oc.*, 5.176 [hereafter cited as *HN*]; Frolow, *Relique*, p. 287.

1101(a)   May   Capture of Caesarea
Baldwin I captured the town of Caesarea. Cross carried by the patriarch,
Daimbert of Pisa.
Sources: AA, VII:56/p. 544; Frolow, *Relique*, p. 288.

1101(b)   7-8 September   Battle of Ramla I
Baldwin I defeated a Fatimid army from Egypt. Cross carried by *abbas quidam*, whom Hagenmeyer identifies as Gerhard, abbot of Schaffhausen (FC, p.
411 n. 18).
Sources: FC, pp. 407-20; AA, VII:66-8/pp. 550-1; WT, pp. 472-4; Ekkehard
of Aura, *Frutolfs und Ekkehards Chroniken und die anonyme Kaiserchronik*,
ed. F.-J. Schmale and I. Schmale-Ott (Darmstadt, 1972), pp. 172-7; *HN*, p.
178; Frolow, *Relique*, p. 288.

1102   27 May   Battle of Jaffa
Baldwin I led an army of Franks and crusaders from the 1101 expedition
against a Fatimid invasion and was defeated near Ramla on 17 May (battle of
Ramla II) and fled to Arsuf. The king then collected reinforcements at Jaffa
and had the Cross brought from Jerusalem, and won a decisive victory over the
Egyptians who had in the meantime advanced to within three miles of Jaffa.
Sources: FC, pp. 446-55; *HN*, pp. 179-80; Frolow, *Relique*, p. 288.

1105   27 August   Battle of Ramla III
Baldwin I defeated the third and final major attempt of the Fatimids to invade
the kingdom of Jerusalem. Cross carried by the patriarch, Evremar of
Chocques.
Sources: FC, pp. 489-501; AA, IX:48-50/pp. 621-4; *HN*, p. 180; WT, pp.
498-500.

1108   Siege of Sidon
Baldwin I besieged Sidon with the help of a large number of ships from the
Italian cities. Albert of Aachen implies that the king had the Cross brought
from Jerusalem at some point.
Sources: AA, X:48/pp. 653-4; Frolow, *Relique*, p. 288.

1113   28 June   Battle of al-Sinnabrah (defeat)
Baldwin I moved to meet an invasion of Galilee led by Mawdud, atabak of
Mosul, and Tughtagin, atabak of Damascus, and was ambushed and defeated
near al-Sinnabrah, south of Lake Tiberias. Neither Fulcher nor William of Tyre
mention the presence of the Cross, but I have argued elsewhere that
formulations used by William of Malmesbury in his account of the battle imply
that the relic was present along with the royal banner.

Sources: FC, pp. 565-73; WT, pp. 523-4; William of Malmesbury, *De gestis regum Anglorum*, 2.451; Murray, 'A Little-Known Member of the Royal Family of Crusader Jerusalem'.

1119(a)   **Defence of Tiberias**
Fulcher's meagre description implies a defensive action against the Turks of Damascus, after which Baldwin II immediately proceeded to the relief of Antioch (see next item). Hagenmeyer (FC, p. 625 n. 5), however, identifies the action with an invasion of the Terre de Suète described in some detail by Albert of Aachen. Cross carried by the patriarch, Warmund of Picquigny.
    Sources: FC, pp. 624-5.

1119(b)   14 August   Battle of Zerdana (*al.* Hab, Tell Danith)
On hearing of the defeat of the Antiochenes at the *Ager Sanguinis* (28 June 1119), Baldwin II marched with Pons of Tripoli to the relief of Antioch, and, joining forces with the Franks of Antioch and Edessa, won a victory over the Artukid emir, Il-Ghazi, near Zerdana. Cross carried by the archbishop of Caesarea, Evremar of Chocques, who preached a sermon before the battle.
    Sources: FC, pp. 624-33; WT, pp. 560-2; Walter the Chancellor, *Bella Antiochena*, ed. H. Hagenmeyer (Innsbruck, 1896), pp. 103-7; *HN*, p. 184; Frolow, *Relique*, p. 288.

1120   June-September   Relief of Antioch
Baldwin II went north to assist Antioch against a fresh incursion by Il-Ghazi, which was repulsed without a major engagement. A considerable section of the nobility was opposed to this expedition, and Patriarch Warmund refused to accompany the Cross.
    Sources: FC, pp. 638-42; WT, p. 564; Frolow, *Relique*, p. 288; H.E. Mayer, 'Jérusalem et Antioche au temps de Baudouin II', *Comptes-rendus de l'Académie des Inscriptions et Belles-Lettres* (1980), pp. 719-30; Murray, 'Baldwin II and his Nobles', p. 67.

1122(a)   **Invasion of Tripoli**
Baldwin II took the Cross with him in his successful attempt to enforce his overlordship on Bertrand, count of Tripoli. This is the sole example of the Cross being used against other Latins, although in the event hostilities did not occur.
    Sources: FC, pp. 646-8; Frolow, *Relique*, p. 288.

1122(b)   August   Relief of Antioch
From Tripoli (see previous item) Baldwin II marched north to assist Antioch against an invasion by the Artukids Il-Ghazi and Nur al-Dawlah Balak. The

king remained in the North, but the Cross was sent back to Jerusalem, where it arrived on 20 September.

Sources: FC, pp. 646-51.

1123(a) 29 May   Battle of Ashdod (*al.* Caco, Ibelin)
During the captivity of Baldwin II, the Fatimids invaded the kingdom, and were defeated by a Jerusalemite army under the constable, Eustace I Granarius, lord of Sidon and Caesarea. From the context it would seem that the Cross was carried by Patriarch Warmund. Frolow wrongly interprets the account of Anselm of Gembloux as referring to a separate action occurring in 1124.

Sources: FC, pp. 661-8; WT, pp. 571-3; Anselm of Gembloux, 'Continuatio Sigeberti Gemblacensis', *MGH SS*, 6.379; Frolow, *Relique*, p. 289 (nos. 11, 12).

1123(b) September   Relief of Kharput
The army of Jerusalem went north to join the Antiochene and Tripolitan forces in an (ultimately fruitless) attempt to rescue Baldwin II and his companions, who had temporarily freed themselves from captivity in the Artukid fortress of Kharput. On arriving at Tell Bashir the armies learned of Baldwin's recapture, and the Jerusalem army returned home.

Sources: FC, pp. 687-90; WT, pp. 570-1.

1124 July   Capture of Tyre
After an investment of five months, the city of Tyre surrendered on 7 July to the army of Jerusalem (under William of Bures, who had replaced Eustace Granarius as constable) and their Venetian allies. Fulcher's formulation implies that the Cross was present at least part of the time, probably with the patriarch, Warmund.

Sources: FC, pp. 745-6.

1137   Relief of Montferrand
Patriarch William, acting as bearer of the Cross and commander of the army, attempted to relieve King Fulk, who was besieged in the town of Montferrand by Zanki.

Sources: WT, pp. 663-70; Frolow, *Relique*, p. 289.

1147   Invasion of Terre de Suète
Baldwin III attempted to take the castle of Bosra from the Damascenes in agreement with its Turkish commander, Altuntash. At one point when danger appeared to threaten, Baldwin III was counselled by some of his chief men to take the best horse in the army and ride to safety 'with the Cross of Salvation in his hand', but did not follow the advice. The Cross was carried by Robert

I, archbishop of Nazareth, who used it to invoke divine aid during the retreat back to Frankish territory.
Sources: WT, pp. 723-33; Frolow, *Relique*, p. 289.

1148   July   **Siege of Damascus**
Baldwin III and the armies of the Second Crusade laid siege to the city of Damascus, but eventually abandoned the investment.
Sources: WT, p. 762; Frolow, *Relique*, p. 289.

1153   July   **Capture of Ascalon**
The Fatimid town of Ascalon surrendered to Baldwin III on 12 July. Cross probably carried by the patriarch, Fulcher.
Sources: WT, pp. 789-805; Frolow, *Relique*, p. 289.

1158   15 July   **Battle of Puthaha**
Baldwin III marched to relieve a cave fortress in the Terre de Suète which was under siege by Nur al-Din, and defeated the enemy in battle at a site near Tiberias. Cross carried by Peter of Barcelona, archbishop of Tyre.
Sources: WT, pp. 841-2; Frolow, *Relique*, p. 289.

1169/71   **Relief of Kerak**
While King Amalric was absent in Cilicia, the constable, Humphrey of Toron, led the army to relieve the siege of Kerak (Petra Deserti) by Nur al-Din, which he abandoned before the arrival of the Franks. Cross carried by the bishop of Bethlehem, Ralph I.
Sources: WT, p. 950.

1170   December   **Relief of Darum**
King Amalric marched to the frontier fortress of Darum which was under attack by Saladin. Cross carried by the patriarch, Amalric of Nesle.
Sources: WT, pp. 936-9; Frolow, *Relique*, p. 289.

1171   **Relief of Beersheba**
Saladin invaded from Egypt to a place known as *Cannetum Turdorum*, situated to the south of Bait Jibrin. King Amalric advanced to Beersheba, but avoided battle, and Saladin moved east to invest Montreal. Cross carried by the patriarch, Amalric.
Sources: WT, pp. 950-1.

1177   25 November   **Battle of Montgisard**
Baldwin IV defeated Saladin and an army which had invaded from Egypt. Cross carried by Albert, bishop of Bethlehem.
Sources: WT, pp. 990-2; Frolow, *Relique*, pp. 289-90.

1179   June   Battle of Marj Ayun (defeat)
Baldwin IV met an invasion of the territory of Sidon by Saladin, and suffered
a major defeat, conceding the field of battle and many captives. While mentioning the presence of the Cross, William of Tyre does not comment on its
lack of efficacy on this occasion.
Sources: WT, pp. 1000-2.

1182(a)   July   Battle of Forbelet
Baldwin IV went to meet an invasion by Saladin from Damascus, and fought
an indecisive battle at this village near the fortress of Belvoir, with heavy
losses on both sides. Cross carried by Baldwin, a canon of the Holy Sepulchre,
who died as a result of the intense heat.
Sources: WT, pp. 1029-32.

1182(b)   October   Invasion of Terre de Suète
Baldwin IV invaded Damascene territory during the absence of Saladin in Iraq.
Cross carried by Patriarch Eraclius.
Sources: WT, pp. 1038-42.

1182(c)   December   Invasion of Terre de Suète
Baldwin IV invaded Damascene territory, again while Saladin was absent in
Iraq.
Sources: WT, pp. 1042-3; Frolow, *Relique*, p. 290.

1183(a)   September-October   Defence of Bethsan
Saladin invaded the region of Bethsan in Galilee. The regent, Guy of Lusignan,
remained inactive with the army at Saffuriyah, probably because many of the
Frankish leaders were unwilling to serve under him.
Sources: WT, pp. 1048-53; Frolow, *Relique*, p. 290; R.C. Smail, 'The
    Predicaments of Guy of Lusignan, 1183-87', in *Outremer: Studies in the
    History of the Crusading Kingdom of Jerusalem presented to Joshua Prawer*,
    ed. B.Z. Kedar, H.E. Mayer and R.C. Smail (Jerusalem, 1982), pp. 159-76;
    B. Hamilton, 'Baldwin the Leper as War Leader', in *From Clermont to
    Jerusalem: The Crusades and Crusader Societies, 1095-1400*, ed. A.V.
    Murray (forthcoming).

1183(b)   December   Relief of Kerak
Baldwin IV marched to relieve this fortress under siege by Saladin, entrusting
command of the army to Raymond III of Tripoli.
Sources: WT, pp. 1055-7, 1059-60; Frolow, *Relique*, p. 290.

1187   4 July   **Battle of Hattin**

Defeat of Guy of Lusignan by Saladin, at which the True Cross was finally lost. Patriarch Eraclius had refused to accompany the Cross.

   Sources: Frolow, *Relique*, pp. 347-9; Cole, 'Christian Perceptions of the Battle of Hattin', and sources listed there; Edbury, *The Conquest of Jerusalem*, pp. 47, 158-60; Kedar, 'The Patriarch Eraclius'.

The South Transept Façade of the Church of the Holy Sepulchre in Jerusalem: An Aspect of 'Rebuilding Zion'

Jaroslav Folda

Among his many contributions to crusader studies, Bernard Hamilton has addressed the holy sites in the context of the Latin kingdom of Jerusalem.[1] In addition, in his important book, *The Latin Church in the Crusader States*, he presented a particularly valuable discussion of the eastern Christians in the crusader states during the twelfth century.[2] With these studies in mind, I would like to offer the following essay in honour of Bernard Hamilton. Using the entrance façade of the church of the Holy Sepulchre as my source, I propose to investigate an art historical issue from perspectives similar to those of Bernard in the works mentioned above.

The Church of the Holy Sepulchre

The crusader church of the Holy Sepulchre in Jerusalem, dedicated on 15 July 1149, has presented scholars with a myriad of problems including the following: (1) reconstructing the original configuration of the crusader church at the time of its completion, (2) understanding the exact dating of its various parts and how much was completed by the time of the dedication, on 15 July 1149, and (3) accounting for the remarkable eclecticism of its architecture and especially the programme of its architectural decoration. In this discussion I shall focus on the south transept façade of the church (Plate 1), its main

---

[1] B. Hamilton, 'The Impact of Crusader Jerusalem on Western Christendom', *Catholic Historical Review* 80 (1994), pp. 695-713; 'Rebuilding Zion: The Holy Places of Jerusalem in the Twelfth Century', in *Renaissance and Renewal in Christian History*, ed. D. Baker, *Studies in Church History* 14 (Oxford, 1977), pp. 105-16.

[2] B. Hamilton, *The Latin Church in the Crusader States: The Secular Church* (London, 1980), pp. 159-211.

entrance, commenting on its original configuration and dating, but concentrating on the interpretation of certain aspects of its programme.[3]

The crusader project to rebuild and redecorate the church of the Holy Sepulchre evolved over a long period of time and included several identifiable components. First, there was the renovation and redecoration of the aedicule of the Holy Sepulchre itself, which began shortly after the First Crusade captured Jerusalem in 1099, and was continued during the first half of the twelfth century, especially after 1119.[4] Second, there was the building of the cloister and conventual buildings for the Augustinian regular canons, which began in 1114 and was probably completed by c. 1120.[5] Third, when the Holy Sepulchre assumed its full function as a state church for royal coronations and burials in 1131, planning apparently began for the reconfiguration of the main holy sites associated with the Sepulchre, Calvary, the Grotto of the Holy Cross and the Prison of Christ into a unified architectural complex with the south transept façade as its main entrance. Construction appears to have been carried out mainly in the 1140s and 1150s.[6]

The South Transept Façade

The south transept façade (Plate 1) was one of the most dramatic new features of the crusader church.[7] Even though it has lost all of its figural decoration

---

[3] I would like to express thanks to my colleague, Alan Borg, for reading this essay and making very helpful and even some cautionary remarks. I am, of course, solely responsible for the interpretation proposed here.

[4] J. Folda, *The Art of the Crusaders in the Holy Land, 1098-1187* (Cambridge and New York, 1995), pp. 79-82.

[5] Folda, *Art of the Crusaders*, pp. 57-60.

[6] Folda, *Art of the Crusaders*, pp. 119, 175-245. Most of the church appears to have been built by the dedication in 1149, but the completion of the south transept façade, e.g., the carving of the figural lintels, and the erection of the campanile probably occurred in the 1150s.

Research continues on the problems of design, construction and dating. Volume 3 of D. Pringle, *The Churches of the Crusader Kingdom of Jerusalem: A Corpus* (in preparation) will deal with these issues, and other scholars, including Robert Ousterhout and Larry Hoey, are working on these problems.

[7] There is a large literature on the problems of the south transept façade of the Holy Sepulchre. Besides my own published remarks, Folda, *Art of the Crusaders*, pp. 214-29, important recent discussions include the following: M. Rosen-Ayalon, 'The Façade of the Holy Sepulchre', *Rivista degli Studi Orientali* 59 (1985), pp. 289-96; H. Buschhausen, 'Die Fassade der Grabeskirche zu Jerusalem', in *Crusader Art in the Twelfth Century*, ed. J. Folda (Oxford, 1982), pp. 71-96; T.S.R. Boase, 'Ecclesiastical Art in the Crusader States in Palestine and Syria', in *A History of the Crusades*, gen. ed. K.M. Setton, 6 vols (Madison, 1969-89), 4.80-4;

over the years, the importance and impressiveness of this façade can still be felt when entering the parvis in front of the church today. Situated between the Franks' chapel to the east, which originally served as a direct entry to the Calvary chapel complex, and the now-truncated campanile to the west, which rises in front of the dome over the rotunda, the south transept façade boldly announces the church of the Holy Sepulchre. Not only does the façade dominate the space of the parvis, masking the fabric of the church behind it including the dome over the crossing (Plate 1), but also it proclaims by its own design and decoration an important and complex message about the church.

As originally planned and executed, the programme of decoration for the façade included figural mosaics in the tympana and the spandrels[8] as well as two figural lintels over the main portals.[9] These figural elements were embedded in a matrix of non-figural architectural sculpture. The latter served to

---

N. Kenaan, 'Local Christian Art in Twelfth-Century Jerusalem', *Israel Exploration Journal* 23 (1973), pp. 167-75, 221-9, all with older bibliography. See now also the very recent article by L.-A. Hunt, 'Artistic and Cultural Inter-Relations between the Christian Communities at the Holy Sepulchre in the 12th Century', in *The Christian Heritage in the Holy Land*, ed. A. O'Mahony et al. (London, 1995), pp. 57-95. This article came into my hands while I was in the process of writing this paper.

[8] The mosaics of the façade, the subjects of which are known only from later pilgrims' accounts, have been lost over the years. Remnants of tesserae are nonetheless visible at the very bottom of the tympanum of the eastern door. The date of these tesserae and their original colouration might be determined with careful study. On these mosaics, see e.g., Folda, *Art of the Crusaders*, pp. 225, 240; Hunt, 'Artistic and Cultural Inter-Relations', p. 73. The identification of these mosaics, their placement and their role in the programme of the south transept façade need further study.

[9] The two lintels were taken down in 1929 for conservation and they are now preserved in the Rockefeller Museum. Unfortunately the treatments of cellulose nitrate which they received then have not succeeded in arresting the deterioration of the stone, and a new project to conserve these lintels is under study in conjunction with the Getty Conservation Institute (Summer 1996). On the lintels, see: Folda, *Art of the Crusaders*, pp. 220-7; M. Lindner, 'Topography and Iconography in Twelfth-Century Jerusalem', in *The Horns of Hattin*, ed. B.Z. Kedar (Jerusalem, 1992), pp. 81-98; B. Kühnel, 'Der Rankenfries am Portal der Grabeskirche zu Jerusalem und die romanische Skulptur in den Abruzzen', *Arte Medievale*, 2nd ser., 1 (1987), pp. 87-121; N. Kenaan-Kedar, 'The Figurative Western Lintel of the Church of the Holy Sepulchre in Jerusalem', in *The Meeting of Two Worlds: Cultural Exchange between East and West during the Period of the Crusades*, ed. V.P. Goss and C.V. Bornstein (Kalamazoo, 1986), pp. 123-31; and L.Y. Rahmani, 'The Eastern Lintel of the Holy Sepulcher', *Israel Exploration Journal* 26 (1976), pp. 120-9, all with older basic bibliography. Hunt, 'Artistic and Cultural Inter-Relations', pp. 72-82, focusses in her article mainly on the figural aspects of the south transept façade in its multicultural setting, and especially on the two lintels. Her views should be considered in conjunction with those cited above.

articulate the architecture and to frame the imagery, but also I would argue that the non-figural sculpture presents important content about the church itself. It is these non-figural aspects of the programme which are the focus of my discussion here.

The south transept façade was dramatically new because no other crusader church had a façade like it, yet it combined features of church architecture East and West in an ambitious project. The south transept façade was designed with a double portal (Plate 2) and paired fenestration over the doors (Plate 3) in a monumental two-storey elevation. The double portal is primarily derived from one of Jerusalem's most celebrated city gates, the Golden Gate.[10] The specific configuration of the two-storey elevation was, however, essentially based on Romanesque architectural design as seen in the entry façades of churches along the pilgrimage routes in the West: see, for example, the south transept portal of the cathedral at Santiago de Compostella or the transept portals of the church of St Sernin at Toulouse.[11] The façade of the Holy Sepulchre differs from all of these sources, however, because of its exclusive use of the broad and graceful Levantine pointed arches and because of its extraordinarily rich repertory of non-figural architectural sculpture.[12] This architectural sculpture further differentiates the façade of the Holy Sepulchre from these other works because the prominent cornices and mouldings 'reach out' on either side to link the façade visually with the Franks' chapel to the east, and the campanile to

---

[10] Kenaan, 'Local Christian Art', pp. 221-2; M. Rosen-Ayalon, *The Early Islamic Monuments of Al-Haram Al-Sharif* (Jerusalem, 1989), pp. 33-41. B. Kühnel, *Crusader Art of the Twelfth Century* (Berlin, 1994), p. 23, also comments: 'It might even be, as suggested by Myriam Rosen-Ayalon ['The Façade of the Holy Sepulchre', pp. 293f.], that the seventh-century Holy Sepulchre ... already had a double portal in the south wall.' We must remember, of course, that a double portal is also a feature of the south transept portals found in certain major churches along the pilgrimage roads in the West. The origin of their double portal entries is not part of our discussion here.

[11] See K.J. Conant, *Carolingian and Romanesque Architecture: 800-1200*, 2nd edn (Harmondsworth, 1990), pp. 165-75, plate 122; H.E. Kubach, *Romanesque Architecture* (New York, 1975), pp. 218, 227. Opinion linking the crusader church with Toulouse and Santiago goes back to C. Enlart, *Les monuments des croisés dans le royaume de Jérusalem: architecture religieuse et civile*, 2 vols (Paris, 1925-28), 2.149.

[12] These arches are a major feature of the crusader church of the Holy Sepulchre. They derive from local sources such as the *Templum Salomonis*/the Aqsa Mosque, and the Cistern of St Helena in Ramla: Folda, *Art of the Crusaders*, p. 213.

The south transept portals of Santiago and St Sernin also have important programmes of non-figural sculpture, but the ensemble on the church of the Holy Sepulchre is quite different and quite distinctive, as we shall discuss below.

the west.[13] Contrast this sculpture in terms of repertory, function and richness with what we know of contemporary crusader façades elsewhere, such as that on the church of Saint Anne in Jerusalem, probably the closest in time and place, dating to the 1130s, that is, shortly before construction began on the church of the Holy Sepulchre.[14]

The unique ensemble of non-figural architectural sculpture which characterizes the façade of the church of the Holy Sepulchre includes the following major elements:[15]

a) The two storeys of the façade are defined by cornices which are virtually identical in design. The upper cornice (Plate 4) articulates the top of the façade in a straight, richly sculptural band constantly bathed in shadow. The lower one (Plate 5) differs from the upper by being indented to 'frame' the portals below and serves as a sort of visual foundation for the somewhat smaller windows above. C. Coüasnon observed that in fact the upper cornice was second-century Roman sculpture of two types which was reused here, a major example of *spolia* employed by the crusaders. The lower cornice was crusader work imitating the upper cornice and, of course, put up first.[16]

---

[13] In fact, neither mouldings nor cornices continue onto either the Franks' chapel porch or the campanile, but instead terminate at the end of the façade. But whereas the lower cornice appears to continue around the Franks' chapel porch, albeit in a slightly different design, the campanile 'breaks' and terminates the upper and lower cornices as well as the upper hood moulding. The upper hood moulding and the upper cornice, by contrast, continue unbroken to the east of the façade, on the upper part of the Calvary chapel complex, which is, of course, integrated into the fabric of the crusader church.

[14] Folda, *Art of the Crusaders*, p. 133, plate 6.6b. Very few crusader churches survive with their façades intact with which to compare that of the church of the Holy Sepulchre. The relative simplicity of, e.g., St Anne's in the 1130s, of what we know of the west façade of the church of the Annunciation in Nazareth dating from the 1170s (Folda, *Art of the Crusaders*, pp. 430-2), and of Notre Dame in Tortosa, dating from the early thirteenth century (P. Deschamps, *Terre Sainte Romane* [Abbaye Ste-Marie de la Pierre-qui-Vire, 1990], fig. 79), make clear, however, how remarkable the south transept façade of the church of the Holy Sepulchre really was. In terms of function, all of these comparative examples were crusader holy sites of some importance, but the church of the Holy Sepulchre was decidedly the most important in that regard and was unique in its role as the state church for royal coronations and burials.

[15] The non-figural sculpture on this façade was variously discussed by a number of French scholars, notably De Vogüé, Enlart and Deschamps, but it was N. Kenaan who focussed attention on the eclectic character of this sculpture and the Near Eastern sources of much of this material in her important study: 'Local Christian Art', pp. 167ff., 221ff.

[16] C. Coüasnon, *The Church of the Holy Sepulchre in Jerusalem* (London, 1974), p. 60.

b) Within each storey the paired arches are articulated with godroons (Plates
    1, 6), the bevelled or cushion-shaped archivolts which help define their
    broad pointed shape. Godroons are particularly effective in generating a
    pattern of rhythmic shadow in the brilliant sunlight of the Mediterranean
    region. Godroons were used for a similar effect on the façade of the church
    of St Anne and may have been the immediate source for those here, but
    they are clearly Near Eastern in origin and derive from Arab sources such
    as the Bab al-Futuh in Cairo.[17]

c) The godroons are strongly emphasized by heavy hood mouldings. But
    whereas the two storeys are united by the unity of the sculptural design of
    the cornices and the godroons, the hood mouldings and the rest of the
    sculpture offer subtle variety. On the first storey, the hood moulding is a
    deeply cut but delicate rosette design (Plate 7) formed with a flat front
    surface curving over a rolled or tubular shape that creates an exquisite
    lace-like effect. Similar rosette mouldings are known from early Christian
    tomb monuments in Syria and parallels with the Golden Gate have also
    been adduced.[18] The hood moulding on the second storey has a floral
    design (Plate 8) with plant shapes consisting of thick curving stems
    terminating in paired fleshy leaves ending in spiral volutes; berries and
    cone shapes are found between the leaves and stalks. The design of this
    moulding is bolder – with flowing curves, more texture, greater three-
    dimensional irregularity of the front surface, and increased open zones for
    shadow – than the tighter, more delicately conceived rosette moulding
    below. This difference apparently responds to their location on the façade
    and how they will be seen: the lower moulding, more refined, is closer to
    the onlooker; the upper one at a greater distance has stronger, more plastic
    forms and greater contrasts of light and dark. The sources of the upper
    moulding appear to be Romanesque in origin. Those who have referred to
    specific parallels have cited Romanesque churches in southern France
    among other possibilities.[19]

---

[17] Folda, *Art of the Crusaders*, p. 225.

[18] Folda, *Art of the Crusaders*, p. 225; Rosen-Ayalon, 'The Façade of the Holy Sepulchre',
pp. 290, 295.

[19] Enlart, *Les monuments des croisés*, 2.163-4, finds comparisons in the narthex of Vézelay
in Romanesque churches of the southwest of France and the Ile de France. Deschamps, *Terre
Sainte Romane*, p. 243, calls this sculpture, 'décor roman fort original'. My colleague, Dr.
Mary Joslin, has proposed interesting parallels with the Saintonge. Kenaan, 'Local Christian
Art', p. 225, does not propose a specific origin for the design. While discussion continues on
the precise parallel, there seems to be no doubt of French Romanesque ancestry.

d) The arches of the façade spring from sets of single, double and triple capitals set on marble columns below, and masonry columns above. The triple capitals appearing on the two lower portals are mainly of the Byzantine wind-blown acanthus type (Plate 10). Parallels with work of the Justinianic period and with San Marco have been mentioned.[20] Kenaan has argued that the capitals flanking the upper windows include variants on the Byzantine wind-blown acanthus type (Plate 9) along with other types including medieval reflections of the 'composite' classical capital and Syrian work of the early Christian period.[21] The overall Byzantine character of these capitals has been noted repeatedly.[22]

e) The imposts of the capitals and the impost moulding to the right of the capitals on the lower storey (Plate 10) constitute the final major component of the non-figural ensemble of sculpture. On the upper level (Plate 9), these imposts are mostly of a stylized upright acanthus leaf design with a classicizing border on the vertical surface above. On the lower storey (Plate 10), the design is characterized by fleshy, flat curving leaves which surround grape clusters or pine cones bordered by a classicizing egg and dart motif along the top, and, along the bottom, by a classicizing bead and reel motif. Kenaan sees this foliate frieze as derived from Syrian sources both in terms of design and placement as an extension of the imposts, and again classically inspired Byzantine sculpture may have been the source.[23]

The identification of these components and their sources is relatively uncontroversial, although certain precisions remain to be achieved, but there are two points to be made. (1) The non-figural sculpture on the façade of the church of the Holy Sepulchre is, for the most part, distinctive among the various products of crusader workshops in mid-twelfth-century Jerusalem, with the obvious exception of the godroons.[24] (2) Numerous significant questions

---

[20] Kenaan, 'Local Christian Art', pp. 222-3, differentiates four different types of which the Byzantine inspired predominate. Boase, 'Ecclesiastical Art', p. 81, finds all of these capitals, 'strongly Byzantine in feeling'. Folda, *Art of the Crusaders*, p. 224.

[21] Kenaan, 'Local Christian Art', pp. 222-3.

[22] These capitals have always been seen as reflecting Byzantine models, but no one has ever suggested they were *spolia*, that is, Byzantine work reused, unlike certain capitals found inside the church.

[23] Kenaan, 'Local Christian Art', pp. 223-4; Rosen-Ayalon, 'The Façade of the Holy Sepulchre', pp. 289-95, suggests, however, that these foliate carvings are crusader imitations of Islamic work.

[24] Compare other work as found on the Haram, on the church of the Ascension and in the workshop of the Hospital of the Knights of St. John, among others. See, Folda, *Art of the Crusaders*, pp. 249-82. It must noted that one or two imposts and capitals on the church of the

remain to be answered about this ensemble. How can the use of such an eclectic array of architectural sculpture be understood? Was this the product of expediency or conscious intention? What explanations can be proposed to understand this remarkably diverse ensemble of non-figural sculpture?

In the first place, the choice of sculpture for such an important part of this supremely important church would surely be the result of careful planning, without clear evidence to the contrary of which there is none. Indeed, given the role this church was intended to fulfil as the ultimate focus of Christian pilgrimage to the Holy Land and as the state church of the Latin kingdom of Jerusalem, and given the important patrons who would have been involved with this project, we can expect that this church would have been configured quite distinctively.[25] In light of this situation, how can we understand the assemblage of such a richly diverse programme?

It can be argued that these sculptures were the product of a richly diverse masons' workshop, and, in a certain sense, this may be correct, but only if we understand the sculptural programme as the intended outcome of a carefully conceived selection of sculpture, not as a matter of expediency due to pressure of time or the mere availability of sculptors doing their best work and using all appropriate materials. The crusader rebuilding of the church of the Holy Sepulchre, of which the decoration of the south transept façade was a significant part, was, after all, the largest and most important undertaking in Jerusalem in the 1140s and 1150s. Furthermore, there was no stated deadline so far as we know; the Second Crusade came and went with little notice taken of this project,[26] and the dedication of the church occurred on 15 July 1149 with part of the project apparently still unfinished. No evidence of haste is apparent, and it is clear that the quality of all the non-figural sculpture is uniformly very high. Under these circumstances, how and why was this non-figural sculpture chosen?

Ascension offer interesting comparisons, but they do not appear to be exactly the same, and there is nothing like the two hood mouldings and the imposts and frieze on the lower story of the church of the Holy Sepulchre elsewhere. This clearly suggests that the south transept façade *non-figural* sculpture was intended to be distinctive.

[25] As patrons we can identify the following likely participants: the patriarchs, and representatives of the regular canons and other religious communities present in the church in the 1130s, 1140s and 1150s, as well as the kings, Fulk (1131-43) and Baldwin III (1143-63), and the powerful queen, Melisende (1131-61).

[26] J. Folda, 'Reflections on Art in Crusader Jerusalem about the Time of the Second Crusade: c. 1140-c. 1150', in *The Second Crusade and the Cistercians*, ed. M. Gervers (New York, 1992), pp. 171-82.

In order to evaluate this problem our sources are essentially the sculptures themselves set in the context of mid-twelfth-century crusader Jerusalem. What significance would these sculptures have had for the crusaders, for the other Christian communities in Jerusalem, and for Christian pilgrims coming to the Holy Sepulchre at this time? In the first instance, the crusaders were rebuilding and decorating the architectural complex of the Holy Sepulchre, which had been initially constructed by Emperor Constantine I in the first half of the fourth century and rebuilt after the destruction of 1009 by the Byzantine Emperor Constantine IX Monomachus in the 1040s. As the main entrance to the newly rebuilt crusader church, the south transept façade (Plate 1) was apparently meant to make a collective statement about the church of the Holy Sepulchre. What were the components of this statement in terms of the non-figural sculpture and how could they be understood?

The reuse of Roman cornice sculpture (Plates 3, 4, 5) both as *spolia* and as models for the masons of the south transept façade clearly suggests that the Roman heritage of this site and this building was meant to be understood. Although Hadrian had built a Roman temple on this site in the second century, it is much more likely that the Roman ancestry referred to by these cornices is that of Constantine who built the Holy Sepulchre as a holy place.[27] The first church of the Holy Sepulchre was an early Christian, Roman building in Jerusalem.

The use of the rosette moulding (Plates 2, 7), strongly related to early Christian tomb monuments in Syria such as those at al-Bara, seems to contain a similar message. In effect the architect/designer/patron here is saying that it is fully appropriate that this monument honouring the empty tomb of the resurrected Christ and for the burial of the crusader kings be decorated this way. Without attempting to say that the rosette had any particular content as a design, the rosette moulding is presented as a fitting component of this ensemble because of its traditional association with tomb buildings in this region from the early Christian period.

The carved capitals (Plates 2, 3, 9, 10) form a major component of the south transept façade decoration and derive their basic types and vocabulary from Byzantine sources. To the extent that there was a Christian presence from the time of the Arab invasion in 638 to the advent of the crusaders in 1099, the

---

[27] B. Brenk, '*Spolia* from Constantine to Charlemagne: Aesthetics versus Ideology', *Dumbarton Oaks Papers* 41 (1987), pp. 103-9, points out that 'Constantine thought the pagan construction materials [from Hadrian's temple of Aphrodite] in Jerusalem to be impure and abstained from using them again' (p. 107). Conceivably the crusaders honoured this same ideal.

church of the Holy Sepulchre was in effect the responsibility of the Byzantine emperor. It was he who rebuilt this church after its destruction in 1009. Thus the Byzantine components of this façade are in effect proclaiming the Byzantine heritage of this building. The church of the Holy Sepulchre was not only a Roman, early Christian building, it was also Byzantine.

The upper hood moulding (Plate 8), the classicizing imposts and the associated foliated frieze (Plates 9, 10) are all Romanesque in the sense of the sculpture being done,'in the manner of the Romans'. As such this Romanesque sculpture, as in a certain sense all of the sculpture on this façade, directly reflects the European classical heritage of the medieval West reinterpreted in these new circumstances, with reference to new Near Eastern stimuli from Syria-Palestine. What is striking is that although this sculpture could be seen as that which was most obviously 'crusader' in terms of its Western character, it is not. It is not because here in the 1140s and 1150s what is crusader is the ensemble of all of the sculpture on this façade, not some narrowly identified parochial output.

Finally, the godroons (Plates 1, 6) clearly proclaim the Near Eastern character of this site by using an Arab vocabulary to articulate the arches of the main entrance façade of this church. The entry here, as with the cases of city gates and other church portals, is given special prominence and is meant to reflect the site and the constituency of this holy place in the Arab Christian world.

In sum, my argument is that this eclectic programme of non-figural sculpture is both a matter of ideology and a matter of aesthetics.[28] It is meant to be an essential part of the programme, proclaiming the function and importance of this façade in regard to the church which the sculpture decorates. It is meant to express the authenticity of this church and its heritage in an immediate, direct way. It is acceptable and correct, that is, it is not only acceptable that this façade aesthetically incorporates sculpture of such different styles from such diverse origins, but it is also desireable and intentional, creatively fusing the sculpture into one harmonious and unique whole. Furthermore, it is meant to address the clientele or constituency of the crusader kingdom and, in particular, this supremely important holy place.

Why did the crusaders choose to decorate the south transept façade in this manner, in striking contrast to contemporary work in the Latin kingdom, or in

---

[28] I am in effect expanding the ideas of Brenk, '*Spolia* from Constantine to Charlemagne', pp. 103-9, on *spolia* to the broader issue of crusader intentions in regard to their conscious eclecticsm, including the use of *spolia*, in certain works of sculpture, painting and architecture.

the West, e.g., the west façades of St Denis or Chartres, or earlier twelfth-century façades of churches on the pilgrimage roads?[29] It is acceptable, correct and desirable for the crusaders to do this because of the nature of their kingdom in terms of its Christian constituency. The non-figural sculpture of the façade of the church of the Holy Sepulchre was a work of crusader creativity writ large, a special case parallel to the kind of aesthetic and ideological production we know in the Melisende Psalter of c. 1135, approximately fifteen years earlier, or in the redecoration of the church of the Nativity at Bethlehem, 1167-69, nearly twenty years later.[30] Like the Melisende Psalter and other major crusader works, the façade of the church of the Holy Sepulchre was the product of a multicultural artistic team carried out for multicultural Christian patrons and for a multicultural pilgrim clientele. Who were these patrons and who were the artists doing the work?

In fact we can say very little about the masons or the sculptors, beyond what the sculpture tells us. It has been suggested that there was a continuous workshop tradition at the church of the Holy Sepulchre from the time of the Byzantine rebuilding.[31] The non-figural sculpture clearly supports this idea and the notion that local Christians, especially Syrians, were involved along with Western-trained masons. There may also have been Muslim masons as well.[32]

---

[29] One of the problems here is the novelty of the idea of a 'programme' in the non-figural sculpture, in contrast to a programme of figural work on a mid-twelfth-century façade, as argued by, e.g., A. Katzenellenbogen, *The Sculptural Programs of Chartres Cathedral* (Baltimore, 1959). Katzenellenbogen basically does not address the rich non-figural sculpture on the west façade portals, for example, and other relevant façades with major non-figural components, such as that at Vézelay (west), or the south transept portals at Santiago de Compostella, are similarly little discussed. In the context of the development of programmes for figural work in monumental stone sculpture in the first half of the twelfth century, we propose that it is possible to have a programme of non-figural sculpture as well.

[30] On the Psalter of Queen Melisende, see Folda, *Art of the Crusaders*, pp. 137-63, and Kühnel, *Crusader Art*, pp. 67-125. For the church of the Nativity in Bethlehem, see Folda, *Art of the Crusaders*, pp. 347-78; L.-A. Hunt, 'Art and Colonialism: The Mosaics of the Church of the Nativity in Bethlehem (1169) and the Problem of "Crusader Art"', *Dumbarton Oaks Papers* 45 (1991), pp. 69-85; Kühnel, *Crusader Art*, pp. 54-9.

[31] R. Ousterhout, 'Rebuilding the Temple: Constantine Monomachus and the Holy Sepulchre', *Journal of the Society of Architectural Historians* 48 (1989), pp. 66-78.

[32] Without knowing more information about the masons/sculptors involved in this project, we cannot rule out the possibility that the 'programme' in the non-figural sculpture I am arguing for here was not partly, or even mainly, the direct result of who was doing the work and what they were best at doing. The main evidence for the idea of a 'programme' in the face of this possibility is the use of *spolia* and the careful imitation of this *spolia*, the striking uniqueness of this façade in terms of the non-figural sculpture, and the comparable nature of crusader art

About the crusader patrons and the wider audience for whom this church was rebuilt and decorated, there are three things to be said from the historical context. First, given the function of the church, both patriarchal and royal patronage were involved: there were two patriarchs, William I (of Flanders, 1131-45), and Fulcher (of Angoulême and Tyre, 1146-57), and two kings, Fulk (of Anjou, 1131-43) and Baldwin III (1143-63), as well as the influential Queen Melisende (1131-61). Second, in addition to this, Bernard Hamilton has made it clear that by the 1140s, the eastern Christian communities were very active in the church of the Holy Sepulchre: '... the Orthodox were not hidden away in a side chapel, but had a large altar in a prominent part of the church at which the Orthodox liturgy was celebrated daily.'[33] The presence of these Orthodox clergy, Syrians and Greeks, and the fact that many royal women in the Latin kingdom, especially Melisende, were Orthodox, clearly indicates that the process of patronage would have recognized the importance of both Eastern and Western Christianity in the project to rebuild and decorate the church of the Holy Sepulchre.[34] Finally, overall this means that Latin and Orthodox Christians were the basic clientele at this crusader holy site, both as clergy and lay persons whether resident or on pilgrimage. Therefore, as planned and executed by crusader patrons, this means that the south transept façade presented an important statement about the church of the Holy Sepulchre in a multicultural visual language intended to reach out to Eastern and Western pilgrims alike. The figural programme on the façade in mosaics and the sculptured lintels must have clearly reflected this East-West, Byzantine-Western Romanesque Christian heritage in striking fashion. The non-figural programme was more subtle, articulating the Eastern aspect in terms of early Christian, Byzantine and Syrian aspects, and the Western in terms of crusader Levantine versions of Romanesque.

Conclusion

The architecture of the crusader church of the Holy Sepulchre is complex and brings together Byzantine, Romanesque and crusader aspects in a unique configuration. The programme of the south transept façade which announces this church at the main point of entry is even more complex.

---

seen in parallel media.

[33] Hamilton, *The Latin Church*, p. 171.

[34] In addition to the discussion of Bernard Hamilton, mentioned above, see also now Hunt, 'Artistic and Cultural Inter-Relations', pp. 63-82.

The rich repertory of sculpture from diverse traditions was a visual expression of the chronological and geographical *oikumene* of Christendom that was specifically relevant to the church of the Holy Sepulchre. It meant that pilgrims visiting the new church received a visual announcement at the entrance which included to some extent the Christian tradition of which they were part. The figural material addressed aspects of pilgrimage, the pilgrims coming to the site, and the presence of Jesus associated with this site and other holy places nearby. The non-figural architectural sculpture expresses important characteristics about the church. Because of its rich eclecticism, an eclecticism which is apparently intentional and carefully planned, the non-figural sculpture not only refers to the authenticity and pedigree of this venerable church, but also speaks out to pilgrims approaching this architectural complex in a multivalent visual language.[35] Thus the south transept façade proclaims the crusader church of the Holy Sepulchre to be, paraphrasing Isaiah, a house of prayer for all Christian peoples.[36]

---

[35] The question of to what extent artists and patrons had a consciousness of historical styles in non-figural architectural sculpture, or otherwise, in the twelfth century is relevant and important here, but it is not one which I can address in this discussion. This issue is obviously very important for the idea of a programme, and it is very relevant in a historical context such as the Latin kingdom of Jerusalem where the juxtaposition of different styles of artistic work was a striking feature of the visual world at this time. What is clear, however, is that each pilgrim could no doubt find those elements in the façade of the church of the Holy Sepulchre that referenced the artistic traditions of his or her own homeland. The role which the richly diverse art of the crusaders had in stimulating greater awareness of differing styles in the twelfth century, in comparison with sensibilities in western Europe, is a topic that remains to be explored.

[36] Isa. 56:7.

Plate 1. South transept façade of the church of the Holy Sepulchre, an overall view.

Plate 2. South transept façade of the church of the Holy Sepulchre: twin portals, lower storey.

Plate 3. South transept façade of the church of the Holy Sepulchre: twin windows, upper storey.

Plate 4. South transept façade of the church of the Holy Sepulchre: cornice, upper storey, right corner.

Plate 5. South transept façade of the church of the Holy Sepulchre: cornice, lower storey, right indentation.

Plate 6. South transept façade of the church of the Holy Sepulchre: godroons, lower storey between the arches.

Plate 7. South transept façade of the church of the Holy Sepulchre: rosette hood moulding, lower storey, right side.

Plate 8. South transept façade of the church of the Holy Sepulchre: foliated hood moulding, upper storey, right side.

Plate 9. South transept façade of the church of the Holy Sepulchre: capitals and imposts, upper storey, central jambs.

Plate 10. South transept façade of the church of the Holy Sepulchre: capitals and imposts, lower storey, left door, left jambs.

A Necessary Evil? Erasmus, the Crusade, and War against the Turks

Norman Housley

Erasmus's writings on the crusade constitute a fascinating addition to the corpus of criticism of the institution and its abuses in the late middle ages and Renaissance. For a man so often accused of inconsistency or ambivalence, Erasmus was strikingly clear in his condemnation of crusading. It was a question of rejection rather than reform. But the matter could not remain there. In common with such contemporaries as Martin Luther, Josse Clichtove and Juan Luis Vives,[1] Erasmus was compelled by the threat posed by the Turks to contemplate the broader issue of if, and how, a war should be conducted against them in defence of his religion.[2] In this respect too the charge of inconsistency would be unfair. What we see instead is a paradox, for Erasmus reluctantly accepted the need to fight while perceiving in the military solution the very antithesis of his religious values. Christianity faced almost as great a threat from its defenders as from its assailants. The intellectual anguish caused by this dilemma contributed in no small measure to the pessimism of Erasmus's last years.[3]

Let us take the crusade first. Certain isolated remarks made before Erasmus achieved fame seem to indicate an acceptance, albeit a conventional one, of the crusading tradition as vested in Christendom's leading secular powers. Writing

---

[1] H. Buchanan, 'Luther and the Turks, 1519-1529', *Archiv für Reformationsgeschichte* 47 (1956), pp. 145-59; W.F. Bense, 'Paris Theologians on War and Peace, 1521-1529', *Church History* 41 (1972), pp. 168-85; R.P. Adams, *The Better Part of Valor: More, Erasmus, Colet, and Vives, on Humanism, War, and Peace, 1496-1535* (Seattle, 1962), pp. 262-4, 285-91.

[2] M. Cytowska, 'Erasme et les Turcs', *Eos* 62 (1974), pp. 311-21; J.-C. Margolin, 'Erasme et la guerre contre les Turcs', *Il pensiero politico* 13 (1980), pp. 3-38.

[3] L.-E. Halkin, *Erasmus: A Critical Biography*, trans. J. Tonkin (Oxford and Cambridge, Mass., 1993), chapters 21-3.

to the great French humanist, Robert Gaguin, in 1495, during Charles VIII's Italian expedition, Erasmus praised the French kings for their mixture of bravery and piety: 'This is why the Christian council of this realm has clearly reserved to itself the role of chief and sole defender of the faith against the armed aggression of the Turk.'[4] Similar language was used, this time about the Holy Roman Emperor, in a letter of February 1503 to Jacob Anthoniszoon;[5] and in his panegyric to Archduke Philip of Austria in the following year Erasmus referred to Spain as 'the sole defensive outpost of the Christian religion', expressing the hope that if Philip had to fight it would not be against Christians but against Turks and Saracens, 'the enemies of Christian peace'.[6]

These were, however, far from being the expression of Erasmus's deep convictions. They were formulaic utterances shaped by the occasions on which they were made: in the first two instances, printed additions to books written in praise of, respectively, French and imperial prestige, and in the third, a panegyric delivered on Philip's return to the Low Countries early in 1504. Even then, it is interesting that Erasmus made no reference to Charles VIII's supposed crusade plans in 1495, nor indeed did Gaguin in a letter to Erasmus written at the same time;[7] while Erasmus's remark about Archduke Philip fighting the Muslims came at the end of a long passage in which the archduke was exhorted not to wage any wars at all. Erasmus was living in Paris in 1495 (at the appalling Collège de Montaigu), but left no signs of being excited by Charles VIII's Italian venture.[8]

More indicative of Erasmus's true feelings was a passing remark made in the preface to his *Moriae encomium*, published in 1511. The preface took the form of a letter to Thomas More, and in defence of his book Erasmus claimed that it was preferable to such hackneyed and superficial activities as speeches in

---

[4] P.S. Allen, H.M. Allen and H.W. Garrod, eds, *Opus epistolarum Des. Erasmi Roterodami*, 11 vols (Oxford, 1906-47) plus index volume (Oxford, 1958), Ep. 45 [hereafter Allen]. *The Collected Works of Erasmus* (Toronto, Buffalo and London, 1974-) [hereafter *CWE*] has so far reached Ep. 1657 in its translation of the letters *(The Correspondence of Erasmus*, trans. R.A.B. Mynors, D.F.S. Thomson and A. Dalzell), following Allen's numbering throughout. In all cases where translated passages are given, for any of Erasmus's works published to date in the *CWE*, I have used their translation; the *CWE* should be consulted also for its excellent, up-to-date critical apparatus.

[5] Allen, Ep. 173.

[6] *Opera omnia Desiderii Erasmi Roterodami* (Amsterdam, New York, Oxford and Tokyo, 1969-), 4(1).30, 83 [hereafter *OODER*] (= *CWE*, 27: *Literary and Educational Writings* 5, ed. A.H.T. Levi, pp. 11, 64).

[7] Allen, Ep. 46, which contains a brief summary of events in Italy to date.

[8] Halkin, *Erasmus*, chapter 3.

praise of rulers (somewhat ironic in the light of his own panegyric of 1504), and orations recommending a crusade against the Turks.[9] As Michael Heath and others have shown, such exhortations were commonplace in the early sixteenth century. The genre was one in which originality was hard to achieve and it laid itself open to such criticisms as this one.[10]

But it was the ambitious plans of Pope Leo X, elected in March 1513, which elicited Erasmus's first detailed commentary on crusading. Erasmus had great hopes of Leo, whom he saw as a peacemaker in contrast to his warmaking predecessor, Julius II. But he had no sympathy at all for Leo X's determination to mount a crusade against the Turks. This placed him in a difficult situation when he wrote to the pope in May 1515 asking Leo's permission to dedicate his edition of Jerome to him. The circumstances ruled out any open condemnation of the crusade, but Erasmus made his views clear enough. The pope's efforts to make peace within Christendom received rhapsodic praise. As for the Turks, if they had to be fought, Leo's great piety would ensure victory. But it would be better to convert them to Christianity than to engage in warfare, and Erasmus's adroit phraseology left open the question of how success would be achieved. 'One day our lion's roar will be too much for them, those monstrous brutes; it comes, it surely comes, the time when even the most ferocious of wild beasts will feel the invincible might of our Leo, mild as he is, and will find themselves unequal to a pontiff whose strength lies in piety rather than armies, who brings immortal powers into battle on his side.'[11]

Selim the Grim's destruction of the Mamluk sultanate in 1516-17 exerted a powerful impetus on Leo X's crusade planning, and by the end of 1517 his proposals had reached the stage of issuing indulgences and levying taxes. Detailed campaign proposals were circulating between the papal, French and imperial courts. On 3 March 1518 Leo appointed four cardinal-legates to preach the crusade in Germany, France, England and Spain. As Erasmus was later to remark, the men chosen were highly capable: Tommaso de Vio (Cajetanus), Bernardo Dovizzi, Lorenzo Campeggio and Giles of Viterbo. On 6 March Leo declared a five-year truce among all the Catholic powers to further the promotion of his crusade.[12]

---

[9] Allen, Ep. 222.

[10] M.J. Heath, *Crusading Commonplaces: La Noue, Lucinge and Rhetoric against the Turks* (Geneva, 1986).

[11] Allen, Ep. 335.

[12] K.M. Setton, 'Pope Leo X and the Turkish Peril', *Proceedings of the American Philosophical Society* 113 (1969), pp. 367-424, especially pp. 391-409; *OODER*, 5(3).68; Allen, Ep. 729.

In a series of letters to various correspondents in February and March 1518, Erasmus was much more forthright in his condemnation of the crusade than he had been in his letter to the pope three years previously. He made it clear that he saw the proposals as pretexts pure and simple. To Johannes Sixtinus, on 22 February, he wrote: 'The pope and the emperor have a new game on foot: they now use war against the Turks as an excuse, though they have something very different in mind. We have reached the limits of despotism and effrontery.'[13] To an unidentified correspondent Erasmus wrote on 5 March of rumours from Switzerland of a Franco-papal plan to expel the Spanish from Naples under cover of the crusade. 'If I mistake not, the pretext is one thing and the purpose another.'[14]

This highly sceptical response to Leo's plans was a natural product of the failure of so much crusade planning in the past, the repeated diversion of crusading funds into secular warfare, and, perhaps most notoriously, the use of the crusade to disguise alliances formed against other Christian powers. The League of Cambrai of December 1508 had been a glaring recent example of the latter.[15] Some contemporaries showed enthusiasm for Leo's crusade project, but Erasmus was far from alone in failing to do so. Richard Pace reported that Henry VIII laughed when he was told of Maximilian's crusade proposals, so clearly were they dictated by Habsburg interests.[16] But James Tracy has shown that in Erasmus's case scepticism was generated by a more immediate and local background. This was his deep disillusionment with Habsburg policy in the Low Countries, especially the recent war against Guelders and the heavy, centralizing taxation which it had cloaked.[17] Popes and princes had shown that they were not to be trusted. As early as 1515, in his commentary on the adage *Dulce bellum inexpertis*, Erasmus voiced the suspicion that financial gain in the pursuit of oppression by both church and state might be

---

[13] Allen, Ep. 775.

[14] Allen, Ep. 781, and see Ep. 786.

[15] C. Shaw, *Julius II: The Warrior Pope* (Oxford and Cambridge, Mass., 1993), pp. 229, 232; K.M. Setton, *The Papacy and the Levant (1204-1571), Memoirs of the American Philosophical Society* 114, 127, 161-2, 4 vols (Philadelphia, 1976-84), 3.54-5.

[16] J.D. Tracy, *The Politics of Erasmus: A Pacifist Intellectual and his Political Milieu* (Toronto, Buffalo and London, 1978), p. 110.

[17] Tracy, *The Politics of Erasmus*, chapters 4-5 et passim. See also the same author's *Holland under Habsburg Rule, 1506-1566: The Formation of a Body Politic* (Berkeley, Los Angeles and Oxford, 1990), chapter 3.

the whole point of Leo's crusade plans.[18] He repeated the charge in the *Institutio principis christiani* a year later.[19] To Beatus Rhenanus, on 13 March 1518, he remarked: 'God help us, what tragic work these princes have in hand! The sense of honour is extinct in public affairs. Despotism has reached its peak. Pope and kings regard the people not as human beings but as beasts for market.'[20]

This latter sentiment well reflected Erasmus's reaction to Leo X's crusade indulgences. They represented trickery of the most outrageous kind, because the papal collectors played down the need for confession and contrition on the part of those who procured them. Erasmus had already attacked the abuses associated with indulgences in his *Moriae encomium*, and in the *Julius exclusus* (first dated edition 1518) he depicted Julius II's soldiers appearing at Heaven's gates and demanding entry on the basis of papal indulgences alone.[21] In one of the letters probably written in the spring of 1518, to John Colet, he commented: 'The Roman curia has abandoned any sense of shame. What could be more shameless than these constant indulgences?'[22] In his critique of indulgences Erasmus was of course far from alone. When he wrote to Thomas More on 5 March 1518 enclosing a copy of Leo X's *Consultationes pro expeditione contra Thurcum*, which had been printed at Augsburg a few weeks earlier, he also dispatched what was almost certainly a copy of Luther's Ninety-Five Theses, from the first Basel printing of late 1517.[23] Erasmus did not consider that indulgences, for the crusade or any other concern, merited such a fierce assault. His attitude was well summarized in a letter to Nicolaas Everaerts in 1521: 'Against indulgence the remedy will be to give nothing, until a better opportunity offers to hound this godless traffic off the stage altogether.'[24]

---

[18] Y. Remy and R. Dunil-Marquebreucq, eds, *Erasme: Dulce bellum inexpertis*, Collection Latomus 8 (Berchem-Brussels, 1953), p. 92. For an English translation, see M. Mann Phillips, *Erasmus on his Times: A Shortened Version of the 'Adages' of Erasmus* (Cambridge, 1967), pp. 107-40, at p. 136.

[19] *OODER*, 4(1).218 (= *CWE*, 27.287: 'We can see that wars of this kind have too frequently been made an excuse to fleece the Christian people — and then nothing else has been done.')

[20] Allen, Ep. 796.

[21] *OODER*, 4(3).122-4, 172 (= *CWE*, 27.114, 138); W.K. Ferguson, *Erasmi opuscula* (The Hague, 1933), pp. 38-124, at p. 78 (= *CWE*, 27.174).

[22] Allen, Ep. 786.

[23] Allen, Ep. 785.

[24] Allen, Ep. 1188. Self-preservation dictated caution: in the same letter Erasmus reported rumours that the advocates of reform were being poisoned. Generally on Erasmus and indulgences, see L.-E. Halkin, 'La Place des indulgences dans la pensée religieuse d'Erasme', *Bulletin de la Société de l'histoire du protestantisme français* 129 (1983), pp. 143-54 (reprinted

Erasmus's letter of 5 March 1518 to More contained his most jocular comments on Leo's crusade plans. 'The pope and the princes have several new plays in rehearsal, using as a pretext a frightful war against the Turks', he remarked. 'I am sorry for those Turks! We Christians must not grow too fierce.' There was to be universal conscription of all married men between the ages of 26 and 50. During the crusade, he informed his friend, it was the pope's desire that the wives of those who were away fighting the Turks should fast every other day, and dress and behave in an abstemious manner. Those men who remained at home were supposed to abstain from sexual intercourse with their wives: 'Nor may they exchange kisses until by the mercy of Christ this terrible war is successfully concluded.'[25] This was a joke at the expense of the uxorious More rather than a reference to an actual papal pronouncement.[26] It was not, however, markedly more fantastic than some of the proposals being made: one, which dated back to at least 1474 but was revived in 1518, envisaged an army of up to half a million men provided and equipped solely by the religious orders.[27]

Normally Erasmus was unable to treat the subject of Leo's crusade as lightly as in this letter to More, for it conflicted at so many points with his firmest religious convictions. Quite apart from the fact that the dissimulation involved on the part of pope and princes was painfully symptomatic of the condition of public affairs, and the peddling of indulgences (particularly by his *bêtes noires*, the mendicant friars) was so abhorrent to him, the very concept of a fighting 'miles christianus' appalled a man who loathed war and regarded soldiers as inherently dehumanized. It was therefore significant that at the same time that he wrote the series of private letters in which he poured scorn on Leo X's crusade plans, Erasmus was working on a new edition of his *Enchiridion militis christiani*, the manual of the true Christian life which he had first published in 1503. Military imagery suffuses the work, as when its author asks: 'Are you not aware, O Christian soldier, that when you were initiated into the mysteries

---

in his *Erasme: sa pensée et son comportement* [London, 1988], Study X); Halkin, *Erasmus*, pp. 146-7, 247-8.

[25] Allen, Ep. 785.

[26] It is interesting that the Erasmus scholar James Tracy originally treated this as a reference to a genuine provision of Leo X, only later seeing it as the joke which it clearly is: *Erasmus: The Growth of a Mind* (Geneva, 1972), p. 176; *The Politics of Erasmus*, pp. 114, 185 n. 25. The reference to universal conscription of *married* men signals the joke.

[27] Setton, 'Pope Leo X', pp. 414-15.

of the life-giving font, you enrolled in the army of Christ, your general?'[28] Actual fighting, however, is roundly condemned: the return to the pre-crusade conception of 'militia Christi' is absolute.[29] In this sense the *Enchiridion* complements the assault on traditional chivalric values carried out by Erasmus and More.[30]

In the preface to this new edition, which was published in August 1518, Erasmus reflected at some length on the planned crusade. He did this more discreetly than in his private correspondence with his friends, and the result was similar in both tone and substance to his letter to Leo X of May 1515. The intentions of those promoting the crusade were questioned rather than openly challenged, and Leo X's zeal was praised: if the pope's plans went awry, it would be because of the deceptions of others. But the 'traffic in indulgences' came in for harsh criticism, and even if the crusade should prove successful, 'the result may extend the kingdom of the pope and his cardinals; it will not extend the kingdom of Christ'.[31]

Leo X continued to promote his crusade until the death of Sultan Selim in 1520 removed the immediate prospect of a Turkish attack. By that point, however, Erasmus's comments on the project had already become infrequent and desultory. In letters to Richard Pace and John Colet in October 1518 he expressed his suspicions about the tax which Maximilian was attempting to secure at the Augsburg Diet for a crusade, even extending his conspiracy theory to include the Turks: 'The princes, together with the pope, and I dare say the Grand Turk as well, are in league against the well-being of the common people.'[32] In view of Erasmus's horror of rebellion, this formed one of his bleakest political pronouncements. In contrast, he was pleased by Wolsey's treaty of London (2 October 1518). He probably did not expect peace in Europe to last long, let alone lead to the crusade envisaged, officially at least, by the treaty's negotiators. But it might function as a deterrent, since

---

[28] *Erasmi opera omnia*, ed. J. Le Clerc, 10 vols (Leiden, 1703-6), 5.3A [hereafter *EOO*], (= *CWE*, 66: *Spiritualia*, ed. J.W. O'Malley, p. 26).

[29] *EOO*, 5.63A-66C (= *CWE*, 66.123-6).

[30] Adams, *The Better Part of Valor*, pp. 75-9, 144-57.

[31] Allen, Ep. 858.

[32] Allen, Epp. 887, 891 (quote). See Ep. 936, 2 April 1519, to John Fisher: 'O that Christ would at long last arise and liberate his people from tyrants of so many kinds. For the end seems likely to be, unless steps are taken, that it would be more tolerable to live under the tyranny of the Turks.'

'nothing renders Christ's people so formidable to the enemies of our religion as concord between princes and between their peoples'.[33]

Soon afterwards the outbreak of the Reformation brought the end of the crusading movement as an expression of Christendom's unity under the spiritual authority of the pope. Confessional conflict did not, however, spell the end of crusading as a military and religious activity, since the Habsburgs continued to enlist papal support for their war against the Ottomans in the shape of crusade indulgences and taxes. The significance of this development did not escape Erasmus. As he wrote to Peter Tomiczki on 2 September 1532, if Charles V was really fighting in the name of all Christendom, then all of his fellow rulers should be involved; otherwise there was the danger of a dynastic war being dressed up in crusading clothes. Was the emperor defending the faith or contending for 'the Hungarian Helen'?[34] On the other hand, Erasmus was fully aware that papal support for Charles V was far from automatic: in April 1531 a correspondent passed on the news that the sultan had informed Ferdinand's envoys of a proposal made after the battle of Pavia by the pope, the French, the Venetians and some of the German princes, that the Ottomans should invade Habsburg lands.[35]

In 1529-30 the crusade preaching associated with Charles V's attempt to raise money to defend Austria came to Erasmus's attention.[36] Some of the scorn which he had displayed towards Leo X's project more than a decade previously was again manifested, and interesting nuggets of detail emerged on the practices involved. Thus in a letter to John Botzheim, written in August 1529, he condemned the fact that 'everywhere the churches are packed with the crimson cross and chest, the papal arms with the tiara are attached to pillars, and some people are even compelled to purchase [indulgences], as is reported to be all but the case in Spain'.[37] This formed part of an invective against decadent practices, including the display of unseemly paintings of the saints, and the singing of inappropriate music in church. However, as Erasmus wrote to Boniface Amerbach a few months later, the magic no longer worked: 'In Flanders the crimson cross has been erected against the Turks. The monks paint pictures of Turkish atrocities, and actively proclaim them. But nobody is

---

[33] Allen, Ep. 964.
[34] Allen, Ep. 2713.
[35] Allen, Ep. 2480.
[36] See L. Gilliodts-van Severen, 'La Croisade de 1530 ordonnée par Charles-Quint', *Bulletin de la Commission royale d'histoire* 16 (1889), pp. 261-82.
[37] Allen, Ep. 2205.

giving a penny'. Such money as was raised would not, in any case, be spent on the war.[38]

It was at this point, in March 1530, that Erasmus wrote and published his *Utilissima consultatio de bello contra Turcos inferendo*.[39] This was his most detailed response to the crisis which had burgeoned since the battle of Mohács in 1526. The circumstances which led him to write it remain unclear. A.G. Weiler has shown that the grounds for viewing the treatise as a response to a specific request for advice from its dedicatee, the Cologne professor of jurisprudence, Johannes Rinck, are not as strong as was once thought.[40] The argument that it was requested by the government of Ferdinand or Charles V to enlist Erasmus's valuable support for the war in Austria is even weaker.[41] Possibly Erasmus felt the need to distance himself from Luther on this subject, as on others: it was probably while writing the *Consultatio* that he asked Boniface Amerbach to send him a copy of Luther's 'libellus de bello adversus Turcas'. This book, which Amerbach duly dispatched, was most likely *Vom kriege widder die Turcken*.[42] On the other hand, it is not impossible that without any external stimulus, Erasmus simply felt the need to state his views on a matter of urgent public concern. Vienna had experienced its first Ottoman siege in the autumn of 1529 and further military action of some sort was widely expected to occur in 1530.[43]

The bulk of the Erasmian case against crusading had already emerged over the years. In the *Consultatio* most of his criticisms were simply reiterated, with no less conviction or panache, although with a discretion dictated by the fact that the work was a public document. He repeated his firm belief that the efficacy of indulgences depended on far more than papal authority: 'They are

---

[38] Allen, Ep. 2256, and see Epp. 2516, 2713. Charles V's regent, Margaret of Austria, complained in a letter on 31 March 1530 that proceeds to date had been disappointing: Gilliodts-van Severen, 'La Croisade de 1530', p. 265.

[39] *OODER*, 5(3).1-82. For commentaries, see M.J. Heath, 'Erasmus and War against the Turks', in *Acta conventus neo-latini turonensis*, ed. J.-C. Margolin (Paris, 1980), pp. 991-9; A.G. Weiler, 'La *Consultatio de bello Turcis inferendo*: une oeuvre de piété politique', in *Actes du colloque international Erasme (Tours, 1986)*, ed. J. Chomarat, A. Godin and J.-C. Margolin (Geneva, 1990), pp. 99-108. Partial translation into French, and accompanying commentary, in J.-C. Margolin, *Guerre et paix dans la pensée d'Erasme* (Paris, 1973), pp. 328-74.

[40] Allen, Ep. 2285; *OODER*, 5(3).4-5.

[41] *OODER*, 5(3).5-6; Cytowska, 'Erasme et les Turcs', p. 317; Margolin, 'Erasme et la guerre contre les Turcs', p. 12.

[42] Allen, Epp. 2279-80; *OODER*, 5(3).21; Margolin, 'Erasme et la guerre contre les Turcs', pp. 12-14.

[43] Allen, Epp. 2249, 2260, 2295, 2328.

deceiving themselves miserably, if they believe that they will go straight to heaven should they happen to fall in battle against the Turks.'[44] But what counted far more than the frame of mind of the soldier was that of the civilian encouraged to purchase indulgences in support of the crusade. For such was the accumulation of distrust that the machinery of preaching the crusade had become totally useless. In phrases very similar to those he had recently employed in his letters to Botzheim and Amerbach, Erasmus wrote that people had too often witnessed the apparatus of indulgences, cross and collecting chest, being set up in their churches, and heard the grandiose promises of religious assemblies, without any result. 'The only winner was money.' Indulgences had been degraded through overuse, and Erasmus claimed (inaccurately, it seems) that an indulgence campaign launched in the recent past by Pope Adrian V for the relief of flood victims in Flanders had provided a notable example of funds which had been generously donated going astray.[45]

Because of this sorry history of dissimulation, men of the undoubted calibre of Cardinal Bessarion, Pope Pius II and most recently Leo X had proved unable to arouse general interest in a crusade. This was even before Luther both launched his onslaught on the spiritual authority of the Roman church and questioned the validity of resistance against the Ottomans, so it was inconceivable that the lack of interest could be remedied now. Interestingly, Erasmus refrained from repeating the ferocious attacks of his earlier writings against clerical involvement in war. He contented himself with remarking that it was 'neither becoming nor in accordance with Scripture or Church law'. Instead he focussed on the fact that it was ineffective. Soldiers did not respond well to clerical leadership, and Mars himself did not favour their efforts.[46]

Clearly the crusade, as preached by Leo X and more recently by Clement VII, was to be rejected. What should replace it as the framework for relations between Christians and Muslims? By the time he wrote the *Consultatio* Erasmus had been pondering this question for about a quarter of a century. His view of the matter was framed by two chief considerations: his hatred for war of any kind, and the apparently inexorable westwards advance of the Turks.

---

[44] *OODER*, 5(3).59.
[45] *OODER*, 5(3).64-7. The indulgence, for Flanders, Zeeland and Friesland, was granted by Pope Leo X in September 1515 and its proceeds were intended to strengthen the dykes rather than assist victims of flooding.
[46] *OODER*, 5(3).66-8, 71-2.

Erasmus was not a doctrinal pacifist.[47] He accepted the right of anybody to defend life, family and property against attack. What he hated were the supremely negative consequences of war, which was destructive of any fruitful activity, including sound religion. As he put it in a famous letter to Wolfgang Capito in February 1517, 'every vestige of true religion, of just laws, of civilized behaviour, of high moral standards and of liberal arts among the incessant clash of arms is either killed outright by a licentious soldiery, or at best is brought to the lowest ebb'.[48] War was beastly, running counter to human physiology and nature. It made no economic sense because its costs always outweighed its questionable benefits. No war could be justified except in spurious terms. The executants of war, soldiers, were the poorest, most wretched and brutalized of people. Secular rulers were encouraged to avoid war under any circumstances, because the most unjust peace was usually preferable to the most just war.[49]

These core themes were developed energetically in a group of Erasmus's most telling works written between 1515 and 1517, especially the adage *Dulce bellum inexpertis* (1515), *Institutio principis christiani* (1516), and *Querela pacis* (1517). There appear to have been several formative influences behind this flood of brilliant polemic on behalf of peace. One, emphasized by the Erasmus scholar L.-E. Halkin, was the deleterious effects of war which Erasmus witnessed in Italy during his visit in 1506-9, and the bellicosity of Pope Julius II.[50] Another, illuminated in a fine study by Robert Adams in 1962, was Erasmus's contacts with fellow humanists Colet and More during his several periods of residence in England from 1499 onwards. In England the association between peace, educational and religious reform, and humanism, seemed clear; it was manifested in such events as the foundation of Corpus

---

[47] Allen, Ep. 1232 makes this clear.

[48] Allen, Ep. 541.

[49] See L.-E. Halkin, 'Erasme, la guerre et la paix', in *Krieg und Friede im Horizont des Renaissancehumanismus* (Weinheim, 1986), pp. 13-44 (reprinted in his *Erasme: sa pensée et son comportement*, Study XV); J.-C. Margolin, *Guerre et paix* (a useful collection of key texts); Adams, *The Better Part of Valor*; Tracy, *The Politics of Erasmus*; J.A. Fernández, 'Erasmus on the Just War', *Journal of the History of Ideas* 34 (1973), pp. 209-26; P. Brachin, '*Vox clamantis in deserto*: refléxions sur le pacifisme d'Erasme', in *Colloquia erasmiana turonensia: douzième stage international d'études humanistes, Tours 1969*, 2 vols (Toronto and Buffalo, 1972), 1.247-75.

[50] See his 'Erasme, la guerre et la paix', p. 16: 'C'est Jules II qui fera de lui un pacifiste ardent et convaincu'; Halkin, *Erasmus*, pp. 66, 267.

Christi College, Oxford, in 1517.[51] By contrast, Erasmus complained in a famous letter to Abbot Antoon van Bergen in March 1514 that the heavy taxes imposed to pay for Henry VIII's French war had 'brought about a sudden change in the character of this island', eroding English generosity and thereby both imperilling the humanist cause and making his own financial position more tenuous.[52]

More recently, James Tracy has emphasized Erasmus's intense interest in events in his native Low Countries. Apart from the distrust of the secular authorities referred to above, the main influence which they exerted on Erasmus's thinking was in terms of the atrocities committed by the mercenaries hired by the warring parties.[53] This crystallized Erasmus's view of the professional soldier as an agent of evil. In the March 1514 letter to Antoon van Bergen mercenaries were condemned as 'murderers, profligates devoted to gambling and rape'.[54] The worst of the mercenaries were the members of the Black Band, whose horrifying sack of Asperen in July 1517 made such a profound impression on Erasmus that he referred to it in the *Consultatio*, thirteen years later.[55] Erasmus never made his peace with the professional soldier. In dialogues written for various editions of the *Colloquies* in the 1520s he constantly pointed out the miseries of the soldier's existence; and at the very end of his life, when he composed a 'soldier's prayer', the best he could manage was a prayer for a bloodless victory achieved through the submission of the enemy.[56]

Only if Europe's rulers pursued peaceful goals could this social evil be contained; politically therefore, Erasmus was at his most optimistic when leading figures, such as Leo X, Francis I and Henry VIII, appeared to be persuaded of the need for peace. In February 1517, when Francis I appeared willing not to exploit his victory at Marignano, the hopeful prospects for peace led Erasmus, albeit briefly, to hail 'the rise of a new kind of golden age'.[57] Such hopes sprang from a broader vision of evangelical rulership outlined a year earlier in

---

[51] Adams, *The Better Part of Valor*, pp. 162 et passim.

[52] Allen, Ep. 288, and cf. Adams, *The Better Part of Valor*, pp. 81-4.

[53] Tracy, *The Politics of Erasmus*, especially chapter 4.

[54] Allen, Ep. 288.

[55] Allen, Epp. 413, 628, 643, 829, 832, 1001; *OODER*, 5(3).52-4.

[56] See 'Militaria' (1522), 'Militis et Cartusiani' (1523) and 'Charon' (1529), *OODER*, 1(3).154-8, 314-19, 575-84; English translation: C.R. Thompson, *The Colloquies of Erasmus* (Chicago and London, 1965), pp. 11-15, 127-33, 388-94. For the soldier's prayer see *EOO*, 5.1204F-1205A, and see Halkin, *Erasmus*, pp. 260-1.

[57] Allen, Ep. 533, and see Epp. 335, 964.

the *Institutio principis christiani*, one of the most high-minded of Erasmus's works. In this the dominance of honour, military prowess and chivalric splendour in the education of princes was condemned in favour of ideals of public service and Christian morality.[58]

Naturally Erasmus was concerned both to demonstrate how firmly his obsession with peace was based on essential Christian principles, and to discredit any association between religion and war. This provoked the concentrated assaults on the scholastic theory of the just war which make it possible to understand how he came to be accused of pacifism.[59] Erasmus eagerly embraced John Colet's rejection of the scholastic approach to Scripture in favour of a historical view which recognized that the church achieved its early expansion by preaching the peaceful message of Christ. Standard texts by St Augustine and St Bernard validating war were therefore irrelevant, especially when they were selectively chosen or quoted out of context.[60] Much more important was the fact that, as Erasmus asserted in the preface to his edition of St Hilary in January 1523: 'The sum and substance of our religion is peace and concord'.[61] As he had written somewhat audaciously to Leo X in 1515: 'To fight the Turks we get no instructions from Christ and no encouragement from the apostles.'[62] Exegetically, of course, this was by no means as straightforward as Erasmus claimed, necessitating some readings (notably of Luke 22: 35-8) which were fully as strained as those of the scholastic commentators.[63]

The other side of the coin was Erasmus's harsh criticism of those clerics who justified or even sanctified the military campaigns of their rulers, preached enthusiastic sermons in camp, and encouraged soldiers to fight in anticipation of a heavenly reward. As Jean-Claude Margolin remarked, Erasmus possessed '[une] horreur congénitale pour la violence mise au service de la foi'.[64] Attacks on this fundamental 'trahison des clercs' feature in all the major tracts on peace. In *Moriae encomium* he savaged the 'learned sycophants [who] put the name of zeal, piety, and valour to this manifest insanity'.[65] In *Dulce*

---

[58] *OODER*, 4(1).136-74 (= *CWE*, 27.206-45).

[59] For rejections of the charge, see Allen, Epp. 858, 1469.

[60] Remy and Dunil-Marquebreucq, *Erasme: Dulce bellum inexpertis*, pp. 74-6 (= Mann Phillips, *Erasmus on his Times*, pp. 29-30). See also Allen, Ep. 288, and Adams, *The Better Part of Valor*, pp. 21-8.

[61] Allen, Ep. 1334.

[62] Allen, Ep. 335.

[63] 'Moriae encomium', *OODER*, 4(3).184 (= *CWE*, 27.145-6).

[64] Margolin, 'Erasme et la guerre contre les Turcs', p. 5.

[65] *OODER* 4(3).174 (= *CWE*, 27.139).

bellum inexpertis Erasmus wrote of the cleric who 'from the sacred pulpit, promises pardon for all the sins committed by those who fight under the banners of his prince', and a few lines later described 'two armies [marching] against each other each carrying the standard of the cross'.[66] The *Querela pacis* contained a lengthy passage, possibly referring to practices followed in England during Henry VIII's war against France in 1512-13, in which the mendicants were accused of inciting troops to violence in the name of Christ.[67] Twelve years later, in his colloquy, *Charon* (1529), Erasmus again took to task those friars who preached that God favoured their rulers and assured soldiers that they would enjoy eternal salvation if they died. 'To the French they preach that God is on the French side: he who has God to protect him cannot be conquered! To the English and Spanish they declare this war is not the Emperor's but God's ... [And] if anyone does get killed, he doesn't perish utterly but flies straight up to heaven, armed just as he was.'[68] The disease affected both head and members: Pope Julius II, who commanded his own troops and whose triumphal entry into Bologna Erasmus witnessed in 1506, aroused his bitter criticism both in the excoriating satire, *Julius exclusus*, and to a lesser extent in correspondence.[69]

What then of the Turks? Erasmus's keen interest in contemporary affairs led him to note in his correspondence most of the major advances which they made. He had a wide network of friends in eastern Europe and his letters in the 1520s in particular were full of references to the progress of the war in Hungary and Austria.[70] Following the death of Louis II of Hungary at the battle of Mohács, Erasmus claimed that the young king had been one of his patrons, and he wrote a treatise on Christian widowhood for Louis's widow, Mary of Habsburg.[71] His references to events in the east were, however,

---

[66] Remy and Dunil-Marquebreucq, *Erasme: Dulce bellum inexpertis*, pp. 40-2 (= Mann Phillips, *Erasmus on his Times*, p. 116).

[67] *OODER*, 4(2).82-4 (= *CWE*, 27.308-9).

[68] *OODER*, 1(3).578 (= Thompson, *Colloquies*, pp. 391-2).

[69] Allen, Epp. 205, 233, 245, 262, 282. On the *Julius exclusus*, see J.K. McConica, 'Erasmus and the "Julius": A Humanist Reflects on the Church', in *The Pursuit of Holiness in Late Medieval and Renaissance Religion*, ed. C. Trinkaus and H.A. Oberman, *Studies in Medieval and Reformation Thought* 10 (Leiden, 1974), pp. 444-71.

[70] For example, Allen, Epp. 1228, 1304, 1310, 1337, 1754, 1762, 1805, 1819, 2005, 2030, 2090, 2177, 2211, 2217, 2230, 2260 (dated 1521-30).

[71] *EOO*, 5.723D-766E (= *CWE*, 66.184-257). See Allen, Ep. 1805.

usually quite short.[72] It is striking that Erasmus showed no real interest in the growth or nature of the Ottoman state. His description of Turkish origins in the *Consultatio* of 1530 was lifted entirely, and uncritically, from a work of Joannes Baptista Egnatius. It was included only to make the didactic point that the Christians had failed to hold back the Turks because of their own sins rather than because of their enemies' military prowess or piety.[73] Furthermore, on numerous occasions when he referred to the Turks Erasmus used them solely as a stick with which to beat his contemporaries. Thus English sailors treated foreign visitors worse than the Turks did; mercenaries in Holland showed 'more than Turkish ferocity'; Christian rulers were so tyrannical that the rule of the sultan could hardly be worse; and Christendom was relapsing into worse-than-Turkish barbarism.[74]

Erasmus's limited degree of interest in the Turks per se was reinforced by his disdain for apocalypticism, which caused so many of his contemporaries to follow and interpret events in eastern Europe with passionate concern.[75] By contrast, only when the threat which the Turks posed was manifest was Erasmus's mind engaged. His proposed solution then, as we have already seen, was the conversion of the Turks to Christianity.[76] In taking this approach he was of course following in the footsteps of other commentators, such as Pius II, in his letter to Sultan Mehmed, and John of Segovia.[77] As in the writings of the latter, a key argument put forward by Erasmus in favour of conversion was that this would be following the example of the early Church, which won over opponents through persuasion and example. 'If a handful of disciples were able to place the entire world under Christ's yoke, armed with nothing but their trust in God and the sword of the [Holy] Spirit, surely we can manage the

---

[72] The siege of Rhodes in 1522-3, for example, seems to have attracted a single, brief reference: Allen, Ep. 1337.

[73] *OODER*, 5(3).11-14, 38-48.

[74] Allen, Epp. 295, 643, 784, 936, 1581 and see Epp. 1584, 1597.

[75] See for example O. Niccoli, *Prophecy and People in Renaissance Italy*, trans. L.G. Cochrane (Princeton, 1990); W. Klaassen, *Living at the End of the Ages: Apocalyptic Expectation in the Radical Reformation* (Lanham, New York and London, 1992).

[76] Above, at n. 11. See also Allen, Epp. 858, 1400. The idea of conversion featured in all the major tracts on peace. See, e.g. 'Institutio principis christiani', *OODER*, 4(1).218 (= *CWE*, 27.287) and 'Querela pacis', *OODER*, 4(2).96 (= *CWE*, 27.319).

[77] D. Cabanelas Rodriguez, *Juan de Segovia y el problema islamico* (Madrid, 1952); Aeneas Silvius Piccolomini, *'Epistola ad Mahomatem II' (Epistle to Mohammed II)*, ed. A.R. Baca, *American University Studies, Series 2: Romance Languages and Literature* 127 (New York, Bern, Frankfurt am Main, Paris, 1990). I am grateful to Ms Nancy Bisaha for the second of these references.

same with Christ's assistance?'[78] His confidence in the peaceful triumph of the Christian message even made him advocate the practice of *convivencia*, anticipating the gradual decay of Islam without the need to suppress it. This, he noted, had been the approach of the early Christian emperors in the case of paganism.[79]

It is hard to view Erasmus's constant pleas for conversion as anything other than a measure of desperation, his exit route from the cul-de-sac fashioned by his loathing for war and the Ottoman advance. He does not appear to have given much sustained thought to the practical problems of missionary work, whether doctrinal, political, organizational or linguistic. He was content with throwaway remarks to the effect that the Turks, as monotheists, were half-Christian anyway; provided that the tenets of Christianity could be communicated to them in a suitably simplified form, there should be no great problem in winning over the other half.[80] There is a painful superficiality in his comment in July 1533 that the Lapps, whose cause he had been urged to take up, should be converted with kindness rather than through conquest and oppressive lordship.[81] The praise which he accorded to King John III of Portugal in 1527 for his sponsorship of missionary work in Africa was no less generalized than his appreciation of the crusading zeal of France's kings in 1495, or his words of praise for Sigismund I of Poland's military successes against the Tatars and Muscovites in 1523, 'which were I suppose more needful than anything else for protecting the boundaries of Christendom'.[82] In much the same way, his views on the possibility of salvation outside the Church were ill-defined.[83]

Of course we must assess Erasmus's works in accordance with his own priorities. What interested him above all else was the reform of Christian society in accordance with humanist ideals, and like so much else the Turkish problem was viewed in this light. In his failure to view the Turks objectively he was, after all, far from unique among his contemporaries. As A.G. Weiler, its most recent editor, has emphasized, the *Consultatio* of 1530 reveals its

---

[78] *OODER*, 5(3).62.

[79] *OODER*, 5(3).82.

[80] *OODER*, 5(3).62; Allen, Ep. 858.

[81] Allen, Ep. 2846, responding to Ep. 2826.

[82] Allen, Epp. 45, 1393, 1800, and see Ep. 1819, in which Sigismund of Poland is praised for his avoidance of war.

[83] G.H. Williams, 'Erasmus and the Reformers on Non-Christian Religions and *salus extra ecclesiam*', in *Action and Conviction in Early Modern Europe*, ed. T.K. Rabb and J.E. Seigel (Princeton, 1969), pp. 324-37.

author's concerns with great clarity.[84] Erasmus himself, in a catalogue of his works printed at the end of the first edition, listed it in the 'ordo quintus, pertinentium ad pietatem'.[85] It is a commentary on Psalm 29, which is a celebration of God's overwhelming power and his providential role. In common with all the other evils of the age, such as syphilis and inflation, the successes of the Turks were inflicted by God as a punishment for Christian sins: 'They owe their victories to our sins, for the evidence makes it plain that when we fought against them, our God was enraged.'[86] For Erasmus, as for others, this was epitomized by the catastrophic defeat at Varna in 1444, which God inflicted on Wladislaw of Poland because the king broke the oath which he had sworn not to attack the Turks; rarely could human sin and divine punishment be so indubitably linked.[87]

In the *Consultatio* Erasmus was at pains to stress that he did not see this as a prescription for passivity in the face of the Turkish onslaught. This was the brush with which he quite unfairly tarred Luther, who by this point had executed a volte face in his views. Ottoman successes constituted, rather, a clear signal from God that Christians should lead better lives. As Erasmus put it in a letter to Peter Gilles in January 1530, in which many of the themes of the *Consultatio* were rehearsed: 'Through so many disasters God is warning us that we should turn back to Him with all our heart and take refuge in the Ark' — the Ark, of course, being Christ's teaching.[88] The Turk within had to be defeated before the Turk without could be dealt with successfully. 'Turkishness' was the failure to live a Christian life, whether on the part of a baptized Christian or an unbeliever. Indeed, the two were complementary, for observation of a reformed Christian society would so impress the Turks (and for that matter the Jews) that their conversion would readily follow.[89] This breathtakingly Eurocentric viewpoint was already on display in the *Enchiridion militis christiani*, in which 'the Turk' was set alongside those baptized Christians who

---

[84] See his 'La *Consultatio de bello Turcis inferendo*', passim.

[85] Allen, Ep. 2283.

[86] *OODER*, 5(3).52.

[87] *OODER*, 5(3).52, 60. As my colleague Nick Davidson has pointed out to me, Christopher Marlowe was to make effective use of the perjured oath in *Tamburlaine*, Part 2, Acts 1-2, in a splendid conflation of Nicopolis, Varna and the 1529 siege of Vienna.

[88] Allen, Ep. 2260, and see *OODER*, 5(3).31, 70. The criticism of Luther is in *OODER*, 5(3).54-8.

[89] Allen, Ep. 858.

were guilty of adultery and sacrilege, and the 'soldier of Christ' was exhorted to direct his hatred not at the man but at the vice.[90]

Erasmus realized full well that conversion was not the answer to an imminent threat of attack, such as seemed likely when he wrote the *Consultatio* in 1530. In these circumstances he counselled resistance. He accepted that this would favour the Habsburgs, at a point when many had good cause to fear any further increase of imperial power. But the alternative was Turkish rule, and that was intolerable. By 1530 Erasmus could no longer write of the Turks in the sprightly tone he had adopted in his letter to More in 1518; events in Hungary and Austria had brought them too close, and even the sceptical Erasmus was affected by stories of Turkish atrocities. The Turks were not just Muslims but barbarians, who inflicted savage massacres, deportations and fiscal oppression on their Christian subjects. The latter were treated not like human beings but animals. This was the same criticism, of course, which Erasmus had levelled against the pope and princes at the time of Leo X's crusade project, but the situation was worse in the Ottoman state, where despotism went unchallenged and neither philosophy nor theology were practised. Conquest by the Turks would entail a descent into barbarism in every way.[91]

Granted that resistance to this threat would constitute a war on behalf of religion, it would succeed only if waged in a spirit of piety, 'if before all else we placate the Lord's wrath, if our intention is unsullied and proper, if our whole trust lies in Christ, if we fight under His banners, if He triumphs in us, if we heed the commands of our God, as if we were attacking the enemy under His eyes'. At first sight this looks like a religious war, and it is striking that a few lines further on Erasmus referred wistfully to St Bernard's description of the early Templars, 'of whom [Bernard] is uncertain whether he should call them monks or knights, such was their moral probity, and their courage in battle'.[92] But in fact there were two crucial differences. First, the fighting itself would not constitute a form of religious observance: Christ's triumph in the warriors would be a spiritual, not a military one. This would not be sanctified violence, which for Erasmus was an obscene oxymoron.[93] Secondly,

---

[90] *EOO*, 5.44F-45A (= *CWE*, 66.94).

[91] *OODER*, 5(3).74-6; above, at n. 20. See Allen, Ep. 2396, for a report on Turkish atrocities, 13 October 1530, and see Ep. 2636.

[92] *OODER*, 5(3).68. See Remy and Dunil-Marquebreucq, *Erasme: Dulce bellum inexpertis*, p. 76: 'Laudavit divus Bernardus bellatores, sed ita laudavit ut nostram omnem damnet militiam.'

[93] I cannot agree with J.-C. Margolin ('Erasme et la guerre contre les Turcs', p. 26), that Erasmus envisaged even the possibility of a holy war.

the war would not be a divinely-mandated one. Erasmus never altered his firm belief that this feature of the Old Testament had been superseded by the new dispensation. The wars of the Israelites should not be viewed as a literal prefigurement of how Christians should behave. If this were the case, he had asked in *Dulce bellum inexpertis*, why did not Christians follow other Jewish practices, such as refraining from the eating of pork?[94]

In the *Consultatio*, for the first time, Erasmus addressed himself to such concrete issues of warfare as leadership and finance. There is no need to discern in this a radical change of mind about the validity of war. Quite simply, it was the first time Erasmus had focussed on the mechanics of warfare. Since the crusading format was condemned, Erasmus looked to Europe's leading secular authorities, Emperor Charles V, King Ferdinand of Hungary, Francis I and Henry VIII, with the moral encouragement of the pope.[95] One of the few positive aspects to the anti-Turkish war was that it would at least stop such rulers fighting amongst themselves. Five years previously, writing to Francis I's sister, Margaret of Angoulême, a few months after the battle of Pavia, Erasmus had tempered his declaration of loyalty to Charles V with the comment: 'Yet I wish his victory had been won over the Turks. What rejoicing there would have been throughout the world if the two greatest monarchs on the earth had made peace and joined their arms to repel the assaults of the enemy on Christ's kingdom.' What is apparent here is less Erasmus's support for war against the Turks than his anguish at the Valois-Habsburg rivalry, which presented him with a personal clash of loyalties as well as symbolizing all the other conflicts within Christendom.[96]

Erasmus's views on how the war against the Turks should be funded were shaped primarily by his firm conviction that all war taxation was oppressive and conducive to tyranny. In this light it is not surprising that Erasmus judged that the war should be financed in the main through secular rulers adopting a more spartan lifestyle at court. This, of course, fitted the treatise's central argument that the war could only succeed if it was preceded by thoroughgoing moral reform at home; in fact Erasmus was recycling suggestions set out in his *Institutio principis christiani*. In addition, once military progress was being made ordinary people would start to make voluntary contributions, so taxation would remain unnecessary. The pattern followed by this expedition would

---

[94] Remy and Dunil-Marquebreucq, *Erasme: Dulce bellum inexpertis*, p. 68 (= Mann Phillips, *Erasmus on his Times*, p. 127).
[95] *OODER*, 5(3).68, 70-1.
[96] Allen, Ep. 1615.

therefore be the opposite of those in the past, when all the energy of the organizers had gone into raising money, and none on making military preparations.[97] Or as Erasmus was to put it in a letter to Peter Tomiczki in 1532, referring to Charles V's crusade plans, 'the recruitment of troops is proceeding slowly, the collection of money with vigour, and few people are predicting good things for this war'.[98]

Erasmus would have been the first to admit the lack of originality and even substance in this section of the *Consultatio*. Many people, he remarked at the start of the treatise, had considered the raising of funds and the issue of leadership, but nobody had given thought to living better lives, 'which is the head of the entire matter'.[99] In the same way that his panegyric of Philip of Austria in 1504 only really came alive when Erasmus exhorted the young archduke to avoid war at all costs, so the 1530 treatise is at its weakest in the part where its author dealt with actual war. No attention at all was accorded to the complex issues of recruitment, goals and strategy which had preoccupied the writers of crusade treatises in the past, had been so much to the forefront of Leo X's planning, and were to concern authors of anti-Turkish tracts for some decades to come.[100] Erasmus was airily, and defensively, dismissive of such technicalities.[101] The reason, surely, was that they entailed thinking about mercenaries, destruction and conquest, and he felt too much distaste for such horrors to go into detail.

Here indeed lay the heart of the Erasmian dilemma. The circle could not be squared. For all his occasional grumbles that he would be better off under the sultan, Erasmus had no doubts about what Turkish rule would entail.[102] He was forced to accept that war, which he had roundly attacked for decades, might in this instance be necessary if the Christian faith and civilization were to survive. But he did not genuinely believe that such a war would be waged by pious Christians purged of their former vices. Nor did he really have the confidence which he claimed to possess in the sincerity of men like Clement VII, Charles V and Ferdinand of Austria. Even if his chosen military commanders were not secretly in league with the Turks (as he had suggested in 1518), and if they steered clear of the decadent practices of crusading, they would still

---

[97] *OODER*, 5(3).72-4, and see *OODER*, 4(1).188-92 (= *CWE*, 27.260-2).

[98] Allen, Ep. 2713.

[99] *OODER*, 5(3).31.

[100] See Heath, *Crusading Commonplaces*, passim.

[101] *OODER*, 5(3).64: 'Tot sumus inquiunt numero, tantum habemus machinarum; his locis aggrediemur, sic et sic fallemus hostem; adsit Deus, non adsit, nostra est victoria.'

[102] For example, Allen, Epp. 1431, 1433, 1437, 3054. See also above, nn. 32, 74.

be waging war, which brought out the worst in people. At best, a war fought for Christianity might be termed a necessary evil. But Erasmus would probably have preferred a rather more forbidding description: that of a medicine which stood a fair chance of killing the patient. Christians confronted the exact reverse of St Bernard's famous dictum, coined four centuries previously, that in one sense or another, the Templars won every battle they fought.[103] As Erasmus put it in a letter to Audomarus Edingus in April 1531: 'My greatest fear is that while some are Lutherans, some Zwinglians, and others Anabaptists, by fighting with the Turks we become Turks ourselves'.[104]

---

[103] 'Liber ad milites Templi de laude novae militiae', *Sancti Bernardi opera*, ed. J. Leclercq, C.H. Talbot and H.M. Rochais, 8 vols (Rome, 1957-77), 3.205-39, at p. 217.
[104] Allen, Ep. 2485.

Index